FOURTH EDITION

IMPLEMENTING CHANGE

Patterns, Principles, and Potholes

GENE E. HALL

University of Nevada, Las Vegas

SHIRLEY M. HORD

Scholar Laureate, Learning Forward

FOREWORDS BY BRUCE JOYCE AND STEPHEN ANDERSON

Boston   Columbus   Indianapolis   New York   San Francisco   Upper Saddle River
Amsterdam   Cape Town   Dubai   London   Madrid   Milan   Munich   Paris   Montreal   Toronto
Delhi   Mexico City   São Paulo   Sydney   Hong Kong   Seoul   Singapore   Taipei   Tokyo

Vice President and Editorial Director:
Jeffery W. Johnston
Senior Acquisitions Editor: Meredith J. Fossel
Editorial Assistant: Krista Slavicek
Executive Field Marketing Manager: Krista Clark
Senior Product Marketing Manager: Christopher Barry
Production Project Manager: Laura Messerly
Senior Operations Specialist: Pat Tonneman
Senior Art Director: Jayne Conte

Cover Designer: Karen Salzbach
Cover Art: Fotolia, © SSilver
Full-Service Project Management: Penny Walker, Aptara®, Inc.
Composition: Aptara®, Inc.
Printer/Binder: Courier/Westford
Cover Printer: Courier/Westford
Text Font: Times LT Std

Credits and acknowledgments for material borrowed from other sources and reproduced, with permission, in this text appear on the appropriate page within the text.

Every effort has been made to provide accurate and current Internet information in this text. However, the Internet and information posted on it are constantly changing, so it is inevitable that some of the Internet addresses listed in this text will change.

Photo Credits: Gene E. Hall (top photo), p. v; Shirley M. Hord (bottom photo), p. v.

Library of Congress Cataloging-in-Publication Data
Hall, Gene E.
  Implementing change: patterns, principles, and potholes/Gene E. Hall, University of Nevada, Las Vegas, Shirley M. Hord, Scholar Laureate, Learning Forward.—Fourth edition.
    pages cm
  ISBN 978-0-13-335192-7
  1. School improvement programs—United States. 2. Educational leadership—United States.
I. Hord, Shirley M. II. Title.
  LB2822.82.H355 2015
  371.2'07—dc23   201304130

2 3 4 5 6 7 8 9 10 V092 16 15

ISBN 10:   0-13-335192-0
ISBN 13: 978-0-13-335192-7

Dedication

We dedicate this book to our many CBAM colleagues and friends around the world from whom we have learned so much. We offer this book as a way of sharing what we have learned along with describing our current questions and dilemmas.

Through continuing collaboration, we can increase everyone's learning about how to most effectively initiate, implement, and sustain change.

Gene E. Hall

Shirley M. Hord

ABOUT THE AUTHORS

Gene E. Hall, PhD, School of Environmental and Public Affairs, University of Nevada, Las Vegas, has been a full professor at four universities and served as the Dean of the College of Education at two universities. Dr. Hall is internationally recognized for his career-long focus on developing new understandings about the change process in organization settings. He regularly serves as a consultant for schools, school districts, businesses, and state leaders on the implementation of various innovations and change processes from a Concerns Based perspective. In addition to his work in the United States, he regularly collaborates with colleagues in other countries and serves on doctoral committees in relation to facilitating, evaluating, and studying change processes. His more recent research has examined relationships between the Change Facilitator Style of leaders and outcomes such as increases in student learning. Dr. Hall has had a parallel academic career in regard to innovation in and national accreditation of teacher education. He is a coauthor of *The Foundations of American Education* (Pearson), now in its 16th edition, and the lead author of *Introduction to Teaching: Making a Difference in Student Learning* (Sage).

Shirley M. Hord, PhD, was the first Scholar Emerita at the Southwest Educational Development Laboratory and is currently Scholar Laureate in association with Learning Forward (previously the National Staff Development Council). She authors articles and books on school-based professional development, school change and improvement, and professional learning communities. A sampling of her publications includes *Learning Together, Leading Together: Changing Schools Through Professional Learning Communities,* Teachers College Press (2004); with Patricia Roy, *Moving NSDC's Staff Development Standards Into Practice: Innovation Configurations,* National Staff Development Council (2003); *Leading Professional Learning Communities: Voices from Research and Practice,* Corwin Press (2008); and with Edward Tobia, *Reclaiming Our Teaching Profession: The Power of Learning in Community,* Teachers College Press (2012) . In addition to working with educators at all levels across the United States, Canada, and Mexico, Dr. Hord serves as an educational consultant worldwide, in Asia, Europe, Australia, and Africa.

PREFACE

Welcome to the fourth edition of *Implementing Change: Patterns, Principles, and Potholes.* That we have had the opportunity to prepare four editions of this book has come as quite a surprise. Through communication with colleagues and readers of the earlier editions, it is clear that many have found the book to be a useful source of ideas for understanding, facilitating, and studying change processes. We have learned from writing each edition, and most certainly have new ideas, stories, and study findings to report.

With so much change happening all around us, it makes sense that a book on change would need change, too. In writing this new edition, a challenge for us as authors has been to make important changes and updates while preserving the foundational content that was so useful in the first three editions. We think we have accomplished both objectives.

NEW TO THIS EDITION

Important changes to this edition include the following.

- As before, the major construct that is the topic of each chapter is *evidence based.* For this edition, up-to-date citations from research have been inserted with each construct, tool, and application.
- The findings from important recent research studies are reported, such as the first studies linking the Change Facilitator Style of school principals with student test scores.
- An entirely new feature is the story of East Lake School District. Instead of each chapter having independent vignettes and anecdotes, the same district and school context with the corresponding staff are used within each chapter. With this approach, it is possible to illustrate how the different constructs and tools can be used simultaneously.
- There is an increased focus on implementing change in schools and school districts. This does not mean that the constructs and tools do not apply in business and other settings. Narrowing the context is intended to keep examples and illustrations simple.
- A set of *Learning Outcomes* are stated at the beginning of each chapter to help the reader focus on the key ideas.
- The flow across the chapters is organized to move from the individual implementer, to teams/groups, to whole organizations (schools/districts), and then to large systems (e.g., states).
- The last chapter comprises over fifty percent new material with a much heavier focus on implementation assessment, program evaluation, and research, as well as exploration of construct interrelationships.

- Also new to the last chapter is an examination of the increasingly important topic, or should we say dilemma, of sustaining change.
- New chapter features include "Applying *the chapter's construct* in Facilitating Implementation" and "Applying *the chapter's construct* in Research and Program Evaluation Studies."
- In this edition, the Concerns Based Adoption Model (CBAM) is used as the overarching framework, with the first eleven chapters examining a particular construct or perspective in depth. The last chapter then applies various combinations of the constructs and perspectives.
- Several increasingly important topics have been added, including *capacity* in Chapter 9, *sustainability* in Chapter 12, and interpreting whole group data in Chapters 4 and 12.

WHY IMPLEMENTING CHANGE CONTINUES TO BE SO IMPORTANT

Change is one of the few constants in our world. There is no escaping the fact that we are living in a time of change. An obvious indicator of continuing change is most certainly the types and uses of technology in our work and in applications such as social media. There are many societal changes too, such as the Arab Spring and the consequences of the many decisions by governments and the courts. There also are continuing changes in our workplaces and our personal lives. Instead of being hapless captives of change, we believe that it is important to understand how change processes work, how to facilitate change, and how to study change. It is not enough to become expert in a particular change; we also need to understand how the change process works.

One clear conclusion that we have offered in the past still holds. Those who initiate change and those who study it should be able to predict much more about what happens during this process than is typically the case. We also should be much better at attending to the needs of the people involved and preventing much that often goes wrong. Hopefully, our attempt to pass on some of what we have learned will be of help to you and the others with whom you are engaged during change.

THE TITLE

The title of this book—*Implementing Change: Patterns, Principles, and Potholes*—is fittingly representative of its content. One of the problems in the field of change is that there is no agreement on the meaning of commonly used terms. For example, the word *change* can be a noun (e.g., the change that is being attempted) or a verb (e.g., changing the culture). The word also can be used to represent the whole of a change effort (e.g., "We have a big change underway!"). Having the term *implementing* as the first word in the title adds an important emphasis. Most changes require some time and effort to make them operational—in other words, to implement them. As you will read throughout this book, we see that successful change begins and ends with understanding the importance of implementation constructs and dynamics.

The terms *patterns, principles,* and *potholes* have been carefully chosen as well. There are patterns in change processes, and most of this book is about describing and naming those patterns. In the study of change, as in the so-called hard sciences, there is widespread agreement on a number of points, or principles. We certainly do not know all that we should; however, some elements of change are understood and agreed on by many of us. All of us know full well that "potholes" may be encountered throughout a change process. Although the inclination is too often to give too much attention to these problems, it is also foolish to ignore them.

PART I: THE CONTEXT FOR IMPLEMENTING CHANGE

The first chapter in each edition has presented a set of *change principles.* In each edition, we have changed some of the principles. Not because they are no longer relevant, but because we have others we want to point out. Each of these principles should be accepted as givens. There is no debate about their validity.

Once you read each you will likely say, "Well, of course. I knew that." However, you also can think of change initiatives in which that change principle was ignored. Just because we know something doesn't mean that we always act accordingly. Incorporating these change principles alone should lead to fewer surprises and more success in your change efforts.

In Chapter 2, we describe another basic change concept, *interventions.* As with other terms, the definition of interventions varies across disciplines. For example, in public health the term is a generic reference to the program that is being adopted. In the Diffusion Perspective, the definition seems to vary between representing the change and supporting actions such as Technical Assistance. In the CBAM perspective, the definition is set: "Actions and events that affect a change process." The change itself is called an *innovation.*

PART II: THE PEOPLE PART OF CHANGE:
THREE DIAGNOSTIC DIMENSIONS: CONCERNS,
USING, AND FIDELITY

An organization or a large system is not changed until the individual members of that unit use the new way. Therefore an important unit of change has to be each implementer. Part II introduces the three *Diagnostic Dimensions* of CBAM (pronounced "see-bam"). Each is an evidence-based construct with related tools that can be used to facilitate, evaluate, and research implementation initiatives.

Chapter 3 introduces ways to think about and appraise the change itself. There can be dramatic differences between what the developer of an innovation has in mind and what is actually implemented. These differences are called *Innovation Configurations.* A second CBAM Diagnostic Dimension addresses the personal side of change. Even when change takes place in organizational settings, personal feelings, moments of joy, and frustrations are part of it. Understanding these *concerns* is addressed in Chapter 4. Chapter 5 is about use and nonuse of innovations. This is not a dichotomous phenomenon. Instead there are different *Levels of Use* as implementers progress from nonuse, to novice user, and on to expert. Change Facilitators and program evaluators should pay close to attention to these different ways of "using" an innovation.

PART III: LEADING CHANGE ACROSS THE ORGANIZATION

The chapters and constructs in this part address factors related to implementing change at the organization level. One of the areas in which our research has continued to advance is understanding and documenting the significant difference that change leaders can make. In Chapter 6, three Change Facilitator (CF) Styles are described. A number of studies have documented the differences in innovation implementation success that are related to how leaders lead. We now have several studies documenting relationships between CF Style and student test scores. In Chapter 7, the importance of understanding organization culture, especially the construction of *Professional Learning Communities (PLCs)*, is examined.

A critical implicit assumption that many make is that managing change processes is controllable by the leaders. However, in reality even the change leaders do not control all parts of the process. We call one key component of the uncontrollable *Intervention Mushrooms,* which is the topic of Chapter 8. Just as the name suggests, this species of intervention grows in the dark and is not controlled by the change leaders. Some are skilled at detecting and addressing Mushrooms, whereas others fail to see them at all. Although we think that this chapter will be of particular interest, an important caution is necessary. The chapter on Mushrooms comes after seven other chapters, each of which presents a construct that needs to be understood *before* it is possible to explore the dynamics of Mushrooms and what can be done about them.

PART IV: DIFFERENT PERSPECTIVES FOR UNDERSTANDING THE BIG PICTURE OF CHANGE: SYSTEMS, DIFFUSION, AND ORGANIZATION DEVELOPMENT

The chapters in Part IV introduce three other perspectives for understanding change that are classics. Each has an extensive history of research, model building, and applications. Each also offers a number of tools that can be used to facilitate, study, and evaluate change efforts. In Chapter 9, *systems and systemic thinking* are the topic. New to this chapter is our proposal to consider capacity and capacity building as important system factors. Chapter 10 introduces another of the classics: *Diffusion.* This perspective had its beginning early in the twentieth century with studies of the varying rates and willingness of farmers and others to adopt innovative practices. It very quickly became obvious that not everyone adopts an innovation at the same time. In Chapter 11, another perspective is introduced: *Organization Development (OD).* This approach focuses on group dynamics and the process skills that can help teams and whole organizations be more effective. Organization Development offers a number of techniques and ways to facilitate change that can be useful.

PART V: COMBINING VIEWS: PERSPECTIVES, CONSTRUCTS, TOOLS, APPLICATIONS, AND IMPLICATIONS

Chapters 1 through 11 build from the individual, to the group, to whole organization and system views. In the last chapter, Chapter 12, we review and extend applications of the constructs that were introduced in the previous chapters. Data sets and findings from several studies are used to illustrate how combinations of change process constructs and measures can be applied. There are conceptual explorations of the relationships among the CBAM Diagnostic Dimensions. The importance of conducting what we call *implementation* assessments is introduced.

Another topic is using recent research findings to understand more about the differences leaders make. Also discussed is the importance of sustaining change. The final topic addresses the importance of ethics in change agentry.

CHAPTER ORGANIZATION

The main topic of each chapter is presented as a key change construct or perspective that is *evidence based*. The construct is introduced along with the supporting research. The measurement tool(s) is described along with summaries of key study findings. Each chapter also has a number of purpose-built features that are intended to help you draw connections between what you know now and what we would like you to understand when you have finished reading each chapter.

To help ground the basic pattern being presented, every chapter begins with several quotes, which will probably be familiar to you. The ideas presented in the chapter illustrate how these quotes can be analyzed in terms of their meaning for change process success. To help you focus on some of the key topics in each chapter, a set of Learning Outcomes is offered near the beginning. Each chapter, except Chapter 12, also contains a story about how that chapter's key ideas could come alive in the East Lake School District.

To aid in remembering key points, with the exceptions of Chapters 1 and 12 each chapter has a box of "Indicators" of the chapter's construct, as well as a table of "Implications for Change Facilitators." This feature lists several succinct suggestions for ways to use the ideas introduced in each chapter. At the end of each chapter are a number of Discussion Questions and two suggestions for "Applications." One set of suggestions is about change facilitating activities that you could try. The other set of suggestions is for research and evaluation activities.

*****

So here it is, the new *Implementing Change* book! We hope that it will help you improve your understanding of the change process. We hope it provides useful ideas and approaches for facilitating change. We also hope we have provided strong examples of how each of the constructs can be used in assessing implementation and in conducting program evaluation and research studies. If you are interested in assessing implementation and research, plenty of ideas are scattered throughout that need to be systematically examined. Let us know what you are thinking of studying and what you learn.

We gratefully acknowledge the encouragement and support of our editor Meredith Fossel and many colleagues at Pearson. It has been a pleasure and honor to work with them over the years and now for this, the fourth edition. One of the other changes with this edition was our having an Editorial Product Manager, Emerson (John) Probst. He has been a terrific help as we have strived to merge files, battle hidden word processing commands, and prepare the best manuscript possible.

We also wish to thank the following reviewers: Kris Bosworth, University of Arizona; John Hamilton, Texas A&M University—Texarkana; and Richard A. King, University of South Florida—Manatee. We have considered and attempted to incorporate nearly all of their suggestions.

G. E. H.

S. M. H.

CONTENTS

CHAPTER 2

**What Actions and Events Are Imperative in Facilitating Implementation?:
Interventions   25**

CHAPTER 4

How Can the Different Feelings and Perceptions About Change Be Understood and Addressed?: Stages of Concern   80

CHAPTER 5

What Are Characteristic Behavioral Profiles of Implementers?: Levels of Use   106

PART III   Leading Change across the Organization   131

CHAPTER 6

<hr>

How Do Leaders Make a Difference in Implementation Success?:
Change Facilitator Styles   133

CHAPTER 7

CHAPTER 8

CHAPTER 9

**How Can Systems Thinking Enhance the Success of Change Efforts?:
Interconnections of Parts That Make a Whole   209**

CHAPTER 10

How Do Communication Activities and Change Agents Affect Implementation?: The Diffusion Perspective   232

CHAPTER 11

**In What Ways Can Team Member Skills and Process Consultants Affect
Implementation?: Organization Development (OD)   254**

**PART V   Combining Views: Perspectives, Constructs, Tools,
Applications, and Implications   280**

CHAPTER 12

How Can Change Constructs Be Combined to Understand, Assess, and Lead Efforts to Implement Change?   282

FOREWORD

PROFESSIONAL DEVELOPMENT AND IMPLEMENTING CHANGE

Bruce Joyce

Let's begin by asking, "Who should buy (or steal) this book?" The answer is *anyone who is interested in educational change.* Shirley Hord and Gene Hall provide essential concepts and strategies for making and understanding changes ranging from simple digital modifications ("Let's make the school a *hot spot.*") to complex innovations in curriculum and instruction ("Let's implement the new core standards in Literacy."). They set out basic substance for novice initiators and managers and provide advanced tools for change veterans and those who would conduct research on educational innovation. All will find stimulation and good sense between the same covers.

Gene and Shirley won't mind if I restate the core concept—*change is learning.* Sometimes the learning is so smooth and easy that you scarcely notice that you have learned, or you are pleased with a small change that takes a minute or two of adjustment but turns out to add convenience. (Remember learning to pump your own gas or when the ATM came to town or somebody invented magnets for refrigerator doors?)

Even very small adjustments in educational procedures have a social dimension. A new arrangement for conferences between teachers and parents involves coordination, notification, and two-way communications. And sometimes a change seems formidable but turns out to be simple. Electronic communication between educators and parents has turned out to be enriching, disappointing the doomsayers who apparently didn't see the rise in social media. Building a massive planetary community makes improving teacher/parent digital talk seem like a small challenge.

The important theme—let's repeat ourselves—is that changes large and small require learning. And, in organizations, that means learning together, which itself, in many places, can require another and complicated level of cooperative learning.

A back story of modifying practice is that a good many types of otherwise comfortable modifications require *giving up* a routine. That sounds OK except that altering even some small behaviors can make us feel uncomfortable, because we *miss* those familiar old things. I am susceptible to this phenomenon; I drive a 20-year old car because I would miss all the little ways I work around her defects.

In education, there is an "other guy" syndrome when it comes to placing the blame for not making needed alterations in practice. In fact, the most powerful-seeming policymakers are actually helpless when it comes to needed innovation, because they haven't created a vigorous learning environment for teachers. The neglect of professional development by top leaders is a consequence of *their* failure to understand that **change is learning**. Just as schools are decades behind in ICT, the rather good new curriculum standards face a perilous future unless states and districts create schools that are, in Bob Schaefer's great terms, centers for inquiry for educators as well as students.

Now, to profit adequately from Shirley and Gene's book, we readers, whatever our roles, have to learn their three basic models that can guide initiators, managers, and participants as a modification in process or equipment comes to town:

- CBAM—the Concerns-Based-Adoption-Model and its framework, Stages of Concern. The model enables us to understand the cognitive and affective phases involved in understanding and implementing new practices. The locomotive of the mind goes from a state of rest, puffs, turns a slow, slipping set of wheels, and gradually moves its burden faster. Real change doesn't go from zero to 60 in ten seconds.
- LoU—Levels of Use—progress from unfamiliarity of something to taking possession of it, using it, and shaping it to fit comfortably. Hall and Hord help us understand ourselves as we move forward.
- Leadership Styles—Initiators, Managers, Responders. Here we have a mirror for leaders. Initiatives are little pools of opportunity. Some leaders splash ahead, cheering us and showing us that the waters are not inhabited by monsters. Some schedule us and gather resources and lead discussions about how to solve problems. Some wait for *us* to swim across. In this area, Gene and Shirley provide concepts that could actually revolutionize the selection and training of leaders.

Consult the book, and these models will be explained and illustrated.

Much more is dealt with in *Implementing Change,* but master these three models and the data-collection tools that accompany them and you will have enhanced understanding and skill in the vitally important area of change in education.

Bruce Joyce
Booksend Laboratories, Saint Simons Island, Georgia

Joyce's most recent book is *Realizing the Promise of the 21st Century*. The ninth edition of *Models of Teaching: The Heart of the Core*, is in press. Both are with Emily Calhoun.

SCHOLARSHIP AND IMPLEMENTING CHANGE

Stephen Anderson

In 1980, I worked for the Southwest Educational Development Laboratory in Austin, Texas, as a research consultant on a federally funded Head Start elementary school improvement project. During that year, the team of teacher trainers I was working with and I attended a three-day workshop at the University of Texas Research and Development Center for Teacher Education. This workshop was delivered by developers of the Concerns Based Adoption Model, including Gene Hall, Susan Loucks, and Beulah Newlove. The relevance and applicability of the CBAM concepts for understanding the process of change in the schools, Head Start Centers, and school districts that we were working with were immediately obvious.

For the last year, I have been serving as a consultant to an ambitious, nationwide, one-laptop-for-all technology integration initiative in Uruguay. The relevance and applicability of the

CBAM concepts to understanding and facilitating the process of change as experienced by Uruguayan classroom teachers and supported by school and system administrators is just as obvious to me today as it was 40 years ago. This observation and comparison could lead one to question whether nothing has been learned by those responsible for planning and facilitating educational change over the past four decades. A more realistic interpretation, however, is that the process of change for those involved has to be re-created every time classroom teachers and other education personnel set out to implement new policies, programs, and practices. Change in practice is more iterative and unpredictable than cumulative in its evolution. The core concepts articulated in the Concerns Based Adoption Model—Stages of Concern, Levels of Use, Innovation Configurations, Change Facilitator Styles, Change Facilitator Interventions, and Intervention Mushrooms— continue to provide a powerful research-based framework for understanding and, ideally, for facilitating the process of change for those involved in efforts to improve education.

In an article published in 1997, I asserted that the Concerns Based Adoption Model was "the most robust and empirically grounded theoretical model for the implementation of educational innovations to come out of education change research in the 1970s and 1980s."[1] I believe that statement still holds. There are distinct bodies of research and literature on different components of the CBAM model—e.g., school leadership and leadership distribution, teacher change (attitudes, practices), professional development, the developmental nature of change over time, and key factors affecting implementation of changes in education policy and practice. What distinguishes CBAM is that it presents an integrated theory of change that incorporates all these components and can be used both to predict and explain the process of change as it plays out in specific contexts for specific initiatives.

Furthermore, as explained in the concluding chapters of this book, the CBAM framework works well when combined with other evidence-based approaches to understanding and facilitating change: systems theory, innovation diffusion, and organizational development. In that article, I observed that most of the published research associated with CBAM illustrated the usefulness of the model and instruments for assessing teacher change (e.g., SoC, LoU) without challenging or adding to the theoretical constructs per se. In this fourth edition of *Implementing Change,* Hall and Hord continue to challenge the research community to test the validity of the theory in different contexts and to problematize and empirically explore the relationships between different components of the theory—e.g., SoC to LoU; LoU to Innovation Configurations; leadership patterns, implementation progress, and student outcomes; and school culture and implementation progress. They highlight their own recent research and cite the results of other CBAM researchers who are pushing its theoretical frontiers in both North American and international contexts. Interesting suggestions for further research appear at the end of each chapter and in the discussion in the concluding chapter.

CBAM-based research is widely practiced, but is not so widely accessible. Much of it is conducted for unpublished doctoral dissertation investigations and as technical reports from evaluations of educational innovations, some of which are cited by Hall and Hord in this book. As a university professor (and CBAM practitioner), for example, I personally supervised a recent doctoral thesis on the implementation of active learning in Bangladeshi primary schools,

[1]Anderson, S. E. (1997). Understanding teacher change: Revisiting the Concerns Based Adoption Model. *Curriculum Inquiry 27*(3), 331–367.

a master's thesis on the implementation of a new citizenship education course in secondary schools in Ecuador, and was a thesis committee member for a doctoral study on teachers' use of Tribes teaching methods in the workplace after completing Tribes training as part of their beginning teacher program. On occasion, I get invited to be an external examiner for doctoral theses that employ CBAM constructs and instruments in Southeast Asia and Australia. All this is to say that researchers continue to actively engage with CBAM around the world, even if findings from that research do not frequently make their way into popular scholarly research journals. I also teach a graduate course on managing classroom change using earlier editions of *Implementing Change* as the textbook. For their assignments, the students, most of whom are practicing classroom teachers and school administrators, select from the suggested application activities at the end of the core chapters on CBAM principles and constructs (e.g., SoC, LoU, IC, change facilitators). I am continually amazed at the results of these small-scale investigations, which demonstrate on an ongoing basis the validity and reliability of CBAM.

It is my sincere hope that the publication of this fourth edition of *Implementing Change* will help extend awareness, use, and further development of the Concerns Based Adoption Model to new generations of education scholars and practitioners in the continuing search for innovation and improvement in teaching and learning in classrooms and school systems around the world.

Stephen Anderson, Professor

Co-Director Comparative, International and Development Education Program
Department of Leadership, Higher and Adult Education
Ontario Institute for Studies in Education University of Toronto
October 2013

PART I

THE CONTEXT FOR IMPLEMENTING CHANGE

The Concerns-Based Adoption Model (CBAM)

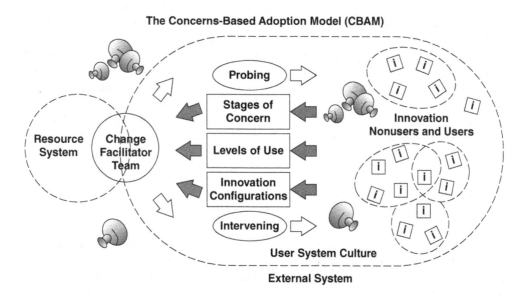

THE BIG PICTURE: DIFFERENT CHANGE PERSPECTIVES

There are several perspectives that can be used to understand, facilitate, and evaluate change processes. Three of these change perspectives (Diffusion, Systems, and Organization Development) have very long histories of research and application. The ideas within each of these perspectives and their implications for leading change efforts are potentially so useful that each perspective has its own chapter in this text.

Another of the change perspectives, the **Concerns-Based Adoption Model (CBAM)**, provides the overall framework and conceptual base for all of the chapters. In the graphic representation of the CBAM there are a number of icons, boxes, arrows, and words. Each represents a key construct that has had decades of research and applications. In total the CBAM graphic is one way to represent the complexities of implementing change that include the individual implementer, change facilitators, the organizational context, and the reality that an organization is located within a larger system context.

The 12 chapters of this text are organized into 5 parts. The chapters in each part present evidence-based constructs that represent key ways of understanding, facilitating, and evaluating change processes. Each chapter introduces a major construct and related perspective for understanding, facilitating, and evaluating change initiatives. Each chapter also provides summaries of related research and examples of how the construct(s) can be used to facilitate and evaluate change processes. The overall flow of the chapters is from examination of individuals, to change leadership, to the organization level, and finally large system change. At several points the interrelationships between the constructs and frames are described as well.

The CBAM graphic is presented with each Part Introduction.The constructs that are described in that part's chapters are highlighted. This is another way to acknowledge that understanding, facilitating, and studying change processes has many elements and factors. Further, these many elements and factors are interconnected: At all times implementing change has to be thought about systemically.

CHAPTERS 1 AND 2: CHANGE PRINCIPLES AND INTERVENTIONS

The first chapter in each edition of this book has presented a set of **Change Principles** that represent basic givens. There is no need to debate the existence and/or the importance of each of these. In this edition, we have updated and emphasized these Change Principles even more. The second chapter is about change facilitating **interventions**, the actions and events that affect how a change process unfolds. Leaders and other facilitators need to plan for and take steps to initiate, support, and monitor implementation efforts. These actions range from the moment-to-moment informal talks and e-mails, to the multiyear accumulation of actions that result in the themes and patterns of change leadership.

To illustrate how the various change constructs and measures can be used, we have developed a case around a hypothetical school district. As part of each chapter we include a feature that describes how the East Lake School District, and some of its schools, apply that chapter's ideas and tools.

INTRODUCING THE STORY: EAST LAKE SCHOOL DISTRICT

East Lake School is a quite typical midsize district serving a community that has economic, ethnic, and cultural diversity. There are 31 schools, which range from high to low socioeconomic status (SES). Across the district, 40% of the students are on free/reduced lunch and 30% are English language learners (ELL). The school board has been surprisingly stable over the last three elections. Although most schools' test scores indicate some growth, there is plenty of room for improvement in certain schools.

Major Change Initiatives

The district is engaged with implementation of several major initiatives. There is an expectation that all schools will be focused on these:

- Instructional Coaches (entering third year)
- Common Core Standards
  English Language Arts (ELA) (entering third year)
  Mathematics (new this year)
  Science (coming next year)
  Depth in Content Knowledge
  Student Argumentation
- The first year of implementing each set of standards includes workshops to "unwrap" the standards
- Formative Assessment (second year), based on Jim Popham's (2008) model
- New Teacher Evaluation (pilot this year)

Key district administrators include:

- Superintendent: Michael ("Call me Mike") Johnson (*Manager/Responder*)

Mike was hired as the superintendent three years ago. The previous superintendent had been state superintendent of the year and later moved to a major district in another state. Mike had been Assistant Superintendent for Facilities, Finance and Human Resources. He is widely known in the community (former high school principal), and is regularly seen at school and community events.

Mike watches closely the budget allocations and has implemented a number of new procedures in order to better track where the funds are spent. He always has time to chat. He listens a lot. His decisions are heavily influenced by "what it will cost" and "is there budget for that?"

- Assistant Superintendent: Leslie Hanson, Ed.D. (*Initiator*)

Dr. Hanson arrived a year ago. She had been Director of Staff Development in a neighboring district. She just finished her dissertation in which she used selected constructs from the Concerns-Based Adoption Model (CBAM) to study a successful districtwide implementation effort. She continually talks her themes:

- Critical thinking
- Problem solving
- Constructivist approaches
- Learner-centered teaching, and
- The importance of having ongoing professional development.

THREE SCHOOLS—A FIRST LOOK

Please note that the labels such as Initiator, Responder, and Manager that are presented after the names below will be defined and discussed in Chapter 6.

Island Park Elementary School

- Principal: Inez Hernandez (*Initiator*; three years in the school)

Ms. Hernandez' first priority is "making sure that 'every-child-is-learning' is at the center of what we do. Every child has a right to receive the very best teaching we can deliver." She continually listens and, after checking with others who might be affected, makes decisions quickly. She has a vision for what Island Park Elementary School should be like in three years. "Our kids will be scoring just as well as those kids in the 'country club' school, especially in problem solving. Our priority this year is to unwrap the math standards and design interim assessments for each grade level."

Island Park does not have an assistant principal but there is an instructional coach, Beverly Denver. Beverly was a teacher in the school, is highly respected, and all teachers say "she really knows her subjects." This is the third year for Beverly to be out of the classroom. "I still miss the kids, and at the same time, I like helping the whole school improve."

River Run Elementary School

- Principal: Ray Raulson (*Responder*; second year in the school)

The previous principal, Mr. Mercer, had been there for six years. He accomplished a major turnaround of what had been a failing school. Mr. Mercer is now Director of Elementary Education in a large urban district. Mr. Raulson's themes include:

"We already have standards!"

"I want everyone to get along."

"We have strong teachers; they know all about teaching."

- Instructional Coach: Mary Sawyer (new to River Run Elementary School this year)

For the last three years, Mary was a Teacher on Special Assignment (TOSA) and served as a mentor to all new special education teachers. Due to the teacher union contract, the district could not keep Mary on as a TOSA. The contract agreement limits this assignment to three years.

Mountain View High School

- Principal: Michael Major (*Manager*; five years in the school)

Mr. Major runs a tight ship. Policies, procedures, budgets, and resources are all accounted for. Routines are in place and the school runs smoothly. Schedules are established well in advance, and even though the staff budget is tight, the school has staggered starts and end times. Principal Major's themes include:

"We have our plans for the year."

"Everyone knows what to do."

- Instructional Coaches: The school has two instructional coaches.

Dick Romano has been in this role for several years. Last year Martin Chin was a middle school math teacher. He is working on his administrator license at the local university. "Someday I want to be a superintendent of an urban district. I loved teaching, but now I want to help other teachers improve their practices."

At this point you have been given a brief introduction to different change perspectives. As you study each chapter you will be learning a lot more. Each chapter introduces a change science construct that is evidence-based. There is extensive research, validation and application of each construct. The East Lake School District story is designed to illustrate how the ideas can come alive. To set the stage a set of principles about change are introduced in Chapter One. There is no reason to debate these. They are givens when it comes to change.

CHAPTER 1

WHAT KEY PATTERNS, PRINCIPLES, AND LESSONS HAVE WE LEARNED ABOUT IMPLEMENTING CHANGE?

We know from past experience that it takes time to institutionalize new practices.
—Michael Major, Principal, Mountain View High School

Learning means you are adjusting to change.
—Art Linkletter on the *Larry King Show,* July 20, 2002

Change means you are adjusting your learning.
—Stephanie Struthers, Director of Professional Learning, East Lake School District

After all this research on classrooms, the inescapable conclusion is that school-based leadership makes a big difference.
—Dr. Leslie Hanson, Assistant Superintendent, East Lake School District

When everything comes together right, change is an energizing and very satisfying experience.
—Inez Hernandez, Principal, Island Park Elementary School

Here we go again. You know how change is. It is like a pendulum, swinging back and forth.
—Sara Johnson, Teacher, Mountain View High School Mathematics Department

WHY A BOOK ON "IMPLEMENTING CHANGE"?

If you are a teacher, an assistant principal, an inner-city district superintendent, a state-level director of traffic or highways, a campus-based school principal, a college dean, or the father in a family—regardless of your role, chances are you have had experiences in suggesting or introducing changes of some sort in your organization. How many times have you been successful in accomplishing those changes, most especially if the changes were not readily agreeable to some of your constituents?

Perhaps you are the human resources manager of a large company. How do you manage the training and development of employees so that they productively take on new and improved behaviors that contribute to the company's bottom line while maintaining employee satisfaction on the job? Perhaps you are responsible for research and evaluation for your school district or a large corporation, or installation of a new approach in the military or government. Your responsibility is to ascertain the effectiveness of new classroom and production floor practices. Each of these new activities requires change. In addition, each must first be in place (implemented) before its effectiveness can be assessed.

For decades—no, millennia (think Machiavelli, *The Prince,* originally published in Italian in 1532, currently available translated, 2005)—leaders have been delivering suggestions, invitations, mandates, and legislation in hopes of changing behaviors, attitudes, knowledge, and understanding. These leaders also have a need to know if their improvement strategies are working. Such actions of introducing, accomplishing or implementing, and assessing change have occurred erratically in the corporate sector, in schools, in medical practice, and in almost every other area of human endeavor. A large part of the required implementation activities have gone unheeded or have resulted in superficial, modest, or poor installation. Too many end with the participants observing, "See, I told you so: This too would pass."

One of the districts we studied addressed this situation head on as they engaged in a major change. When administrators recognized the mixed feelings of the staff, they immediately planned for, announced, and delivered assistance and support for implementing the current change. They also designed and put into place a monitoring system that provided bimonthly feedback on the status of implementation. These actions sent strong signals to the staff that the new program was here to stay and that the administration would back it over time.

In an era of abundant research findings and examples of tested and improved practices that can lead to better products and processes, there is a surprising and woeful lack of finding these new ideas, products, and processes in use in our homes, schools, and workplaces. Advertising and marketing activities extol the virtues of everything from the latest fad diet to how to teach phonics. Many of these products and processes are discarded after a brief period of experimentation and no immediate or visible success. What is the problem here?

For the past 40 years, the authors of this text have been leaders of an international team of researchers studying the change process in schools, colleges, businesses, and government agencies. We have been systematically charting what happens to people and organizations when they are involved in change. We have learned a lot about the challenges, the problems, and what it takes to be successful. Our research approach is different from that of others in a number of ways, including our primary focus on the people at the front lines who have to implement the expected change. Our secondary focus has been on how leaders can facilitate change.

In our 76 combined years of research and practice efforts to discover, support, and assist schools and other organizations in their efforts to improve, we have observed and shared the successes of those schools and businesses that have managed and guided change efforts from their abstract promise to their successful reality. We have observed also, despite our most urgent and encouraging support and assistance, organizations adopting new programs and processes year after year, quickly rejecting each as they failed to deliver on their promise. Our keen observations, rigorous studies, and multiple experiences have led us to articulate some basic principles about the process of change.

The original team for these research efforts came together in the late 1960s at the University of Texas at Austin. From 1970 to 1986, this group studied the change process in schools and universities as part of the agenda of the Research and Development Center for Teacher Education. Along the way, researchers from the United States, Belgium, the Netherlands, Australia, Canada, Taiwan, Hong Kong, and several other countries joined in verifying the concepts and extending the research agenda. Now in place is an international network of change-process researchers who have conducted studies related to the concepts and principles presented here. We initiate the discussion of change and implementation in this book by a brief explication and review of these time-tested principles.

REFLECTION QUESTIONS

As you think about your experiences, what have you learned about change? What is one principle of change that you would identify?

LEARNING OUTCOMES

After reading this chapter, the learner should be able to:

1. Describe how change and learning are related.
2. Specify the role required of leaders in the process of change.
3. Explain the significance of interventions to the success of change efforts.
4. Suggest how top-down mandates can work.

PRINCIPLES OF CHANGE

One important result of our long-term collaborative research agenda is that we now can draw some conclusions about what happens when people and organizations are engaged in change. A number of patterns have been observed repeatedly, and some have developed into major themes, or basic *principles*, and we do mean *principles*. As in the so-called hard sciences, enough is now known about some aspects of the change process that we can state a series of principles that are true for all cases.

The Change Principles presented in this chapter are the "givens" underlying all that will be presented in subsequent chapters. From our point of view, these principles are no longer debatable points, for they summarize predictable aspects of change.

Before introducing selected principles about change, a caveat is needed: Each principle is not mutually exclusive, and at first reading some may seem inconsistent with others. These principles do not cover all aspects of change. (Otherwise we would not need the other chapters in this book.) Instead, they address selected aspects of the change process in which the patterns are clear. Acknowledging that these principles are foundational to our way of thinking about change will save you time in trying to discover our implicit assumptions. In addition, understanding them should help you in predicting key aspects of change efforts with which you are engaged.

We need to emphasize that at all levels—individual, organizational, and system— change is highly complex, multivariate, and dynamic. If it weren't so complicated, it would not be nearly as much fun to study, facilitate, and experience. So let's begin our journey of bringing order to change by introducing a set of principles about change that each of us has understood implicitly but probably not verbalized. Interestingly, we predict that you will be able to describe personal change experiences in which each of these principles has been ignored or violated. Certainly, your future change efforts can be more successful if these principles are acknowledged.

Change Principle 1: Change Is Learning—It's as Simple and Complicated as That

To *improve* the speed of transportation from one place to another, one might decide to make a *change* and use a bicycle; to become a skillful bicycle rider requires *learning* about the pedals, handlebars, balance, the rules of the road, and laws governing the conduct of persons using public highways and neighborhood paths and sidewalks. This is an example easy to understand and to visualize. It is also easy to understand that having a caring father or 11-year-old brother to guide the learning, to provide feedback about how to sit astride the vehicle, and how to rotate the pedals so that the wheels turn efficiently can add measurably to the quality and reduce significantly the time required for the learning.

In the marketplace, matters are not quite so simple. For example, a shoe store manager, noting that the quality of her merchandise and the appeal of the salesroom equaled those of her nearest competitor who was besting her in shoe sales, wondered if her sales staff lacked in their approach to customers. She engaged a colleague to check this and discovered that the competing store's staff expressed a warmer attitude toward customers and expressed and conveyed more knowledge about the merchandise. It was obvious to this manager that something must be done to *improve* staff/customer relations.

Her first attempt to *change* her staff's knowledge and skills was to bring them together for coffee before the store opened and share a report from the Business League about research results that identified how sales personnel should act to make successful sales. The staff appreciated the fine coffee and rolls but expressed a lack of knowing what to do to behave as the research findings indicated. "Well," the manager contemplated, "I guess they will need *to learn* how to act in these new ways."

In three successive meetings, the staff met to study new behaviors, to see them demonstrated, to practice them on each other, and to receive feedback from the business consultant who was instructing them. Everyone was delighted when shoe sales increased, as did the commissions of the staff.

To make things better (improved) in the family setting, in the marketplace, and in the classroom, *change* is introduced, and *learning* makes it possible to make the change (see Figure 1.1). Each change initiative represents a new opportunity to learn. Each change initiative has its own cycle. Over time we experience a series of change cycles: change-improvement- learning + change-improvement-learning + . . . Even when there is little improvement there still is learning from the experience. Another important feature in Figure 1.1 is that two spirals are displayed. This is symbolic of an on-the-ground reality that is often ignored. In most settings most of the time there is more than one change process unfolding at the same time. This means more opportunities for learning. It also represents the potential of there being more confusion, less change success and less learning.

In the two examples provided, the changes and their learning needs are fairly easy to understand and to accomplish. But let's visit a mathematics classroom embarking on a school improvement effort—one expected to enable students to increase their abilities in critical thinking, in problem solving, and in teamwork. Before these new outcomes (changes) can be realized in the students, the instructional staff must change their teaching. Changing to a new way of teaching mathematics is not an easy effort.

One of the authors still vividly recalls a long-ago classroom teaching experience. The district mathematics curriculum coordinator introduced and expected that all teachers would

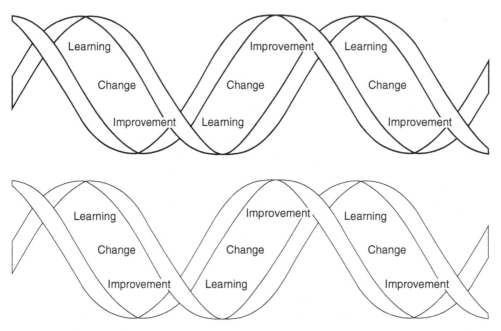

FIGURE 1.1   Learning: The Basis for Improvement

Source: Created by James L. Roussin & Mark Roussin, Stillwater, MN

implement and use a new inquiry-oriented math curriculum that provided students with a large degree of self-guided instruction. To support the teachers in this new approach to teaching math, teacher's guides for the curriculum were distributed, and teachers were directed to access staff development to learn about how to teach the new program by sitting alone in front of their residential televisions with the teacher's guide in their hands—not a very powerful learning strategy.

Subsequently, this teacher's mathematics guide became permanently affixed to her left arm. Following this "teacher-proof" set of teaching directions worked well when the students responded with understanding and the correct answers. However, when students didn't understand or respond correctly, the teacher did not know what to do for she had little depth of understanding of the process for this kind of instruction. Fortunately for all in this classroom, one of the intellectually gifted sixth-grade students understood the situation and the curriculum and taught the teacher! *Learning* enabled the teacher to *change* her practices and to use the *improved* and more effective program with students. (As a side note, in this same vignette, many teachers did not have access to the learning that enabled them to use the program. After trials and frustration with the program, they reverted to their old practices—a common result in such scenarios.)

Professional learning is a critical component embedded in the change process. Research focused on change process and on professional development reveals parallel findings, both of which identify the imperative of learning in order to use improved programs, processes, and practices.

Change Principle 2: Change Is a Process, Not an Event

The very first assumption in our studies of change in the early 1970s was that change is a process, not an event (Hall, Wallace, & Dossett, 1973). In other words, change is not accomplished by having a one-time announcement by an executive leader, a two-day training workshop for teachers in August, the delivery of the new curriculum/technology to the office, or a combination of these actions. Instead, change is a process through which people and organizations move as they gradually learn, come to understand, and become skilled and competent in the use of new ways.

Our research and that of others documents that most changes in education take three to five years to be implemented at a high level (for example, see George, Hall, & Uchiyama, 2000; Hall & Loucks, 1977; Hall & Rutherford, 1976). Further, for each new unit (e.g., school, business, or state) that undertakes the change, the process will take three to five years. For each new adopting unit, the clock begins at the beginning. There are very few shortcuts. However, the use of the constructs and tools presented in this book will significantly reduce the time needed to achieve a higher level of implementation. Failure to address key aspects of the change process can either add years to, or even prevent, the achievement of successful implementation.

Unfortunately, too many policy makers at all levels refuse to accept the principle that change is a process, not an event, and continue to insist that *their* changes be implemented before their next election, which typically is within two years. This "event mentality" has serious consequences for participants in the change process. For example, the press to make change quickly means that there is neither time to learn about and come to understand the new way nor time to grieve the loss of the old way.

Have you ever realized that grief is a key part of change? Chances are that when people must change, they have to stop doing some things that they know how to do well and in fact like doing, which creates a sense of sadness. What many leaders see as resistance to change may in large part be grief over the loss of favorite and comfortable ways of acting (Bridges, 2009). We recall following a new science program implementation, in which the second-grade teachers literally wept over losing their egg-hatching unit. This personal side of change will be examined in depth in Chapter 4.

Although many other implications of this principle will be developed in subsequent chapters, one that is important to note here has to do with planning for change. The strategic plan for change will look very different depending on whether it is assumed that change is a process or an event. If the assumption is that change is a process, then the plan for change will be strategic in nature. It will allow at least three to five years for full implementation and will budget the resources needed to support formal learning and on-site coaching for the duration of this phase. There will be policies that address the need for multiyear implementation support, and each year data will be collected about the change process. Such data will serve to inform the leaders in supporting planning for and facilitating implementation in subsequent years.

If the assumption is that change is an event, the plan for implementation will be tactical in nature. It will have a short-term focus typically centering on one formal training session for teachers before school begins, no on-site coaching or follow-up, and perhaps a first-year summative evaluation to see if the new approach is making a significant difference. As will be described in later chapters, one typical consequence of not finding any significant differences in the first or second year of implementation is the mistaken conclusion that the new approach does not work, when in fact there was not enough time and support for implementation so that it might work.

Examples of an event mentality also can be seen in the formal steps taken in the typical school improvement process: developing the plan utilizes several steps, and implementation requires just one. If school improvement were being thought of as a process, instead of an event, it would be called school "improving," and there would be several sets of actions across the implementation phase. The event mentality was well expressed by one assistant superintendent who exclaimed in the spring of the first year of implementation, "What do you mean, that teachers need more training? We bought them the books. Can't they read?"

Change Principle 3: The School Is the Primary Organizational Unit for Change

Although we have emphasized and will continue to emphasize the importance of understanding the dynamics of individuals in change, the key organizational unit for making change successful is the school. The school's staff and its leaders will make or break any change effort, regardless of whether the change is initiated from the inside or outside. However, the school is not an island; rather, it is part of district, state, and/or federal systems of education. The school can and must do a lot for itself, but it also must move in concert with and be supported by the other components of the system.

Note the assertion that schools need outside support. Change is a complex, dynamic, and resource-consuming endeavor. No single organization, be it a school or a national corporation, is likely to have all the expertise and resources needed to succeed in change. As will be emphasized in later chapters, *external* change facilitators, as well as supports from other parts of the system, are necessary. This is why, too frequently, the concept of site-based management does a disservice to organizations such as schools. Change processes are easier and chances of sustained success are increased as the school staff understands more about how to use external resources. Change becomes easier as those external to the school recognize the importance of their roles in facilitating change success in each school.

Everyone—teachers and principals in the school and personnel in the district office—must consider and understand how a school learns and advances as a change process unfolds. Many of the same interventions, such as providing teachers (and principals) with professional learning about their role with the innovation, can in fact be made throughout a district, especially during the first year of implementation. However, by the second year and beyond, different schools will be moving at different rates and will have different change successes and challenges. Thus, at least some of the key interventions will need to be uniquely targeted for each school.

Change Principle 4: Organizations Adopt Change—Individuals Implement Change

Although everyone wants to talk about such broad concepts as reform, policy, systems, and accountability, successful change starts and ends at the individual level. An entire organization does not change until each member has changed. Another way to say this is that there is an individual aspect to organizational change. Even when the change is introduced to every member of the organization at the same time, the rate of learning to make the change and of developing skill and competence in using it will vary individually. Some people will grasp the new way immediately, although most will need some additional time, and a few will avoid making the change for a very long time. Rogers (2003) has called this third group "laggards." Even when the change is mandated, some individuals will delay implementation. One implication of this principle is that leaders of organizational change processes need to devise ways to anticipate and facilitate change at the individual level.

This principle does not mean that all of the interventions (e.g., on-site coaching or a telephone hotline to address specific questions) in a change process must be addressed at the individual level. Nor does it mean that every individual will be at a different point in the process. People respond to and implement change in typical patterns that will be described in the following chapters. Change process leaders can and should anticipate many of these patterns. Many interventions should be targeted toward subgroups (e.g., principals being given an advance overview about what the change entails), and many others should be aimed at the organization as a whole. Still, since there is an individual element to how the change process unfolds, many of the interventions must be done with and for individuals, for there can be no change in outcomes until each individual implements the new practice.

Organizations are under heavy pressure to increase performance. In business, the press is to increase productivity, quality, and sales. In schools, the bottom line is the expectation to have ever-increasing student scores on standardized tests. To improve performance, many policy makers and executives are placing heavy emphasis on evaluating the end results. For schools, this is seen in the widespread focus on high-stakes testing. Annual testing of students has been mandated along with negative consequences for schools that do not show adequate increases in test scores. An implicit assumption with this approach to change seems to be that schools will incorporate the necessary changes to make test scores go up. However, little support is being made available to schools to implement these changes.

Figure 1.2 illustrates this problem. Imagine a setting where there is a very large and deep chasm with schools engaged in current practice located on the left cliff. On the right side of the chasm are the increases in student outcomes that are desired. Strategies that focus only on the right side fail to acknowledge several realities associated with implementing change. First, if there are no changes in practice, there is little reason to expect a change in outcomes. As principals often observe, "If you always do what you have always done, you will continue to get what you always have gotten." The second failure is in relation to Change Principle 2: Change is a process, not an event. If it takes three to five years to implement new practices to a high level, then it is highly unlikely that positive increases in outcomes will occur during the first or second year of implementation. In the scene shown in Figure 1.2, with an event mentality, practitioners are being asked to make a *Giant Leap*. They are being directed to improve outcomes without any support for learning how to change their current practices and thus improve.

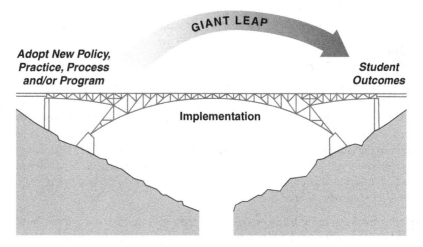

FIGURE 1.2   Implementation Bridge   Without an Implementation Bridge, individuals and organizations must make a giant leap

In order for change to be successful, an *Implementation Bridge* is necessary. Each member of the organization has to move across the Implementation Bridge. As they learn to change their practices, there can be changes in outcomes. Without an Implementation Bridge, there is little reason to expect positive change in outcomes. Instead, there are likely to be casualties as attempts to make the giant leap fail. Individuals and whole organizations may fall into the chasm.

Each chapter in this book will present research-based constructs and tools that can be used to facilitate individuals and organizations in moving across the bridge. The constructs and tools also can be used to measure the extent to which they have moved across the bridge. These implementation assessment data can then be correlated with outcome measures. Ideally, outcomes should be higher for those individuals and organizations that have moved further across the bridge. This was the case in one large study of implementation of standards-based teaching of mathematics (George, Hall, & Uchiyama, 2000). Students in classrooms with teachers who had moved further along with implementation had higher test scores.

REFLECTION QUESTIONS

Why would you wish for your children (or grandchildren) to be assigned to a teacher who is a continuous learner, one who is consistently updating his/her knowledge base? In what ways might the school support this learning?

Change Principle 5: Interventions Are Key to the Success of the Change Process

As individuals plan and lead change processes, they tend to be preoccupied with the innovation and its use. They often do not think about the various actions and events that they and others could take to influence the process; these actions are known as *interventions*. Training workshops are perhaps the most obvious type of intervention. Although workshops are important, the research studies cited in this book document many other kinds of interventions that are significant also—some that are even more crucial to achieving change success!

Pothole Warning

The term training workshops is used with great frequency. If we train horses and dogs, what do we really mean by a training workshop for educators?

Pothole Repair

*It seems to us that the term **training** is not very appropriate for its application to the human species. The knowledge and skills that are required for some designated task must be "developed" in each individual. And what about the term workshops? Here, it appears that we are really using this term to refer to large group learning sessions. In the case of either term, what is needed is an understanding that these activities are interventions that support individuals in gaining the requisite capacities for behaving in new ways. Without these interventions, whatever they are labeled, the change is doomed unless attention is given to them.*

Interventions come in different sizes. Interestingly, the most important interventions are the little ones, which most leaders forget to do or forget about having done. When change is successful, it is the quantity of the little things that makes the final difference. One of the major types of small interventions is what we call the *One-Legged Interview*. One frequent opportunity for One-Legged Interviews to occur is when a teacher and a principal meet in the corridor as each is headed to a different classroom. If they do not interact or if they have a social chat, these encounters are lost opportunities for innovation-related interventions. However, if the principal or teacher initiates a brief discussion about the innovation—"How's it going with _____?"—then a One-Legged Interview type of intervention is taking place.

We use the term *one-legged* to indicate that these interventions are brief since both the teacher and the principal probably have to be somewhere else when the next bell rings. Yet a moment was taken to talk about the teacher's involvement with the innovation. The research reported in later chapters consistently indicates that teachers are more successful with change in schools where there are statistically significantly more One-Legged Interviews.

We will share more about One-Legged Interviews in Chapter 2 on interventions. Here, the point is that it is critical to distinguish between the concepts of *innovations* and *interventions*. Change leaders tend to think only about innovations (the change itself), and not to think sufficiently about interventions (the actions taken to facilitate implementation) in terms of an overall plan for and during the unfolding of the change effort; and many fail to appreciate the value of small interventions.

Change Principle 6: Appropriate Interventions Reduce Resistance to Change

One of the big questions about change has to do with dealing with resistance. In most change efforts some people will *appear* to be resisting and some may be actively sabotaging the effort (note "appear to be" and "may be"). The first step is to determine the reason for the apparent resistance. Often what appears to be resistance is the individual working through the sense of loss for having to stop doing something that was comfortable. A second form of resistance is grounded in having serious questions about whether the change will really be an improvement. This questioning may be due to limited understanding about the change, or it may be based in solid reasoning and evidence. Some see a third form of resistance—several contemporary writers have stated in one way or another that change is painful, and they assert that this pain must be endured as a natural part of the change process. These authors might leave you feeling that only the masochist likes change, but this does not have to be the case.

Each of the three cases for apparent resistance has very different underlying reasons. In most situations, addressing the resistance requires attending to individual differences (Change Principle 4). To address these concerns requires very different interventions. *If* the process is facilitated well, learning about the change and its implementation can be productive, and it certainly does not have to hurt or even be dreaded. Of course, there are moments of frustration and times of grieving over what is being lost. However, if there is major pain in change, chances are strong that the leadership for the change effort has not understood what is entailed and required to facilitate the process well. In each of the following chapters, basic constructs, measures, research findings, and case examples will be introduced and used to describe ways of more effectively facilitating change. If these tools are understood and used well, there should be little resistance or pain—and large gains.

 REFLECTION QUESTIONS

Think about a change effort in which you have been involved. Were any individuals involved resistant to the change? Which of the three explanations might apply to these individuals? Or, is there a fourth explanation for their attitude?

Change Principle 7: District- and School-Based Leadership Is Essential to Long-Term Change Success

A central theme of advocates for bottom-up change is that those nearest the action have the best ideas of how to accomplish the change. Many implementers believe that they do not need any involvement from or with those above them. But here again, the findings of research and experience argue for a different conclusion.

Many of us have had firsthand experience with trying to implement some sort of innovative effort from the bottom. A classic example for the authors of this book was when we first worked together as teacher education faculty members. We were hired to create and implement an experimental teacher education program based on the Teacher Concerns model of Frances Fuller (1969). We and several others formed a multidisciplinary faculty team that developed and operated an experimental teacher education program that was truly an innovation bundle, one that included innovations such as professors teaming, an all-day blocked schedule for teacher education candidates, early field experiences, and a partnership of principals and teachers. In short, it incorporated many of the innovations that are found in what are now called professional development schools.

Although the teacher education program was very successful and became well known nationally and internationally, it expired after five years. It did not become the regular teacher education program at our university, nor did it have much direct influence on the traditional teacher education program. Why was that?

As faculty, we were at the proverbial bottom of the organization. As long as we had the energy, we were able to work collaboratively to develop and implement our innovation bundle. Although that bundle turned out to be successful, over time our faculty colleagues in the regular programs and the administration of the university did not actively support the continuation of the bundle, nor the implementation of any of the specific innovations into the regular programs. Without their direct support, in the end the innovation withered and was forgotten.

The point here is not to analyze what we might have done to garner more upper-level administrator support (which we will do in other chapters). Rather, our objective is to use firsthand experience to show that although the "bottom" may be able to launch and sustain an innovative effort for several years, if higher level decision makers do not engage in ongoing active support, it is more than likely that the change effort will cease.

In many ways Change Principle 7 is a corollary of Change Principle 8, since everyone along the policy-to-practice continuum has a role to play if change is going to be successful. Yes, teachers and professors can create, share with others, and implement new practices. Yes, administrators have to do things on a day-to-day basis that are supportive and provide continuous learning about the innovation opportunities. (Remember those One-Legged Interviews?) Administrators also have to secure the necessary infrastructure changes and long-term resource supports if use of an innovation is to continue indefinitely. And finally, yes, policymakers need to design polices that legitimize infrastructure changes and innovative practices and encourage continued use of the innovation.

Change Principle 8: Facilitating Change Is a Team Effort

In this book we will emphasize repeatedly the importance of facilitating the change process, which means that leadership must be ongoing for change to be successful. In Chapter 6 we

TABLE 1.1 The Policy-to-Practice Continuum

FEDERAL	STATE	DISTRICT	SCHOOL	CLASSROOM
President	Governor	Superintendent	Principal	Teacher
Secretary of Education	Commissioner of Education	Board of Education	Site Council	
Congress	Legislature			

will describe different Change Facilitator styles and the significance of each. Embedded in all of this and in many of the principles presented here is the core belief that change is a team effort. Just as in Change Principle 3 we stressed that no school is an island, we argue here that collaboration is also necessary among those responsible for leading change efforts.

Although in Change Principle 7 we describe the crucial role of the school principal, we want to emphasize that many others also have a responsibility to help change efforts succeed. Indeed, other administrators play important roles, as do frontline users and nonusers of the innovation. Teachers, for example, play a critical leadership role in whether or not change is successful. We really are in this phenomenon together, and all must help to facilitate the process.

Team leadership for change extends far beyond the school site. In many ways all of the actors across the Policy-to-Practice Continuum (see Table 1.1) are contributors to change success. Each of these role groups has the potential to strongly influence what happens at the local site and with individual users. State and federal executives and policy makers obviously have the potential to affect change in schools. Each time there is an election, voters hear about the "education" governor/president. Administrators and staff in the school district office can make important contributions to efforts to move across the Implementation Bridge. Each of these "external" roles can, and do, make significant differences in the degree of success of change. Colleagues in a school make a difference, too, as they learn about the change together. When teachers and others inside the organization share successes and challenges, implementation efforts can be more successful.

 ### REFLECTION QUESTIONS

Consider a change project in which you were part of the team that supported and facilitated the effort. What roles did you and the other team members represent? What support and assistance did you and the team offer that contributed to the success of the project?

Change Principle 9: Mandates Can Work

Change Principle 5 introduced the concept of interventions and gave special attention to a category of small interventions called One-Legged Interviews. Among the number of other types of interventions that will be described in later chapters, one of the more common is known as a *strategy*. A mandate is one kind of strategy that is used widely. Although mandates are continually criticized as being ineffective because of their top-down orientation, they can work quite well. With a mandate the priority is clear and there is an expectation that the innovation will be implemented. The mandate strategy fails when the only time the change process is supported is at the initial announcement of the mandate. When a mandate is accompanied by continuing communication, ongoing learning, on-site coaching, and time for implementation, it can work. As with many change strategies, the mandate has garnered a bad name—but not because the strategy itself is flawed, but because it is not supported over time with the other necessary interventions.

Change Principle 10: Both Internal and External Factors Greatly Influence Implementation Success

There are a number of factors that affect how successful each school will be in implementing change. Internal factors include the history of past attempts to change as well as characteristics of the current innovation. An additional factor is the recognition that no school is a fully independent operation (Change Principle 3). There are external pressures and expectations that cannot be ignored. How the internal and external factors are interpreted and applied becomes the key to implementation success.

Internal factors can easily be divided into two major sets:

1. *Physical features* of the setting, such as size, resources, spaces, technology, and schedules. Each feature can be either an important support or a hindrance. If the schedules facilitate implementers collaborating, there will be more teamwork. If technology can be used with ease, there will be more uses of it.
2. *People factors* include beliefs, attitudes, values, perceptions, and expertise. Of course leadership (Change Principle 7) and the depth of distributed leadership (Change Principle 8) are key factors. The organization culture and related norms are a set of internal factors that most certainly affect change success. For example, a staff that believes that adult learning is important and openly shares successes and failures will be more successful in implementing new approaches.

External factors most certainly include the multiple policies and procedures related to accountability that must be addressed. Characteristics of the surrounding community and the socioeconomic status of families are other obvious external factors. The amount of direct support and advocacy from supervisors, such as district superintendents, also are key factors. At the same time, as important and influential as these external factors may be, there are significant differences in how the people internal to the school interpret them.

In some schools, external factors drive everything: "The state makes us do this." In other schools within the same external environment, the internal interpretations can be quite different: "This is the policy. However, it doesn't say that we can't do it this other way."

Pothole Warning

With no interaction with the staff, the administrator/principal of the school determines that the staff should adopt a new mathematics curriculum that targets students' self-initiated learning. The program is announced to the staff, and they are provided with two days of staff development to support this adoption. The principal announces that there will be an evaluation of the new program at the end of the current semester.

Pothole Repair

Wow! Do you feel revolution in the air? This internal mandate will fail. Alternatively, the professional learning community school is an internal structure/strategy in which the entire staff—administrators and teachers—come together to study student performance data in order to decide collectively where attention needs to be given for increasing student learning, and what innovation or new programs/processes will be selected to address the needs of the students. Related is the attention by internal and external facilitators needed for providing the interventions necessary to support the staff in learning to use the new way.

Change Principle 11: Adopting, Implementing, and Sustaining Are Different Phases of the Change Process

In the distant past, and unfortunately in too many instances today, a decision is announced with the expectation that by the first day of the new school year, a change is made; although it is doubtful that life was ever really that simple. Today, especially given the complexity of most innovations, assuming change by simply announcing the adoption decision is bound to result in little success.

Understanding that change is a process (Change Principle 2) and that an Implementation Bridge is necessary is becoming widely prevalent. However, there seems to be less appreciation for the length of time it takes for most implementers to move across the bridge. In schools and in higher education, it commonly takes three to five years to fully implement a major reform initiative. True transformational changes can take even longer.

There is a rich history of research related to adoption and implementation. We know a lot about how to facilitate implementers moving onto and across the bridge. We have a lot less experience with understanding how to sustain use of the new way. Staying across the bridge and continuing to use the new way with quality requires structural changes as well as ongoing attention by both internal and external leaders.

Change Principle 12: And Finally, Focus! Focus! Focus!

It does not require multiple academic degrees to understand that multiple change efforts require multiple resources, and multiple amounts of attention and energy with multiple actions, to utilize formative and summative evaluations of the efforts to assure successful implementation. These elements require consistent, enduring, and uninterrupted attention to the goals and intended results of each change initiative. Consider the childhood fable of the Tortoise and the Hare's race. The Hare had a top-notch portfolio of talents and capacities that would surely enable him to win. For whatever reason, the Hare, possibly thinking of his superior skills and advantage, charged blithely ahead, skipping down the race path, admiring the blooming shrubs and flowers, thoughtfully picking some fragrant gardenia blossoms that might assist him in becoming better acquainted with Missy Blondine Rabbit. Meanwhile the Tortoise was consistently plodding along—with all attention given to the end marker that was the goal of the race. We know the result: The distractions allowed by the Hare gave the race to the Tortoise, who remained steadfast in her singular resolve to reach the end and win.

One might also recall Larry Lezotte (premier leader of Effective Schools research and practice) who advocated for schools and districts to exercise "organized abandonment," to carefully consider the primary goal of their improvement efforts, and eliminate all change initiatives that had accumulated but that did not support the major identified goal (1991, p. 4). This leaves the priority goal's challenge with all available resources to achieve its desired results. Jim Collins, Stanford Graduate School of Business, corporate leadership guru, author/lecturer, and researcher of business practices, in his book *Good to Great* (2001) admonishes change leaders to follow the "hedgehog concept"; that is, do one thing and do it well. In other words, keep the focus on the primary goal to be achieved. This is done, Collins maintains, through conscious choice (determining the precise goal to be achieved) and discipline (saying "no" to any opportunities that distract from the identified goal).

EAST LAKE SCHOOL DISTRICT'S STORY

The East Lake School District was introduced in Part I that precedes this chapter.

EAST LAKE IS ABOUT TO EXPERIENCE AN EPIPHANY ...

Mike Johnson, superintendent of East Lake School District, returned home after attending Mountain View High School's basketball game in the school's gymnasium. Mike felt especially obligated to remain for the whole game and see it to its successful conclusion on their home court (Mountain View won!); at a game a week earlier, a player on the visiting team suffered a possible concussion as the result of a fall on the gym's newly waxed and slippery surface. At their residence, Mike and his wife briefly shared anecdotes of the day and evening. Brenda Johnson had attended the community's Leadership Council for Tomorrow's monthly evening meeting. After hearing of the safe and successful basketball game, Brenda asked Mike if he had ever heard of the Hedgehog Concept, a topic that had consumed 30 minutes of her meeting and had been led by a supporter of the concept. Mike acknowledged that the topic was not familiar to him.

The next day Mike attended the Rotary Club's weekly luncheon, where the supporter of the Hedgehog Concept was the speaker. She promoted enthusiastically and at length the concept on how any business or organization can select one critical goal or objective to pursue and then employ the discipline to remove any and all obstacles that could cause distraction or lack of attention to the identified goal. Mike gave little attention to this message until after the meeting, when a visiting superintendent from a neighboring district called Mike's attention to the possible virtues and successful outcomes of such an approach.

Back in his office at 2:00 p.m., Mike was visited by Principals Inez Hernandez and Michael Major, who had been privy to the "gossip, rumor, and here-say" communication network in the district. They wondered if the superintendent had learned about "Hedgehogs and stuff" that was traveling around several of the schools. The visitors had copies of a paper written about it, one of which they left on the superintendent's desk. Mike declared innocence about Hedgehogs, and the conversation moved on to other topics. But at 3:30 p.m. on that day, a very important announcement arrived at the superintendent's office. The Director of Facilities, Transportation, and Budgets rushed in with a sheaf of papers to inform his boss that the state legislature had just removed 5 billion dollars out of the fund earmarked for schools. This move was to support the state's "arrogant" governor's interest in expanding his small business project and to contribute to the budget shortfall of the state.

This news meant a serious problem for the district. The director wondered to the superintendent if the district could afford to continue to support all the initiatives that the district had undertaken in the past couple of years, given the serious possibility of reduced state level funding.

After the director departed, Mike called in the assistant superintendent, Dr. Hanson, and asked her about Hedgehogs. "Do you mean," Dr. Hanson asked, "Jim Collins's message in his book *Good to Great* that suggests to the corporate sector that they not follow the typical business ideas for developing a successful business? Actually, I read that book for one of my recent courses. The metaphor is from a 1953 essay about Tolstoy's view of history that was written by Isaiah Berlin. He compared foxes, who are fascinated by many things, to hedgehogs, who tie everything to one whole system."

EAST LAKE SCHOOL DISTRICT'S STORY (CONTINUED)

Mike replied, "I think we should call a meeting immediately of our principals and school board to consider the impact of the legislature's decision and our district's work on school improvement. Let's try out this metaphor along with Hall and Hord's Change Principles. We really have to focus. And also, invite our budget director."

"Yes, sir," she said and left to arrange and organize for the meeting.

A TURNING POINT MEETING

Copies of the paper, left for the superintendent by the two principals, as well as a thick report of the district's state student test scores; status reports of the district's multiple change initiatives (which were not very pithy, given the nearly nonexistent monitoring of the individual efforts); a handout of the Change Principles; and the business office's copy of the legislative action marked each seat and were noted by the attendants as they convened for the meeting.

Three and a half hours later, Mike complimented the group on their meticulous examination of the data that were supplied. He further shared his appreciation for their uninterrupted attention to the task before them, including how to manage the district's efforts to consistently improve the schools' effectiveness so that all students learned well and how to deal with the looming financial crisis. He was effusive in his endorsement of the decision that they had collectively agreed on: The district would push full throttle ahead on adopting and implementing the new standards-based mathematics curriculum, and they would show how the other efforts were related, although those efforts would be of lower priority until time and resources became available for their full support.

Mike explained, "We will address the highly important mathematics curriculum since our student data tell us of its compelling need for attention in the district. Since it is tied to the Common Core Standards, this will also tie to the state's policy that directs all districts to create a plan to tie teacher evaluation to growth scores. Our next step is to convene a meeting of our community stakeholders to explain to them the situation, the rationale for our decision, and to request their support and advocacy. Leslie has provided each of us with a copy of research-grounded Change Principles for consideration. Please review these principles and be prepared to discuss their application to our new effort. You will note that we have already addressed Principle 12."

REFLECTION AND APPLICATION OF THE CHANGE PRINCIPLES

At the next meeting a week later, there was general consensus about how the Change Principles fit the district's situation and what needed to be done. Inez Hernandez (Island Park's principal) started by summarizing several of the principles. "Four of the principles might efficiently and effectively be considered collectively by East Lake: Principle 3, the school is the primary organizational unit for change; Principle 4, the organization may adopt a change, but it is up to the individuals who are expected to use the change to implement it; Principle 2, change is a process, not a one-time provision of an event such as a large-group learning session (workshop); and Principle 1, that change is based on learning about a change and how to use it. These four principles focus on *who* will be involved in implementation and on the initial *time and effort* that will be required for implementation."

Dr. Hanson said, "Our district's leaders should give early attention to address Principle 1 in order to launch the learning about the new mathematics change and how to use it. Research has instructed us that this principle and its learning is a multistep process initiated by hearing about or reading about the change, followed by a demonstration or modeling of the change, after which the potential implementers engage in practicing the new "way" and are given feedback. Ultimately, these individuals transfer the newly developing skills and capacities into the classroom where coaching is provided. These individualized coaching sessions are provided to eliminate incorrect behaviors and to improve the developing practices so that the novice (at the outset) now becomes expert in using the innovation."

EAST LAKE SCHOOL DISTRICT'S STORY (CONTINUED)

Assistant Superintendent Leslie Hanson added, "All of the principles work 'hand in glove,' for none of the principles operates in isolation from the others, but in tandem—that is, together. Our district and school leaders will require effective lessons in the use and application of these principles in their journey to school improvement through changes in classroom practice."

Superintendent Johnson followed, "Consider another grouping of the principles for our district: Principle 5, interventions are key to the success of change; Principle 6, interventions to support the change must be appropriate; Principle 7, leadership is essential (for assessing, planning, coordinating, supporting, and providing the interventions) for facilitating the change process; and Principle 8, this facilitation is a team effort. These principles attend to the interventions designed to facilitate implementation, which is context-specific, as Principle 10 reminds us. Significantly, the successful use of these principles is dependent on contextual factors, as is Principle 9, that mandates can work. Surprise!"

The superintendent continued, "Principle 11 maintains that the phases of the change process should be kept fully in mind during the adopting phase, followed by implementing; and when implementation has occurred, the now not-so-new change is sustained as it becomes part of routine practice. We are now discontinuing our efforts to keep all the balls of multiple change efforts in the air simultaneously. We need to keep in mind that for our folks, this new direction will be seen as a big change. We need to be sure to be clear about the situation and the reasoning behind our plan.

"In short, we are taking the advice of the Hedgehog and have identified a single highly significant innovation on which we will discipline ourselves to give undistracted focus and attention for the next three to five years."

The superintendent summed up the consensus: "This will be a big change for our district. We need to keep in mind that just adopting this focusing strategy is only the first phase. We now have to work on getting everyone on to and ultimately across the Implementation Bridge. The district has taken what would have been our first advice: to clarify and focus on only one new big-ticket effort at change and then proceed to consider carefully the concepts, strategies, and tools that will enable this district, its schools, and its educators to become more effective in using this innovation in order to provide a quality education for all our students."

CRITIQUE QUESTIONS OF EAST LAKE DISTRICT'S STORY

1. If Change Principles 1, 2, and 4 had been operating in this district, what differences would they have made?
2. What would you advise should be done next in this district?
3. If an innovation requires three to five years for quality implementation, how would you have managed the six initiatives held by this district?

SUMMARY

We have shared in this chapter a dozen principles important for consideration in the implementation of change. In order to provide a brief introduction to others about these principles, these talking points might be used:

1. A fundamental understanding required for the adoption and implementation of any change, or innovation, is that those who will be involved with it, whether using it or supporting others in using it, must learn what the new "way" is, and how to use it appropriately and productively.

2. Change is not a one-time event, but, rather, typically a three-to-five year process that can only be successful with consistent attention and focus on the learning and implementing needs of the participants.

3. While it is individuals who implement changes, the school is the primary organizational unit that adopts the change with the expectation that all members will take it on board and install it at a quality level; the district may introduce and "oversee" the change at the schools, but until each individual in each school has personally implemented it, change cannot be said to be implemented.

4. Interventions will dictate the success of the change effort, and appropriate interventions reduce resistance to adoption and implementation.

5. Leadership at the school and district levels is essential to successful change, and increased success occurs when the leaders take action as a team.

6. Surprise! Mandates can work as a successful approach to change—if communication, learning, and support are provided across the adoption and implementation stages.

7. Both internal factors (such as *physical* features of resources, schedules, space, technology; and *people* characteristics such as attitudes, values, expertise) and external factors (policies, regulations, community demographics) influence implementation; the wise change leaders give these factors careful and thoughtful attention.

8. Implementation leaders should never forget that there are clear phases to any change process—adopting, implementing, and sustaining—with each requiring its unique attention and support.

9. Too many change leaders, thinking that more is better, allow multiple change efforts to crowd into the district system and its schools; the wise leaders identify one vital change at a time upon which to focus resources and staff attention and effort, in order to produce the success of their most vital initiative.

DISCUSSION QUESTIONS

1. Identify, at this point, the Change Principles with which you most strongly agree. Are there any with which you strongly disagree? Why?

2. If a change effort is unsuccessful, which principles might be most "at fault"? Explain your answer.

3. Change Principle 6 addresses resistance to change. Is resistance ever appropriate or useful?

   If yes, explain why.

4. Describe a change experience that you have had or are experiencing. Point out how the 12 different principles relate. Do any of them explain why specific things went well and what is, or was, problematic?

APPLYING THE PRINCIPLES IN FACILITATING IMPLEMENTATION

1. Convene two or three persons in leadership roles in a school district or other type of organization. Ask them to review the 12 Change Principles and request that they describe how each principle is being addressed. Do they identify one or more principles that they have not addressed?

2. Select a school or other type of organization, and learn about its effort to implement a major innovation. Make a chart of the internal and external leaders of the change process. What types of facilitating interventions is each person making? To what extent are the individuals working as a team?

APPLYING THE PRINCIPLES IN RESEARCH OR PROGRAM EVALUATION STUDIES

1. In a school district where a districtwide innovation such as a new curriculum or perhaps a new technology has been introduced, conduct a survey, or interview leaders of a sample of schools. The survey should be constructed to solicit information about which of the Change Principles guided the introduction and implementation of the innovation, and which of the principles seemed to have been missed.

   Construct a chart on a large piece of chart paper, listing the 12 principles with a brief description of each principle down the left (vertical) side. On the horizontal continuum, place the name of each of the surveyed schools at the top of the column. Under the name of each school, make two columns, labeling one *Principal* and the second *Teachers*. This prepares your chart on which you will record your findings by filling in the cells with information obtained from the principal and the teachers that you interview and/or survey.

2. Interview a principal and several teachers individually (this should be done confidentially–do not reveal your sources). Solicit from them indicators of the presence or absence of each of the Change Principles. Compare the responses of the teachers with the administrator. Share the results with the administrator and other persons responsible for facilitating the implementation effort.

3. For a particular change initiative, such as a school/district improvement plan, conduct an Implementation Assessment for the purpose of seeing to what extent all of the Change Principles have been addressed. Share the results (above) with the central office staff responsible for implementation. If there is agreement, assess the implementation effort at several future times, such as every four months, to ascertain if/what interventions have been provided that address each of the principles. At the conclusion, share the results with this group.

LEARNING MORE ABOUT CHANGE PRINCIPLES

Abrahamson, E. (2004). *Change without pain*. Boston, MA: Harvard Business Press.

Deutschman, S. (2007). *Change or die*. New York, NY: HarperCollins.

Kotter, J. (2005). *Our iceberg is melting*. New York, NY: St. Martin's Press.

Kotter, J. (2008). *A sense of urgency*. Boston, MA: Harvard Business Press.

Reigeluth, C. M., & Garfinkle, R. J. (1994). *Systemic change in education*. Englewood Cliffs, NJ: Educational Technology Publications.

Sarason, S. B. (1996). *Revisiting "The culture of the school and the problem of change."* New York, NY: Teachers College Press.

CHAPTER 2

WHAT ACTIONS AND EVENTS ARE IMPERATIVE IN FACILITATING IMPLEMENTATION?

Interventions

Oh, my! I have just been called by the assistant superintendent to participate with a planning committee for introducing the new standards-based mathematics curriculum. I don't know whether to be thrilled or terrified!

—Josh Searight, Mathematics Department Head, Mountain View High School

I am so pleased. Our school improvement team just finished writing a grant for $50,000 that will supply resource materials and equipment for our new science program.

—Assistant Principal, Mountain View High School

What should I do next? The teachers have been to the fall series of three workshops and still don't understand how to operate the mathematics tutoring process. It appears that one-to-one help is now needed.

—Counselor, River Run Elementary School

Interdisciplinary curriculum development has required a significant amount of time and resources across these first three years, but it is well launched in our school, and we are preparing to report to the board about our efforts.

—Michael Johnson, Superintendent, East Lake School District

You know, the staff doesn't seem to really get it. What can I do to help them "see" my vision for our new curriculum that will surely make a great deal of difference in our students' mathematics achievement?

—Beverly Denver, Instructional Coach, Island Park Elementary School

All too often, the public, education professionals, and policy makers assume that change just happens. We are reminded of two theories articulated by Chin and Benne (1969):

1. The rational empirical approach to change postulated that a good program or process provided to good people would find its way into their practice. (The clue here is *good*.)
2. The power coercive approach maintained that a good program or policy delivered to good people through the offices of a power or authoritarian figure would certainly ensure change in practice. (The key here is *power* and its influence.)

Even today these two approaches tend to be employed by would-be change agents who assume that change will just happen if an attractive or needed innovation is presented (or mandated). Typically overlooked by such would-be reformers is an understanding that most change implementers have full-time jobs and don't have the opportunity to carefully and methodically design a self-changing approach. Difficulties also arise if the innovation is complex and vastly unfamiliar to the persons who are expected to adopt and implement it.

What we know from our own research and review of the literature on successful school change is that the ongoing actions of leaders and others are needed in a major way to support implementers. The main purpose of this book is to help would-be change facilitators to understand and learn how to apply a set of research-verified constructs and tools that can be used to develop the insights and skills needed to achieve successful change. Through our studies and firsthand experiences with supporting change in schools, businesses, and other organizations, we have assembled a large set of success stories. An important element of these successes has been notes about the rich variety and abundance of actions that leaders and other facilitators can do. Such ways of thinking about and describing change-facilitating actions are the topics of this chapter.

LEARNING OUTCOMES

After reading this chapter, the learner should be able to:

1. Identify and describe actions and events that become interventions.
2. Specify potential persons who deliver interventions.
3. Explain why interventions are really necessary.
4. Identify and describe six basic kinds of interventions needed for supporting successful change initiatives.
5. Report additional kinds of interventions that may be considered by facilitators.
6. Advocate for different sizes of interventions that researchers and practitioners use for studying and planning change.

INTERVENTION DEFINITION

Already you will have noticed our frequent use of the term *intervention*. This term has several meanings, which can lead to some confusion. In some disciplines, such as the health sciences and community development, the meaning of the term is a combination of the change, that is, innovation, and the various actions related to adopting the change, such as technical assistance. Here, the meaning is limited to the actions that affect change processes. As you will see, we use the term with great regularity in this book. The actions of leaders and others are so critical to change process success that we have devoted a great deal of time to analyzing what is done and the differences that interventions can make. Facilitators provide the interventions that can increase the potential for the success of change or allow it to fail. Thus, we think it is important to understand this term as we use it. Our explanation and definition follow; please hear our voice.

A white paper for one of our earlier studies reported on our efforts to develop a definition of the construct "intervention." After extensive fieldwork and research team debate, we settled on the following:

> Any *action* or *event* that influences the individual(s) involved or expected to be involved in the process of change is an intervention. (Hall & Hord, 1984)

Notice the use of the terms *action* and *event*. An action is deemed to be planned and focused deliberately on an individual, group, or all users or prospective users of a program or practice (see Table 2.1). Such an action could be sending an article about the use of math manipulatives to all primary teachers who teach mathematics. Discussion in a staff meeting about how implementation is going is another intervention. Complaining to a colleague also could be an intervention.

An event, on the other hand, is something that occurs outside the deliberations and plans of the change process. Has this ever happened to your effort? We have observed that events do indeed influence the process of change, so we have included them in our definition of intervention. Events that we have observed in our work include the following:

- A blizzard that prevented all truckers from delivering necessary equipment for a district's new astronomy program.
- A fire in the intermediate service center's print shop that caused a 3-week delay in getting materials for the high school's drug-prevention initiative.
- A learning styles consultant's bike accident on a mountain trail that resulted in rescheduling campus-based facilitators' preparations and planning for the project.

Each of these events was not planned; however, each affected change process progress.

Another important element—whether it is an action or an event—is that an intervention's influence may be positive or negative. In some of the preceding examples, the influence was intended to be positive, while the examples of events all suggest negative consequences.

TABLE 2.1   Definition of an Intervention

	An intervention is an	
Action	or	Event
	that is	
Planned	or	Unplanned
and that influences individuals (either positively or negatively) in the process of change.		

TABLE 2.2   **Indicators of the Intervention Construct**

1. If a central office curriculum coordinator brings microscopes to a teacher who is implementing a new life-science curriculum, this is an intervention to support the teacher's use of the change.

2. If a university professor coaches three principals in developing instructional leadership skills by meeting with them each week across a school year, this is an intervention on behalf of the principals' developing new roles.

3. If a principal conducts a staff development session about formative assessment, the principal has provided an intervention.

4. If a superintendent sends an e-mail or hosts a party for all district staff in recognition of a success, that is an intervention.

5. When two teachers meet in the parking lot and talk about the innovation, that too is an intervention.

This does not mean that all actions are positive or that all events are negative. A refusal to approve funding for a how-to workshop (action) can be negative, whereas a flat tire that forces teachers to carpool (event) and thereby have the opportunity to share success stories could be positive (see Table 2.2).

Pothole Warning

Be very sensitive and observant to the unplanned events that will almost always creep into the change process. Beware that their influence can be negative— or not.

Pothole Repair

Keeping your ear to the ground and your hand on the pulse will be very helpful in forestalling unfortunate negative events that cause change projects to flounder. On the other hand, maintaining a close watch as implementation unfolds can afford the possibility of identifying events that have a positive influence; these then should be capitalized upon and repeated for their continuing effect.

THE SIZE OF INTERVENTIONS

We have seen and recorded wide-ranging types and sizes of interventions—from quite simple and short-term actions to multiyear strategic plans. An example of a short-term intervention would be a One-Legged Interview, such as when a school improvement team member stops by to say hello to another teacher and then asks if she has any needs regarding the new technology. Another, more complex example is a change facilitator observing an implementer and providing feedback on his use of a new instructional strategy. An intervention's simplicity or complexity may be analyzed, and this, as well as the various levels of interventions that constitute a typology of interventions that facilitators can consider in their work, is addressed in the remainder of this chapter.

REFLECTION QUESTIONS

Consider a change project with which you are familiar. Identify an action and an event that occurred during implementation. Who, or what, contributed the action and the event? What were the results of each action and event?

SOURCES OF INTERVENTIONS

Who are the deliverers of interventions? Policy makers and executives are quick to claim responsibility for many change initiatives. The research on and stories about successful school change are almost unanimous in identifying the principal as the primary catalyst and facilitator of site-based change. And yet, as we have documented in our studies, the principal is not the only source of interventions.

It is easy to assume that principals and superintendents, because of their positions, are the primary change facilitators. Although this is desirable, it is not always true. Frequently, they are a minimal source of change process–related interventions. Even when they are involved, almost inevitably, because of the multiple roles that administrators have, others are the major sources of interventions (see Table 2.3).

We suggest that innovation-related interventions and change facilitation support and assistance may be delivered by any person who assumes the role and responsibilities of the change facilitator (whether implicitly or explicitly). In other words, there are many possible and actual sources of change-related interventions.

One important implication is that many change effort participants, including implementers, do not realize that they take actions that influence an individual, a group, or perhaps the entire change effort. Another implication is that many people can be involved in the delivery of planned interventions. One significant result is that the burden of support and assistance to the users and nonusers is distributed. Responsibility for change leadership can be shared. This is important in view of the limited time that people typically have to invest in facilitating change. Sharing change-facilitating responsibilities means that the role is not necessarily positional but becomes operationally defined by what is done and by whom, which is the focus of the discussion that follows.

REFLECTION QUESTIONS

Think back to your involvement in a change effort. Recall any and all individuals who supplied help and assistance in the implementation of the change. What roles did these individuals represent? Were they administrators? Teachers? Coaches? Parents? Others?

TABLE 2.3   **Sources of Interventions**

CAMPUS	DISTRICT	COMMUNITY	GOVERNMENTS
Principals	Superintendent	Parents	Policy makers
Key teachers	Curriculum coordinators	Business	State board/Legislature/Congress
Counselor	Instructional supervisors	Representatives	Governor/President
Students		School board	Voters

SIX FUNCTIONS OF INTERVENTIONS

Many organizations, leaders, and consultants have been committed to implementation of various changes and improvements. Considerable time and attention are given to implementing change through such efforts as developing school/district improvement plans. Although planning activities for change seem generally to receive great attention, thinking through the details of delivering key interventions frequently falls in the cracks. Up-front planning for the launch of a new initiative can be very well thought-out, but often there remains an implicit assumption that implementation is an event.

Think back to the metaphor of the Implementation Bridge. The Giant Leap (shown in Figure 1.2) illustrates what happens when we assume that adoption automatically results in immediate student gains. As obvious as this metaphor may be, too often change leaders do not plan for the actions that will facilitate implementers getting across the bridge. Instead there is an expectation that somehow change unfolds magically. Unfortunately, this scenario is far too often exercised in our schools, universities, and other organizations. This approach is seen every year with the announcement of another "fix" that is to be adopted with little funding, limited resources, and an expectation that change will be accomplished in a relatively short time period.

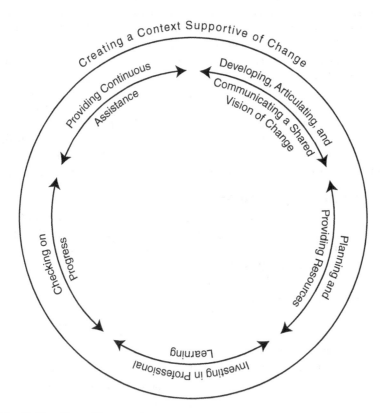

FIGURE 2.1 Six Functions of Interventions

Thinking in depth about interventions is critical for all organizations and especially for school success in implementing today's complex innovations and comprehensive reforms. To respond to this issue and to provide an example of the Implementation Bridge across a chasm, the staff of the Southwest Educational Development Laboratory (SEDL) undertook a broad review of the leadership and change-facilitation literature.

Their first objective was to identify relevant research-based concepts and information that could support the development of effective facilitative leaders for school improvement projects. To help these busy practitioners get to the center of change-facilitation work, and to share strategies for moving implementers across the Giant Leap's chasm, this wide-ranging review of the literature focused on the actions and behaviors of leaders who were facilitating change (Hord, 1992a)—in other words, on interventions. What could be more important, the staff asked, than assisting potential facilitators in understanding the demands of the role and the strategic interventions required for advancing the change effort?

The literature review resulted in identifying a broad array of interventions, which were organized into six *Functions* (see Figure 2.1). A major source of this information came from earlier CBAM research, specifically the Principal/Teacher Interaction (PTI) study reported by Hord and Huling-Austin (1986) and the conceptualization of Game Plan Components in an Intervention Taxonomy done by Hall and Hord (1984). These six Functions were deemed necessary for making change happen. In many ways they constitute the job description for change facilitators, whether they are assigned to local schools and districts or to state departments of education and other organizations. The ultimate purpose has been to think about the importance of different types and sizes of interventions that are necessary to realize successful change in organizations. Since the original identification of these six Functions, they have been continuously reviewed and revised through ongoing literature reviews, especially the research on successful change (Hord, Rutherford, Huling-Austin, & Hall, 2004). These six Functions, which CBAM devotees have come to refer to as the "six sacred strategies," are introduced next.

Function I: Developing, Articulating, and Communicating a Shared Vision of the Intended Change

A first step in moving toward a changed and improved future is the development of a shared dream or vision of what will be—such as a vision of the future that increases student outcomes. The goal of increased student outcomes could result from specific changes or innovations that are selected for adoption and implementation. Many change efforts fail because the participants do not share mental images or pictures of what classroom and/or school practice will look like when an identified change is implemented to a high quality. Picturing the change in operation provides the target for beginning the change journey. A part of this process can be creating an Innovation Configuration (IC) Map of the change—a useful way of defining what the change/innovation will look like when it is actually and actively in operation in its intended setting (see Chapter 3).

The elements of the shared vision of change must be as clearly defined as possible, and facilitators must continuously communicate this vision to enable implementers to move toward high-quality implementation. When implementers have a shared vision, facilitators can be consistent in supporting individuals and groups.

Specific facilitator interventions for developing a shared change vision could include but are not limited to engaging the school staff and community in identifying its beliefs and values regarding the purposes of the school, determining areas of the school program in need of change and improvement, selecting solutions to address the areas in need, and collectively developing clear mental images of the solution (i.e., the vision of change) when it is in operation in the school or classrooms.

The shared vision can be communicated in multiple settings: on the school's or district's Web site, in school and district newsletters, at school board and other community meetings, at the local coffee shop, and even on the golf course. The idea is to continually remind all constituents, in various ways, of the vision and where the school is in relationship to realizing it. Related is the understanding that attention to the vision must be provided throughout the process of change in order to capture and capitalize on (or diminish) evolving changes in the vision. For further material on vision and on the six Functions of basic interventions, see the Additional Readings/Resources at the end of this chapter.

Function II: Planning and Providing Resources

When an initial vision for change has been established (the vision can certainly evolve and change as the school staff experiences, learns, and gains more expertise), planning for its realization is both possible and necessary. All logistical factors and resource allocations, along with policy implications, must be considered. Although it seems obvious, the planning and provision of resources represent an important means by which implementers are enabled to initiate implementation and sustain the change process. We have observed change efforts that lacked necessary resources, which forestalled the expected beginning of the change process and in the end doomed the entire effort.

We frequently observe school districts and other organizations that have well-articulated policies for selecting innovations. What we find missing is the equally important set of policies that address how implementation is to be supported and achieved. We also regularly see failures to plan for *sustaining* use of the innovation once it is implemented.

Planning is not a one-time event. Like a holiday trip, destinations sometimes change, and unexpected additions frequently may be made for increased effectiveness and/or satisfaction. Thus, although a plan is essential for understanding where the change journey begins, it should never be considered as cast in concrete. Likewise, the resource requirements for a change are altered across time as implementers become more expert in the use of an innovation and as the configuration of use may make differing demands. Not to be forgotten is the regular depletion of program materials and equipment and the need for updating supplies to teachers and students.

Other types of resources also require planning. One of the most important and most typically lacking is time: time for planning, time for professional development, time for sharing, and projecting the time (years) it will take to achieve high levels of use. Also important, of course, is time for facilitators to do *their* work. School administrators would do well to plan dedicated time for one or more skilled facilitators to coach and address Stages of Concern (SoC) (Chapter 4) and Levels of Use (LoU) (Chapter 5). Scheduling time for implementers to meet to discuss successes and share solutions to problems has proven to be valuable, also.

Other specific actions of facilitators related to this Function include developing policies related to implementation (if they are not already in place), establishing rules and guidelines by which implementation progress will be assessed and monitored, staffing new roles and/or realigning existing ones, scheduling meetings and other regular and nonregular events, seeking and acquiring materials and equipment, providing space, and accessing funds needed for the new program or practice.

Function III: Investing in Professional Learning

Change means developing new understandings and doing things in new ways. If faculty members are to use new curricular programs or instructional practices, they must learn how to do that. Thus, *learning* is the basis of and the corollary to change (see Change Principle 1, Chapter 1). Formal training and other forms of professional and personal development, then, are essential to preparing implementers for the change. And, when change is viewed as a process, learning opportunities for implementers should be ongoing as they develop more expertise in using the innovation. All too frequently, training workshops are scheduled only at the beginning of a change effort. We know that Task concerns do not become intense until after use begins. Therefore, Stages of Concern can be used to design and shape the development and learning sessions in the preimplementation period of preparation as well as during implementation, when implementers are changing from novices to mature users of the new practices (as is discussed in Chapter 4). Note also that different levels of information and understanding are characteristic of people's behaviors at each Level of Use (see Chapter 5).

Leaders of the change effort will need to consider the following interventions, and others, in the learning and development category: scheduling learning and development sessions across time as the implementers move from novice to expert; identifying and contracting with consultants (internal and external); providing information about the change; teaching the skills required of the innovation; developing positive attitudes about use of the new program; holding workshops; modeling and demonstrating innovation use; and clarifying misconceptions about the program or practice. With this Function, the interventions are formal, organized, and scheduled, that is, provided as large-group learning sessions. Professional learning interventions at the individual and small-group levels are addressed in Function V below.

It is important that learning and development be concerns-based and focused on the vision for the change. When implementers' current concerns are addressed, implementers gain the information and learn the skills necessary to use the new way well. Too often, professional development has been vague and off-target in relation to the current concerns of those out on the bridge. With a focus on the staff's concerns about its new program and practices, and on the vision of what the change will look like in operation, investing in professional learning will pay large dividends.

Function IV: Checking Progress

Because change does not happen overnight, the process must be continuously assessed and monitored. Even though a clear articulation of the change has been expressed and material and human resources have been provided, the change journey is not without its bumps and detours. A significant set of facilitator interventions should focus on keeping a hand on the pulse of change. One-Legged Interviews are an excellent way to check with implementers to identify emerging needs, clarify questions, and solve small problems. Not only does this enable the facilitator to assess progress, it also signals continuing interest to the implementers that their efforts are worthy of notice and support.

Decision makers and regulatory agencies have always known that what is measured or monitored is given more attention. A change effort will be given more attention if facilitators continually check on how implementation is progressing.

More often than not, the change effort is lost when the leaders fail to routinely check on progress. Important checking actions include gathering data about the concerns of each implementer; collecting information about the developing knowledge and skills of implementers; collecting feedback at the end of workshops and providing feedback on the feedback; talking informally with users about their progress; and, at regular intervals, systematically measuring, analyzing, and interpreting SoC, LoU, and IC (see Chapters 3, 4, and 5). It is important that data collected about implementation be analyzed, carefully interpreted, and used to guide subsequent interventions.

Function V: Providing Continuous Assistance

Assisting is directly coupled with assessing, as discussed earlier. When concerns, needs, and problems are identified, a response is required that resolves the issue. Assistance may take the form of supplying additional materials that address a mechanical use problem, providing formal or informal learning activities that address Impact concerns, teaming with implementers to demonstrate refinements, and peer observations. It makes sense to assess progress in order to identify needs and then to provide assistance to respond to the needs. This coupling of *assessing* and *assisting* is labeled *coaching, consulting,* or *follow-up* and typically occurs with individuals or very small groups of implementers. These are crucial interventions.

A very important assisting action is to stop by and simply ask, "How's it going?" Additional actions include responding to individuals' questions and confusions, encouraging individuals in their use of the innovation, assisting single and small-group implementers in problem solving, providing follow-up and technical assistance, conducting quick conversations about the implementers' use and reinforcing what they are doing, and celebrating successes both small and large, publicly and privately.

The importance of the coaching role should not be underemphasized. We have observed repeatedly that when an expert coach, such as a master teacher, has assigned time (several days each week) to coach implementers, Task concerns (i.e., Stage 3 Management) do not become intense. In other words, during the first year(s) of implementation, the typical wave motion of high Task concerns can be reduced (see Chapter 4) when coaching is provided.

Function VI: Creating a Context Supportive of Change

Increased attention is currently being paid to the context, climate, and/or culture of the school and district and how these factors influence the workplace and, subsequently, how professionals respond to change initiatives. For example, Boyd (1992b), in a review of the literature on context that supports or inhibits change, defined two components of context. One is the *physical,* or nonorganic, aspects of an organization: its building facilities, schedules, policies, and the like. The second component is the *people* element: the beliefs and values held by the members and the norms that guide their behavior, relationships, attitudes, and so on. Although the context is identified by its two parts, the parts are interactive and influence each other. For example, a small faculty in a small facility (but one with an available meeting space) will find it much easier to come together to interact and build trust than would a much larger faculty spread over multiple buildings. A supportive context decreases the isolation of the staff; provides for the continuing increase of its capabilities; nurtures positive relationships among all the staff, students, and parents/community members; and urges the unceasing quest for increased effectiveness so that students benefit. (For further discussion of the characteristics of a supportive context for change, see Chapter 7.)

In such a context the participants value change as a means for improving their effectiveness and seek changes in order to improve their practice. Boyd (1992a) reports that school leaders can take actions, such as those listed in Table 2.4, to create this context.

In summary, the six Functions of interventions provide a useful framework for developing the knowledge and organizing the skills that facilitators need to plan for change, monitor progress, and evaluate outcomes (see Table 2.5).

REFLECTION QUESTIONS

Have your experiences with change projects contained these six Functions? If any were omitted, did this omission have any effect on results? If so, how?

TABLE 2.4   Strategies to Use in Creating a Supportive Context (Boyd, 1992b)

1. *Shaping the structural features of the context* by manipulating schedules and structures (such as faculty meetings) so that people can come together and share improvement ideas, by allocating resources to support the improvement effort, and by developing policies for enhancing staff capacity.

2. *Modeling* the behaviors and norms desired of the staff by interacting and cooperating in a significant way with all staff, by working with focus and commitment, and by being highly visible in the daily routines that they hope the staff will emulate.

3. *Teaching and coaching* by reading, studying, and subsequently sharing materials that will nurture and develop the staff's expertise; by attending professional development activities with the staff; and by attending conferences and sharing materials with the staff.

4. *Addressing conflict* by facing it rather than avoiding it, and thus using conflict as a vehicle to resolve disputes and build unity.

5. *Selecting, rewarding, and censuring staff* by recognizing their work publicly and privately, by inviting the staff to share their efforts and experiences related to improvement goals, and by insisting that staff commit to school goals through the selection and termination processes.

TABLE 2.5 Implications of Interventions for Change Leaders and Facilitators

1. Successful implementation of new policies, programs, processes, practices, and even new personnel does not just happen.

2. Assuming that simply announcing such changes is sufficient (nearly all of the time) leads to little or no implementation or, at best, very superficial implementation.

3. Interventions both small and large can make the difference.

4. Although principals and other leaders have been identified as change facilitators or significant suppliers of interventions, others also take many of these actions. Whoever assumes the role and responsibilities—whether they are teachers, parents, central office personnel, community members, or others—can and does provide change process–related interventions.

5. Many types of interventions must be provided to ensure the success of change. The most effective facilitators acquaint themselves with and use their knowledge of interventions in planning, monitoring, and assisting their organization's efforts to change and improve.

6. Because change is accomplished at the individual level, facilitators need to use diagnostic tools for shaping the interventions supplied to individuals as well as providing groups with the array of interventions necessary to ensure each implementer's success. At the same time, other interventions need to be targeted toward the whole organization or system.

7. Since *learning* new information, skills, and behaviors is at the heart of any change project, facilitators would do well to keep this basic premise in mind as they consider, design, and deliver the interventions necessary for change process success.

ADDITIONAL KINDS OF INTERVENTIONS

Four of the six basic intervention types discussed—planning and providing resources (developing supportive organizational arrangements), investing in professional learning (training), checking on progress (monitoring and evaluation), and providing continuous assistance (providing consultation and reinforcement)—accounted for the majority of interventions identified in earlier CBAM studies; the original CBAM names are shown in parentheses (Hall & Hord, 1984, 1987; Hord & Huling-Austin, 1986; Hord et al., 2004). Two of the six categories of interventions—developing a shared vision of the change and creating a context for change—were identified by Hord (1992a).

The CBAM studies revealed two additional components that are less frequently given attention but are quite important in change efforts, especially for larger systems: communicating externally and disseminating information. We examine the importance of these interventions next.

Communicating Externally

An important but often neglected set of interventions are those actions taken to keep individuals and groups external to the implementation site informed about what is happening. To gain their support or approval, these groups need to be informed by the on-site participants. One of the quotes at the beginning of this chapter reports that the change effort on interdisciplinary curriculum is going well and that a report on progress will be made to the board. It is easy to understand the politically and economically astute reasons for communicating externally to such an influential group, but too often too little is done, or it is done too late.

Activities related to this category of interventions include describing the change, its purpose, and its benefits to those outside the current adopting organization; not only having a Web site but keeping it up to date; and making presentations at various district and community meetings. At the local level, external communications could include keeping the external *SAC* members of the site council and the PTO/PTA informed about progress and setbacks, informing all possible constituents about progress, and developing a campaign to gain the support of the public and other relevant groups.

Disseminating Information

Efforts to share information about the new program or practice, and to let others know of its value and positive impact with the intention of persuading them to adopt the program, are dissemination interventions. These interventions are important first steps in "going to scale." In broadcasting the virtues of the innovation, broader support and influence may be gained as well, but in this category the primary intent is to inform prospective adopters from other sites.

To accomplish the purpose of this category, the facilitators engage in various activities, including e-mailing descriptive information to external persons, colleagues, friends, and others who might be interested; making presentations at regional and national meetings; encouraging others to adopt the innovation by reporting its benefits; making large-group presentations about the innovation to potential adopters; providing free sample materials; and training expert colleagues to represent the innovation.

Note that it is not necessary to do disseminating interventions in order to have change success at the home site. As a matter of fact, spending too much time on disseminating, especially early in implementation, can be a distraction and draw needed energy and resources away from the project. Early dissemination also runs the risk of appearing premature, since everything may not work out as expected. Four or 5 years into a change process can be an excellent time to begin disseminating actions, for at this point those actions can serve to reward and expand the perspectives of successful implementers while increasing visibility for all.

REFLECTION QUESTIONS

Imagine that you are assigned the task of communicating externally about your change effort. Who would you target for this purpose? What might your talking points be? How would you know if you have been successful?

EAST LAKE SCHOOL DISTRICT'S STORY: DEVELOPING THE INTERVENTION GAME PLAN

EAST LAKE USES THE "BRIDGE" TO CONSIDER ITS INTERVENTION GAME PLAN . . .

Superintendent Mike Johnson had been considerably disconcerted by the events of the first days chapter (Chapter 1) of East Lake's story. However, he was greatly pleased by the district's and school administrative staff's attending to the challenges before them, and making a careful and deliberate decision. Further, he congratulated himself again for having brought Leslie on board as the assistant superintendent. She and he would spend the next half day creating the agenda for the stakeholders

(continued)

EAST LAKE SCHOOL DISTRICT'S STORY (CONTINUED)

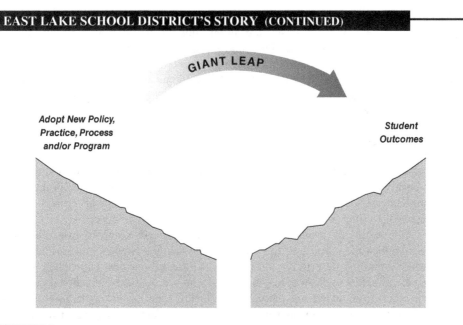

FIGURE 2.2

meeting, and he would deputize her to create a small committee to produce the first draft of an Implementation Game Plan.

As Mike reviewed the Change Principles provided by Leslie, his attention was caught by Principle 4 and the eye-catching graphic of the Giant Leap (Figure 1.2). Mike admitted to himself that he and the district had been guilty of the message of the graphic. There were times when the district had adopted new programs and policies without providing appropriate and ongoing support for the staff in order to assure that the new programs would be fully implemented. This explained to Mike why little improvement in student results had been accomplished after taking on these new programs and their practices. He assumed that Leslie and her team would not let that happen this time.

Ten days later, Leslie and her team invited Mike to an "unveiling" meeting to share with him their ideas and the intervention plan they had drafted, which would be used with all the stakeholders of the district. Consideration was given to addressing all individuals who would be involved with the standards-based mathematics program priority, including interested parents and community members. At their first meeting, Leslie had shared a new set of ideas with the Implementation Game Plan Committee—a paper from one of her recent grad-level courses that focused directly on the actions required to enable implementation and to subsequently achieve change process success. She and the committee were very enthusiastic about their use of the paper's messages and the plan that they had sketched out.

Leslie explained to the game plan committee that they were utilizing the work of researchers who had identified six "Functions" necessary for successful implementation. She noted that the committee had been noticeably impressed with the Giant Leap graphic in their Change Principles material, and that they had found the "Implementation Bridge" metaphor to be a very persuasive way to think about putting the newly defined mathematics curriculum in place in the schools.

"Thus," she said to Mike, "we have crafted our plan and its explanation through use of the Implementation Bridge. If you will, please, Inez [Island Park principal], manage the PowerPoint for our presentation."

EAST LAKE SCHOOL DISTRICT'S STORY (CONTINUED)

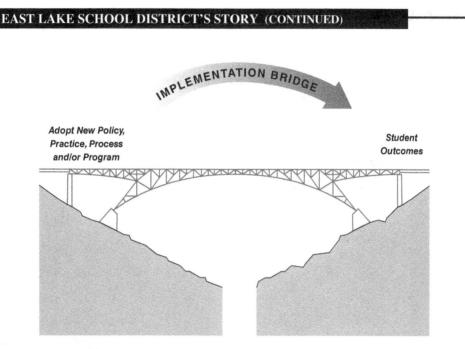

FIGURE 2.3

The Giant Leap was flashed on the screen.

"What you see here," Leslie explained, "is the first step in the implementation process: the determination of *what* is the new program, process, or practice that we will use to improve our students' mathematical reasoning, critical thinking, and problem-solving skills. But you will notice that the new practices and the students are woefully unconnected—thus, the Giant Leap to get over the chasm that separates the two entities. It is sad to say that there are more than one or two schools, districts, and additional educational and other organizations that assume that the introduction of a new program somehow automatically produces new outcomes.

"There is an old American saying, 'You can't cross 20 feet in two big jumps'—another foolish assumption. Or if you do so, it is at your peril. So, what to do?

"There needs to be a bridge for crossing the chasm, and although it is named the Implementation Bridge, it gives no indication about what it is or how to implement the new program or move it to the students. But in the next slide, important new elements are introduced:

"The school's principal and teachers are now in the picture, although their simple existence cannot promise implementation success. But we now know that there is a program to be taken on board and that our educators have a role to play that will target students. Still, how to get the program across the bridge? Of course, you knew we had an answer; please show the next slide.

"We now have our six research-tested Intervention Game Plan Functions, labeled by most change facilitators as strategies. These constitute a heavy load on the bridge, but they serve as the heart and muscle for reaching successful change. Let us look at these six Functions/Strategies to see how they will carry the new program across the bridge to the principals and teachers, and through them, subsequently, to students."

(continued)

EAST LAKE SCHOOL DISTRICT'S STORY (CONTINUED)

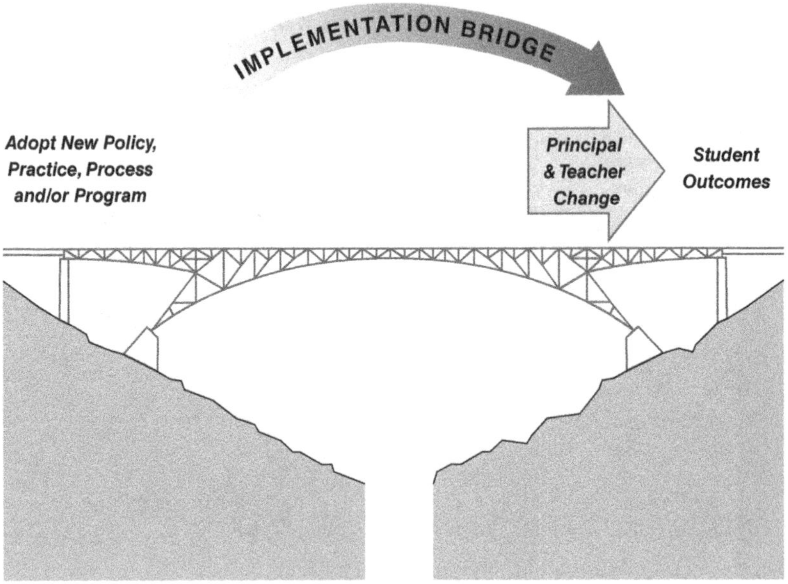

IMPLEMENTATION BRIDGE

Adopt New Policy,
Practice, Process
and/or Program

Principal
& Teacher
Change

Student
Outcomes

FIGURE 2.4

FUNCTION VI: CREATE A CONTEXT SUPPORTIVE OF CHANGE

"This strategy (that we have identified as Function VI and placed at the end of the list of Functions) demands a multitude of activities. Ideally, this Function should not have to be addressed at the beginning of a change effort. Such a context should already have been a permanent part of the climate/culture of the schools and district. If such a context does not exist, a few ideas for generating this positive climate are to use actions that allow for relationship building, such as making clear to the implementers that they are doing important work; developing trust between and among all the individuals doing the implementation; and recognizing and applauding the efforts of each person who is giving time, attention, and energy to the school's efforts to improve. When things fail or go wrong, help individuals to see it as an opportunity for learning, changing, and trying again."

Superintendent Mike was listening closely to these ideas, for he recognized their importance in the workplace. When individuals have the opportunity to learn and grow in an atmosphere of mutual trust and respect, the challenging work of implementing new practices is diminished. Mike started thinking that he must be a cheerleader, coach, and champion of all the "troops," especially as they head into the fray of change.

FUNCTION I: DEVELOP A SHARED VISION

Working on the context is never finished, but an initial strategy directed at the implementation of the new mathematics curriculum, or any new practice and imperative for any successful change, is to create a precisely clear mental image of the change as it is expected to appear after its high-quality

EAST LAKE SCHOOL DISTRICT'S STORY (CONTINUED)

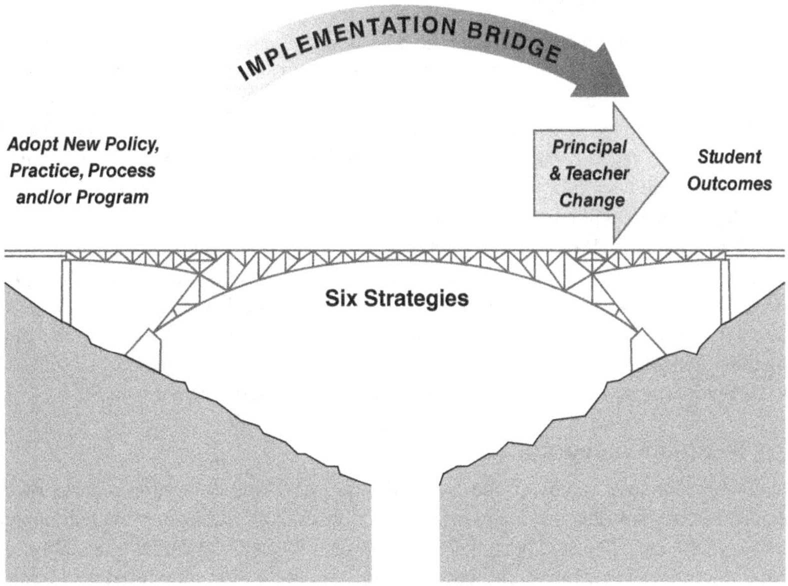
IMPLEMENTATION BRIDGE
Adopt New Policy, Practice, Process and/or Program
Principal & Teacher Change
Student Outcomes
Six Strategies

FIGURE 2.5

implementation. This provides the target for the implementers' work, and the tool that we recommend is the Innovation Configuration Map (see Chapter 3) that indicates in action language what an observer would see in classrooms when the innovation (in this story, a very innovative way of approaching teaching and learning of mathematics) is in use.

"Excuse me, Leslie, could I ask a question?" queried Martin Chin, the new instructional coach at the high school.

"Of course," Leslie replied.

"I am already lost. Does everyone else know about this configuration thing?"

"No, Martin, we will all be engaging in a great deal of learning—how to think differently and learn about new tools and techniques to use as we implement our new program. We will all be learning together, and that will be incredibly exciting—I promise!"

FUNCTION II: PLAN AND PROVIDE RESOURCES

"Because we will be very explicit about our vision of our change, we can use that for planning for the implementation; we can also, for the same reason, be able to identify our needs, such as time, space, materials, and human resources. We may determine that we will benefit from engaging a consultant to help us learn, or we may travel a short distance to see this curriculum in action in another school. The important thing is that our vision text will enable us to be fairly clear and comprehensive about creating our plan and for listing our resources to use the plan."

(continued)

EAST LAKE SCHOOL DISTRICT'S STORY (CONTINUED)

FUNCTION III: INVEST IN LEARNING

"In the materials that we are studying and using to help us with implementation, we have heard several times that learning is the basis for change. So, the term *invest* is interesting. Why would we use the idea of investing related to learning?"

Ray Raulson raised his hand. "Well, I watch the stock market at times, and occasionally I put some money into some stocks—that is, I invest it, with the hope that I will get a big return on my investment. I'm not sure what it means to 'invest in learning,' unless it suggests that investing in our learning and that of others will pay some dividends."

"I think you nailed it, Ray. Since learning is the key to the success of the change process, we will be learning a great deal about the new math—what it is and how to use it. That will require a big investment of time and commitment in order to maintain continuous learning about it. But we can be assured that it will pay off in our new knowledge and skills in teaching math. And notice again that the principal and teacher are the factors that most immediately impact students. All our educators must be excellent learners of the new program in order to use it well with students."

FUNCTION IV: CHECK ON PROGRESS

"Probably the most ignored strategy of the six is this one—checking on progress. If we assume that when a change has been offered and a day-or-two-long 'workshop' has been provided, implementation will proceed, we have defeated ourselves at the outset," Inez shared with her neighbor.

"It has often been said," her colleague reported, "that what gets monitored gets done. While we hate to acknowledge this, it certainly holds some merit. So, how do we do this monitoring?"

A major purpose of the concepts and tools of the Concerns-Based Adoption Model (CBAM) is to serve this precise purpose. Change leaders and facilitators must be keenly aware of the progress that is being made and where each individual is in the process.

"So, Leslie, are you saying that we will be 'snooping' around to watch what our staff is doing?" asked high school principal Michael Major. "We've never done this before and I am now worrying about how this will go over with the staff that has been working quite independently."

"That is a good point, Mike; we have some suggestions and we will explain very openly about how the checking progress will be done, and how the staff will collaborate in assessing where they are with implementing the new program. And we will describe to all staff how checking progress connects with this Function/Strategy."

FUNCTION V: PROVIDE CONTINUOUS ASSISTANCE

"Coaches who assist and support star athletes (even famous standout golfers, for example) engage in the follow-up work of supplying continuous support to individuals and groups, based on the assessments of how it is going. The combination of checking on progress and providing assistance is essentially the role of instructional coaches in schools. The dual actions of checking or assessing progress and giving assistance based on the assessment are the key to a successfully implemented innovation. This role is imperative, and it deserves to be introduced to our staff in such a way that they recognize its helpful benefits and its value.

"We will plan this introduction to the staff very carefully, and we expect that the principal of each school will be fully involved in this introduction and, as their time permits, their engagement in developing the skills to check progress and couple that with appropriate feedback and continuous assistance. In this way each staff member can develop the knowledge and skills for implementing this innovation. But we have one more significant figure to share and explain.

EAST LAKE SCHOOL DISTRICT'S STORY (CONTINUED)

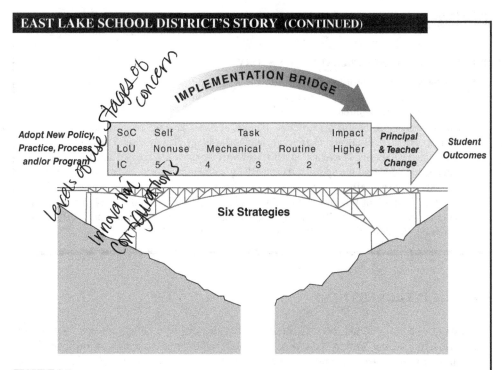

FIGURE 2.6

"You now see another layer of the comprehensive approach that we will take to address implementation. The six strategies are important for moving the new program across the bridge, but in order for the strategies to work well, we will use several diagnostic tools that will help us in crafting the strategies for their greatest support and impact on our implementation process. One of the tools shown on the top line in the box is Stages of Concern (SoC), which we will learn about in Chapter 4 of this book which is guiding our work for implementing our new curriculum. The middle line in the box represents Levels of Use (LoU), which is the focus of attention in Chapter 5, and the bottom line reflects Innovation Configurations (IC), featured in Chapter 3.

We will use this volume in a book study. We can use its research-based concepts and tools to assess implementation and support and guide our work. It will help us to personalize our work with all who are involved in implementation, so that this process is successful and our students benefit from the new knowledge and skills of our principals and teachers. We will take measured steps and sufficient time for everyone to learn the new mathematics curriculum and how to use it, so as not to rush pell-mell and fall off the bridge. We are ready to engage in this work with you. We are committing the next three years to steady and focused work so that each of us, as good learners, can become successfully prepared to use the new curriculum for the benefit of our students. Now, we have reserved 30 minutes for a question-and-answer period after we have a break and a small snack."

Needless to say, after this carefully planned and creatively presented session, to decompress Leslie had a long, soaking bath with fragrant oils and a glass of white wine the moment she reached her home that evening.

(continued)

EAST LAKE SCHOOL DISTRICT'S STORY (CONTINUED)

CRITIQUE QUESTIONS FOR EAST LAKE'S STORY

1. In what ways do the story and figures support your understanding of the vital need for planning by developing an Intervention Game Plan? How could the slides be used to analyze the status of the already-introduced innovations?
2. Change leaders/facilitators all too often assume, or don't have the requisite knowledge and skills to assess, their clients' capacity to implement innovative processes and practices. To what extent will Leslie's presentation help the mostly inexperienced school and district administrators to understand the needs of their teaching colleagues for appropriate interventions to support their change efforts?
3. Can the "lessons" of this story be used to explain to parent and community groups about the time and resources needed for implementing new programs that will promote students' increasing success in the academic subjects? How might it be tailored for them?

SIZES OF INTERVENTIONS

In our extensive longitudinal research studies, it became clear that interventions come in different sizes. Some interventions take years to unfold, while others are over in minutes. Some interventions affect everyone, while others affect only one person. Our ideas about the different sizes of interventions were introduced and described in an Intervention Taxonomy (Hall & Hord, 1984). Brief descriptions of this part of our intervention framework are presented next and summarized in Table 2.6. Although these were developed for research purposes, many experienced change facilitators have found them to be instructive and useful.

Policies

Since they affect the whole organization/system and exist typically for an extended amount of time (years), the policies of an organization must be taken into account when planning for change or when studying a planned change project. Policies that have long been in place, as well as new ones, can affect a change initiative. For example, a long-standing policy could include contract specifications that restrict staff development to the school day. This then becomes an intervention that affects having after-school sessions to support implementation

TABLE 2.6   The Relative Size of Interventions

Policies: Decisions that affect the whole organization for an extended period
Game Plan Components: Major functional groupings of interventions
Strategies: Interventions that operationalize the Game Plan Components into actions
Tactics: Sets of small actions that compose the Strategies
Incidents: Brief in-time actions that focus on one or a few users or nonusers, and that may or may not add up to Tactics

of a new program. Or there may be a policy that prohibits staff development during the school day, thus requiring its scheduling for after the formal school hours, with stipends being paid to the teachers who participate. Such overarching policies can have significant and far-reaching influence on a change process. Facilitators ignore them at their risk.

REFLECTION QUESTIONS

Have you considered how policies from the federal, state, and district levels can impact implementation? Have you had the experience with ignoring a policy that later resulted in a problem for the change effort? How could this have been avoided? What do you do now?

GAME PLAN COMPONENTS

Previously in this chapter, the large clustering of interventions was referred to as "Functions." Our original thinking had been to use the metaphor of the coach who prepares an overall plan ahead of the game. Within the game plan are various "plays" and strategies anticipating what will be done on offense and defense. Just as with a coach, we believe that as the game (of change) unfolds, leaders need to make adjustments in their Intervention Game Plan. We have changed the name of the major intervention groupings from "Game Plan Components" to "Functions." This name change places more emphasis on the purpose of each intervention grouping. With either term, Functions or Game Plan Components, the message is to think about the big picture and then to plan interventions within each grouping. Each Function/ Component is composed of a variety of interventions. One way to sort all of these interventions is by size. Larger interventions can take years to fully unfold. Very small interventions can be over in minutes.

Strategies

Strategies, in our research nomenclature, are an accumulation of smaller interventions that over time accomplish specific change process objectives. They can be thought of as the sets of interventions that operationalize a particular Game Plan Component/Function. Strategies impact a large number of implementers and take long periods of time. For example, under the Game Plan Component of Monitoring and Evaluation (also known as Checking Progress), the Strategy of one principal, who was closely guiding and supporting change in his school, was to collect samples of students' work every Friday. While collecting the samples, the principal talked with each teacher and was able to assess students' work. This was done with half the staff each Friday, so that over the course of two weeks, all students' work and all classroom teachers were involved in Checking Progress. This Strategy led to another Strategy, Providing Consultation and Reinforcement (Providing Assistance). Subsequent to Checking Progress, the need for Providing Assistance was clear—help was needed for the teachers in working with those students whose work indicated low performance. These Strategies mutually informed the teachers about additional possibilities for student work and reinforced and/or encouraged various teachers and students in their use of the innovation.

Tactics

This intervention is defined as a set of small, interrelated actions. A day-long workshop would be a Tactic that is part of the Strategy of "Designing and Providing Training" sessions across the first year of implementation. The Strategy is, in turn, part of the Game Plan Component/Function of Training.

Other examples of Tactics are visiting each implementer in his or her classroom over a three-day period to solicit concerns about training sessions for the new computers, and scheduling a consultant to be in the school for a week to provide technical assistance to any teacher who indicates interest.

Incidents

We have learned with certainty how significant the small and more individualized interventions known as Incidents are. They are short in duration, focus typically on one or just a few implementers, and mostly occur informally. This is not to say that they are unplanned, for they are so powerful that they should be on the mind of every facilitator. It is in these little day-to-day, moment-to-moment actions (which frequently take the form of the One-Legged Interview described in Chapter 1) that the change effort is most frequently won or, unfortunately, lost. We have observed repeatedly in schools and other types of organizations that where there are significantly more Incident interventions there is significantly greater implementation success due to this personalized help and support. Opportunities are abundant for enacting Incident interventions, such as the following:

- When meeting a user or nonuser in the hallway, the facilitator can offer comments to support his or her hard work with the innovation or to increase his or her interest in learning about it.
- At the staff mailbox, the facilitator can share requested information with the person who is early into use of a new program.
- Crossing the parking lot to go home, three teachers share examples of what their students have been doing.
- In the staff lounge, the facilitator shares a brochure about forthcoming professional development sessions.

The effective facilitator uses these small interactions to "check on progress" and also as an opportunity to provide customized encouragement and assistance. If the change process planners or policy makers think only of the Tactic of workshops as the key interventions for a change effort, the implementers will be shortchanged. Incident interventions are the building blocks that make Tactics, which combine to make Strategies, which in combination come to represent each Game Plan Component/Function. It is in these one-to-one interventions that individuals and small groups have many of their more idiosyncratic—yet vastly important—concerns given attention. As the title of the classic song says, "Little Things Mean a Lot."

 Pothole Warning

So, you have assumed that giving the change effort participants the guide and materials, as well as sending them to a day-and-a-half large-group learning session, has prepared them to adopt and implement the new curriculum. And

you now are surprised when you visit classrooms to find the new materials stashed at the bottom of shelves or unopened on the back-of-the-room worktable. Alas!

Pothole Repair

Recruit several teacher leaders, provide them a crash course in facilitating change, and engage them in conducting One-Legged Interviews to learn where the staff are in terms of implementation. Identify those who have managed to begin implementation and invite their assistance in helping buddy teachers to get started. Then reserve time with your teacher leaders to plan a set of Incident- and Tactic-level interventions to support the staff in learning how to use the new curriculum and to begin its use. You might also reread the previous section on the six Game Plan Components/Functions. Which ones have not been emphasized enough?

THE ANATOMY OF INTERVENTIONS

An even more specific analysis of interventions can be done. The framework for this was developed with our colleagues to quantify the internal elements of interventions. Since this framework is a way to examine the internal parts of interventions, we call it the Anatomy of Interventions (Hall & Hord, 1987). This is a framework for analysis of the Source, Target, Function, Medium, Flow, and Location of each intervention (see Table 2.7).

Such an analysis and coding of interventions across time makes it possible to ascertain who is providing intervention actions to whom, for what purpose, how, and when. Thus, redundancies and gaps may be identified and corrections taken so that all persons involved receive the supportive interventions that are needed. This type of analysis also becomes documentation of who is doing more and of what types of interventions are being used.

The Source of an intervention is the person who is initiating the action, and the Target is the person (or persons) who receives the action. In our studies, it is clear that principals and others in a leadership role are the most frequent Sources of interventions. SoC, LoU, and IC, which we will learn about in the next several chapters, provide diagnostic data that are useful in designing interventions that will be relevant and effective for each Target. Function is the purpose of the action and, interestingly, an intervention can have multiple Functions, which can be quite useful.

Documenting the Source, Target, and Function of a sample of interventions can reveal important information about who is being given attention in a change effort, by whom, and for what purpose. Redundancies (which do not occur very often) and gaps in the provision of intervention actions may be revealed also. For research purposes, these three subparts—along

TABLE 2.7   Internal Elements of Incident Interventions

Source: Person(s) providing the action
Target: Person(s) receiving the action
Function: Purpose of the action
Medium: Means by which the intervention is delivered (telephone, face-to-face, etc.)
Flow: Directionality of the intervention action (one-way, interactive, etc.)
Location: Where the action took place

with Medium, Flow, and Location—may be coded using a set of carefully defined codes and coding rules. (See Hall and Hord, 1987, for additional information.)

REFLECTION QUESTIONS

When might you use the Anatomy of Interventions in a change project? How would you apply this tool in your project?

Using Another Change Construct to Generate Interventions

Thinking about interventions in general and the Functions of interventions most certainly is important. An expanded approach would be to use one or more of the many other research-based change constructs as a heuristic. For example, the construct of Innovation Configurations, which will be introduced in Chapter 3, provides a very important diagnostic base for constructing interventions. As implementers move across the bridge, interventions are needed to facilitate their achieving fidelity in using the innovation. Beginning examples of how these ideas can be interrelated to identify interventions is presented in Table 2.8. Combining implementation assessment information about current practice with the Functions of interventions can be a very powerful approach to facilitating change.

TABLE 2.8   Using an Innovation Configuration Map to Generate Interventions

1. The six Functions of interventions provide a practical framework facilitators can use in supporting and guiding change initiatives. These are the "sacred six" kinds of actions demanded for the success of change projects.
2. An interesting way of generating specific interventions for each Function is to employ an Innovation Configuration Map as a guide (Chapter 3). Function I is the articulation of a shared vision of the intended change when it is implemented in a high-quality way. The IC Map is the written product that represents the creation of a shared vision of the change. When this IC Map is completed, it can be used for designing the Function II interventions: Planning and Providing Resources. The map indicates the desired outcomes—what actions are taking place in the innovation's setting—and is the point of reference for making an action plan to reach those desired outcomes. It can also be referenced to determine fiscal and human resources needed to reach the desired outcomes, or the vision of the change.
3. Referring to the IC Map provides clarity for identifying professional development for staff (Function III) needed to reach the actions delineated on the map. Professional developers use the map to target critical components that require knowledge and skill development. But that is not the end of the change process, though many seem to believe that if initial training is provided the process is complete—which is not true.
4. An IC Map can be used with Function IV, Checking Progress. The facilitator uses the map to ascertain where each individual is in the change effort. Then Function V, Providing Continuous Assistance, may be planned for coaching implementers in moving closer to the Ideal Variation of each Component on the map.
5. An IC Map may not directly address Function VI, Creating a Context Supportive of Change. But a map of such a context for change could be produced to guide the facilitator in designing interventions to enable the creation of a more supportive context in the organization.

SUMMARY

The concepts and actions (interventions) described in this chapter were created and designed with change facilitators in mind. To share these ideas briefly with others, these talking points can be used:

1. It is imperative that leaders of change efforts become aware of the role of interventions in implementing change.
2. In those change processes that are supported by statistically significant, more innovation-related Incident interventions, teachers have greater implementation success.
3. Interventions have been sorted into six Functions that can be used in planning for and monitoring change initiatives.
4. Initiating effective interventions should be ongoing. Without continuing facilitating actions, many members of an organization work in isolation and fail to develop full use of the innovation. As we admonish in our workshops, "Change facilitators, *do* something."

DISCUSSION QUESTIONS

1. What preparation relative to interventions should be provided to a person who will serve as a change facilitator? Would your prescription be different if the facilitator were based at the school, district, or state level?

2. What length of time should be considered in developing the Intervention Game Plan for implementing a transformational change such as changing from a teacher-centered to a learner-centered approach? Which Functions will require more time and effort?

3. How might the song title "Little Things Mean a Lot" apply to interventions?

4. How might a campus-based practitioner, a state policy maker, or a researcher employ the information on interventions in this chapter?

5. Which of this chapter's intervention concepts are most applicable to the corporate world or private sector?

APPLYING THE INTERVENTION IDEAS IN FACILITATING IMPLEMENTATION

1. Obtain a school/district improvement plan or a strategic plan for another organization. Which intervention Functions are addressed, and which are absent? Based on the plan, what is our prediction about the likely degree of implementation success?

2. Develop a plan for making a presentation to a school board using the six basic Functions of interventions as a framework. Make your story that each type of Function needs attention and resources in order to further advance a particular change process.

3. Develop a plan of interventions to be supplied to a school or business whose staff will be implementing a complex innovation. Be as thorough and comprehensive as possible, identifying key strategies within each Game Plan Component/Function and examples of relevant Incidents.

APPLYING INTERVENTIONS IN RESEARCH OR PROGRAM EVALUATION STUDIES

1. For 1 month, document all the interventions provided for implementation of a priority innovation in one organization. Use the Anatomy of Interventions to analyze the interventions in terms of their Source, Target, and Function. Share the results with the implementation facilitators. Then record their subsequent interventions to ascertain if they are acting in ways related to the study results.

2. Collect baseline data on the extent of implementation in two settings. Document the interventions provided to both settings. Analyze each setting's interventions in terms of Functions, Strategies, and Tactics. How does each Intervention Game Plan seem to relate to the extent of implementation? What would you recommend be done to increase implementation success?

LEARNING MORE ABOUT INTERVENTIONS

Folkman, J. (2006). *The power of feedback: 35 principles for turning feedback from others into personal and professional change.* Hoboken, NJ: Wiley.

Gawande, A. (2007). *Better: A surgeon's notes on performance.* New York: Picador.

Hargreaves, A., & Shirley, D. (2009). *The fourth way.* Thousand Oaks, CA: Corwin Press.

Hord, S. M., & Roussin, J. L. (2013). *Implementing change through learning: Concerns-based concepts, tools and strategies for guiding change.* Thousand Oaks, CA: Corwin Press.

Professional development focused on developing the knowledge base and skills of facilitators related to the six Intervention Functions is available as a three-day institute. For information about *Leadership for Changing Schools,* contact SEDL, Austin, Texas, 800.476.6861.

A leader's guide, videotapes, audiotapes, and copy for handouts and transparencies from the *Leadership for Changing Schools* institute is available as a stand-alone set of materials and activities. For information, contact SEDL, 800.476.6861.

PART II

THE PEOPLE PART OF CHANGE

Three Diagnostic Dimensions: Concerns, Using, and Fidelity

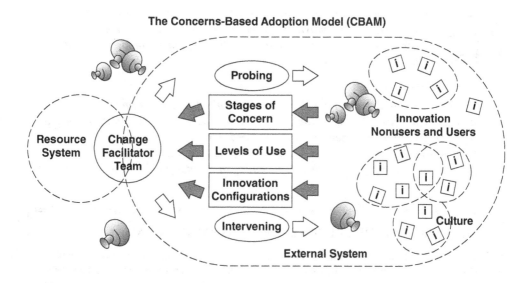

The Concerns-Based Adoption Model (CBAM)

Change Principle 4 states that individuals must implement the innovation before one can say that the organization as a whole has changed. For individuals implementing change is a complex and personal experience. Meaningful change requires learning new knowledge and skills. There will be moments of frustration and also joy. Most of today's innovations are complex and there likely will be components that have nuanced characteristics, which makes achieving full implementation challenging.

Researchers have identified three different constructs that can be used to understand, facilitate, and evaluate change at the individual level. Each of these dimensions can be *diagnostic* in that they can be used to assess the current extent of implementation. Each dimension can be used in *planning* the next action steps to further advance implementation. In addition, each dimension is important to apply in *evaluation and research* studies. Each of the next three chapters addresses one of these constructs.

Chapter 3: How Can We Clarify the Change? Innovation Configurations

Chapter 4: How Can the Different Feelings and Perceptions about Change Be Understood and Addressed? Stages of Concern

Chapter 5: Are There Characteristic Behavioral Profiles of Implementers? Levels of Use

Pothole Warning!

Most of the descriptions of each construct presented in the next three chapters are about how individuals experience change. Do not conclude that the constructs do not apply to groups, or all the members of an organization, or system.

Pothole Repair:

Each of the Diagnostic Dimensions can be applied to groups and all members of an organization/system. One easy way is to use each construct to anticipate how like groups will be experiencing a change process. If one or more of the measuring tools has been used to collect data at the individual level, then aggregate the data for different subgroups, such as a department, or in total for the entire organization/ system.

■ ■ ■ ■ ■ ▬▬▬▬▬▬▬▬▬▬▬▬▬▬▬▬▬▬▬▬▬▬▬▬▬▬▬▬▬

EAST LAKE SCHOOL DISTRICT'S STORY, PLANNING AHEAD

In Chapter 2, Dr. Hanson used a sequence of slides to apply the Implementation Bridge metaphor to how the district would proceed to focus and assess change process progress. In the final slide she referenced Stages of Concern, Levels of Use and Innovation Configurations. You will learn about each of these constructs in the next three chapters.

CHAPTER 3

HOW CAN WE CLARIFY THE CHANGE?

Innovation Configurations

I have just visited three third-grade classrooms to observe the teachers using the new curriculum. Two of them are operating as expected, but the third is way off base.

—Inez Hernandez, Island Park Elementary School principal

Why can't they (teachers) just do the lessons as designed and do them as we described in the workshop? When you go out in the field, you will not believe some of the things that are going on.

—Susan Lewis, Mathematics curriculum developer

Mrs. Lewis, the math expert, was in my classroom yesterday. She said the students were doing a good job of using mathematical language! To tell you the truth, I wasn't sure we would ever get to this point.

—Josh Searight, Department Chair, Mountain View High School

Well, the teacher's guide is so clear and the training gave me the opportunity to practice, so I understand what is expected. I am able to do all of the activities in each lesson just as they are described in the guide and how I saw them in the video examples.

—Betty Hollister, Island Park Elementary School teacher

My volunteer group is trying hard to explain to new members what our roles are as teachers' aides—what can we do to describe it better?

—East Lake District parent volunteer

For teachers and others who are expected to implement new practices, all too frequently a problem is lack of clarity about what they are being asked to do. Even when training and materials are provided, there is a big leap from preparing to do something to actually doing it. In the end, what teachers do in the classroom may bear little resemblance to what the creator(s) of the change had in mind originally. All of the teachers may call it the same thing, but in practice what they do may look very different. In this chapter we will examine the *innovation*—the change itself. How to describe an innovation and how to measure its various forms in use are central themes. A key purpose of this chapter is to introduce a construct, a tool, and a process that can be used to construct a common understanding of what a change can look like when fully implemented.

EAST LAKE SCHOOL DISTRICT'S STORY, PART I: IMPLEMENTATION OF THE MATHEMATICS PROGRAM BEGINS

East Lake prepares to move into the first step of its game plan . . .

Superintendent Johnson was pleased with the results of Leslie and Inez's presentation of the actions needed to fully implement a new program. He invited the two of them to a 20-minute meeting the following morning in his office.

GETTING STARTED

After pouring a cup of coffee for them, Mike Johnson complimented Leslie and Inez on a successful meeting with the schools' principals and coaches. "What is our next step?" he inquired. The three brainstormed and determined that it was time to expand the planning team to include more principals and coaches, as well as teacher leaders/classroom teachers. They thought that it is important for everyone to have a connection to this change initiative and to understand how it will aid them in their work of developing enhanced mathematics skills and understanding for students. They identified additional educators to expand the leadership team: Director of Professional Learning, Stephanie Struthers; instructional coach Beverly Denver and Joseph Vance (kindergarten teacher) of Island Park Elementary School; Mary Sawyer (coach), sixth grade teacher Pamela Stone, and Principal Ray Raulson of River Run Elementary School; Principal Michael Major, mathematics department head Josh Searight, and Michael Chin (coach) of Mountain View High School.

Leslie asked if these personnel could be given release time and substitutes to handle their campus duties or possibly a stipend to meet for several daylong Saturdays to work on a long-range plan. Superintendent Johnson gave his approval, directed this information to his secretary, and asked her to set up meeting space and times for the Mathematics Game Plan Team to meet.

MATH TEAM GOES INTO ITS FIRST HUDDLE

Ten days later, on a bright Saturday morning, Leslie greeted the expanded Team with a deliciously aromatic egg soufflé, biscuits, and gallons of coffee. She thanked the members for bringing material that they thought might be relevant to their plan for introducing and implementing the new math program. "Our state is one of the 45 that have adopted the Common Core State Standards for mathematics, so, rather obviously, that material is what we will focus on—in addition to ideas that you have gleaned from your perusal of the new mathematics standards. We are especially glad that Stephanie Struthers, our Director of Professional Learning, High School Math Department Chair Josh Searight, and Joe Vance, kindergarten teacher, participated in a two-hour webinar earlier this week, to gain an introduction to the CCSS Mathematics. They will serve as point people—liaisons for communication, sharing of materials, scheduling meetings, and will generally be in charge of supporting our effort. But each and every one of us has much learning to do about the new math; that means we will all be expected to serve each other in our mutual endeavors."

"I am really glad to be invited to serve on this team," Principal Ray Raulson said, "but I really need to know just what is this new math, and how is it different from what we have been doing. If I can understand that, I will be able to focus my head in that direction."

teach how I live it would teach our would teach our we best practices to

EAST LAKE SCHOOL DISTRICT'S STORY, PART I (CONTINUED)

"Exactly," Joe Vance agreed, "I can't seem to 'get it' even though I participated in the webinar."

"The first thing that we have to understand is that across the U.S., our curriculum has been stretched very broadly, which means that we are trying to teach a curriculum that is a mile wide, and consequently an inch deep. The new approach is to narrow the focus so that we are teaching at less breadth and more depth . . . but, this is a very simplistic explanation," Stephanie responded. "The Common Core standards will clearly define what students are expected to learn, rather than what teachers are expected to teach, though these two activities cannot, of course, be separated. It will employ a constructivist approach to teaching and learning."

"Oh, what does that mean? Will it prepare our students for college level math, if we use this approach, rather than the lecture-type of teaching that we commonly use?" inquired Josh, high school math department chair.

"Yeah," Joe worried, "how does this all work? The webinar was only introductory in its presentation, and it raised more questions than answers, as typical, I guess, when you are dealing with something new."

"Well," Stephanie replied, "constructivist teaching is a path to increasing students' critical thinking and problem-solving skills. One of the eight practices of the "Core" is students' development of deep understanding of mathematical concepts so that they are able to critique the reasoning of others' explanations. Wouldn't that be something if our students could become mathematicians—able to explain the "bottom line" on what subtraction really means as a mathematical operation, or long division. As it is now, students learn a rote way to do long division problems and have no underlying understanding about what all those actions that they do really mean. I think this can be really exciting. I am beginning to understand that all of us will be into learning all about this ourselves before we can teach it to students, and that could be very cool."

Coach Mary Sawyer joined the conversation, "You know, I am just recalling . . . one of our teachers who is working on her master's degree, was sharing in the teachers' lounge the other day about a tool that one of her professors in her course on change had introduced. It was something about '*configurations*' or such, and I thought I understood it had something to do with introducing new programs or processes . . . I wonder about that, and if it could help."

"Indeed," Leslie chimed in, "that is a part of the work that I was doing on my dissertation, but I didn't use that tool. Nonetheless, I am certain that you are correct, and we will look into that." And they did, and the rest of this chapter discusses what they learned. Read on to learn about their discoveries.

CRITIQUE QUESTIONS OF EAST LAKE'S STORY

1. Are these the appropriate educators to add to the Game Plan Team? Why, or why not?
2. What do you see being the major objectives for this committee? In other words what questions should they address and products should they produce?
3. After the Team gains the information they are seeking, what would you recommend as the next action steps in their plan?

LEARNING OUTCOMES

After reading this chapter, the learner should be able to:

1. Specify what an intended change is supposed to look like once it is fully implemented.
2. Explain key issues that may result from a lack of clarity about how to use an innovation.
3. Describe how a clear vision of a change can serve as a road map to successful implementation.

4. Understand how to determine key Components of an innovation, develop "word picture" descriptions of Component Variations, and construct an Innovation Configuration (IC) Map.
5. Use the construct of Innovation Configurations to explore issues and implications for assessing Fidelity of Implementation (FOI).
6. List the multiple uses of an IC Map.

THE CHANGE: WHAT IT IS AND IS NOT

A major reason that widespread change often occurs only modestly across a school/district is that the implementers, facilitators, and policymakers do not fully understand what the change is or what it will look like when it is implemented in the envisioned way. When there is such confusion, principals and other facilitators may give conflicting signals, and teachers will create their own versions of the change as they try to understand and use the materials and/or processes that have been advocated. Evaluators then have serious difficulties in appraising whether the new way is better than the old, or as Charters and Jones (1973) opined, it is likely to be the "appraisal of a non-event." This is particularly problematic when what is being done under the name of the innovation is different in various classrooms. This phenomenon led those of us working with the Concerns Based Adoption Model (CBAM) to add a third diagnostic dimension—Innovation Configurations (IC) (Hall & Loucks, 1981)—and that is the topic of this chapter.

Before describing Innovation Configurations, a definitional issue must be addressed. For any change or innovation there will be one or more architects, or creators. They may be national expert(s) or local developer(s). Frequently the creators of an innovation are curriculum experts from outside the school or district, such as a national project or publishing house. Other changes emerge when a local team or committee of teachers, who have experimented in their classrooms, develop an approach that they wish to share with others. Still other changes are driven by local school boards, state legislatures, and federal policies; some are even initiated by court decisions. In the CBAM approach to change, we have used the term *developer* to represent any and all of these sources.

REFLECTION QUESTIONS

What difference would it make, if any, whether a new program or practice— e.g., an innovation—was created by a local or external developer? Have you had the experience of working with both a local and a national developer? What comparisons can you make about these two sources of change?

INNOVATION ADAPTATION

The construct of Innovation Configurations (IC) addresses both the idealized images of a change created by a developer as well as the various operational forms of the change that can be observed when it is being implemented. The focus, in the IC Diagnostic Dimension, is on developing and applying word-picture descriptions of what the use of an innovation can look like. That is, how does it look in *operation,* what are individuals *doing* related to the innovation?

Previously, a typical means of determining whether a new program or process was being used was to count how many classrooms contained the program materials. Alternatively, *use* of the new way would be assumed because the teachers had participated in a workshop or the principal would report that teachers were doing it.

The uncertainty of whether there was high-quality use of a new program or process was discovered early in the original CBAM verification studies. The implementation of two innovations was being studied: teacher teaming in elementary schools and college professors' use of instructional modules. In each case, when the so-called users were asked to describe what they were doing, a surprising range of practices was outlined, but in all cases the interviewees would claim to be using the same innovation. For example, when teachers in Texas, Nebraska, and Massachusetts were asked to describe their teams, they provided very different pictures of the innovation of teaming:

> *Team Texas* consisted of three teachers and two aides who served approximately 110 students. They "teamed" all day and were housed in a pod that was equivalent in size to three classrooms. The students were taught by all of the teachers, and each teacher took the lead in planning for one subject area.

> *Team Nebraska* consisted of three teachers, each of whom had a homeroom class. For half the day, students would move from classroom to classroom as they were grouped and regrouped for lessons. Teachers kept their own students for the afternoon. Teachers specialized in teaching all students particular subjects.

> *Team Massachusetts* consisted of two teachers, each of whom had a regular classroom with 25 to 30 students. The teachers exchanged lesson plans once a month, but each kept and taught his or her own students all day.

As these examples illustrate, how the change is thought about in theory may bear little resemblance to the activities that are done in classrooms under the name of that innovation. In each of the schools just described, the teachers were quick to say, "Oh, yes, we are teaming," but what they were doing under the name of teaming was very different.

An early conclusion in our studies was that users of innovations tend to adapt, and in some cases mutate, innovations. In other words, the innovation *in action* can take on many different operational forms or *configurations.* Once the phenomenon of IC is recognized and accepted as a natural part of the change process, a number of implications emerge. For example, the outcomes from the use of different configurations of an innovation will likely vary. Users of some configurations will be associated with higher outcomes than those using other configurations. And, to improve their implementation, it is likely that users will need targeted training and coaching on particular aspects of the innovation, depending on which configurations are in use.

There is a philosophical issue here also. To what extent is there a need to advocate for close adherence to the developer's intended model (i.e., a "fidelity" approach)? When, or should, all users be doing the same thing? In other words, how necessary and appropriate is a fidelity model of change? The concept of IC and its related measurement procedure help address these questions.

The purpose here is not to make judgments about how good or bad it may be to adapt an innovation. Instead, the goal is to point out that (a) in most change efforts innovation adaptation will occur, (b) there is a way to chart these adaptations, and (c) these adaptations have direct and indirect implications for facilitating and assessing change initiatives. In the concluding section of this chapter, we return to issues related to fidelity and some of their implications, but first, we describe IC as a concept and its Mapping procedure.

REFLECTION QUESTIONS

Have you been an implementer in a change project and found yourself adding to or not doing some parts of the new program? What motivated your making these changes?

INNOVATION CONFIGURATIONS AS A CONSTRUCT

Anyone who has been involved in change recognizes the phenomenon of IC. The tendency to adapt, modify, and/or mutate aspects of innovations is a natural part of the change process; it is neither malicious nor even explicitly planned. It happens for a number of interrelated reasons, beginning with uncertainty about what is supposed to be done. Most people, especially teachers, want to do the "right" thing. Therefore, when teachers are asked to use an innovation, they will try. The problems begin when the details of how to do it are not made clear.

In nearly all cases the innovation as operationalized by different users will vary along a continuum from being very close to what the developer had in mind to a distant zone where what is being done is nearly unrecognizable. Creating different configurations of an innovation is not unique to education. For example, consider cars as the innovation.

As Figure 3.1 illustrates, and as any parking lot confirms, a car can be and has been significantly adapted from an initial conception of a two-door sedan. A whole range of "configurations" can be observed, ranging from changes in color, to the addition of mag wheels, to rebuilding as a race car, to some forms that some might claim are cars about which the rest of us would say, "No, those are not cars!"

FIGURE 3.1   A Continuum of Innovation . . .

REFLECTION QUESTIONS

Think of an innovation that you were expected to put into practice. Where did you start, and how did you know when you had full implementation? Did you have any uncertainty about the expectations for your implementation effort?

This same continuum of configurations exists for innovations, except that determining what is and is not the innovation is more difficult than with the car example. All too frequently the developers of an innovation have not thought clearly about what use of their change will really entail. They have thought more about philosophy (we use a constructivist model) and what is needed to support its implementation (you must have five days of training and use these materials). In addition, because teachers (like the rest of us) are always short on time, they will tend to reduce the amount of change and effort they have to invest whenever they can. If there is limited training and support for the change, it is likely that it will not be fully or faithfully implemented. Although the implementers may genuinely believe that they are using the innovation, an expert observing their practices may conclude, "Hmm, the way they are doing it is not what the developer intended."

The different possible configurations of innovations are easy to picture. Take, for example, the innovation of integrated use of technology. What is envisioned here is classroom use by students and teachers of various forms of technology for information retrieval, processing, and communication. Some of the relatively simple configurations that could be observed include (a) classrooms with only a few computers with no Web access, which are used mainly for drill and practice, (b) classrooms with computers that are linked within the school and include CD-ROM databases but no Web access, (c) classrooms with computers with Web access, projection devices, and video where students work individually with their own laptops and in groups to research, plan, develop, and communicate presentations about their learning, and (d) schools in which all computers are in a lab or media center and used on an assigned schedule for groups of students.

Once it is recognized and accepted that there will be different configurations of an innovation, an important next issue is how to describe those configurations. Answering this question entails development of an IC Map.

MAPPING INNOVATION CONFIGURATIONS

The scenarios described in the previous section are very familiar to teachers, principals, other leaders, and program evaluators. The situation in which teachers are not sure about what they are to do occurs in part because innovation developers have a hard time imagining the extent to which their innovation can be adapted. Another reason for the uncertainty is that change facilitators and teachers do not have clear images and descriptions about what the use of the innovation can look like. To address these needs, we have developed a process and tool that can be used to visualize and assess the different configurations that are likely to be found for any particular innovation. We call the process *Innovation Configuration Mapping* and the resultant tool an *Innovation Configuration Map*.

Elements of Innovation Configuration Maps

The concept of a map was deliberately chosen for this work because, just as a road map shows different ways for getting from one place to another, so does an Innovation Configuration Map. A highway map will picture interstate highways, U.S. highways, and county roads. These are alternate routes, all of which make it possible to complete the trip. The IC Map does the same thing for change facilitators and users of innovations by identifying the major Components of an innovation and then describing the observable Variations of each component. The IC Map is composed of "word picture" descriptions of the different possible operational forms of an innovation or change.

Pothole Warning

Do not assume that just because every staff member attended the two-hour session where the innovation was described that they all hold the same image of what it is—especially if it was described in general terms.

Pothole Repair

How to enable everyone to hold a common and authentic vision of the new practice is the challenge. Precision in describing what use looks like is the key, and the operable term. Read on. The IC tool can address this challenge.

IC Map Components.   Consider the very simple IC Map component presented in Figure 3.2, which describes the units that a teacher presents. In the *a* Variation, all units and most activities are taught. The quantity of units and activities that are taught decreases in the other Variations, with the *e* Variation describing the classroom where none of the units or activities are taught. Even without naming a specific program, it is possible to use this component with its different variation descriptions to visualize different degrees of coverage of units and activities.

The purpose of the IC Map is to present carefully developed descriptions of the core components and the different ways (i.e., the Variations) it could be made operational. An IC Map will have a number of Components (typically 6 to 12), and each component will have a number of Variations (typically 2 to 6). The number of components will vary depending on the complexity of the innovation and the amount of detail needed. There is a trade-off between the number of components and the level of detail represented. In an IC Map with fewer components, each component will have more information, which at some point makes

FIGURE 3.2   A Simple IC Map Component (from The Science Program)

THE TEACHER . . .

COMPONENT 1: TEACHES THE SCIENCE ACTIVITIES AND UNITS

(A)	(B)	(C)	(D)	(E)
Teaches all units and most activities.	Teaches most units and activities.	Teaches some units.	Teaches a few selected activities.	Teaches no units or activities.

the descriptions so very dense that it is not easy to visualize because of the detail. On the other hand, an IC Map with many components may be too finely ground and becomes tedious. In the end, the team that develops an IC Map has to decide what is best for its situation.

The major goal in writing each component statement and each variation description is to be as visual and action oriented as possible. The better the word pictures, the easier it will be for teachers, principals, program evaluators, and others to see what successful use of the innovation entails. This cannot be overstated.

Developing Clear Word-Picture Descriptions.   The IC Map component presented in Figure 3.2 was deliberately chosen because of its simplicity. Richer IC Map Components are shown in Figure 3.3. The components were selected from the Instructor Profile for Fast Trac II (Novak, 1992), a 10-week course for business entrepreneurs. In this project that was being disseminated by the Center for Entrepreneurial Leadership of the Kauffman Foundation, there was interest in developing an IC Map that depicted the role of the course instructor. This IC Map was used as part of the quality control check as the course was disseminated nationally. The resultant IC Map was used to select content for instructor training since instructors were to be skilled in doing each of the map's components. The map was also used by the instructors in planning and self-reflection, and by trained assessors in determining instructor certification by viewing videotapes of their classes.

One of the interesting aspects of the Fast Trac IC Map was that the "innovation" was about the role of the course instructor. An IC Map could have been developed around the role of workshop participants or around what they, as entrepreneurs, applied from the course to their businesses. Deciding which innovation user to focus on for IC Mapping is a critical first step.

Note in Figure 3.3 how the Variation descriptions in Component 2 are stated. The basic component is the same as in Figure 3.2, but each Variation is more descriptive. However, as IC Mapping expert Paul Borchardt would say (personal communication, November 10, 2003), this is still a "boring" component, since it basically just evolves from "all" (*a*) to "a little" (*d*). A component of this type could be made much richer by adding a second dimension, or practice, that increased in occurrence from *b* to *d*. For example, the dimension of excessive time being spent on one or two modules could gradually increase across the variation descriptions. Alternatively, a "small and skinny" continuum could be used, indicating "all" to "little" that could be easily checked off.

A much higher quality example of an IC Map Component and its variations is Component 11 in Figure 3.3. Note how the word-picture descriptions of each variation are richer and how four different dimensions—variety, type, relevance, and length—are addressed in each variation. An IC Map notation technique is to present a key word for each dimension (in italics) within brackets following the component label.

Indicating Ranges of Quality and Fidelity.   Figures 3.2 and 3.3 illustrate a number of additional features of IC Map Components. One is the implicit value in the sequencing of the variations. As one moves from the *e* Variation toward the *a* Variation, the behaviors and practices described increasingly approach the more ideal practices as viewed by the innovation developer or some consensus group, usually those who developed the IC Map. This sequence, having the ideal "a" variation to the left is the reverse of what is done with most

FIGURE 3.3 Two IC Map Components for the Instructor's Role in the Fast Trac II Course for Business Entrepreneurs

FAST TRAC II COURSE INNOVATION CONFIGURATION MAP

Site ____________ Session ____________ Instructor ____________ Observer ____________ Date ________________

A. FULL COURSE OVERVIEW

2) Balanced Coverage of the Six Core Modules —Entrepreneurial Mind-set —Management & Organization —Finance [*6 covered, equal emphasis*]
—Legal Entities —Marketing —Negotiations

(a)	(b)	(c)	(d)	(e)	(f)
All six modules are developed and with equal emphasis.	All six modules are developed but with one or more given less emphasis.	One or more modules are not systematically addressed.	One or two modules become the course.		

LECTURE SEGMENT

11) Use of Examples by the Instructor during the Lecture (Variety, Type, Relevance, and Length)

(a)	(b)	(c)	(d)	(e)	(f)
Examples are used throughout. Examples are interesting, varied, to the point, and congruent with the issue or topic at hand. Examples include retail/service/manufacturing and participants' expertise with examples from their businesses.	Examples presented are to the point and congruent. Variety is limited in terms of retail/service/manufacturing and participants' businesses.	Examples and stories are not always relevant to the issue or topic at hand and tend to be drawn out, or a few businesses are overused as examples. Examples may not be clearly explained.	So many examples and war stories are shared that complete coverage of the points is hindered.	So many examples and war stories particular to the instructor's personal experience are shared that there is little variety and complete coverage of the point is hindered.	There are few examples and/or all of the examples are based in one or two businesses.

Source: Reprinted by permission from the Kauffman Center for Entrepreneurial Leadership at the Ewing Marion Kauffman Foundation.

ideal | acceptable | unacceptable

scoring rubrics. One of the reasons for this is to have the map reader "see" the ideal variation first. Laying the component variations along such a continuum from more to less desirable can be very helpful. Note that this IC Mapping technique can be used to implicitly signify when some variations are valued more highly than others. The authors of this text are not arguing for or against such a fidelity perspective but merely showing how it can be noted on the IC Map.

Another IC Mapping technique that can be helpful with a fidelity perspective is use of what we call *fidelity lines,* which are represented by the vertical dashed and solid lines between certain variations of the components in Figure 3.3. A solid line signifies that all of the variations to the right have been judged to be "unacceptable" ways of doing that component; all of those to the left of the dashed line are considered "ideal" practices, whereas those between the solid and dashed lines are viewed as "acceptable." Determining the placement of these lines in this case was done by the Fast Trac course developers. Whether to have lines and where to place them are important decisions for IC Mapping groups. No matter who is to make the decision about the inclusion of fidelity lines, *no lines should be added until after the IC Map has been through several revisions and has been used in data collection.* The insertion of fidelity lines should not be arbitrary or capricious. The rationale should be strong, and, hopefully, empirical data should support their placement.

On the other hand, over time, the lines could be shifted to represent goals (for accomplishment) as the innovation users become more familiar and experienced with using the innovation and are ready to move to the more sophisticated or ideal variations toward the left of the map. Being flexible with the lines in this way also reduces the users' anxiety, for it communicates that they are not expected to become expert immediately but that they may move through the variations with the help of their facilitator and colleagues.

Student IC Map Components.   One of the first decisions in IC Mapping is to determine which role(s) will be the focus of the map. For example, as mentioned, the Fast Trac map shown in Figure 3.3 could have focused on the participants or the regional dissemination administrators instead of the instructors. IC Maps can deal not just with the role of the teachers and their use of the materials, but also with the role of the students. When multiple roles are to be mapped, it is important that each role has its own map. Mixing roles across a map promotes confusion and reduces reliability.

For example, Figure 3.4 describes one aspect of student performance in a constructivist approach to teaching mathematics (Alquist & Hendrickson, 1999), which is based on the first set of standards of the National Council of Mathematics. Figure 3.5 is a student component from the IC Map for standards-based education that was developed in Douglas County School District in Colorado. The rich and observable descriptions of each variation in these examples were the result of intense and sustained effort.

For the clearest and most straightforward depiction of innovation use, developing IC Maps for each role group (i.e., students, others) is strongly advised. The IC Maps for the various role groups can be shared so that there is understanding across the organization about *who* is expected to do *what.* The IC Map gives individuals an immediate and complete picture of expectations for them. This approach also makes clear the desired ends. IC Maps that describe student behaviors help teachers in deciding their own practices. "If students are to be doing 'a,' then if I do X they will do 'a'."

FIGURE 3.4 Student IC Map Components for Learning Mathematics

INNOVATION CONFIGURATION MAP FOR THE TEACHING AND LEARNING OF MATHEMATICS DODDS-HESSEN DISTRICT SUPERINTENDENT'S OFFICE, RHEIN MAIN, GERMANY

DRAFT	DRAFT	DRAFT	DRAFT

B. Engagement with Task/Investigation

3) Student Engaged in Mathematical Tasks Throughout the Lesson [Engagement, Time]

a	b	c	d
Most students are engaged in mathematical tasks, most of the time.	Most students are engaged in mathematical tasks, part of the time.	Some students are engaged in mathematical tasks. Many are off task most of the time.	Few students are engaged any of the time.

4) Students' Understanding of Problem-Solving Strategies [Knowing Your Goal, Where You Are Now, Knowing the Steps to Get to the Goal, Reflection]

a	b	c	d	e
Students view the open-ended problem as a whole and analyze its parts. They create, select, and test a range of strategies. Students reflect upon the reasonableness of the strategies and the solution.	Students grasp the open- and close-ended problem as a whole and analyze its parts. Students pick an established/ traditional strategy to try to solve the problem, which is applied without considering alternatives. Students reflect upon the reasonableness of the solution but not the strategy.	Students approach the open-ended problem as a whole but do not have a clear understanding of the parts. The primary focus is on getting an answer. The students' reflection is on whether the answer is right rather than the reasonableness of the strategy.	Students approach open-ended problems as unconnected/unrelated parts and do not see the problem as a whole. Students may manipulate materials and numbers, but they are not clear about the reason/ purpose. If observable, reflection is about procedures.	Students calculate and compute using rote and routine procedures. Students are not clear about the final goal or the relationship of the tasks to that goal. There is little or no reflection about what is being learned.

Property of Hessen DSO, Unit 7565 Box 29, APO AE 09050—Contact the authors of the IC Map for the latest version.

DRAFT

Source: From "Mapping the Configurations of Mathematics Teaching" by A. Alquist and M. Hendrickson, 1999, *Journal of Classroom Interaction*, 34(1), 18–26. Reprinted by permission.

FIGURE 3.5 Student IC Map Component for Standards-Based Education

5) Student Ownership and Understanding of Learning (*Understanding of Standards or Checkpoints, Understanding of Progress in Relation to Standards or Checkpoints, Understanding of What Is Needed to Improve Performance in Order to Achieve Standards or Checkpoints*)

a	B	c	D	e
Students **understand** what they are **expected to know and be able to do** and can **articulate in specific terms** what it means to reach the standards or checkpoints. They can **describe where they are** in regard to the standard and know what they **need to improve** to achieve it.	Students **understand** what they are **expected to know and be able to do and can articulate in specific terms** what it means to reach the standards or check-points. They can **describe where they are** in regard to the standards or checkpoints, but are **unclear what they need to do** to achieve them.	Students can use the **"language" of standards.** They **can state the standards and checkpoints** that they are expected to learn, but they are **unclear about where they are** in meeting the standards or checkpoints or about what **to do** to achieve them.	Students' focus is on **the requirements of the class and grade** they receive.	Students' focus is on the **current activity.**

Examples:

a	B	c	D	e
"I know that we are studying primary source materials as they relate to the Holocaust and that's why we are reading *The Diary of Anne Frank.* I know that we will be evaluating and interpreting sources for their usefulness in understanding the Holocaust. I am pretty good at locating primary sources, but I have trouble knowing whether they are really quality sources. My teacher has shown some interesting ways to judge the quality of a source, but I need some more practice with them."	"I know that we are studying primary source materials as related to the Holocaust, and that's why we are reading *The Diary of Anne Frank.* I know that we will be evaluating and interpreting sources for their usefulness in understanding the Holocaust. I can find sources, but I am not sure how to evaluate their relevance and quality. I am not sure what I'll need to do to become proficient in evaluating these sources."	"I know that we are studying how to select and evaluate primary source materials as related to the Holocaust. I'm not sure exactly what I'll need to know about primary sources, or if I am any good at using them."	"We are studying how to use primary source materials. I need to get at least a B on the final report"	"We are reading *The Diary of Anne Frank,* and I will be writing some kind of report when we are finished."

Adapted: From Douglas County School District Re-1, Castle Rock, Colorado (April, 1999).

FIGURE 3.6 Cross Walk of Four Role Groups for Learning Forward's Standards for Professional Learning

LEARNING COMMUNITIES

TEACHER	COACH	SCHOOL LEADERSHIP TEAM	PRINCIPAL
1.1 Engage in continuous improvement			
Desired outcome 1.1.1: Develops capacity to apply the sevenstep cycle of continuous improvement.	**Desired outcome 1.1.1:** Develops own and others' capacity to apply the seven-step cycle of continuous improvement.	**Desired outcome 1.1.1:** Develops own and others' capacity to apply the seven-step cycle of continuous improvement.	**Desired outcome 1.1.1:** Develops own and others' capacity to apply the seven-step cycle of continuous improvement.
Desired outcome 1.1.2: Applies the cycle of continuous improvement with fidelity in professional learning.	**Desired outcome 1.1.2:** Applies the cycle of continuous improvement with fidelity to facilitate professional learning.	**Desired outcome 1.1.2:** Applies the cycle of continuous improvement with fidelity to decisions about professional learning.	**Desired outcome 1.1.2:** Applies the cycle of continuous improvement with fidelity to lead professional learning.
		Desired outcome 1.1.3: Supports application of the cycle of continuous improvement.	
1.2 Develop collective responsibility			
Desired outcome 1.2.1: Advances collective responsibility.	**Desired outcome 1.2.1:** Advances collective responsibility.	**Desired outcome 1.2.1:** Advances collective responsibility.	**Desired outcome 1.2.1:** Advances collective responsibility.
Desired outcome 1.2.2: Engages with colleagues to meet the needs of all students.	**Desired outcome 1.2.2:** Fosters engagement of all colleagues in meeting the needs of all students.	**Desired outcome 1.2.2:** Fosters engagement of all staff in meeting the needs of all students.	**Desired outcome 1.2.2:** Fosters engagement of all staff in meeting the needs of all students.
Desired outcome 1.2.3: Models collective responsibility by participating in learning communities.	**Desired outcome 1.2.3:** Models collective responsibility by participating in learning communities.	**Desired outcome 1.2.3:** Models collective responsibility by participating in learning communities.	**Desired outcome 1.2.3:** Models collective responsibility by participating in learning communities.
1.3 Create alignment and accountability			
Desired outcome 1.3.1: Aligns professional learning with school goals.	**Desired outcome 1.3.1:** Aligns professional learning with school goals.	**Desired outcome 1.3.1:** Aligns professional learning with school and system goals.	**Desired outcome 1.3.1:** Aligns professional learning with school and system goals.
	Desired outcome 1.3.2: Supports colleagues to use the cycle of continuous improvement to achieve professional learning goals.	**Desired outcome 1.3.2:** Monitors the use of the cycle of continuous improvement to achieve professional learning goals.	**Desired outcome 1.3.2:** Monitors the use of the cycle of continuous improvement to achieve professional learning goals.

Source: From *Moving NSDC's Staff Development Standards into Practice: Innovation Configurations*, by Shirley Hord and Pat Roy (Roy & Hord, 2003). Reprinted with permission of the National Staff Development Council, www.nsdc.org. All rights reserved.

Connecting IC Maps across Role Groups – A "Crosswalk".   As noted above, clarity is increased when only one role group is the focus of a map. On the other hand, a tool that indicates how various components are shared across role groups can be highly useful, and provides understanding across the organization about *who* is expected to do *what*. This approach was taken in the creation of IC Maps to represent/reflect what each of four school-based groups (principal, teacher, coach, and school leadership team) were expected to be doing in implementing the Standards for Professional Learning, revised from earlier articulations of standards for staff development. For an extended period of time (years), the standards had languished in their printed documents when the Learning Forward executive director suggested that maps be constructed to give each of the "players" rich word-pictures of their role (Roy & Hord, 2003). In 2011, the standards were revised to account for the research results that had accrued, and a new set of IC maps was created. These maps describe expectations for conducting professional development that exemplify the now-seven Learning Forward standards for professional learning (Learning Forward, 2011). Figure 3.6, the Cross Walk, is the result of organizing all the desired outcomes (in these maps, *desired outcomes* is the term used for *components;* there are no variations in the Cross Walk) of all four role groups of the school-based educators.

The desired outcomes of teachers are presented as the first column in the Cross Walk. Then the desired outcomes of the other role groups are placed horizontal to the teachers in order to show which desired outcomes relate to each other. This depiction suggests how the four role groups (principal, teacher, coach, and school leadership team) support and enable the achievement of the desired outcomes for teachers.

The idea is to read horizontally, beginning with the teacher. The numerals of the outcomes can refer the reader back to the ICs presented in the book of maps). Notice that in some rows of desired outcomes, all squares are not filled. This effort with the Cross Walk is to illustrate the systemic approach to professional development and the role that all educators play.

More Complex and Richer IC Map Components.   When the need and available time are present, IC Map components can be made even more complex and richer. In one such project, the innovation itself was very subtle and complex, and developing each component had to be done in ways that built in the nuances of the philosophy of the developer as well as clear descriptions of how this approach would be seen in classroom practices. The innovation, the Essential Curriculum, is an educational program that provides children and young people with the knowledge and skills that will directly assist them in their development as capable and ethical people (Dunn & Borchardt, 1998). Although the program contains lessons and activities, its philosophy of how people should treat each other is expected to be expressed in the classroom throughout the day. Because of this, the IC Map includes components that describe practices during a lesson as well as others that address practices to be used throughout the day.

To help teachers, change facilitators, and evaluators who assess implementation of the Essential process, the IC Map components became much more complex. One of those components is presented in Figure 3.7. This IC Map Component contains a number of readily apparent differences compared to our previous examples. First, the range of variations is greater with a common dimensionality built into each one that deals with how holistically the teacher is integrating use of the program's principles. The *f* variation, for example, describes

FIGURE 3.7 A Dense and Complex IC Map Component with Indicators

THE ESSENTIAL CURRICULUM IC MAP

II. All Day in the Classroom

D. Teacher

6) The Principles and Concepts are applied throughout the day by the teacher [*Teacher Application, All*].

Consistent reliance on and integration of program	Deliberate and conscious application of principles and concepts	Emphasizes selected principles and concepts	Program delivery as designed	Presentation of parts and pieces at random	Non-use	Opposition to principles and concepts
(Complete Integration)	(Deliberate Application)	(Selected Emphasis)	(Motions)	(Parts and Pieces)	(Nothing)	(Antithesis)
(a)	(b)	(c)	(d)	(e)	(f)	(g)
Principles and concepts are integrated without conscious effort into activities of the day. ▪ Teacher and students acknowledge mistakes in words, including "Oops, I goofed." ▪ Teachers teach students through steps of correcting errors seamlessly. ▪ Students have "driver's licenses" and "drive" to other parts of the building using self-control. The license can be suspended for lack of self-control.	All principles and concepts are developed and consciously applied throughout the day. ▪ When opportunities arise, teacher and students draw connections to and apply specific principles and concepts. ▪ When faced with opportunities, teacher and students talk out loud about the relevant principle or concepts.	Selected principles and concepts are emphasized and applied appropriately throughout the day. ▪ Teacher leads students in applying principles of "self-control" but does not refer to other concepts. ▪ Teacher recognizes opportunities around "making mistakes" but misses opportunities related to other principles and concepts.	Lessons are taught, but no extrapolations to situations outside the Essential lesson context. ▪ When obvious opportunities to refer to principles and concepts arise, teacher does not make connection. ▪ Teacher handles fight on playground without reference to any Essential principle.	Some activities are purposefully selected to teach the concept. ▪ Tap and Trade game is played without principles being taught. ▪ Social studies curriculum happens to lend itself to the selection of Essential lessons.		Principles and concepts applied in classroom are antithetical to Essential curriculum ▪ Praise is used indiscriminately (unearned). ▪ Self-esteem activities teach principles and concepts counter to Essential's principles. ▪ "In this classroom we will not make mistakes." ▪ "I can give my students self-esteem." ▪ Mistakes are punished without any processing.

Source: From *The Essential Curriculum,* The Teel Institute, Kansas City, Missouri. Reprinted by permission of the Kauffman Center for Entrepreneurial Leadership at the Ewing Marion Kauffman Foundation.

the case when nothing that is related to that component is observed. The *g* variation addresses behaviors and actions that are actually antithetical to the intent of the program, which is information that can be very helpful. Another important addition to this component is the open-ended list of examples under each variation description. Although they will not represent all that is in a particular variation, nor will they necessarily be exclusive to that variation, they do describe the kinds of behaviors that are indicative of it.

Here is something to consider: You have undoubtedly tried to read and understand highly detailed road maps that make it frustratingly difficult to plainly see the bigger and clearer picture. You may want to consider two or three iterations of an IC Map—that is, a first map of an innovation might provide the major components and their variations in rich language so that one develops an initial mental image of the innovation in action. This map then may also serve as a monitoring instrument to track where and how the individual implementers are progressing. Then, on the reverse side of the document page, a more detailed map may be portrayed that provides to the implementer and the facilitator further information and useful explanation, and so on. Using this approach reduces user and implementer anxiety and frustration.

REFLECTION QUESTIONS

Whew! There's a lot of information here about IC Maps. Take a moment to recall a time when you were expected to change your practice by implementing a new way of "doing." Was there clear description of what your role was to be? If so, was that helpful to you? If not, what were your results?

The Process of Developing an IC Map

Developing an IC Map is a challenging endeavor. It also is energizing for those who really are interested in successful implementation of an innovation. The process includes moments of discovery about the intent of a particular innovation and how it should be used, as well as the initial struggle to figure out what the components are and then how to develop useful word-picture descriptions for each variation. Additional rewards come when the first draft of the IC Map is shared with interested teachers, principals, and other change facilitators. Often, this is the first time they will have seen written descriptions of what they will be doing when using the innovation.

Frequently, the first reaction of people who examine an IC Map is to be impressed by the ease of understanding that appears to be there. This reaction tends to come from individuals who are not yet involved with implementing the innovation. If the individuals are users of the innovation they are likely to do a self-assessment of where they would place themselves on each Component's Variations. A still different reaction is to consider some of the other variation descriptions and whether they should try them. The IC mappers receive very helpful feedback from these dialogues, which can be used in further refining the map.

Team Work Is Best.   Developing an IC Map is definitely an interactive process. An individual working alone is very unlikely to construct a map that is as useful as one that evolves from a team effort. Typically, three to seven key people (who are to some degree knowledgeable about the innovation) work together and over time (in total five or six days will be needed) to devise a complete first draft of an IC Map. One of the major outcomes of this interactive process is that the IC mappers develop a consensus about what the innovation should look like when it is in use. Up to that time, they likely will not have been using the same terms and mental images of use. This regularly observed lack of explicit agreement in understanding adds greatly to teachers' confusion about what they are supposed to be doing. Teachers have a difficult time when their principal, district office staff, and outside experts work from different implicit mental images of what ideal use looks like.

To engage in IC Mapping, establish a team of four to eight key personnel that includes roles such as lead teachers, principals, innovation experts, and relevant district personnel. It will help immensely to have a team facilitator who is expert in developing IC Maps. It normally takes 4 or 5 days to develop a solid first draft. If the innovation is large, in other words it is an *innovation bundle*, then establish separate groups to map each innovation within the bundle.

Through the process and dialogue, clarity increases about what use of the innovation looks like and how they are to use it. This results in participants developing precise expectations, a feeling of contributing to the innovation that they will use, and commitment to the innovation's implementation. In other words, the participants will have "buy-in."

REFLECTION QUESTIONS

Have you had the opportunities to experience both of these initial processes: (a) being part of an IC Map construction team and (b) receiving an IC Map with suggestions for its use? How does this compare with your not being provided with a clear image of what ideal use should look like? What advantages did each approach provide? What different reactions and feelings did each of the approaches stimulate?

Broad Spectrum Search.   The general process that is followed in developing an IC Map is presented in Figure 3.8.

The beginning steps entail reviewing all of the available printed material and then interviewing the innovation developer and/or experts. Following this, a range of classrooms where the innovation and similar practices are in use should be observed. It is important to observe a variety of classrooms because an IC Map needs to have word-picture descriptions that cover all possible variations. The key questions that should be asked throughout this process are:

1. What does the innovation *look like* when it is in use?
2. What would I *see* in classrooms where it is used well (and not as well)?
3. What will teachers *and* students *be doing* when the innovation is in use?
4. What are the *interactions*?
5. What does the classroom *look like*?

Operational, not Philosophy.   A key part of IC Mapping is the orientation that is taken. The focus is on developing pictures of the *operational forms* of the innovation, not statements of its philosophy or a listing of its implementation requirements. Innovation creators have a tendency to focus on implementation requirements. They may say something like, "You have to use these materials and spend at least 30 minutes doing so every day." However, this is the wrong answer for those building the IC Map. Instead they need to know *how* those materials are being used and *what* happens during the 30 minutes. A separate list of Implementation Requirements may be created to care for these items and keep them from becoming lost in the process.

Mind/Web Charting.   The initial document review, interviews, and observations should lead to generating possible components that represent the major parts of the innovation. One useful

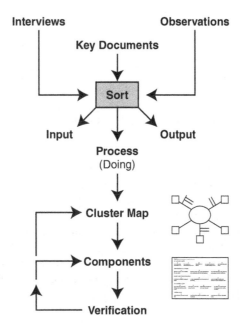

Note: This is a dynamic, interactive, consensus-building process.

FIGURE 3.8   The IC Mapping Process

way to explore possible Components and Variations is to place all possibilities on chart paper as a web or mind map. Mappers then delete suggestions that are irrelevant and add others deemed significant. The suggestions that are similar or alike are clustered, and those most core and central become the potential IC Map Components. The label for each Component should be clear, crisp, and as descriptive as you can make it. The first goal is to develop a holistic organizing scheme of possible components that represent what the innovation is like when it is used.

Drafting Components and Variations.   The next step is the task of agreeing on which components are key and should be developed. The selected components should represent *critical aspects of innovation use, not those typical to good teaching in general.* Then comes the intense work of negotiating the wording of components and component variations. Once a draft is complete, it should be tested in what we call the first "dose of reality." Typically around the third day of IC Map development it is worthwhile to try the draft out in several classrooms. Without exception, when IC mappers try out their first full draft, they discover a number of points that need clarification. They also are likely to discover that other components need to be mapped.

Identifying Dimensions.   One other useful IC Mapping technique is to examine the *dimensions* that comprise each Component. Each Variation has several ideas within it. The typical *a* Variation will have three to five ideas. The *b* Variation will contain four of these dimensions. The *c* and *d* will have less or none of the ideas that were part of the *a*. If this is all, then it will be what is done with most rubrics. There is a progression from "all" to "some" to "none" of the idea. This structure in rubrics is readily observed since the ideal variation will have more words, with the quantity of words tapering off as less of the best practice is present. An IC Map

*Learning leads to more questioning

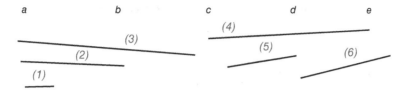

FIGURE 3.9   Structure of Dimensions within IC Map Component

has another set of dimensions that build up as the Variations flow from *c* to *e* and *f*. In most change processes the absence of using the innovation does not mean that nothing is happening. The implementer is doing something else, most likely the old way. The *d – f* Variations are descriptions of what is being done instead. Figure 3.9 is an illustration of how dimensions can flow across the Variations of a Component. As you can see in the example figures, the identification of dimensions is done in italics as part of each Component's title.

Developing an IC Map is a highly interactive and iterative process (see Table 3.1). Our experience has been that innovation developers cannot develop high-quality IC Maps by themselves. They see their innovation holistically and the idea of breaking out components is

TABLE 3.1   Indicators of Innovation Configurations

1. The wise IC "mapper" will always type the word *DRAFT* on each page of the IC Map, as it is under development. Map maker(s) should type his/her name and the date of the current draft on each page. This reduces the confusion when searching for the most recent version of the IC Map.

2. The Variation descriptions will taper off from the ideal as they move from *a* to *c* to *d* . At the right end of the Variation continuum is a description of what is being done instead of what would be done if this component of the innovation were being used. Typically the *e* and *f* variations will be descriptions of the "old" way. Thus, on the map, a reviewer will see a range of variations that describe the user's actions from the "old" to the "new." Keep in mind that the *d* and *e* variations are not "bad" or pejorative descriptions; they are descriptions of decreasing fidelity to the innovation, and/or alternative practices that represent other ways of doing things.

3. A completed IC Map should serve as a record of how an innovation is being used. The Map's purpose is not to explain how the information about practice is to be collected; this may be done by interview, observation, or user self-assessment.

4. Some caution is needed in terms of reliability and validity, especially for certain types of IC Map Components. For example, there will be much lower validity for a teaching process component that is self-assessed than for one that is recorded by a trained observer.

5. Rich descriptive word pictures should be created for each Variation. Address the presence or absence of each dimension within each Variation. Care should be taken for having too few or too many dimensions in a Variation. Rarely should a Variation consist of only one dimension or more than four. Fidelity lines may be inserted only *after* the IC Map has been through several iterations of drafts and testing, and is viewed as a stable document.

6. Debate and consensus-building among the mappers is key. Talk about "what do you mean" and "what would I see" is critical to developing a useful and valid IC Map.

difficult and often uncomfortable. "You can't look at that (part) by itself; it all fits together!" An earlier technical document on IC Mapping (Heck, Stiegelbauer, Hall, & Loucks, 1981) may be of some help. A more significant resource is the more current technical manual (Hord, Stiegelbauer, Hall, & George, 2006). The Guiding Principles of IC Mapping also provide additional technical information and tips to consider in reviewing map drafts.

INNOVATION CONFIGURATIONS: APPLICATIONS AND IMPLICATIONS

The Innovation Configuration concept and IC Maps have many applications and implications. We have selected a few to introduce here to stimulate further thought about this important aspect of the change process. The points that are included address some facets of facilitating change processes, conducting research, and drafting IC Maps.

Using IC Maps to Clarify the Change *How fully shared?*

Once an IC Map is developed, it should be shared with all of the potential and current users of the innovation and with all change facilitators. This was done, for example, for the nine innovation bundles in the Kentucky Education Reform Act. Under the leadership of Roger Pankratz and the Kentucky Institute of Education Research, each of nine cross-state constituent teams of 6 to 10 members met for a week to develop the first drafts of the IC Maps. Each team was assigned one bundle. The resulting copies of their IC Maps were then sent to all 1,230 schools in the state. This was the first time that teachers and principals had word-picture descriptions of what they would be doing under the labels of each of the reform initiatives.

Using IC Maps to Guide Construction of a Professional Learning Community

In Professional Learning Communities (PLCs), the concept and the work (Chapter 7) involve command of substantial information and understanding about how to create the desired structures and strategies in schools. Although some information about each structure may be accessible, much more would be desirable. One tool for increasing understanding would be change facilitators' creation of IC Maps of PLC (Hord & Tobia, 2012), or other reform structures or practices. The resultant maps could be used to guide and support development of the PLC and also be used by facilitators and program evaluators to assess the extent of implementation at various points in time. In this way, interventions that support participants could be related to how far they have moved on the map in terms of each component. For example, interventions could be cataloged as they relate to the development of each of the six dimensions of PLC (components) in the map (Hord & Tobia, 2012).

Using IC Maps to Plan Implementation Supports

An IC Map is also a diagnostic tool for planning professional development. For example, a large number of teachers could be observed and an IC Map marked for each to indicate their progress in implementation, with the information then summarized by component. The summary would be a tally of how many teachers were at each of the variations for each component. Then it would be possible to identify those components for which implementation was going well (i.e., many teachers using *a* and *b* Variations) and any components where implementation was lagging (i.e., many teachers using *d* and *e* Variations). This information could be used to plan large group learning sessions to address less well-implemented components.

Coaching with IC Maps

IC Maps can be a useful coaching tool as well. Principals and other change facilitators observe classrooms to provide help to teachers, but often they are not given guidelines and specifics about what to look for. The IC Map provides a set of descriptions that can be used to focus their observations. There might also be a pre-observation discussion during which the teacher and the facilitator agree that certain IC Map Components will be targeted during the observation. If a student IC Map is used that focuses on what the students are doing, teachers are less likely to perceive the use of an IC Map as an evaluation threat. In all cases, if the focus is kept on the innovation instead of the teacher, personal concerns will be lower.

Using IC Maps for Self-Reflection

One of the most important uses of IC Maps is for self-assessment and reflection. Each component variation should be a word picture description of one way that component could be made operational. As was suggested above, unlike most rubrics, with an IC Map the *d* and *e* variations are not merely less of the *a or b* variation; instead they represent other possible practices. When an implementer, such as a teacher, compares his or her current practice with the variation descriptions, she or he will be able to place themselves at one of the variations along the continuum. In addition, by studying the other variations they can see what they can do differently to get closer to the *a* variation.

Table 3.2 is a summary of key themes and implications of Innovation Configurations for Change Facilitators and leaders.

TABLE 3.2   Implications of Innovation Configurations for Change Leaders and Facilitators

Change leaders and facilitators of change use IC maps to:

1. Describe what the innovation is, to communicate specific expectations of implementers, and to establish goals to be achieved at a designated time.

2. Develop a common vocabulary for dialogue about the innovation.

3. Offer an array of best practices for the innovation, and to specify the "ideal."

4. Gauge the level of implementation of an innovation in an identified unit (grade level, school, all district schools), and provide the means by which leaders can discuss progress of various groups.

5. Enable the identification of resources and support for innovation implementation and sustainability.

6. Guide the focus of professional development.

7. Promote individuals' reflection and self-assessment of his/her practice.

8. Provide the basis for altering/differentiating the IC, based on context.

EAST LAKE SCHOOL DISTRICT'S STORY, PART II

After the second Saturday's all-day meeting with the Game Plan Team, Josh, high school department chair and Joe, kindergarten teacher, were driving home and discussing the day's work.

JOSH: This work of creating an IC map is challenging, but I think I am finally beginning to understand what's most critical in the new CCSS-based math that we will teach.

JOE: The neat thing about it is that we are developing one consensus vision that we can use all the way through the grades. Then, when kids move from one school to another, they will not be lost in trying to find themselves in a different text and curriculum.

JOSH: It's a new way for me to teach. I have been very accustomed to using more teacher direction: I tell the students what and how, and then set them to practicing related problems. It was pretty easy, once you became familiar with the text and its sequence of learning objectives for the students.

JOE: What I like about this new way is that it will provide even my kindergarten students the opportunity to be thoughtful about math. The student IC Map component about "using mathematical language" is really good. It means that I have to learn how to stimulate them to be thoughtful, critical thinkers, and problem solvers. That is really exciting to me, but I am wondering how this is going to go over with parents. It will be a really big change from how they learned mathematics.

JOSH: And, say, that brings up an issue . . . we will need to plan how to share this with parents. And, of course, we can't do that before we reach full determination about the components of this new math . . . thinking and re-thinking to identify the most critical components—the major pieces, to me, is the trickiest part; they require very thoughtful analysis skills.

JOE: And, then, of course, we will also plan how to share meaningfully with our teacher colleagues.

JOSH: There is a whole lot more work to be done!

CRITIQUE QUESTIONS OF EAST LAKE DISTRICT'S STORY

1. Josh and Joe are thinking about the creation of an IC map for the new math curriculum, and they discuss sharing the map with parents. Why, or why not, would it be a good idea to share with parents, and when might you do it?
2. Would you ever want to share the IC Map with students? Why or why not?

REFLECTION QUESTIONS

In the past, how have you shared with students what is expected with a new program/innovation? Were you able to provide descriptions of what it looked like in operation? Or, did you present more about the philosophy or overall approach, or say nothing?

USING IC MAPS IN RESEARCH, PROGRAM EVALUATION, AND IMPLEMENTATION ASSESSMENTS

A serious problem in most research and evaluation studies has been the failure to document implementation before making judgments about the effects of various treatments, programs, and innovations. Typically, implementation is assumed to have occurred if teachers were trained or the materials were purchased. Our view is that without direct determination of the extent of implementation by each implementer, any study findings will be suspect. Also, any comparison classrooms have to be checked to see if components of the innovation are in use there. Often they will be doing the same thing, but have a different name for it. Without direct measurements of presence and absence of components of the innovation, it is highly risky to be drawing inferences about the effects of a particular program or innovation. An IC Map provides one clear and direct way to record the actual extent and quality of what has been implemented in treatment and comparison classrooms and schools.

Testing Fidelity of Implementation Against Student Outcomes

In a number of earlier research studies, IC Maps were developed and data collected to assess the extent of implementation. For example, Bridge (1995) conducted a number of studies of the implementation of the Integrated Primary program in Kentucky. The *a* variations were formulated using the state's reform initiative and the standards of the National Association for the Education of Young Children. Bridge found that children had higher achievement in primary-grade classrooms with higher levels (i.e., more *a* and *b* variations) of implementation of the developmentally appropriate practices. Koon (1995) had similar findings in a study of the extent of implementation of YESS! Mini-Society (Kourilsky, 1983), an innovation designed to introduce concepts of business and entrepreneurship to students. The IC Map sampled in Figure 3.4 was developed and used in a major study of implementation of constructive teaching of mathematics. In that study too, there was a positive relationship between higher fidelity classrooms and student test scores (George, Hall, & Uchiyama, 2000).

The Fidelity Enigma.   Each of the studies just cited reflected a fidelity orientation. The innovation developers had established expectations of which practices were preferable. In each study the IC Maps were developed accordingly and higher student outcomes were associated with higher fidelity implementations. An issue that merits discussion is when and whether it is appropriate to ask for or insist on high-fidelity use of an innovation. From one point of view teachers are being told what to do, which reduces their teaching freedom. On the other hand, if student gains are higher when the innovation is used in specified ways, should not teachers be expected to use the verified practices? Although we do not have a simple or universally applicable answer to this critical question, we believe that it must be openly asked, discussed, and addressed in each change effort.

Pothole Warning

The issue of fidelity is a real stickler. Without it, implementation is left to each implementer's imagination or to assumptions. How can we attribute student gains to new programs when it is possible that the programs were not fully operational in each classroom? At the same time, to what extent should teacher creativity be curtailed?

Pothole Repair

With the construct of Innovation Configuration, each of these questions can be more carefully considered. Formative and summative evaluation studies must begin with assessing the extent of the innovation's implementation in each classroom where use is expected. This assessment must be done in comparison classrooms too. Leaders should also consider and balance the demands for fidelity with the extent to which (and around which Components) teacher creativity is to be encouraged.

Identifying Critical Components and Their Relationship to Student Outcomes

In the study of standards-based teaching and learning of mathematics, the relationship between fidelity of implementation of particular IC Map components and student outcomes was examined (George, Hall, & Uchiyama, 2000). In the first analysis, hierarchical clustering was used to group classrooms as being high (*a* and *b* variations), medium (*c* variations), or low (*d* and *e* variations) fidelity. In this study the highest fidelity implementations had significantly higher student test scores. A further statistical analysis by IC Map component identified one component in particular as being associated with higher student test scores ("Teacher use of direct instruction"). Empirical findings of this type could be used by the change facilitators to design key workshops and other forms of support that would enhance implementation of the most critical component(s).

SUMMARY

In this chapter we introduced the idea that an innovation can be made operational in many different forms or "configurations." We advocated developing IC Maps and openly sharing the drafts with all parties. Along the way we pointed out some of the conceptual, operational, and philosophical implications of this process. For introducing these ideas to others, you may find these Talking Points useful:

- One of the important benefits of developing an IC Map is the consensus building that it encourages. Without such agreement, various leaders and change facilitators all too frequently deliver different messages; this adds to the confusion and frustration about the change.
- Change processes will be more efficient and effective when careful consideration is given to what ideal implementation should look like from the outset. This is not to say that images and values of the innovation cannot change with time.
- It is important to type *DRAFT* on each page of the IC Map.
- When a variety of configurations is implemented, it is unlikely that significant gains in student learning will be detected across all classrooms.

- The IC Map is a multi-purpose tool that change leaders, implementers, and program evaluators can use to decrease ambiguity.
- Evaluators and researchers need to specify which configurations have been implemented in "treatment" groups and in any comparison groups.

DISCUSSION QUESTIONS

1. Describe an experience that you have had during which the innovation as used was different from what the developer had intended. Why did this occur?

2. What key steps would you take to introduce the idea of developing an IC Map to a school/district staff?

3. How could a teacher use an IC Map?

4. How could a principal use an IC Map?

5. How could a corporation or small business use an IC Map?

6. What do you see as an important implication of IC for evaluation and research studies?

APPLYING INNOVATION CONFIGURATIONS IN FACILITATING IMPLEMENTATION

1. Develop two or three configuration components, with their variations, for an innovation that you know. Try out the draft of your IC Map by interviewing a principal, or one or two teachers (independently), about use of the innovation. What did you learn about the innovation and its implementation from this experience?

2. Critique an IC Map that someone else has developed. Can you visualize the ideal use of the innovation from studying the map? Which variation descriptions present clear word pictures? What are the dimensions within each variation? Does each component contain a reasonable number of variations? Which would you suggest be changed or clarified?

3. Make a presentation to your Board of Trustees about the desirability of creating IC Maps to support passage of the district's bond issue. In addition to the Trustees, what other individuals should have an IC Map to guide their work in this promotion? Explain why.

APPLYING INNOVATION CONFIGURATIONS IN RESEARCH AND PROGRAM EVALUATION STUDIES

1. Focusing professional development around the Critical Components on an IC Map is seen as an important way to increase fidelity of implementation. Create an IC Map of an impending curriculum to be implemented. Use the map to track implementation progress. Identify interventions that the facilitators are providing and examine how closely they relate to Critical Components. To what extent is there a relationship between the progress of implementation and the interventions that are made?

2. Identify parents of two teenagers who cannot seem to maintain tidy bedrooms, despite regular demands, scoldings, bribes, and threats. Invite the parent to describe or write a paragraph about their expectations related to the condition of their teen's bedroom. Engage the parent and his/her child in constructing an IC Map of a "reasonably" tidy bedroom. The following are examples of possible components:

   a. Makes the bed daily
   b. Places soiled clothes in the hamper
   c. Takes uneaten food, dishes, and utensils to the kitchen and garbage container

   Additional components could be added, but keep it fairly simple. Develop variations for each of the components. The maps of the two families could be quite different; they should represent the components of interest in each family. Coach the parents in how to introduce the maps to their children, indicating that each student will use the "map" collaboratively with his/her parent to record the journey to a tidy personal living space. After 2 weeks, interview the parents to ascertain how the map is working. Is the student using it? Has the appearance of the room changed? Now ask the parents to leave the monitoring in the students' hands with no parental interference for 2 weeks. Interview the parents to learn if progress continues or decreases. The idea is to learn how an IC Map might be applied to family life and to discover if this is a reliable means for changing behavior with less stress and trauma.

LEARNING MORE ABOUT INNOVATION CONFIGURATIONS

Hord, S. M., & Roussin, J. L. (2013). *Implementing change through learning: Concerns-based concepts, tools, and strategies for guiding change.* Thousand Oaks, CA: Corwin Press.

This hands-on practical book uses a series of powerful Learning Map activities to guide and support individuals and teams in developing the knowledge and skills for using the concepts, strategies, and tools of the Concerns-Based Adoption Model (CBAM) to manage their change efforts successfully. This is the "how to" book of CBAM.

Learning Forward. (2012). *Standards into practice: School-based roles. Innovation Configuration maps for Standards for Professional Learning.* Oxford, OH: Author.

This volume of Innovation Configuration maps de-mystifies and details, in the action words of the IC map text, the vision of what the Standards for Professional Learning look like in practice. In this first volume, the roles of teacher, coach, school leadership team, and principal, as they relate to the Standards, are depicted.

For accessing training in the use of and creation of IC Maps, contact the authors or Southwest Educational Development Laboratory (SEDL), 4700 Mueller Boulevard, Austin, Texas 78723, (800) 476–6861.

HOW CAN THE DIFFERENT FEELINGS AND PERCEPTIONS ABOUT CHANGE BE UNDERSTOOD AND ADDRESSED?

Stages of Concern

My kids have been doing terrific in using mathematics language to probe the reasoning of others. Now José and I are talking about bringing our two classes together to see how well they do in checking the reasoning of others.

—Kim White, fifth-grade teacher at Island Park Elementary School, in reference to Common Core Standards

I don't have time to go see what she is doing. I still have to plan for how I will work with this new approach tomorrow.

—Pamela Stone, new sixth-grade teacher at River Run Elementary School

Oh, oh! What is the principal talking about now? Will I have to stop using what I have been doing and start doing this new stuff?

—Mary Jo Rodriquez, Social Studies Teacher, thoughts upon hearing Mr. Major (principal) mention students doing formative assessments

I haven't thought about it. I have so many other things going on.

—Helen Morse, Mountain View High School English Department Chair, who also has yearbook staff to advise and a new prep to prepare

The preceding quotes are all too familiar to those of us who have spent time in schools working with teachers and others engaged in change. Many feelings and perceptions are expressed. Many more are only whispered or left unspoken. No matter how promising and wonderful the innovation, no matter how strong the support, implementers will still have moments of self-doubt about whether they can—and even whether they want to—succeed with the new approach. Moments of euphoria are experienced when the change works well, and at other times success seems impossible.

We all know what it is like during the first year of doing something new and different. We tire more easily. We need more time to prepare. And we can't predict everything that will happen. We never feel like we are really on top of matters. Yet after several years the new becomes familiar and readily doable. Our thoughts shift from the struggles of figuring out what to do to the satisfactions of seeing what happens with students and of talking with others about the benefits of the change and about how to fine-tune it to work even better.

Across all of these experiences an affective dimension can be observed, for we are not just doing but continually thinking and feeling about how the change is working, how well we are doing, and what effects it is having. This personal side of change is experienced by everyone—executives, parents, students, sales representatives, secretaries, and governors— whenever we are involved in implementing change.

The construct for understanding the personal side of change is **Stages of Concern (SoC)**. In this chapter the concerns construct is described, three ways of measuring concerns are introduced, and most importantly, effective and less effective ways of addressing the different concerns are examined.

LEARNING OUTCOMES

After reading this chapter, the learner should be able to:

1. Describe the different feelings and perceptions that emerge as part of the change process.
2. Name and describe each of the seven Stages of Concern (SoC).
3. Introduce to others the idea of concerns and describe the three ways to assess SoC.
4. Draw some of the more typical SoC profiles and interpret their meaning.
5. Propose different change interventions that would be appropriate and inappropriate for addressing each Stage of Concern.
6. Consider both individual and group SoC profiles in designing change-facilitating interventions.

THE PERSONAL SIDE OF CHANGE

Pothole Warning

Personal feelings and perceptions can very easily upset a change process.

Pothole Repair

Sometimes it is more important to attend to the personal aspects of change than it is to singularly focus on use of the innovation.

Feelings and perceptions about an innovation and/or a change process can help or disrupt. When people are excited about a promising change, they will try it. But if they perceive threat or loss, people will hold back from engaging with the process. These feelings and perceptions can be sorted and classified into what we call *concerns*. In fact, extensive research is available about how our feelings and perceptions evolve as a change process unfolds. We have named this construct *Stages of Concern (SoC).* Information about SoC provides the diagnostic basis for taking steps to advance an implementation effort. Also, through many studies, three different ways of measuring concerns have been established.

Understanding the SoC and using the assessment techniques can result in significantly more effective one-on-one coaching, more relevant workshops, and strategic plans that take into account the personal side of change processes. Understanding and use of SoC can result in efforts to implement change being more personalized and effective. Description of the SoC, the assessment techniques, and how to facilitate change processes in *concerns-based* ways are the central topics of this chapter.

Different Types of Concerns

The idea of calling one's feelings and perceptions *concerns* was originally proposed by Frances Fuller (1969), a counseling psychologist at The University of Texas at Austin who took an interest in student teachers as a result of teaching their required educational psychology course. When she started teaching the course, she worked diligently to make it a good one, but the evaluations at the end of the semester showed that 97 out of the 100 students rated the course as "irrelevant" and "a waste of time."

Fuller was an exceptional educator. As Howard Jones, a colleague of ours from the University of Houston, likes to tell, she did not react as you might expect to the students' evaluation of her course. Instead of being completely discouraged, she asked, "What did I do that turned those three students on?" This was a breakthrough question. When she looked at the 3 students who had rated the course positively, she found that they, unlike the other 97, had had some sort of previous experience with children. They had either taught a church class or were parents already. Thus, they had a different background with which to understand and appreciate the introductory course on educational psychology. Fuller hypothesized that their *concerns* were different as a result of their experiences.

Fuller's Unrelated, Self, Task, and Impact Concerns

Fuller proceeded to conduct a series of in-depth studies of the concerns of student teachers. She then proposed a model outlining how, with increasing experience in a teacher education program, the student teacher's concerns moved through four levels: Unrelated, Self, Task, and Impact.

Unrelated concerns are found most frequently among student teachers who have not had any direct contact with school-age children or clinical experiences in school settings. Their concerns do not center on teaching or teaching-related issues. Instead, they more typically focus on college life (e.g., "I hope I can get a ticket to the concert"). They might be concerned about courses removed from professional education (e.g., "I hope I pass that geography course"). These teacher candidates do have concerns, but they are not teaching related.

Self-concerns tend to be most prevalent when teacher education candidates begin to engage with more intense clinical experiences, especially at the beginning of student teaching. They now have concerns about teaching, but with an egocentric frame of reference. Their thoughts focus on how the experience will affect themselves. Beginning student teachers with Self-concerns will be asking questions such as "Where do I park my car when

I get to the school?" "Can I go in the teachers' lounge?" and "Will I get along with my cooperating teacher so that I get a good grade?" These expressions indicate concerns about teaching, but with a focus on themselves rather than on the act of teaching or the needs of children.

Task concerns show up quite soon after the start of student teaching, as the actual work of teaching becomes central. Typical expressions include "Oh! I am so tired. I had to stay up until midnight grading papers." "When three groups are going at once, my head is spinning, and I don't know where to turn next!" "These materials break too easily—there are pieces everywhere, and they just play with them!"

Impact concerns are the ultimate goal for student teachers, teachers, and professors. At this level, the concerns focus on what is happening with students and what the teacher can do to be more effective in improving student learning. Improving teaching and student learning are what the talk and thought are about: "My students are doing great; they now understand why I gave them that assignment!" "I am thinking of adding some new interest centers. They might attract those children who don't seem to get it this other way." "There is a workshop next Saturday on involving kids with special needs in cooperative groups. I am going to take it."

In her studies, Fuller found that over two thirds of the concerns of preservice teachers were in the Self and Task areas, whereas two thirds of the concerns of experienced teachers were in the Task and Impact areas. She also observed that at any given time teachers may have concerns at several levels, but that they tend to concentrate in one particular area.

Connecting Concerns to Teacher Education

The Concerns of Teacher model was used to propose a different design and flow for teacher education programs, which was named *personalized teacher education* (Fuller, 1970; Fuller & Bown, 1975). Fuller believed that becoming a teacher entailed *personalogical development,* or the development of one's own style and philosophy. The best way to achieve this end was to address the candidate's concerns when she or he had them. In the design of a teacher education program, this means offering the courses and field experiences in a sequence that parallels the developing concerns of the students, rather than in a sequence that parallels the professors' concerns.

For example, when teacher education students have Self-concerns is the time for early field experiences, low-ratio teaching activities, and the parts of educational psychology courses that address how children of the same age as those being observed learn. For students with Task concerns, the timing is ripe for the how-to components of methods, especially classroom management. The history and philosophy aspects of teacher education are seen by the candidates as being much more relevant when offered near the end of their program. This personalized approach does not mean that all content that is important from the professors' point of view is left out. Instead, the information is provided when it is most relevant to the students' developing interests and perceived needs—in other words, their concerns.

 REFLECTION QUESTION

How well did your concerns with teacher education or a similar program match up with Fuller's Teacher Concerns model?

CONCERNS ABOUT THE CHANGE PROCESS

Our years of experience with studying and leading implementation efforts has clearly documented that the concerns phenomena that Frances Fuller had identified are limited neither to college students going through teacher education programs nor to teachers. In fact, everyone involved in change exhibits the same dynamics in terms of feelings and perceptions.

The same *Unrelated, Self, Task,* and *Impact* pattern of concerns is found in people involved with all types of innovations and change processes. In addition, choosing the types of interventions that are to be done to facilitate the change process is based on the same personalization model. Instead of connecting college courses to concerns, Change Facilitators are making interventions that should be addressing implementers' concerns. In fact, if the example is simply changed from learning to teach to implementing a new program/process, the same types of concerns are typically heard:

> *Unrelated (now called Unconcerned):* I am not really interested in _____ [this innovation]. My mind is on . . .
>
> *Self:* I don't know if I can do this. Also, I am concerned about what my boss thinks.
>
> *Task:* Using this material is taking all of my time. You can't imagine all the pieces and steps that are entailed in just doing one activity!
>
> *Impact:* Yesterday, I was talking with Mary Beth. Both of us have found that with the new approach, all of the students are engaged in the activities and are picking up on the concepts much more quickly.

As these quotes illustrate and the findings from our research and that of our colleagues document (see, for example, Dunn & Rakes, 2010; Persichitte & Bauer, 1996; Saunders, 2012; Shieh, 1996; Van den Berg & Vandenberghe, 1981), the same types of concerns exist when people are engaged with any change. Further, the personalized idea about what the leaders need to say and do is the same. Interventions to facilitate change must be aligned with the concerns of those who are engaged with the change. For example, when teachers are in the first year of implementing an innovation such as standards-based education, they have many Task concerns. The most valued and effective facilitator is a teacher or consultant who is highly experienced, knows the details and mechanics of using the innovation, and can offer specific how-to tips. Teachers with intense Task concerns don't want to hear about the philosophy; they want help in making the innovation work more smoothly. The more abstract and subtle aspects of innovation use are of greater interest to teachers with Impact concerns.

Pothole Warning

What should a leader do when a teacher says, "Why should I do this, anyway? It too will pass"?

Pothole Repair

This may be a hint of Self-concern ("I don't know what it is" or "What will it mean for me?"), or perhaps it is an indication of more intense lack of concern ("I have a lot of other things on my plate right now"). Either way, rather than telling the teacher, "This is different," first ask them to explain why they feel the way they do.

Identifying and Defining the Stages of Concern (SoC)

An important early step in our research was to construct a definition of the term *concern*. For our purposes, one of the strengths of this term is that it does not have a narrow, specific meaning. Each person is able to think about concerns in terms of his or her own perceptions and ruminations. In our cross-cultural studies, one of the most important decisions was selecting the equivalent word. For example, in Dutch we selected the word in the salutation "To whom it may be of concern."

Concerns Definition.   The agreed-upon definition of the term *concern* is this:

> The composite representation of the feelings, preoccupation, thought, and consideration given to a particular issue or task is called *concern*. Depending on our personal make-up, knowledge, and experiences, each person perceives and mentally contends with a given issue differently; thus there are different kinds of concerns. The issue may be interpreted as an outside threat to one's well being, or it may be seen as rewarding. There may be an overwhelming feeling of confusion and lack of information about what "it" is. There may be ruminations about the effects. The demand to consider the issue may be self-imposed in the form of a goal or objective that we wish to reach, or the pressure that results in increased attention to the issue may be external. In response to the demand, our minds explore ways, means, potential barriers, possible actions, risks, and rewards in relation to the demand. All in all, the mental activity composed of questioning, analyzing, and re-analyzing, considering alternative actions and reactions, and anticipating consequences is *concern*.
>
> To be concerned means to be in a mentally aroused state about something. The intensity of the arousal will depend on the person's past experiences and associations with the subject of the arousal, as well as [on] how close to the person and how immediate the issue is perceived as being. Close personal involvement is likely to mean more intense (i.e., more highly aroused) concern which will be reflected in greatly increased mental activity, thought, worry, analysis, and anticipation. Through all of this, it is the person's perceptions that stimulate concerns, not necessarily the reality of the situation. (Hall, George, & Rutherford, 1979, p. 5)

Stages of Concern Defined.   Through our research, we have identified and confirmed a set of seven specific categories of concerns about the innovation that we call *Stages of Concern* (SoC; pronounced "ess-oh-see" not "sock"!), as presented in Table 4.1. With further study

TABLE 4.1   Stages of Concern: Typical Expressions of Concern About the Innovation

	STAGES OF CONCERN	EXPRESSIONS OF CONCERN
IMPACT	6 Refocusing	I have some ideas about something that would work even better.
	5 Collaboration	I am concerned about relating what I am doing with what my co-workers are doing.
	4 Consequence	How is my use affecting clients?
TASK	3 Management	I seem to be spending all of my time getting materials ready.
SELF	2 Personal	How will using it affect me?
	1 Informational	I would like to know more about it.
UNRELATED	0 Unconcerned	I am more concerned about some other things.

TABLE 4.2   Stages of Concern About the Innovation: Paragraph Definitions

Impact	**6 Refocusing:** The focus is on the exploration of more universal benefits from the innovation, including the possibility of major changes or replacement with a more powerful alternative. Individual has definite ideas about alternatives to the proposed or existing form of the innovation.
	5 Collaboration: The focus is on coordination and cooperation with others regarding use of the innovation.
	4 Consequence: Attention focuses on impact of the innovation on "clients" in the immediate sphere of influence.
Task	**3 Management:** Attention is focused on the processes and tasks of using the innovation and the best use of information and resources. Issues related to efficiency, organizing, managing, scheduling, and time demands are utmost.
Self	**2 Personal:** Individual is uncertain about the demands of the innovation, his/her inadequacy to meet those demands, and his/her role with the innovation. This includes analysis of his/her role in relation to the reward structure of the organization, decision making, and consideration of potential conflicts with existing structures or personal commitment. Financial or status implications of the program for self and colleagues may also be reflected.
	1 Informational: A general awareness of the innovation and interest in learning more detail about it is indicated. The person seems to be unworried about himself/herself in relation to the innovation. She/he is interested in substantive aspects of the innovation in a selfless manner, such as general characteristics, effects, and requirements for use.
Unrelated	**0 Unconcerned:** Little concern about or involvement with the innovation is indicated. Concern about other thing(s) is more intense.

Source: Stages of concern about innovation: Hall et al., Report No. 3032 © 1979

and application in schools, colleges, and, to a lesser extent, businesses, we and our colleagues developed paragraph definitions for each of the SoC, which are presented in Table 4.2. Note that the original ideas of Unrelated, Self, Task, and Impact have been preserved, but, based on the research findings, the Self and Impact areas have been clarified by distinguishing stages within each. Self-concerns are now divided into two stages—Informational and Personal— and Impact concerns into three—Consequence, Collaboration, and Refocusing.

If you think about it, these stages make intuitive sense, and you certainly hear people express these kinds of concerns. For example, at the beginning of the change process teachers (and others) say:

> *Well, at this point I don't know much about it, other than we have been told that we will be adopting it (Stage 1 Informational). I don't know what the principal thinks about our doing this (Stage 2 Personal), or if he even knows about it (Stage 1 Informational). I just hope that I don't have to stop doing what I have been doing and start all over again (Stage 2 Personal). I hope that we learn more at the next faculty meeting (Stage 1 Informational).*

All of these concerns are in the *Self* area, but they represent two component parts. The person knows a little, but would like to know more (Stage 1 Informational) and is concerned about where he or she stands in terms of the principal's knowledge and position. The person is also wondering about what he or she will have to give up when the innovation arrives (Stage 2 Personal).

Pothole Warning

Don't forget about those who are enthusiastic about the change.

Pothole Repair

Having intense Impact concerns is ideal. Unfortunately, all too often leaders overly focus on those with Self and Task concerns. Be sure to take time to compliment and support those with Impact concerns.

Impact concerns are even more complex. Stage 4 Consequence deals with increasing effectiveness and impact in one's own use of the innovation; Stage 5 Collaboration focuses on concern about working with one or more colleagues so that together there can be more impact; and Stage 6 Refocusing indicates that the person has ideas about a more effective alternative. Remember that the overarching theme of Stages 4, 5, and 6 is always concern about improving the *impact* of the innovation on clients/students.

REFLECTION QUESTIONS

How does the SoC idea fit with your experiences with change? What are some examples of your concerns?

WHY ARE THEY CALLED STAGES OF CONCERN?

The research studies clearly document a quasi-developmental path to the concerns as a change process unfolds. However, the ideal flow to concerns is not always guaranteed, nor does it always move in one direction. *If* the innovation is appropriate, *if* there is sufficient time, *if* the leaders are initiating, and *if* the change process is carefully facilitated, then implementers will move from early Self-concerns to Task concerns (during the first years of use) and, ultimately, to Impact concerns (after 3 to 5 years).

Unfortunately, all of these *ifs* are not always present. More often than not, the support needed for the change process over time is not forthcoming, or the leaders fail to facilitate effectively, or, in the case of schools, the district, state, and federal governments annually add more innovations to the point where none can be fully implemented. In these situations, concerns do not progress from Self to Task to Impact. Instead, progress is arrested, with Stage 3 Management concerns continuing to be intense. If these conditions do not change, in time many teachers return to Self-concerns.

In the first conception of the Concerns-Based Adoption Model (CBAM), the term *Stages of Concern* was deliberately chosen to reflect the idealized, developmental approach to change that we value (see Hall, Wallace, & Dossett, 1973). Unfortunately, in most instances, as we pointed out in Chapter 1, change is not viewed and treated as a process, but as an event. When this event mentality is applied, the stage model breaks down, and people are forced into sustained Self and/or Task concerns. This is why we call the stages "quasi" developmental.

CAN THERE BE CONCERNS AT MORE THAN ONE STAGE?

When presenting the SoC, we are frequently asked if it is possible to have concerns at more than one stage at the same time. Of course it is possible! In fact, most of the time a person will have intense concerns at more than one stage. For example, although a teacher may have intense Task (Stage 3 Management) concerns, concerns about students are still influencing his or her instructional decision making. In general, people have a conglomeration of concerns representing several of the stages, with some more strongly felt than others and some absent all together.

Graphically, we represent this conglomeration or array of concerns of varying intensities by using a *concerns profile*. By representing the SoC on the horizontal axis and the relative intensity of concerns on the vertical, a general picture of a person's concerns can be displayed. The peaks indicate stages that are more intense, and the valleys show those that are less intense.

Different, commonly observed scenarios can be envisaged using concerns profiles. For example, we have already described the first-year user of an innovation with intense Stage 3 Management concerns. That person's concerns profile would have a peak on Stage 3, whereas the other stages would be lower. If the person were also a first- or second-year teacher, he or she might have more intense Stage 2 Personal concerns about surviving the evaluation process and receiving continuing appointment. In this case the concerns profile would likely have two peaks, one for Stage 3 Management concerns and a second peak for Stage 2 Personal concerns.

Another teacher might be very experienced and truly a master teacher. His or her concerns profile could be most intense on Stage 3 Management concerns, too, relative to first-time use of major change. But her or his second-most intense stage could be Stage 4 Consequence, indicating more concern about how use of the innovation is affecting his or her students.

Many combinations of concerns can be imagined and have been observed. In each case, once the profile of concerns has been identified, the important work can begin. As interesting as it is to see and attempt to analyze a concerns profile, the crucial step is in using understanding of SoC to make *concerns-based interventions*. Facilitators need to take steps to resolve the Self and Task concerns and facilitate the arousal of Impact concerns. Examples of relevant and inappropriate interventions for each SoC are presented in Appendix 4A.

HOW DO CONCERNS CHANGE OVER TIME?

SoC profiles are a very informative way to illustrate movement and nonmovement during a change process. When concerns profiles are collected at different points in time, each is a snapshot of that moment. The time series of profiles becomes a motion picture of how concerns evolved and, hopefully, developed. These snapshots represent one way of assessing how far across the Implementation Bridge (remember Figure 1.2?) each individual, group, and organization has progressed.

As the term *stages* implies, and as the numbering of the stages suggests, there is a hypothesized pattern to the evolution of concerns profiles when the change process unfolds

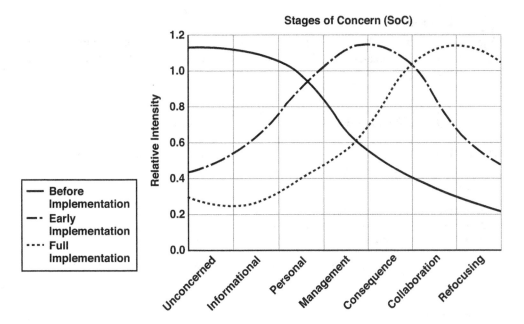

FIGURE 4.1   Ideal "Wave Motion" Development of Stages of Concern

successfully. This progression takes the form of a "wave motion" of intensities that begins with Self-concerns being most intense prior to first use of the innovation. Then, as implementation begins, Task concerns become more intense, and Self-concerns gradually reduce in intensity. With time (3 to 5 years), Impact concerns can increase in intensity as the Self and Task concerns decrease. A graphic representation of this wave motion pattern is presented in Figure 4.1.

However, as we all know, this idealized evolution does not always occur. Attempting to change humans in an organizational context is a very complex, dynamic, and, in many ways, subtle enterprise. Still, by looking for the patterns, being knowledgeable about what has been learned about change, and being grounded in the uniqueness and intricacies of the situation, it is indeed possible to plan and facilitate a change process in ways that result in concerns unfolding in the manner shown in Figure 4.1. But since there is a high likelihood that convoluted turns and unexpected happenings will occur along the way, Change Facilitators must continuously engage in monitoring and adjusting.

 ### Pothole Warning

If the personal side of change is not seen as important or needing to be addressed as a change process unfolds, then the entire effort may be lost.

Pothole Repair

Not only are there likely to be increasing doubts about the change, but there can be more resistance. Attending to Stage 1 Informational concerns early and often is very important.

REFLECTION QUESTIONS

Have you ever been part of a change process where the "wave motion" flow to Stages of Concern took place? What were keys to moving from Self to Task to Impact concerns?

TECHNIQUES FOR ASSESSING STAGES OF CONCERN

The monitoring of the change process should include regular and ongoing assessment of the SoC of all participants, including the Change Facilitators. There are three ways to assess concerns:

1. One-Legged Interview (OLI)
2. Open-Ended Concerns Statement (oeSoC)
3. SoC Questionnaire (SoCQ)

Each of these techniques has its strengths and appropriate uses, as well as its inherent weaknesses.

INDICATORS OF STAGES OF CONCERN

1. Self-concerns around uncertainty about how change will affect "me" and whether or not "I" can do it are part of all change processes. Feelings of uncertainty and potential threat may not be expressed, but most likely are present.
2. Teachers and others with Stage 4 Consequence concerns are thinking about how their use of the innovation is impacting students and what can be done to have even better outcomes. Although these are the types of concerns that we wish educators had all the time, they are unfortunately less frequent than we would like. There are so many demands that there seems to never be enough time to get Task concerns resolved. The Self and Task concern teachers demand attention, while the Impact concern teachers go ahead and do good work. Be sure to take time to visit with and support the Impact concern teachers. They will find your interest supportive and you will feel better by being around some of the success stories.
3. Stage 5 Collaboration concerns, in combination with Stage 4 Consequence concerns, are rare in any organization, including schools. When a number of employees have such concerns, it strongly indicates that the leader has been doing something special. In terms of interventions, do all that you can to nurture and support these Impact concerns. Intense Stage 4 Consequence and Stage 5 Collaboration are very strong indicators that a Professional Learning Community (PLC) (see Chapter 7) type of organizational culture is in place.
4. The SoC can be applied to both individuals and to groups. In fact, this chapter deliberately does not identify which are being discussed. The concepts and thinking are the same for both. However, because group SoC profiles are by definition an average, they can mask individual differences.

The One-Legged Interview (OLI)

Many past CBAM research studies have carefully documented the numerous interventions that school principals, school improvement teams, lead teachers, staff developers, and others have used to facilitate a change process (Entrekin, 1991; Hall, Hord, & Griffin, 1980; Schiller, 1991a, 1991b; Shieh, 1996; Staessens, 1993; Vandenberghe, 1988). One of the major findings has been that schools that are more successful in change have statistically significantly more of the very small, almost unnoticed interventions that we call *Incidents* (see Chapter 2 for more information about interventions). Most of these take the form of a brief conversation between a Change Facilitator and an implementer about use of the innovation, which we call *One-Legged Interviews (OLIs)*.

The busy work of schools leaves little time for extended conversation; everything happens on the run. The clock is ticking, the bells are ringing, and the students are moving. When the adults do meet, the available time is short. Maybe a couple of minutes allow for a quick chat as they pass in the hall, go to the office to pick up their mail, or gather in the lounge during the lunch period.

Because the time available is so brief, you must make it count. CBAM research shows that these brief moments are *critical opportunities* to assess and address SoC. The quantity of innovation-related One-Legged Interviews is a strong indicator of the final degree of implementation success.

One interesting insight into the concept of One-Legged Interviews came when a principal suggested that we should call them "flamingo interviews." This seemed like a good idea until, when telling a Floridian about the suggestion, she pointed out that, yes, a flamingo does stand on one leg, but it also puts it head under its wing! This would not be a very effective way to assess concerns.

The important beginning of a One-Legged Interview is to encourage the client (e.g., a teacher) to describe what he or she is doing and how the client feels about what he or she is doing, or thinking of doing, with the innovation. The facilitator should not assume that he or she understands the situation, but instead should ask and listen.

> *How's it going today with _____?*
> *What do you see as strengths and weaknesses of this approach?*
> *Tell me more.*

The trained facilitator can quickly hear and, if necessary, probe lightly to clarify the concerns. Following this quick diagnosis, the second part of the OLI is for the facilitator to do something to address in some way the indicated concerns. This is an important time to keep the "wave motion" in mind. The focus of the intervention must be on helping to resolve current concerns while anticipating the potential arousal of others.

Using the One-Legged Interview to assess concerns has advantages and disadvantages. Advantages include that it can take place whenever you are in conversation, whether it is face-to-face, by telephone, or through an e-mail exchange. Also, it is unobtrusive, with none of the obvious probing involved in survey methods. Another strength is that the facilitator shows interest in what the teacher is doing, which in and of itself is supportive.

The major disadvantage of OLI is limits to accuracy. Different facilitators can hear the same words and offer very different interpretations. So be very careful about leaping to conclusions based on a diagnosis derived from a single One-Legged Interview. Specifics must be checked out and, as with all concerns-based diagnoses, treated as tentative until more is known.

The Open-Ended Concerns Statement

The first systematic measure of concerns that Frances Fuller used was to ask teacher education students to write a description of their concerns, which was then content analyzed. This open-ended statement has continued to be helpful, and collecting the information is straightforward. Respondents can use a blank piece of paper or be surveyed online. The following request is made:

When you think about [the innovation], what concerns do you have?
Please be frank, and answer in complete sentences.

1.

2.

3.

The responses are then collected and the content is analyzed. The first step is to read the statement all the way through to determine if the *overall theme* reflects Unrelated, Self, Task, or Impact concerns. The statement is then reread and a specific SoC is assigned to each sentence. Most of the time, each sentence will fall inside the overall assessment of Unrelated, Self, Task, or Impact. Note that the individual sentence scores are not totaled and averaged. There is no such thing as a "3.5 concern" or a "5.7 average concern." Instead, the entire statement is judged holistically.

This technique has a number of strengths. An obvious one is that the concerns are in the respondents' own words. Also, this technique can be used at any time. For example, if a staff meeting or workshop is coming up, ask the participants to submit an Open-Ended Concerns Statement in advance. This information can then be used to plan the meeting or workshop so that it responds to the expressed concerns. Participants can thus have input in a nonthreatening way.

As with the One-Legged Interview, the open-ended format has disadvantages. One is that different respondents will provide different amounts of information. One person may write three paragraphs, whereas another may write only one sentence. Some people will only provide a list of topics instead of complete sentences, which means no concerns statement is available to be scored. Some people will turn in a blank page, which is very hard to interpret. The other major problem with Open-Ended Concerns Statements is reliability. Even thoroughly trained judges have difficulty in agreeing on how to rate some statements. But for most staff-development and meeting situations, for which an estimate of concerns is useful, the open-ended statement and One-Legged Interview are excellent tools.

The Stages of Concern Questionnaire (SoCQ)

The most rigorous technique for measuring concerns is the Stages of Concern Questionnaire (SoCQ) (Form 075), which is a 35-item questionnaire that has strong reliability estimates (test/retest reliabilities range from .65 to .86) and internal consistency (alpha-coefficients range from .66 to .83). The SoCQ was constructed to apply to all educational innovations. (We have other forms of the SoCQ for use in other settings, such as business.) The questionnaire items stay the same, with the only change being the insertion of the name of the specific innovation on the cover page. In addition to the paper-pencil form, SEDL has a well-developed online form (www.SEDL.org).

Responses to the SoCQ can be used to construct concerns profiles. The questionnaire has been designed so that a raw score is calculated for each stage; a graphic representation of the data can be made using a percentile table for conversions.

Copies of the SoC Questionnaire and the SoC Quick Scoring Device are included as Appendices 4.B and 4.C in this book. A technical manual, *Measuring Implementation in Schools: The Stages of Concern Questionnaire* (George, Hall, & Stiegelbauer, 2006), includes additional scoring and interpretation information, as well as guidelines for appropriate applications. *An important caution:* No one should consider using the SoCQ without study and direct access to this important reference.

The original SoCQ was developed several decades ago (Hall et al., 1979). It has had extensive use in studies, as a guide for staff development, and for facilitating implementation processes. In 2006 the SoCQ items and statistics were revisited and the new version (Form 075) was established. This form has an even stronger record of effectiveness.

The advantages of the SoCQ for assessing concerns include strong reliability and validity, and the capability to develop concerns profiles. The SoCQ is particularly useful for formal implementation studies. One disadvantage is that respondents do not like too-frequent requests to fill out this, or any other, questionnaire. This most formal way of assessing SoC should be used sparingly. Normally in our school studies, we will use the SoCQ twice a year (e.g., early October and late April). Sometimes we have gone to a third assessment in January. We always include space for an open-ended statement on the last page to give the respondents another opportunity to point out something they may think is being missed.

 REFLECTION QUESTION

When in a change process would you want to use each of the three ways of measuring SoC?

Change Facilitator Stages of Concern Questionnaire

A special form of the concerns questionnaire, *Change Facilitator Stages of Concern Questionnaire* (CFSoCQ), was developed for use with principals, staff developers, and others who have a role in facilitating implementation (Hall, Newlove, George, Rutherford, & Hord, 1991). This questionnaire is not for use with those who are the front-line implementers of the innovation. The CFSoCQ is designed to assess the concerns from the perspective of the leaders and other supporters of the implementers. The CFSoC stages have been defined and these definitions are used to interpret CFSoCQ profiles in the same manner as is done to interpret SoCQ profiles.

Pothole Warning

Any changes to the wording of the 35 items on the SoCQ will endanger reliability and/or validity.

Pothole Repair

Do not change the wording of the 35 items on the SoCQ.

EAST LAKE SCHOOL DISTRICT'S STORY: WHAT ARE THE CONCERNS AT THIS TIME?

Dr. Hanson, assistant superintendent, has been thinking about how best to use the upcoming districtwide staff development day. In the past, for some of these days, the district would bring in a nationally recognized speaker. However, Mike (superintendent) is concerned about paying out "so much money" in travel and consulting fees. "How about letting each school plan their own professional development (PD) day?" Dr. Hanson knows from experience that doing that in some schools would just lead to deterioration in what is accomplished during the day.

In order to get a better reading on where people are, she sent out an online SoCQ survey that asked teachers to indicate what their current concerns were about this year's move to Common Core Standards in mathematics. She reviewed the resultant Stage of Concern profiles and planned what to do from here.

In reviewing the data (See Figure 4.2), Dr. Hanson saw that profiles for elementary, middle, and high school were basically the same. This suggests that, in general, across schools teachers are at about the same point in implementation. When the overall SoC profile is compared with the SoC wave motion (Figure 4.2), the district is at early implementation. Task concerns are the most intense, with Self-concerns (Stage 1 Informational and Stage 2 Personal) somewhat lower. Three other important aspects of the district SoC profile are these:

1. Stage 0 Unconcerned scores are more intense, especially for the high school and middle school teachers. This indicates that they are concerned about things other than standards and math. The Stage 0 score for the elementary school teachers suggests that they are more intensely engaged with implementing the math standards.
2. Impact concerns (Stage 4 Consequence and Stage 5 Collaboration) are low. This should be expected in the first year of implementation.
3. However, there is clear "tailing up" on Stage 6 Refocusing. There are some strong ideas about something that needs to be different.

Dr. Hanson, in consultation with the district's mathematics coordinator and director of staff development, decides on the following:

a. The upcoming PD day should be districtwide.
b. Between now and that day, each of them did a number of One-Legged-Interviews with teachers and principals to find out what is behind the "tailing up" on Stage 6 Refocusing. What was heard, loud and clear, was more general frustration about there being too much to do (High Stage 0 and Stage 3) rather than specific concerns about the math standards effort. "Every year they keep dumping more on us." "We need time to get on top of all this stuff."
c. Based on what was heard, the districtwide PD day agenda included several parts. First to speak was Superintendent Johnson, who expressed understanding about so much going on. "I will do my best to not have more coming down on you over the next year." To address Task concerns,

EAST LAKE SCHOOL DISTRICT'S STORY (CONTINUED)

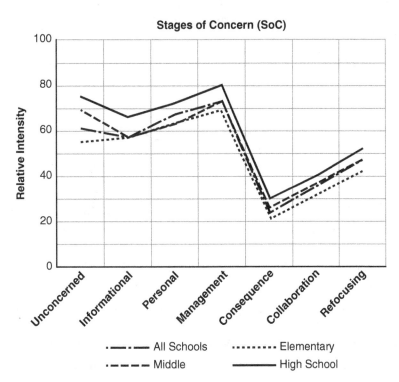

FIGURE 4.2   Districtwide SoC Profiles About Implementing Math Common Core Standards

the rest of the morning included "review" of mathematics content and having several highly respected math teachers share how they organized class periods. For the afternoon, teachers were grouped by level of schooling and grade levels. The topics included unwrapping the specific standards and lessons that would be coming up over the next two months. The other key topic was exploration of the kinds of formative assessments that teachers *and students* could be doing.

SECOND YEAR: SCHOOL-SPECIFIC SoC ABOUT FORMATIVE ASSESSMENT

In January teachers were surveyed about their concerns with regard to implementing formative assessment strategies. This initiative had been launched the year before. Curiously, halfway through the second year of implementation, the SoC profiles about formative assessments were markedly different from school to school (see Figure 4.3). This means that rather than doing the same intervention districtwide, support needs to be customized school by school.

ISLAND PARK ELEMENTARY SCHOOL

The SoC profile for Island Park indicates that teachers already have more intense Stage 4 Consequence concerns, and the Self and Task concerns are down. It is worth noting that Stage 5 Collaboration concerns are second-highest. When the math coordinator shared this SoC profile with Inez Hernandez (principal), she immediately pounced on the Stage 5 Collaboration concerns.

(continued)

EAST LAKE SCHOOL DISTRICT'S STORY (CONTINUED)

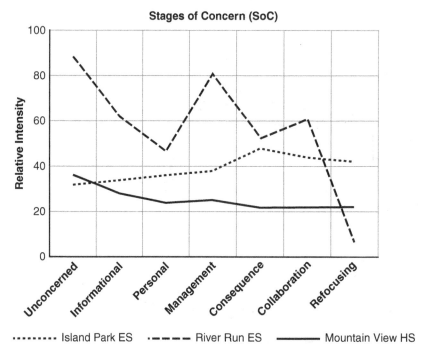

FIGURE 4.3   Teacher Concerns in Different Schools in the Second Year of Implementing Formative Assessments

"We need to do more teaming in this school. For this year I have made the schedule so the special teachers have all the kids for each grade level at the same time. This gives all the teachers at that grade level a common prep period. During that period I have each grade level working on ways to have students do more self-assessing. The kids are beginning to understand how to self-assess their learning, but we need to keep working on it. Even kindergarten kids can do this, if we help them. At our schoolwide staff meetings I want the whole school to share across grade levels about what they are doing to help their kids relate their current understandings to the standards and benchmarks."

RIVER RUN ELEMENTARY SCHOOL

When the SoC profile for River Run was shared with Ray Raulson (principal), his immediate response was "The teachers already have too much to do. Where is the time supposed to come from? Some of the teachers are really complaining about having to take time for the PD day." "By the way, did you go fishing over the three-day weekend?" "No, I . . ." "Well, you should have; I caught three big ones." "Back to the teacher concerns. What do you think we should do from here?" "We have had standards for years. Besides, teachers tell me that elementary school students are too young to do self-assessing." "How about we use the PD day to look at data about student assessment? We can ask each teacher to bring examples of strong and weak student performance on particular math standards. Then we can work on development of some common assessments and explore ways to help students understand where they are. I will bring one or two teachers from other schools (thinking Island Park) who can show what they are doing."

EAST LAKE SCHOOL DISTRICT'S STORY (CONTINUED)

MOUNTAIN VIEW HIGH SCHOOL

Principal Major hastily looked at the SoC profile. "It figures. The teachers have so many other things to do and be concerned about. Class sizes are up and we have had to cut some of the electives. In most departments, the teachers have always been testing students. Between unit tests, term tests, the required homework, and projects, teachers have plenty of information when it comes to assigning grades." The math coordinator asked, "What about the degree to which teachers and students are doing their own formative assessments? For example, do you see most of the teachers making adjustments during instruction?" "Some are, some are not." "Let's have the PD session focus on how to organize assessments so that teachers have less to do and students take more responsibility. I have several good activities and two videos that illustrate students doing self-assessments that are linked to the standards.

"Also, I plan to meet with math department teachers before the PD session. Let's begin the PD session by introducing some assessment techniques that can be used in all subjects. Then we will have the other district curriculum coordinators do discipline-specific breakout sessions." "OK with me, but I already had set the agenda for the meeting. So I will need at least an hour to go over scheduling for next year." Mr. Major then added, "You know, I can see some of the other reasons that the teachers have this concerns profile. For example, the science fair is coming up, the English teachers are working on the yearbook, and we are in basketball finals. We also are finalizing the schedule for next year. As always, in a big high school there is a lot going on."

EAST LAKE CASE CRITIQUE QUESTIONS

1. What characteristics of the interventions to be used in the districtwide PD day made them especially relevant to the identified SoC?
2. What characteristics of the school-specific interventions make them concerns based?
3. What would need to happen in a school like River Run Elementary School to resolve the continuing high Task concerns with "tailing up" on Stage 6 Refocusing?
4. The arousal of Impact concerns is important. What could be done to arouse Stage 4 Consequence concerns in Mountain View High School? What else could be done to support the sustaining of Impact concerns in Island Park Elementary School?

Characteristic Stages of Concern Profiles

Many of the commonly observed SoC profiles are easy to interpret by studying the technical manuals and developing an understanding of concerns theory. Some profiles are in fact "classic"; we have seen them many times, and their meaning is well understood. A couple of these are presented here to illustrate our thinking about diagnosis and implications for concerns-based intervening.

SoC "Wave Motion"

The first step in interpreting any SoC profile is to compare the overall shape to those in Figure 4.1, the SoC wave motion. Does the profile more closely represent the Self, Task, or Impact profile? Or is it more of a combination?

Following examination of the overall profile shape, it is important to look for the peaks and valleys. It does not matter if the overall profile is at the 80th percentile or the 20th; it is the overall shape that must be considered first. It is the high and low points on that profile that are the key points of reference. This is when the full SoC definitions (Table 4.2) become important.

A peak on a profile indicates that the type of concerns that are described for that stage are intense, whereas a valley shows that there is little or no concern for that stage. When there is a peak at more than one stage, the profile must be interpreted by combining the definitions for those stages.

Most SoC profile analyses can stop here. However, to illustrate that there is always more to be learned about concerns theory and assessment, a couple of the more interesting variations in concerns profiles are described next. For each profile we offer a brief interpretation and ideas about the types of interventions that would make sense.

Impact Concerns Profile

High Stage 4 Consequence and Stage 5 Collaboration in a concerns profile (see Figure 4.4) represent the ideal goal of a concerns-based implementation effort. After all, the essence of good schooling is teachers with high Impact concerns about the effects on students of their use of the innovation (Stage 4 Consequence) and about linking with other teachers in using the innovation (Stage 5 Collaboration). These are characteristics of a Professional Learning Community (PLC) (see Chapter 7) at its best. The early research of Judith Warren Little, as

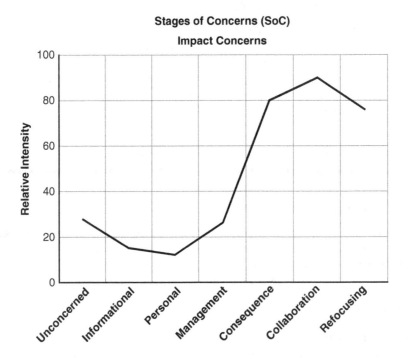

FIGURE 4.4   The Ultimate Goal of Concerns-Based Implementation Is Development of Impact Concerns.

well as the more recent studies, confirms the importance of collegiality for teachers and their students (Little & McLaughlin, 1993; Thessin & Starr, 2011). Unfortunately, finding individual teachers and school staffs that reflect this concerns profile is rare. To develop to this point means that change truly has been treated as a process, that the innovation has been given sufficient time to be implemented, that there has been a principal with an Initiator Change Facilitator Style (see Chapter 6), and that the innovation, or more likely an innovation bundle, was significant and matched the school's vision well.

Intervening to address Impact concerns should include a celebration. Clearly the teachers and the principal have been hard at work and doing some special things. They should be congratulated, supported, and cherished. Also, this is a fragile system state. A change in a key player (e.g., the superintendent or the principal) or the arrival of some new mandate from the school board, state, or federal government can sidetrack and undercut the synergy and momentum that have been built. Therefore, a second set of interventions should be designed to protect and encourage the continuation of the Impact concerns, with a special emphasis on facilitating the sustaining of Collaboration concerns.

The "Big W" Concerns Profile

By way of contrast, there are other SoC profiles that indicate challenges with achieving implementation success. For example, the "Big W" concerns profile (so named for its configuration of peaks and valleys) has been observed all too frequently (see Figure 4.5). In this profile,

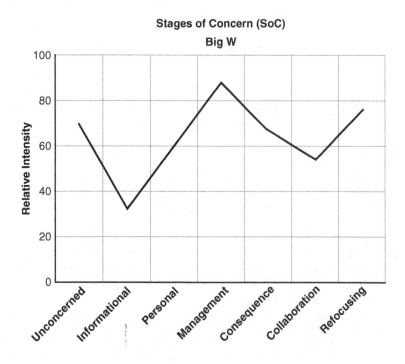

FIGURE 4.5   The "Big W" Concerns Profile

Stage 3 Management concerns are very intense, whereas Stages 1 Informational, 2 Personal, 4 Consequence, and 5 Collaboration are of much lower intensity. This profile would not be so significant if it were not for the "tailing up" on Stage 6 Refocusing. This combination of peaks and valleys indicates that some ideas are strongly held about what ought to be done *differently* with this innovation and/or the change process (Stage 6 Refocusing). These views are related to the very high (and unresolved) Stage 3 Management concerns. Teachers with this profile can be quite adamant about their situation and how things should be changed.

More than a One-Legged Interview will be needed to address the underlying cause of the Big W concerns profile. We know from a number of studies that this concerns profile is frequently found in schools where the principal has displayed the Responder Change Facilitator Style (see Chapter 6). When this is the case, part of the intervention plan may need to be strengthening the principal's support related to use of the innovation.

INTERPRETING GROUP SoC PROFILES

Individual SoC profiles can be combined to see the overall concerns of a team, whole school, or district. Interpretation of a group SoC profile is done in the same way as with individuals. However, it is important to keep in mind that a group profile will be the average of individuals and any subgroups. For example, if one person is very high on Stage 1 Informational concerns and others are low, then the group score will be in the middle. In this type of finding, the interpretation of the group profile would not be representative of the concerns of either subgroup.

> **IMPLICATIONS OF STAGES OF CONCERN FOR CHANGE LEADERS AND FACILITATORS**
>
> 1. Assume that all change processes will begin with most everyone having more intense Self (Stage 1 Informational and Stage 2 Personal) concerns. From the very beginning, before implementation, purposeful interventions should be done to address these concerns.
> 2. Personal concerns (Stage 2) are a very natural reaction when we are first confronted with change. Ignoring or condemning people who have high levels of Personal concerns will not make the concerns go away. Anticipating the potential arousal of Personal concerns is the important prior step.
> 3. The first time an innovation is used is when Task (Stage 3 Management) concerns will become most intense. Providing an on-site implementation coach, a how-to-do-it Web site, and a where-to-ask questions source should be planned for and kept in place throughout at least the first year.
> 4. An important condition for the arousal of Impact concerns (Stage 4 Consequence, Stage 5 Collaboration) is first facilitating the resolution of Self and Task concerns.
> 5. Concerns-based interventions can be targeted toward all implementers, especially during the early phases of the change process. As implementation progresses, key organization units (such as individual schools and departments) will be progressing at their own pace. This becomes the time when more interventions will need to be customized for each implementing unit, for example, individual schools.

When a large number of SoC profiles are available, they can be sorted into subgroups according to common characteristics. For example, Matthews, Marshall, and Milne (2000) had in excess of 700 SoC profiles from teachers engaged in their first year of use of laptop computers. One of us examined each SoC profile and was able to place them in one of six subgroupings. The resultant report addressed the whole group and characteristic concerns of each subgroup.

INDICATIONS OF RESISTANCE IN SoC PROFILES

We haven't yet talked about resistance, which is a natural part of change. In the CBAM work, most of what is called *resistance* will show up in the SoC diagnostic dimension, especially Self-concerns. Here again, we advocate listening before intervening. Often, what Change Facilitators see as resistance are aspects of Stage 2 Personal concerns (see Figure 4.6). There is an uncertainty about what will be expected and self-doubts about one's ability to succeed with the new way. There may also be some grieving over the loss of things that were currently being done successfully. Another aspect of this, which is all too frequently overlooked, is the failure to have addressed, early on, Stage 1 Informational concerns. When people don't know what is happening, it is perfectly normal for Stage 2 Personal concerns to become more intense. The less information provided, the higher the Stage 2 Personal concerns will be.

At the beginning of a change process, when Self-concerns are more intense, be sure to use many channels to communicate what is coming. Communication must start during the spring, before implementation is to begin. Also, don't simply make a one-time announcement

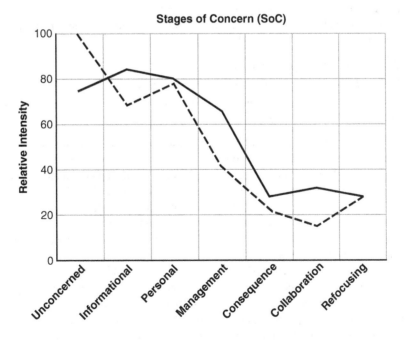

FIGURE 4.6   Comparison of Positive and Distrustful Self-Concern SoC Profiles

and expect everyone to get the message. People with Stage 1 Informational concerns need to receive small bits of information, repeated across time. They do not want all of the details at once. And don't forget their Stage 2 Personal concerns; they want to hear enthusiasm and promises of continuing commitment to and support for the change.

Understanding Resistance in Terms of SoC

Of course, there can be real resisters. The reasons for their position are varied. Some may simply not understand the proposed innovation. Others may have a different agenda or a real philosophical disagreement with the innovation. Sadly, there may be one or two who have serious problems elsewhere in their lives, which none of us are equipped to handle. Figure 4.6 shows the characteristics of these concerns. This SoC profile has the general overall shape of Self-concerns (remember Figure 4.1), but Stage 2 Personal concerns are especially intense, and there is a slight "tailing up" of Stage 6 Refocusing. This profile suggests lack of understanding of, and possibly hostility to, the change.

Pothole Warning

Mandates automatically lead to significantly higher Stage 2 Personal concerns. Failure to anticipate this condition can be fatal to change initiatives.

Pothole Repair

As was pointed out in Chapter 1, mandates can work but only when greater attention is given to addressing Self (Stage 1 Informational and Stage 2 Personal) concerns. More effort must be given to providing information that is clear and consistent.

Let's look more closely at some of the dynamics of resistance. Figure 4.6 presents both the typical positive Self-concerns profile and a characteristic hostile nonuser profile. Consider some of the standard comments of the hostile nonuser:

"Where is the research to show that this is better?"

"We've always done it this way. All you have done is put a new name on it."

"Ah. This is just old wine in new bottles. You know how education is. It's just a pendulum swinging back and forth from fad to fad."

The tendency of Change Facilitators is to react to such attitudes by saying something like "Oh, no. This really *is* different." However, from a concerns profile perspective, this is the wrong intervention. What the facilitator is hearing is the "tailing up" on Stage 6 Refocusing—that is, strongly held ideas about how things ought to be different. But which SoC is the highest? Stage 2 Personal is highest, and right behind this is Stage 1 Informational. The indication is that the so-called resister actually does not have enough information about the innovation and thus is personally uncomfortable about it. So telling this person that this innovation really is different is *interpreted* (see Chapter 8) as follows: "You are telling me that I don't know what I am talking about and that further threatens me." The result is less ability to listen, still higher Stage 2 Personal concerns, and probably stronger "tailing up" on Stage 6 Refocusing.

A better intervention approach (although there is no quick cure once this profile is established) would be to express empathy and understanding for the person's concerns. Don't attempt to explain a lot in the first contact. Try to have a series of One-Legged Interviews to get a sense of what is producing this concerns profile, and then gradually provide pieces of information about the change, the change process, and how they will be supported. There is no simple remedy for this, or for many other concerns profiles. However, what needs to be done to facilitate change in most cases is relatively straightforward: provide information, resources, and support that are aligned with the person's concerns.

More About Concerns-Based Interventions

Although much of the discussion of SoC to this point has focused on individuals, keep in mind that SoC also is regularly applied to groups, a whole school staff, or a larger system. As one example, read this chapter's East Lake School District story to get an idea of how SoC can be applied across a school and a districtwide change process. In this story example, interventions that would be appropriate for addressing each SoC are described. Keep in mind, however, that some interventions will not be appropriate. Examples of appropriate and inappropriate interventions are presented in Appendix 4.A.

Stages of Concern also can be useful in developing school/district improvement plans and in strategic planning. When initial planning is being done, action steps and the time line can be based on the SoC wave motion. As change processes unfold, data about SoC can be used in planning future implementation support steps. The same SoC information can be used by program evaluators to measure progress across the Implementation Bridge.

Also, we know that SoC is a cross-cultural phenomenon. For example, Shieh (1996) was the first to systematically identify the same categories of concerns in teachers in Taiwan. Earlier, Van den Berg and Vandenberghe (1981) developed Dutch language measures and documented SoC in Belgium and the Netherlands. Hargreaves, Moyles, Merry, Paterson, Pell, and Esarte-Sarries (2003) studied teacher concerns in the United Kingdom. In a large study in Cyprus, Christou, Eliophotou-Menon, and Philippou (2004) documented relationships between teacher SoC and implementation of a mathematics curriculum. Cheung, Hattie, and Ng (2001) and Cheung and Yip (2004) have examined SoC in Hong Kong. Also, SoC has been studied extensively in regard to the implementation of technology (see, for example, Yuliang & Huang, 2005).

 REFLECTION QUESTION

For most innovations, such as new curriculum approaches and new technology, it typically takes 3 to 5 years for the SoC wave motion to unfold for a whole school/district staff. What length of time would you expect with a transformational innovation such as changing from teaching-centered to student-learning-centered instruction?

SUMMARY

In this chapter we have introduced the Stages of Concern construct to examine the personal side of change. Important talking points include:

1. Feelings, emotions, worries, moments of joy, and varying perceptions are important elements of all change processes.

2. Stages of Concern (SoC) provide a research-verified construct for identifying and describing the different feelings and perceptions people can experience when implementing change.

3. There are three ways to assess Stages of Concern: One-Legged Interviewing, Open-Ended Concerns Statements, and the Stages of Concern Questionnaire.

4. The SoC wave motion represents the ideal pattern for the arousal and resolution of Stages of Concern as a successful change process unfolds.

5. There will be greater success when the change-facilitating interventions are aligned with Stages of Concern.

6. In a concerns-based world, the arousal and sustaining of Impact concerns, especially at Stage 4 Consequence and Stage 5 Collaboration, is the goal.

7. Stages of Concern can be applied to individuals, groups, whole organizations, and large social systems.

8. As a last reminder, be sure to obtain the SoCQ technical manual (George et al., 2006) and, if possible, participate in a training session before initiating a major effort using SoC.

DISCUSSION QUESTIONS

1. In your experiences with implementing change, which Stage of Concern have you found to be the most frequent?

2. If the ideal is having teachers with Impact concerns, what can be done to support the arousal and sustaining of Stage 4 Consequence concerns? What would need to be added to address Stage 5 Collaboration?

3. What happens to people's concerns when the leader has intense Stage 2 Personal concerns? How do interactions change?

4. Think about one of the great teachers you have had. In general, what were his or her most intense SoC?

5. In your experience, which professional development sessions and workshops did you consider to be the best and the worst? In looking back, how well did each match with your concerns at the time?

APPLYING STAGES OF CONCERN IN FACILITATING IMPLEMENTATION

1. Attend a workshop and observe the concerns of the participants. How well did the content and process of the workshop match their concerns?

2. Collect and analyze Open-Ended Concerns Statements from people who will be attending a staff meeting or workshop. Analyze the statements. (If possible, obtain a copy of Newlove and Hall's [1976] manual to help with this.) Develop a recommendation about what should be done and how best to address the participants' concerns.

3. Conduct a One-Legged Interview with a person, and then ask someone else who understands SoC to do the same, with the same individual. See how well your assessments of the person's concerns match. What would be your recommendation about what to do to address that person's current SoC?

APPLYING STAGES OF CONCERN IN RESEARCH AND PROGRAM EVALUATION

Note: Before conducting any study, be sure to obtain a copy of the appropriate technical manual and study it closely. Also, contact one of the authors of this text when you have questions.

1. *Evaluating a Professional Development Session:* Measure the SoC before and after a PD session. How well did the session address the participants' concerns?

2. *Monitoring Implementation Progress:* At a key time, such as halfway through the first year of implementation, assess SoC using the SoCQ and an Open-Ended Concerns Statement. Use these data to plan the next steps of implementation support.

3. *Longitudinal Study of a Major Change Effort:* Plan for and collect SoC data once or twice a year for several years. Use the findings to plan next steps and to review how far across the Implementation Bridge each individual department and whole school has progressed.

4. *Summative Evaluations:* A key issue that must be addressed in most evaluation studies has to do with determining the outcomes of the change. Before judgments can be made about the value of an innovation in terms of outcomes such as student learning, an assessment should be made of how far along implementation has progressed. SoC is one important indicator. In theory, outcomes should be higher as each implementer moves from Unconcerned to Self, to Task, and ultimately to Impact concerns.

5. *Basic Research Question:* A basic area for research would be to learn more about what is entailed in arousal and resolution of concerns. Frances Fuller (1969, 1970) hypothesized that arousal of a concern was more of an affective experience and resolution came about through cognitive experiences. We need to know a lot more about this topic.

LEARNING MORE ABOUT STAGES OF CONCERN

SEDL in Austin, TX, is a repository for basic documents related to the Concerns-Based Adoption Model and SoC. SEDL also has an online form of the SoCQ and related scoring services.

For measuring teacher SoC, use the Stages of Concern Questionnaire (Form 075). George, A. A., Hall, G. E., & Stiegelbauer, S. M. (2006). *Measuring implementation in schools: The Stages of Concern Questionnaire.* Austin, TX: Southwest Educational Development Laboratory.

For measuring change leaders concerns, use the Change Facilitator Stages of Concern Questionnaire (CFSoCQ). Hall, G. E., Newlove, B. W., George, A. A., Rutherford, W. L., & Hord, S. M. (1991). *Measuring change facilitator Stages of Concern: A manual for use of the CFSoC Questionnaire.* Austin, TX: Southwest Educational Development Laboratory.

For interpreting written descriptions of concerns, refer to Newlove, B. W., & Hall, G. E. (1976). *A manual for assessing open-ended statements of concern about the innovation* (Report No. 3029). Austin: The University of Texas, Research and Development Center for Teacher Education. (ERIC Document Reproduction Service No. ED 144) Also available from the Southwest Educational Development Laboratory, Austin, TX. 207.

CHAPTER 5

WHAT ARE CHARACTERISTIC BEHAVIORAL PROFILES OF IMPLEMENTERS?

Levels of Use

Mercy! Is this new software product as good as they are saying? They are always bringing new tools, but this one sounds good, and I am going online to see if I can learn more about it, and if it will do anything for our department.

—Harriet Jones, East Lake central office, Social Studies Coordinator

I am happy to report that I have worked the bugs out of how to use math manipulatives with third graders, and I have a system that works!

—Betty Hollister, third-grade teacher, Island Park Elementary School

Can you help me order the equipment for the sophomore earth science units? I'm getting things ready to start in September.

— Paul Borchardt, high school science teacher, Mountain View High School

I telephoned a colleague at another school to inquire about the problem-based mathematics program his school is using and whether it stimulates the kids in critical thinking.

—Middle School Math Department Chair, East Lake District

Another teacher and I have worked together with this approach. The changes that we have made this year are really helping students to succeed.

—Malcolm Sanchez, fifth-grade teacher, Island Park Elementary School

Many assume that if individuals have a new program, process, or product in their possession, they will be using it. Through our research studies we have learned that use of a new program is not automatic, nor is it a matter of some persons using it and others not. Use of new programs or processes is not a simple case of "Yes, he's using it" or "No, she is not." Instead of simply looking for use/nonuse, the real question is *"How* is she or he using it?"

There are a number of different approaches to *using* an innovation. Each approach represents a unique behavioral profile of how nonusers and users can be engaging with the innovation.

In the past, the typical view about use of new programs, instructional methods, organizational structures, or other innovations was to base measurement on whether the materials and/or equipment required were present. Little attention was given to whether the materials ever left the storage closet or, instead, held up a flowerpot.

The implicit assumption was that initial professional development plus materials equaled use. Our observations and studies have documented a number of different behavioral patterns for nonusers and users. To understand this phenomenon of the change process, the **Levels of Use** was born.

Stages of Concern. Levels of Use. The terms have a deceptively similar ring. However, we are about to make a significant conceptual switch, for whereas Stages of Concern (SoC) addresses the *affective* side of change—people's reactions, feelings, perceptions, and attitudes— Levels of Use (LoU) has to do with *behaviors* and portrays *how* people are acting with respect to a specified change.

This chapter will explore the behaviors of people as they seek to learn about new practices and other changes or, perhaps, ignore such matters entirely. This construct addresses behavior as individuals adopt and implement new ideas and innovations. Eight Levels of Use (LoU) will be defined and explained, and examples will be used to illustrate each of the eight. LoU is a third Diagnostic Dimension of the Concerns Based Adoption Model (CBAM). The behaviors of so-called users and nonusers is another frame for assessing where people are along the Implementation Bridge.

The LoU framework makes it possible to understand and predict what is likely to occur as a change initiative unfolds. Facilitators who understand and apply the LoU construct and its measures are able to provide appropriate interventions that will be relevant and helpful to those involved, or expected to be involved, in change. In addition, LoU is a very important framework for evaluators and researchers. A critical step in determining whether a new approach is making a difference is to determine first if, and how, the innovation is being used. Otherwise, as Charters and Jones (1973) observed, there is a risk of evaluating "nonevents."

LEARNING OUTCOMES

After reading this chapter, the learner should be able to:

1. Explain the construct of Levels of Use (LoU).
2. Identify the benefits that LoU can provide in evaluation of change efforts.
3. Describe how an individual's LoU can be assessed.
4. Illustrate what a person looks like at each of the LoU.
5. Demonstrate how LoU can be applied to facilitating change initiatives.
6. Describe implications of LoU for research and evaluation studies.

THE LEVELS OF USE CONSTRUCT

Eight classifications, or behavioral profiles, of how people act or behave in relation to an innovation have been identified and verified through research. Since LoU deals with behaviors, it was possible to develop operational definitions for each level (see Table 5.1) (Hall, Loucks, Rutherford, & Newlove, 1975). These definitions enable a change facilitator or evaluator to make clearer distinctions within the traditional dichotomy of use/nonuse. The construct can be applied to individuals, aggregation of individuals, whole organizations such as schools, and large systems.

The first distinction to be made is whether the individual is a user or a nonuser. Three nonuse and five use behavioral profiles have been identified. Each is described briefly in the following subsections, along with suggestions about appropriate interventions.

Nonusers

Three very different types of nonusers have been identified, in terms of their actions with a change. It is important to understand the behavioral distinctions among them, since the support and assistance that are appropriate for each will vary accordingly. In addition, although the behaviors of each are quite different, all three describe nonusers of the change.

Level of Use 0 Nonuse.   When a person knows very little or nothing at all about an innovation or change, and exhibits no behavior related to it, that person is said to be at LoU 0 Nonuse.

TABLE 5.1   Levels of Use of the Innovation

	VI	**Renewal:** State in which the user re-evaluates the quality of use of the innovation, seeks major modifications of or alternatives to present innovation to achieve increased impact on clients, examines new developments in the field, and explores new goals for self and the system.
	V	**Integration:** State in which the user is combining his or her own efforts to use the innovation with related activities of colleagues to achieve a collective impact on clients within their common sphere of influence.
Users	**IVB**	**Refinement:** State in which the user varies the use of the innovation to increase impact on clients within immediate sphere of influence. Variations are based on knowledge of both short- and long-term consequences for clients.
	IVA	**Routine:** Use of the innovation is stabilized. Few if any changes are being made in ongoing use. Little preparation or thought is being given to improving innovation use or its consequences.
	III	**Mechanical Use:** State in which the user focuses most effort on the short-term, day-to-day use of the innovation, with little time for reflection. Changes in use are made more to meet user needs than client needs. The user is primarily engaged in a stepwise attempt to master the tasks required for the innovation, often resulting in disjointed and superficial use.
	II	**Preparation:** State in which the user is preparing for first use of the innovation.
Nonusers	**I**	**Orientation:** State in which the user has recently acquired or is acquiring information about the innovation and/or has recently explored or is exploring its value orientation and its demands upon user and user system.
	0	**Nonuse:** State in which the user has little or no knowledge of the innovation, has no involvement with the innovation, and is doing nothing toward becoming involved.

Source: LoU has been described and presented in many publications. An important resource for obtaining more detailed information about LoU is Hall, Dirksen, and George (2006).

Further, if the LoU 0 person has any knowledge of the innovation, it may be inaccurate. They take no action in regard to the innovation. For example, if they receive a brochure in the mail, they don't read it. If there is an orientation presentation about the innovation, he or she does not attend, or (if required to attend) spends the time texting or engages in some other form of off-task activity. Again, no action is taken related to the change.

If it is not important for such an individual to participate with the particular change, a facilitator may ignore this person. However, if the person is expected to be involved, the facilitator's challenge is to design and deliver interventions that stimulate interest and support movement to learn about the change. LoU 0 Nonuse people are potentially an excellent source of data for the evaluator who is looking for a comparison or control group. However, unbeknown to many change facilitators and evaluators, significant proportions of LoU 0 people are regularly found in *treatment* groups.

Level of Use I Orientation.   When a person takes action to learn about an innovation, or exhibits interest in knowing more about it, he or she is characterized as being at LoU I Orientation. Typical LoU I behaviors include attending an overview session about the innovation, examining a Web site or materials displayed by a vendor, asking questions of colleagues, or e-mailing a vendor to obtain descriptive materials about various approaches that might work. The behaviors are related to learning more about the innovation, but no decision has been made to use it.

The facilitator will find it easy to respond to such a person, since he or she is actively looking for information. Thus, relevant interventions include providing information in the most provocative and interesting manner possible so that adoption and use will be encouraged.

Level of Use II Preparation.   An individual who has decided to use the new program or process and names a time to begin is at LoU II Preparation. At this level, use has not started, but the intention and a specific start-up time have been indicated. The person typically is studying, attending introductory workshops, and preparing materials for initial use.

It could be that the decision to begin use has been made for the individual—for instance, by a state or district policy that mandates action or by the principal in concert with faculty peers who are pressing for use. In any case, although how the decision is made is of interest, it does not figure into LoU, which focuses on behaviors. Obviously, the facilitator's role is to be as supportive as possible, providing assistance so that when use does begin, it can proceed as efficiently and smoothly as possible.

These three classifications of nonusers have been verified through studies of change efforts in K–12 schools, universities, medical schools, and business settings. Because the three levels represent three different behavioral profiles, they provide understanding and guidance to change facilitators in supporting each individual in his or her actions to learn about, consider, and prepare for first use of an innovation. Strategic planners should keep in mind that in order for an entire organization or macrosystem to change, the individual members will need time and appropriate interventions to move beyond these nonuse levels.

In research and evaluation studies, all three of these LoU will be classified as nonusers. As was noted above, all too frequently we find a noticeable number of these individuals in the group that is assumed to be using the innovation.

Users

Implementation may be said to start in earnest when users and their clients (i.e., company staff, teachers, and students) begin use of the innovation. Five LoU of users have been identified and described. A key in making these distinctions is the type of adaptations that are being made by the user in relation to his or her use of the innovation, or in the innovation itself. How this plays out will be discernible as each of the five levels is described in the following subsections. Keep in mind that although these descriptions are presented in a sequence that is logical, each person will not necessarily follow the sequence. Each LoU is independent of the other; LoU is not a straight-line hierarchy.

Level of Use III Mechanical Use.   At this level, use of the innovation is disjointed and inefficient. This LoU is characterized by experimentation in schedules and organization in order to make the innovation work more easily for him or her. There is continual referral to the users' manual, and planning is day-to-day and minute-to-minute. Adaptations are made in managing time, materials, and other logistics. There is a short-term, day-to-day focus on planning and a general inefficiency in how the innovation is used. This user is making adaptations in his or her use (or in the innovation itself) in order to master his or her use of the new practice.

The facilitator's task is to help LoU III Mechanical Use implementers with the frequently harrowing experiences of finding and organizing materials, and having time to plan for use while managing classrooms and students. The lack of knowledge about what will happen next affects such users' efforts to make innovation use more efficient for them.

Successful facilitators of LoU III Mechanical Use are those who are willing to do all sorts of seemingly low-level, nitty-gritty tasks to help the implementer achieve short-term success in use. They offer many how-to tips. They send out e-mails with organization suggestions. They may publish a Web site or set up a telephone hotline to answer mechanical-use questions as they arise.

Successful facilitators have been known to organize materials in the closet, co-plan with the teacher, run and fetch what is needed, bring in substitute materials when glitches occur, and co-teach or demonstrate teaching in the LoU III teacher's classroom. As noted in the discussion of adaptations, LoU III implementers are making changes in their use of the innovation in order to find a system that works for them. A knowledgeable and experienced facilitator can be a highly significant source of help.

Level of Use IVA Routine.   At this level, the implementer has mastered the innovation and its use and has established a regular way of working with it. LoU IVA users do not plan to make any adaptations or changes; instead, use is stabilized. These users may be heard to comment, "Why should I change? My way is working fine." Thus, the LoU IVA person is making no adaptations. Note that this does not mean that the Configuration (see Chapter 3) they are using is of high fidelity. LoU IVA users have routines in place and are not making any changes at this time in their use of the innovation.

The facilitator may conclude that this user needs no help, since use is established. In this case, congratulations and some celebratory symbol from the facilitator could be a wise response. On the other hand, a discussion with the user, or an observation to determine how this person's use aligns with the ideal variation on an IC Map (see Chapter 3), could be very informative and ultimately lead to a new set of actions—perhaps a move toward LoU IVB.

Level of Use IVB Refinement.   Some users begin to observe and wonder about how well their use of the innovation is working for the benefit of their clients (in the case of classrooms, this would be students). Based on their reflection and assessment, they make adaptations in the innovation or in their use of it with the intention of increasing client benefits. These actions signify LoU IVB Refinement. The key here is making adaptations for the client's benefit (not for the benefit of the user, as in LoU III). Note again how the types of adaptations help in understanding and distinguishing each LoU.

The facilitator is typically welcomed warmly by the LoU IVB person, who is looking for new ways to make the program as successful as possible for students. Since the LoU IVB user is wondering how well the program is working, a key action of the facilitator could be to suggest or to help the teacher find assessment or evaluation tools or rubrics to use in checking student work. Conversation about the adaptations or adjustments that are under consideration also would be helpful to the LoU IVB user. Providing journal articles and examples of what other users have done will be useful too.

Level of Use V Integration.   The LoU V Integration person, like the LoU IVB individual, is making adaptations for the purpose of increasing the benefit for clients, but the LoU V action is done in concert with one or more users. The collaboration is between users, not between a user and a resource person such as a counselor, librarian, or principal. The two or more users collegially plan and carry out adaptations in their use of the innovation that will benefit their students.

LoU V is a significant phase for the evolution of a change process and for the professional culture of the school. Change facilitators should do all that they can to nurture and facilitate its development and continuation. The facilitator's task is to make it possible for people who wish to work together to do so. Thus, making accommodations in the schedule so that the LoU V users can have concurrent planning periods, changing office or classroom assignments, and other logistical arrangements should be done in order to support two or more users working together.

It should be noted that some users wish to work together to better manage the new program and its demands and to increase the users' efficiency and decrease the workloads that new programs frequently demand. This can be a wise means of providing additional help and support to peers. However, this reason for working together is part of LoU III Mechanical Use, not LoU V, which entails collaborating to make adaptations in use for *client* benefits, not *user* benefits.

Level of Use VI Renewal.   At LoU VI Renewal, the user is exploring or implementing some means to modify the innovation in major ways or to replace it altogether. The modification may constitute one very significant addition or adjustment, or it may comprise multiple small adaptations that add up to significant change. In either case, the adaptation is intended to benefit clients. Again, making the adjustments is central, and it is the size or number of adaptations that places a person at this level. Curiously, persons at LoU VI make up a small part (2.5%) of the CBAM database.

Facilitators for persons at this level may applaud them and stay out of their way. These users may want access to additional materials or resources that will translate their adaptations into reality. For example, the LoU VI individual might be invited to provide professional development activities for and with others to share a possible new direction. Or the user may be asked to join a design team that is planning an entirely new replacement program or a revision of the current program. On the other hand, if the program is meant (through the decision of someone in authority) to be used without changes in its design, the facilitator may find himself or herself in the position of having to tactfully explain that the proposed LoU VI adaptations are not in line with the expectations of the school, district, or state.

In summary, the operational definitions for each LoU are behavior based and action oriented. LoU does not focus on attitudes or feelings; SoC does that. Because these actions can be observed, facilitators find the LoU construct and definitions useful for observing and analyzing what users are doing, for better understanding their needs, and for further facilitating implementation.

Assessing LoU is critical in evaluation and research studies. Otherwise, there is no certainty that the so-called treatment group only contains users and that there really are no users in the control group. Also, in longitudinal studies we regularly find that the majority of first-time implementers will be at LoU III Mechanical Use. As we will examine in depth in Chapter 12, these "users" are not likely the best subjects to have in summative evaluations. By definition, their use is inefficient and not output oriented.

REFLECTION QUESTIONS

Consider the eight LoU. At which levels do you think a facilitator's support would be most critical? Why would that be the case?

ASSESSING LEVEL OF USE

Whereas information about a person's SoC may be obtained in several ways (see Chapter 4), LoU may be assessed only through long-term observation or use of a specially designed Focused Interview Protocol. Various researchers and others have attempted to develop a paper-and-pencil measure to determine LoU, although we have consistently stated that it will not work. Measuring behaviors through self-report (as is done in assessing feelings through the SoC Questionnaire) is like trying to decipher semaphore signals by listening to a radio. In summary, using a questionnaire to rate behaviors, and to make the distinctions across the levels, is not possible.

Using Decision Points to Distinguish Each LoU

In the above introduction of LoU, the factor of adaptations was used as an abbreviated way to describe each LoU. In fact, we were using a set of Decision Points (see Table 5.2) that provide a key basis for determining LoU. Each Decision Point describes critical behaviors that are associated with a particular LoU.

TABLE 5.2   **Levels of Use of the Innovation with Decision Points**

Level VI, Renewal: State in which the user re-evaluates the quality of use of the innovation, seeks major modifications of or alternatives to present innovation to achieve increased impact on clients, examines new developments in the field, and explores new goals for self and the organization.

Decision Point F: Begins exploring alternatives to or major modifications of the innovation presently in use.

Level V, Integration: State in which the user is combining his or her own efforts to use the innovation with related activities of colleagues to achieve a collective impact on clients within their common sphere of influence.

Decision Point E: Initiates changes in use of the innovation for benefit of clients based on input from and in coordination with colleagues.

Level IVB, Refinement: State in which the user varies use of the innovation to increase the impact on clients within his or her immediate sphere of influence. Variations in use are based on knowledge of both short- and long-term consequences for clients.

Decision Point D-2: Changes use of the innovation to increase client outcomes based on formal or informal evaluation.

Level IVA, Routine: Use of the innovation is stabilized. Few if any changes in use are made. Little preparation or thought is given to improving innovation use or its consequences.

Decision Point D-1: Establishes a routine pattern of use.

Level III, Mechanical Use: State in which the user focuses most efforts on the short-term, day-to-day use of the innovation, with little time for reflection. Changes in use are made more to meet user needs than the needs of clients. The user is primarily engaged in an attempt to master tasks required to use the innovation. These attempts often result in disjointed and superficial use.

Decision Point C: Makes user-oriented changes.

Level II, Preparation: State in which the user is preparing for first use of the innovation.

Decision Point B: Makes a decision to use the innovation by establishing a time to begin.

Level I, Orientation: State in which the individual has acquired or is acquiring information about the innovation and/or has explored its value orientation and what it will require.

Decision Point A: Takes action to learn more detailed information about the innovation.

Level 0, Nonuse: State in which the individual has little or no knowledge of the innovation and no involvement with it, and is doing nothing to become involved.

Source: LoU has been described and presented in many publications. An important resource for obtaining more detailed information about LoU is Hall, Dirksen, and George (2006).

Measuring Levels of Use

The two Configurations of LoU Interviews are (a) the LoU One-Legged Interview for facilitators and (b) the LoU Focused Interview (Hall, Dirksen, & George, 2006; Loucks, Newlove, & Hall, 1975) for research and evaluation. The underlying structure for both LoU interview procedures is based in the Decision Points. The interviewer asks a series of questions in order to gain examples of the interviewee's innovation-related behaviors. The reported behaviors are checked against the Decision Points. For example, a teacher who is looking for an innovation-related resource that would help certain struggling students is indicative of Decision Point D-2, "Making changes to increase client outcomes." The interviewee who is using the innovation, but not looking for anything related to it, would be an indication of Decision Point D-1.

The difference in the two interviews is the breadth and depth of seeking behavioral indicators. In the One-Legged Interview, if the interviewee reports behaviors that are clearly indicative of one of the Decision Points, the facilitator can move on to intervening in some way. However, in the full LoU Focused Interview, there will be further intensive searching for additional behavior examples.

Branching Design of the LoU Interview

The overall design of the LoU interview is a branching format (see Figure 5.1). The Decision Points provide the keys to determining which questions to ask and where to move the interview next. The initial question in both LoU interviews is "Are you using the innovation?" The answer separates nonusers from users, and depending on the response, the "no" or "yes" branch is followed. This is the design of a "focused" interview. All branches, that is, levels, do not have to be asked about, just the branch that follows up from answers to the previous questions.

Using the branch design as the guide, the interviewer determines which of the three types of nonusers or five types of users the individual may be. The key in the interview is to stimulate the person to describe and provide examples of behaviors that he or she is taking in relation to the innovation. The interviewer then refers to the Decision Points and LoU definitions to determine the person's LoU. Facilitators can use this assessment as a diagnostic guide for structuring support and assistance. Evaluators and researchers will use the assessment to determine how far across the Implementation Bridge implementers have progressed.

The LoU One-Legged Interview

In a One-Legged LoU Interview (which in the past some called the "branching interview"), the facilitator visits with the user in a brief and informal way to gain an estimate of his or her LoU in order to offer appropriate assistance. The determining part of the interview is intended to be brief, but sufficient to gauge the interviewee's LoU. The One-Legged LoU Interview is not about fully substantiating the rating. Briefly, the purpose of this conversation is for the facilitator to make a quick assessment of a person's LoU and to do something that will facilitate further use of the innovation.

Pothole Warning

Use of the One-Legged LoU Interview cannot provide the rigorous information required for evaluation of an implementation effort. Nor can this data-collection tool produce results that are acceptable for research studies. Beware of this temptation.

Pothole Repair

To gain more reliable and valid data for research and evaluation purposes, the full LoU Focused Interview must be used.

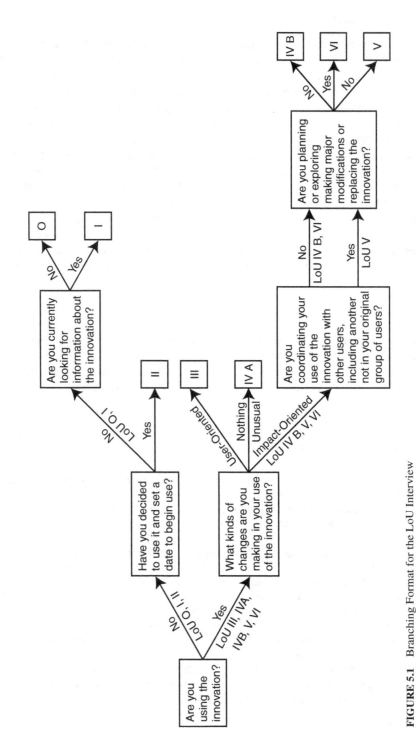

FIGURE 5.1 Branching Format for the LoU Interview

Source: LoU has been described and presented in many publications. An important resource for obtaining more detailed information about LoU is Hall, Dirksen, and George (2006).

The LoU Focused Interview

For research, assessment, and evaluation studies, more rigorous and detailed data are needed. For these purposes, the prospective LoU interviewer undergoes a three-day training and certification program to be qualified in using the LoU Interview Protocol. A full LoU interview takes 30 minutes or less and appears to the interviewee to be an interested discussion of what the person is doing, or not doing, in relation to an innovation. The LoU interview is based on the LoU definitions, the Decision Points, and a more detailed set of indicators of each LoU called *Categories*. The interview protocol includes a set of required questions that must be asked. The trained LoU interviewer has demonstrated mastery of three skills: He or she must (1) fully know and understand the construct; (2) ask the required questions and be able to probe to seek examples of behaviors indicative of LoU; and (3) be able to rate LoU interviews with reliability.

The ultimate product of this interview process is an overall determination of the person's LoU. As part of the process, a matrix-type rating sheet is filled out that becomes a more descriptive account of the individual's innovation-related behaviors. The LoU Interview Protocol and rating procedure are summarized in two training manuals (Hall, Dirksen, & George, 2006; Loucks et al., 1975).

LoU Categories

In measuring any variable, it is important to have multiple data points. There will be greater reliability and more confidence in the final determination when there is agreement across multiple data points. This need with the LoU Focused Interview has been accomplished with the identification of sets of indicators of each level, which are called Categories. The seven

---

INDICATORS OF LEVELS OF USE

1. With any innovation, each person exhibits some kinds of behaviors and thus can be identified as being at a certain LoU.
2. The Decision Points that operationalize the levels and the information related to Categories contribute to the overall description of an individual's LoU.
3. It is not appropriate to assume that a first-time user will be at Level III Mechanical Use. Nor should it be assumed that a person who has used the innovation several times will not be at LoU III.
4. The Levels of Use Focused Interview protocol has been established for reliable and valid measurement of Levels of Use.
5. A written format will not work to measure behavior. The only alternative to the LoU interview would be extended ethnographic fieldwork using the LoU Chart as the observation and interview guide, which is what was done in the original LoU interview validity study (Hall & Loucks, 1977).
6. The LoU are presented in a logical sequence, but this is not always followed by everyone. Typically, people move sequentially from LoU 0 to LoU IVA and then may move up, move down, or stay at LoU IVA.

TABLE 5.3   Levels of Use Categories

Knowledge: That which the user knows about characteristics of the innovation, how to use it, and consequences of its use. This is cognitive knowledge related to using the innovation, not feelings or attitudes.

Acquiring Information: Solicits information about the innovation in a variety of ways, including questioning resource persons, corresponding with resource agencies, reviewing printed materials, and making visits.

Sharing: Discusses the innovation with others. Shares plans, ideas, resources, outcomes, and problems related to its use.

Assessing: Examines the potential or actual use of the innovation or some aspects of it. This can be a mental assessment or can involve actual collection and analysis of data.

Planning: Designs and outlines short- and/or long-range steps to be taken during the process of innovation adoption (i.e., aligns resources, schedules activities, meets with others to organize and/or coordinate use of the innovation).

Status Reporting: Describes personal stand at the present time in relation to use of the innovation.

Performing: Carries out the actions and activities entailed in operationalizing the innovation.

Categories are Knowledge, Acquiring Information, Sharing, Assessing, Planning, Status Reporting, and Performing (see Table 5.3). In combination, the Categories represent the whole of Levels of Use. Each Category represents a subset of indicators.

Knowledge.   This Category reflects the individual's practical and theoretical understanding of the change: its characteristics or elements, how to use it, its potential effects, and the advantages and disadvantages of variations in its use. Unlike the other Categories, which relate to the implementer's behavior, this cognitive dimension is not expressed as a behavior. Rather, the Knowledge Category reflects the degree of complexity and sophistication of one's understanding of the innovation and its use: The higher the LoU, the more complex the Knowledge schema.

Acquiring Information.   This Category focuses on actions taken to seek information about the innovation through such behaviors as questioning colleagues and others, reviewing printed materials supplied by a vendor, visiting sites where the innovation is in place, or searching Web sites.

Sharing.   Sharing reflects what individuals tell others about their innovation use (or nonuse), including related ideas, problems, successes, and plans. This Category is most easily learned through observation. Sharing is when one person tells another what they are doing, or not doing, related to the innovation. This Category should not be used when the person is asking others something about the innovation. Those behaviors are placed under the Acquiring Information Category.

Assessing.   Exploring actual or potential innovation use to determine its strengths and weaknesses is the focus of Assessing. Informally or formally collecting and analyzing data about what is being done and their effects are examples of Assessing. However, Assessing may also be only mental reflection about use of the innovation.

Planning.   Thinking ahead to design, and outlining short- and long-term actions to take related to use of the innovation, constitutes Planning. The individual is looking beyond today's use to the next steps.

Status Reporting.   This Category entails the individual's reporting his or her own views of his or her overall use of the innovation. The information derived from the interviewer's questions in this Category provides a general description of the person's LoU.

Performing.   The Performing Category is for those concrete indicators of actions during the time of actual use of the innovation. In the LoU interview, specific examples of behaviors will be rated in the Performing Category.

Pothole Warning

Many students of LoU find understanding and verbalizing the distinction between Status Reporting and Performing difficult; consequently, they mix them up.

Pothole Repair

It might be prudent to carry a pocket index card with the definitions and an example of Status Reporting (general telling) and Performing (specific example of action) in order to have these descriptions handy, and to keep in mind adding to one's repertoire more examples of each.

One of the interesting aspects of the LoU Categories is that all, with the exception of Performing, represent actions relative to innovation use that occur outside the actual moments of delivery. As is obvious, much activity related to using innovations occurs beyond the classroom, or use site, and significant time and activity are invested in such behaviors.

Operational Definition of LoU—The LoU Chart

How the levels and Categories relate (for further explanation, see Hall & Hord, 1987) is depicted in the LoU Chart (see Appendix 4A), which is the full operational definition of Levels of Use. For each LoU, the types of behaviors within each Category are different. Description of these behaviors is found at the intersection of the horizontal row that describes a particular LoU with the vertical column that addresses each Category. The trained LoU interviewer is skilled at asking questions that allow the user to describe what he or she is doing in relation to each Category. The trained LoU interviewer can also relate information obtained in an interview to the Decision Points. Each of these smaller ratings is then integrated holistically to determine the overall LoU.

REFLECTION QUESTIONS

How might you manage "differentiated" interventions for a large group who are at different Levels of Use? In what situations would you intervene on the whole group, for example, all of a district's middle school teachers, and when would you want to address subgroups?

APPLYING LEVELS OF USE

The three major ways in which LoU can be employed are (a) planning for the next steps in a change process, (b) facilitating the change process, and (c) conducting evaluation and research studies. The first two can be considered formative uses; the latter can be formative and/or summative.

Facilitating Change Using LoU

LoU is not only an important tool for facilitators and evaluators to apply daily; it also can be used to guide strategic planning. Such plans include timelines that project phasing and likely development of each Level of Use, and then identifying related intervention strategies. Levels of Use provide planners with an evidence-based metric for understanding the status of each group and individual, and for determining appropriate support for advancing the change process.

Using LoU in General.   For facilitating purposes, a beginning application of LoU can be simply keeping the construct in mind and anticipating likely scenarios. More concrete is having an estimate of a sample of an individual's current LoU, which can be obtained through One-Legged Interviewing. Frequently, it is desirable to obtain an estimate for a group or whole system—for instance, all the eighth-grade teachers, or an academic department in a high school. This can be done by interviewing the individuals and aggregating the data. This assessment is followed by provision of interventions for the group. Similarly, data could be collected by sampling individuals across a school or large system. These same steps can be applied to large-system planning, such as a statewide reform initiative. If district and even state data are desired, representative sampling could be done across the unit. Regardless of the size of the system, consideration of each LoU and the likely overall development of LoU can be used as guides to planning.

We strongly believe that each person's LoU and success with a change are in large measure influenced by the facilitation he or she receives individually, and as part of subgroups and groups. If no support and facilitating interventions are offered, many will never fully implement the innovation, and others will remain nonusers. For example, those who are at LoU III Mechanical Use need interventions that will help them move beyond this level, or they may adapt the innovation (see Decision Point C) to make it easier for them to manage, or they may stop using the new practice altogether.

Interventions for Nonusers.   From a strategic perspective, assuming that all potential implementers across a system should ultimately be users, the facilitator's first challenge is to plan for intervening in ways that support all individuals in moving from LoU 0 Nonuse to LoU I Orientation. Although, ideally, intended users would have been involved to some degree in deciding to adopt or to develop the innovation, this is frequently not the case. The facilitators, therefore, may need to begin by making people aware of the impending innovation and expectations regarding implementation. The first objective is to stimulate people to actively seek information (Decision Point A), thus moving them to LoU I Orientation. Keep in mind, however, that each person must move through Decision Point A in order to be characterized as being at LoU I Orientation.

At LoU I Orientation and LoU II Preparation, information is needed about the purposes and requirements of the change as well as the timelines for implementation. This information should be general so as not to be overwhelming, yet specific enough to allow people to move to the next level. At these nonuse levels, people also need information about required materials and equipment—their purchase and preparation—and about how to get started. The advice should be practical, with only a moderate amount of attention to theory.

Interventions for Users.   As use is initiated, most if not all first-time users of an innovation will be at LoU III Mechanical Use. Their typical behaviors reflect concerted effort to find and organize materials. Effort is invested in searching for time to plan for new ideas and put them into practice. These users try multiple ways of handling various parts of the innovation. There are unanticipated innovation-related surprises as well as a short-term focus on Planning (e.g., for the next day). (Keep in mind behaviors indicative of Decision Point C.) LoU III users typically need help in finding, ordering, and organizing themselves and structural aspects of innovation use.

Help in finding the time for managing these logistics, and anticipating what comes next with use of the innovation, is imperative. Facilitators and administrators who can do these coaching activities will significantly reduce the amount of time that implementers remain at LoU III. Conducting how-to workshops, modeling, and providing guidance in structuring tasks can help, as can Web sites and chat rooms. Making it possible for users with common problems to meet with an experienced user to ask technical questions is another effective intervention that will be well received.

If implementers have appropriate facilitative assistance and time, they typically move to LoU IVA Routine. They have established a way to use the innovation that works for them and their students or other clients. By definition, LoU IVA users do not experiment with the program further (Performing), make no adaptations in the program or in their way of delivering it (Decision Point D-1), and state that they plan to continue their current use in the same way (Planning). This is an especially important time to check on Innovation Configurations (see Chapter 3).

If the LoU IVA user's Innovation Configuration (IC) meets the expectations set forth in the goals of the change effort, one appropriate intervention is to celebrate. Give praise and other types of recognition to reinforce the person's efforts. If, on the other hand, a user is using a less-than-desirable Configuration of the innovation and has become stable (LoU IVA Routine) in this pattern, the facilitator may need to encourage further refinements in use. Interventions to help the user continue to change may be in order at the same time that encouragement is being provided.

Pothole Warning

Oh, dear! I will need to help these people get "unstuck" if they are stabilized in a pattern of using the new program that is not desirable (i.e., LoU IVA with a poor Configuration). What a challenge!

Pothole Repair

One intervention to consider is taking these implementers to observe another person(s) who demonstrates exemplary practice. Before such a visit is arranged, consider how to discuss this with the "needy" user so that the visit will produce a positive effect on use.

IMPLICATIONS OF LEVELS OF USE FOR CHANGE LEADERS AND FACILITATORS

In this section there is significant discussion and multiple suggestions of interventions that may be employed at each LoU to support and enhance the effective implementation of new programs, practices, or processes. These ideas, however, should not be used in a cookbook fashion. Therefore, it is very important for the change facilitator to understand that it will take time and practice to become knowledgeable and skilled in facilitating change using LoU.

1. The facilitator should have deep content knowledge of the innovation, understanding its essential components and characteristics as well as its philosophical (and historical, perhaps) basis, the assumptions that accompany it, and the purposes or goals for which it may be used (see Chapter 3). A facilitator with a superficial knowledge base will have limited understanding for interpreting what each person is doing in a particular LoU.
2. In addition to knowing the innovation, the facilitator must have a deep understanding of the LoU construct and the operational definitions of each of the levels. This requires careful and thorough knowledge and skills development about the construct and its behavioral indicators. Being able to accurately recognize and identify users' (and nonusers') behaviors associated with each level is obviously important. To do this, training followed by practice and feedback to refine such identification skills is needed.
3. The effective facilitator knows well not only the innovation and the LoU construct, but also how to probe during the interview process in order to obtain useful information—and to supply or suggest relevant interventions that enable the individual to move to higher Levels of Use. These skills and qualities have direct implications for the preparation and competence of facilitators to use LoU in change efforts.

LoU IVB Refinement users are typically a pleasure for facilitators. These people are searching for new materials, activities, or other refinements in use of the innovation that will benefit their students (Acquiring Information). Importantly, they are also mentally assessing how well the innovation and their use of it are working in relation to their students (Assessing). Thus, these users welcome suggestions for assessing effectiveness and new ideas for improving varied aspects of the program or practice. Putting them in contact with others to access new information is a key intervention. Bringing others to visit them to see their ideas at work is confirming and rewarding. In addition, LoU IVB users may be potential facilitators.

If individuals are interacting with other users to coordinate their use and are making efforts to work together for their clients' benefit (Decision Point E), they are diagnosed as LoU V Integration. Through collaboration, they are making adaptations in their use for client gains. For example, a LoU V teacher is working with another teacher to collectively regroup students in order to take advantage of their interests and to accommodate differing ability levels. The facilitator, for example, the principal, supports the LoU V teachers by making it possible for them to more easily coordinate their efforts (by restructuring schedules, space, etc.).

Time for planning together will be of utmost importance. If the integration involves several people, developing their skills in shared decision making could be relevant too.

Normally, not a lot of a facilitator's time is directed to LoU VI Renewal users. In typical change efforts, very few people reach this level, and those who do have typically done so by virtue of their own creative abilities and energy. Further, these users are interested in significantly modifying the innovation, which may or may not mesh with the planned goals of the change effort. These users can be a very positive force in change because they have alternative ideas, and because their ideas are focused on improved outcomes for their clients. They could, however, be moving in a completely different direction from the one the innovation's designer intended. Their work should thus be either supported and applauded or channeled in more productive ways that are consistent with the organization's goals. "How does what you are exploring relate to the School Improvement Plan?"

Using Levels of Use in Research and Evaluation Studies

To measure LoU in evaluation and research studies, the three-day formal training and certification steps are necessary. The Certified Levels of Use Interviewer has demonstrated knowledge and skill in three areas: (1) knowing and understanding the construct of Levels of Use (the LoU Chart), (2) using the established LoU Interview Protocol *as stated* and doing follow-up probing effectively, and (3) rating LoU interviews reliably. This training is especially important given the understandable caution about rating people based on "self-report."

LoU is an operationally defined construct, which makes using a Focused Interview Protocol the right tool. The training program results in LoU interviewers who can use the construct definition, as well as Decision Points and Categories to reliably and validly determine each individual's LoU in each of the Categories and overall.

LoU ratings can be used to address study questions such as these: How far across the Implementation Bridge has the change effort progressed? How effective was the implementation plan? How effective have been the facilitation interventions? Which LoU should be the priority for the next implementation facilitation interventions? Has institutionalization been achieved? and When connected with outcome data (such as test scores), how much gain results from use of the innovation?

As was mentioned earlier, it is critical that Levels of Use also be assessed in any comparison/control groups. Otherwise, there is no way of knowing that both study groups are pure. For example, in one of our first LoU studies we found in the schools charged with implementing the innovation that only 80% of the teachers were users. This was at the end of three years of concerted support! We also found that 49% of the teachers in the designated comparison schools were users! No wonder the test indicated "no significant differences." However, when we compared users against nonusers, regardless of school assignment, there were differences at the .005 level in favor of the innovation (Hall & Loucks, 1977).

Another implication for research and evaluation studies has to do with timing and sampling. For example, many summative evaluation and treatment/control studies are conducted with first-time implementers. Our studies consistently document that most first-time users will be at LoU III Mechanical Use. By definition, these implementers are not proficient users of the innovation. It seems likely that their output/outcomes will be lower. Outcome studies should be done with LoU IVA Routine and higher users.

We will present more about applications of LoU in research and evaluation studies in Chapter 12. In doing such studies, it is crucial to assess LoU in the control/comparison group as well as in the treatment group. We almost guarantee that both groups will contain a mix of users and nonusers.

REFLECTION QUESTIONS

In your situation, when would you want to use the One-Legged Interview and when the LoU Focused Interview? On what basis would you make this decision?

SIDELIGHTS ABOUT LoU

Two final little items: You might have noticed that SoC uses Arabic numerals for its naming system, whereas LoU employs Roman numerals. This is simply an effort to further differentiate the two concepts and their classifications. Similarly, we always refer to *stages* with concerns and *levels* with LoU.

You might have wondered why LoU IV is the only level divided into two sections, LoU IVA and LoU IVB. The answer is one of history and pragmatics. The initial LoU verification study was launched with only seven levels: 0 through VI. Each level addressed taking some sort of actions related to the innovation. As the research team came back from the initial round of interviewing, the need for an additional classification became very apparent. A large number of people "out there" were users, but they were not making any changes in their use! Another LoU was discovered. Since we were into a large field study and had organized data as they related to the LoU Chart, we decided to not try to rearrange all the higher levels. It would have required us to relearn levels and codes. Instead, we split LoU IV into two levels, IVA Routine and IVB Refinement.

EAST LAKE SCHOOL DISTRICT'S STORY

In this installment of the East Lake story, we will use the algebra and geometry teacher team as an example of LoU in a change process—and to acknowledge one of the ways teachers collaborate to become more effective in order to produce increased student-successful learning. And, rather than supplying analysis at the end of the installment, we will analyze this team as we learn its story.

TIME SERIES: LoU SNAPSHOTS OF A MATHEMATICS TEACHER TEAM

Students of CBAM have suggested that it is easier to understand LoU if the example of a "real, live person" is provided for each level. Therefore, we introduce Louise, Lois, Leroy, and Laurie—a team of algebra and geometry classroom teachers at Mountain View High School. We will trace this team through all the LoU, describing the team at each LoU, including the Decision Points. But please remain aware that seldom in reality do people move hierarchically from one level to the next. Sometimes individuals may skip a level, move back to a lower level, or reach a level and move no further. At other times users may drop the innovation entirely (this is not rare, particularly at LoU III) if she or he receives no help and becomes increasingly unable to make sense of the change or to use it efficiently.

(continued)

EAST LAKE SCHOOL DISTRICT'S STORY (CONTINUED)

Louise, Lois, and Leroy came to the high school within a two-year period and have been in the math department for four years. Each is considered a good teacher by the students and is respected by peer teachers. They teach algebra and geometry much as they did at the beginning of their teaching careers—which in total comprises 15 years of teaching high school students.

During the summer, the three mathematics teachers, along with the principal, interviewed and hired Laurie (who had recently completed her master's degree) to join the "A and G" (algebra and geometry) teachers. After Laurie happily agreed to the new job and departed, and the interview team members were chatting among themselves, the principal told the math teachers that he had heard that the state board of education was recommending (actually, mandating) that high schools begin *now* to prepare for adopting the new Common Core State Standards in mathematics. Principal Major commented that since the district had already decided to adopt the new standards and give this new curriculum undivided focus, he was asking the teachers, "What do you think?"

Louise and Lois expressed a lack of information and interest, and Leroy admitted that he knew a "smattering" about this curriculum, but hadn't looked into it, and was not sure what it was all about (LoU 0 Knowledge). Further, Leroy and his colleagues reported about their current areas of attention: He had just purchased a new home and planted a new lawn; Lois was busily occupied with preparations for the school year that would begin shortly; Louise was deeply engaged in planning a holiday trip to Hawaii before school began. None of the three gave further attention to the new math core curriculum (LoU 0 Performing); none asked the principal any questions (LoU 0 Acquiring Information).

[Overall, Louise, Lois, and Leroy are at LoU 0 Nonuse with regard to the math Common Core curriculum.]

At the end of September, the gentle autumn rains had come to Leroy's lawn, and to his classroom came a student from another high school in the city. This student asked Leroy if the class would be using the new math Common Core process. Leroy said, "No, I don't think we'll do that this year." However, the topic came up again on Saturday, when he was playing doubles tennis with Laurie and some teacher colleagues from another high school.

One of the opposing players, who taught math at a nearby private school, mentioned going to an orientation session on math Common Core and asked Leroy and Laurie what they thought. Leroy recalled and described his new student's question, and Laurie chatted with some energy about what she had learned briefly about math Common Core during her last college course. She urged Leroy to call a meeting of their A and G team, and to access enough materials from their willing tennis partner for all four of their team to review (LoU I Acquiring Information and Performing).

[Because Leroy and Laurie have taken action to learn more about Common Core (Decision Point A), they have moved to Level I Orientation. Their teammates, Louise and Lois, remain at LoU 0 since they are completely unaware of the Common Core at this time. Laurie's idea to involve all the team in learning about this new approach to teaching mathematics to their students may have a hint of LoU V, but they are not yet users of the innovation.]

The four members of the A and G team (they became known as the "joined-at-the-hip mathematics quartet") began to meet regularly for 30 minutes before school on Tuesday, Wednesday, and Thursday. Louise and Lois joined Leroy and Laurie in examining the materials accessed from their tennis partner; they may now be characterized as LoU I, Acquiring Information, Assessing, and Performing. The team found the approach, philosophy, and learning outcomes of the Common Core to be exciting and very relevant for their students' use. They wondered if their students had the skills to engage in this new self-initiated and constructivist approach to their learning (LoU I Assessing). This meant that the A and G team dug deeply into a variety of data sources to ascertain if they and their students were prepared for the new curriculum. Louise and Lois became particularly eager to determine how well their students could solve problems and engage in critical thinking, as well as

EAST LAKE SCHOOL DISTRICT'S STORY (CONTINUED)

develop reasoned arguments with fellow students about their solutions to math problems (a "shift" that characterizes the new Common Core standards).

Principal Major supported the quartet's expression of interest and encouraged them to learn more. "After all, this curriculum has now been adopted by the district, so it is a good idea to get started on it," he commented (Decision Point B, LoU II). The group found the materials to be highly interesting (LoU I Assessing), and talked with their department chair and called the district math coordinator to find out what was available in the school and district relative to core curriculum for math (LoU II Acquiring Information). The principal suggested that they visit the private-school math teacher from whom they had obtained the initial material and who had begun implementing this new curriculum.

Subsequently, all four teachers attended a district workshop/learning session focused on math Common Core and became quite excited about the ideas (LoU II Acquiring Information, Assessing, and Performing). They shared what they were learning with their math department chair (LoU II Sharing). Subsequently, the quartet decided they would attend a series of three more sessions to learn more (Acquiring Information, Performing, and indications of Decision Point B).

Principal Major reported that the school's budget would support teachers who would attend these workshops that focused on the Common Core, "for we are adopting it now." The four teachers decided that they would be the pioneers of the new curriculum, provided they could learn enough to get started by the spring semester (LoU II Planning, Decision Point B).

[Because the A and G team have decided to use the new curriculum and have set a specific time to begin (Decision Point B), they are at LoU II Preparation.]

Louise, Leroy, Lois, and Laurie attended the workshops and considered them to be quite good. They thought that the philosophy and approach were well articulated and that they provided a meaningful basis for selecting materials and choosing activities for students (LoU II Assessing). They began collegially to collect materials and to make lesson plans for their classes that would engage in the new curriculum (LoU II Performing). Further, Louise and colleagues and the other workshop participants were networking and sharing tips on how to get started—even though some people were from rural areas some distance away from the city (LoU II Sharing and Acquiring Information).

On schedule, after the December holiday break, the A and G team initiated use of the new curriculum with a class that each team member had identified to be their first endeavor.

It was a good time, but it was also a maddening time. The A and G team had cooperatively prepared all the suggested materials to teach the first activities, but were unsure about how to organize their classrooms for this new, more student-oriented learning model (LoU III Knowledge and Assessing). They worried about how to design and create the formative assessments for this curriculum (LoU III Knowledge), even though the idea of formative assessments had been introduced in the schools.

The students were excited by the new approach and clamored to be quite independent in all phases of their new student-initiated math projects, whereas the A and G team were trying to keep up with finding and providing materials, activities, and ideas (LoU III Planning and Performing). They made a number of unproductive phone calls to publishers of the curriculum to enlist their support and advice on projects (LoU III Acquiring Information). The team shared, "Everything seems to take more time than I had anticipated" (LoU III Status Reporting). A crisis almost occurred one day when one of the four teachers had not prepared sufficiently for the class, and a school board member stopped by.

Parents telephoned, and some came to their student's class to find out what was going on, which was a mixed blessing for the team in the midst of all that they were trying so hard to do. The parent inquiries were both useful and distracting. It took significant time to explain this new way of learning math, the importance of its intended results, and their children's role in this approach to learning. The team tried to train one of the parents to explain to others, but this required more of

(continued)

EAST LAKE SCHOOL DISTRICT'S STORY (CONTINUED)

their time than was helpful, so they dropped this idea (LoU III Performing). The principal checked in regularly, providing support and ordering materials that were needed. Somehow the foursome made it to spring break.

[Because the team are using the innovation and making user-oriented changes (Decision Point C), their overall rating is LoU III Mechanical Use.]

During spring break, Louise, Lois, Leroy, and Laurie were in touch with one another several times and reflected on their work with the new curriculum, and how disappointing its use had been (LoU III Assessing). They decided that they definitely would not expand it to other classes until they had ironed out the wrinkles, that in the remainder of the semester they would slow the pace, and that there would be a great deal more planning (LoU III Planning). The team decided to invite the students to reflect on their experience, and together they would correct their errors and discuss frustrations. The teachers decided also to present some math problems to their classes in two ways: the way that the students had worked on math the previous year, and the "new" way. They would ask the students to compare what and how they were learning in each case, and they fervently hoped that a rich discussion and students' appreciation of the new method would emerge, so that the students would be more effectively engaged (LoU III Planning). They talked this over with the district math coordinator, who supported their assessment and plans (LoU III Sharing).

At the end of the school year, the A and G team breathed a sigh of relief. They felt they had accomplished a reasonable introduction of the math Common Core, and that they and the students were beginning to catch on (LoU III Assessing). The team members had asked each other to visit their classrooms to observe and take notes, and then to hold a consultation at the end of the day to discuss the notes and share feedback. They visited one another's classrooms several times to give pointers and ideas about arrangements and management of the classroom (LoU III Acquiring Information and Sharing). This had helped a great deal. Having each other visit and give critiques had been especially meaningful. [Note that this behavior is not indicative of LoU V Integration. The purpose is to address the teachers' efforts and efficiencies.] The team and their students assessed the triumphs and traumas of the introduction of the new math, and all felt that they had made significant strides in how to address this new way of teaching and learning math successfully (LoU III Assessing). Further, the principal congratulated the students and the team publicly on their efforts.

In the fall, the A and G team continued to use the new curriculum with their incoming algebra and geometry classes, using the improved methods that they and their students had developed during the spring. They decided to make no adaptations in the way they would work with students for the fall semester; they would use the spring version (LoU IVA Performing).

[Because the team have determined a satisfactory way to use the new math curriculum and are repeating their approach in the fall (Decision Point D-1), they are at LoU IVA Routine.]

During the following spring semester, Lois, Louise, Leroy, and Lauren saw that their classes were working well. But they were concerned and interested in the students developing more critical thinking skills and the ability to articulate with accuracy and precision their mental "moves" in which they engaged when solving a complex mathematical problem (LoU IVB Assessing). After much discussion, they planned for the students in each of their classrooms to pair up to solve a problem, then discuss how they would share their solution with other classmates, and be ready for the other students to ask pithy questions, which they should stand ready to answer (LoU IVB Planning). This new activity, the team rationalized, could give the students some space to do creative problem solving and critical thinking, and to engage in reasonable discourse about their solution. The A and G team felt this additional responsibility would improve the students' understanding of the fundamentals of mathematics, and of how to think about mathematical processes as mathematicians do (LoU IVB Assessing and Performing). It did indeed make the students feel very empowered

EAST LAKE SCHOOL DISTRICT'S STORY (CONTINUED)

and capable. This move also was applauded by the parents, who saw it as an opportunity for their children to develop poise and confidence while sharing their thinking with others.

[Because the team have adapted their use of the innovation to increase client outcomes (Decision Point D-2), they are at LoU IVB Refinement.]

In May, the principal dropped a hint to the local newspaper's editor, a friend in the Rotary Club, who picked up on the story of the team working so well with the Common Core math standards and with students. The editor sent a reporter to investigate. The A and G team suggested that the reporter also interview some of the students' parents. The discussion between the four teachers and the reporter after the interviews focused on the plethora of publications bemoaning the shortage of mathematicians in jobs requiring math, science, and technology-related skills.

Later that night, Louise had an idea: In the fall, why couldn't she and the team organize the senior students into cross-classroom task forces that would explore this problem, and then plan for how the students might visit the middle schools to interest students in pursuing math as their special area of study in high school and into college? To do this well, they should talk with Helen Morse (chair of the English Department) and several of her teachers. "After all, we all have the same students. They have been working with formative assessments and have Common Core standards too." She shared her idea with the team the next day, and they began planning for how these activities could happen and how they could partner with the English Department (LoU V Planning). The senior students, who would now be reorganized into committees from across the two departments according to their interest in the various components of this project, would be allowed to develop plans and procedures for their part of the project, although they would be monitored carefully by their teachers.

At the beginning of the fall semester, Louise, Laurie, Leroy, and Lois, along with Helen and two other English teachers, had their classes meet together during the home room period in the media center, where there was space to accommodate them. Louise, Leroy, and Helen worked in depth with various groups of students while Lois, Laurie, and the two English teachers floated to facilitate and support the others. The teachers did extensive planning for this expanded team-taught, blocked cohort of students (LoU V Planning). They would frequently exchange assignments so that each played various roles with the students, keeping their work fresh and their ideas stimulating to the students (LoU V Performing). They occasionally invited the principal to actively participate in their project.

[Because the team have initiated a student-oriented change that entails working with some other implementers (outside of their original team) in relation to the math curriculum innovation, they have behaviors at Decision Point E, which means they are at LoU V Integration.]

The A and G team were quite pleased with their work with the other teachers and how it was positively affecting students (LoU V Assessing). Their students completed their work with students from the other classrooms in a mostly orderly and productive manner. All students developed and shared scripts of their presentations about their mathematical solutions. They invited parents and the faculty of the town's junior college to observe their mathematical presentations. The combined team of teachers were very excited about working together across their subject areas and with the students (LoU V Performance).

During her family's Thanksgiving gathering, Laurie sat next to her ninth-grade niece at the luncheon feast. The niece attends school in a neighboring state, and was quite unaware of the type of math that Laurie was sharing with her. Stimulated by the gift of some computers and related equipment from her uncle, during the next several weeks Laurie began to chat with her team members about the niece who was not experiencing the fundamentals of the math that they were providing to their freshman-through-senior high school students. They began to wonder how their students might use e-mail to connect with students out of their district, to share and provide learning for those who were not involved in such challenging math (LoU VI Assessing).

(continued)

EAST LAKE SCHOOL DISTRICT'S STORY (CONTINUED)

They conferred with Principal Major about the possibility of giving this challenge to their students. He did not deter them, but he did remind them that they had a school schedule to maintain and a curriculum to teach, and that time might not be available. The teachers explained to him that this was a significant opportunity for their students to communicate to other students what they were learning, thus sharing and reinforcing their own learning. "Well," Principal Major replied, "that is a really big ticket, and quite an interesting addition to your mathematics curriculum. If you think you can make it work, okay." The team decided that their students from across their classrooms would communicate by e-mail, and be in on exploring and creating a schedule. They would then use their technology to share information and teach the "newbie" students, report needs, brainstorm solutions, develop plans, give critiques of each other's ideas, and share results of their interactions.

[Because the A and G team have explored and are preparing to implement a major modification in challenging activities that they provide for their students' gain (Decision Point F), they are at Level VI Renewal.]

This is not the end of this team's story, and we will meet them again in Chapter 7.

CRITIQUE QUESTIONS OF EAST LAKE DISTRICT'S STORY

1. Consider the timeline of this team's journey through LoU. What reaction, if any, do you have to the pace of the A and G team's movement?
2. What, if anything, should the team's principal and/or curriculum supervisor do with and for the team now?
3. How did the Categories and Decision Points lead to the overall LoU ratings? Explain your reasoning.

SUMMARY

In this chapter, the Levels of Use construct, behaviors, related tools, and uses by change facilitators, researchers, and evaluators have been described. Several talking points may be used to share this information with others:

1. LoU is one of three Diagnostic Dimensions of the CBAM. It focuses on what people are doing, not feelings and perceptions.
2. The Decision Points provide a means for precisely identifying individuals at the various levels.
3. The LoU Categories further define the construct and provide more fine-grained data points for determining each level.
4. Two procedures may be used to assess LoU: (1) the One-Legged Interview, which is informal and used for facilitation purposes; and (2) the LoU Focused Interview, which is more rigorous, and is used for research and evaluation.
5. LoU can be used in planning for change, as well as in assessing progress.
6. In research and evaluation studies, it is important to document LoU in both treatment and comparison samples.

DISCUSSION QUESTIONS

1. How would you use Levels of Use to assess staff's knowledge and skills as they are introduced to and gradually become skilled at using a new technology procedure or process?

2. Describe an experience you have had with a change wherein you experienced different LoUs.

3. Place the different LoU on the Implementation Bridge. Which LoU represent behaviors before one is on the bridge, and which represent being all the way across?

4. Use examples to illustrate and discuss how the Categories expand the descriptions of each LoU.

5. What do you see as the similarities and differences between the two major ways of measuring LoU?

6. Think of an innovation, such as technology- or problem-based learning. How could LoU be used as a tool to monitor its implementation?

7. How might teachers' LoU of a new math program be used to explain student outcome scores across three years of implementing the program?

APPLYING LEVELS OF USE IN FACILITATING IMPLEMENTATION

1. Interview three people (e.g., teachers) about an innovation. Use the LoU One-Legged Interview to estimate each individual's LoU, and then make an appropriate intervention for each. If you can't find three teachers, use classmates or friends. Remember that they don't have to be users for you to assess their LoU.

2. Plan how LoU could be employed at the school district or state level to assess implementation of a systemwide school improvement project. How often would you want to formally measure LoU?

3. Identify a change effort that is in its early stages on your campus or in your workplace. Explain how you would use LoU to develop and guide a three-year implementation plan.

4. Consider the Innovation Configuration (IC) of your new product or practice (in operation) (see Chapter 3). Describe how you would use the IC in tandem with an LoU interview to learn the status of implementation of your school or district's progress.

APPLYING LEVELS OF USE IN RESEARCH AND PROGRAM EVALUATION STUDIES

1. One area that needs further study has to do with the rate at which people move from level to level. One approach to addressing this topic would be to identify a sample of people as they engage with an innovation and assess their Level of Use at regular intervals. It also would be important to learn more about the types of interventions that are supplied to all groups and individuals. Analyses of these data most certainly will lead to new insights into why there is more or less movement in LoU.

2. Clearly, there need to be more studies that explore relationships between LoU and outcomes. So far, most of the studies have documented increases in outcomes with those who are users according to LoU. However, the relationships are not always linear. At some point it seems likely that there will be a study that finds decreased outcomes when there is use of the innovation. Explaining that finding will be interesting, indeed.

LEARNING MORE ABOUT LEVELS OF USE

For access to training for either the LoU One-Legged Interview technique or the LoU Focused Interview, contact the authors.

Guskey, T. R. (2000). Participant use of new knowledge and skills, Chapter 7, in *Evaluating professional development*. Thousand Oaks, CA: Corwin Press.

> Tom Guskey was one of the first evaluation experts to recognize the value of applications of Levels of Use to evaluation of professional development. In a five-step process, step 4 is the exploration of participants' use of new knowledge and skills, and Levels of Use provides interview protocols to determine the degree to which and how participants are applying or using their newly gained knowledge and skills from their professional development learning sessions.

Hord, S. M., & Roussin, J. L. (2013). *Implementing change through learning: Concerns-based concepts, tools, and strategies for guiding change*. Thousand Oaks, CA: Corwin Press.

> This hands-on practical book uses a series of powerful Learning Map activities to guide and support individuals and teams in developing the knowledge and skills for using the concepts, strategies, and tools of the Concerns Based Adoption Model (CBAM) to manage their change efforts successfully. This is the "how-to" book of CBAM.

PART III

LEADING CHANGE ACROSS
THE ORGANIZATION

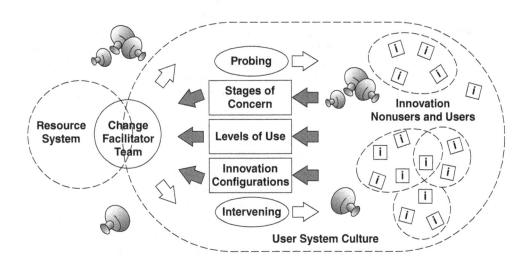

CHANGE FACILITATOR STYLE, ORGANIZATION CULTURE, AND INTERVENTION MUSHROOMS

The three chapters in Part II presented three evidence-based constructs and measures for understanding, facilitating, and evaluating change processes from the perspective of the implementers. There is a personal side to change (Stages of Concern), and there are steps in moving from nonuse to novice to expert (Levels of Use). Also, complex changes are not likely to be implemented initially with high fidelity. Instead there will be adaptations and partial implementations (Innovation Configurations). Each of these constructs can be applied to individuals, groups, and whole organizations. Each represents on-the-ground perspectives.

The perspective of the next three chapters is organization-wide. In Chapter 1, Change Principle 3 said that the school, or other organization, is the primary unit of change. Individuals implement innovations, but it is the organization as a whole that accomplishes change. We use the term *organization* loosely here. There are many types of organizations, including schools, social agencies, national companies, and government departments, where the constructs presented in the next three chapters can be applied.

In Part III, each of the next three chapters addresses one of the now highlighted areas of the CBAM graphic. Chapter 6—*How Do Leaders Make a Difference in Implementation Success?*—presents three different *Change Facilitator Styles*. The research is clear; leaders make a significant difference in change process success. The three Change Facilitator (CF) Styles introduced in this chapter have been closely examined. Each of the CF Styles is described, a measure for assessing CF Style is introduced, and findings from research studies are summarized. One of the styles is consistently found to be correlated with less implementation success. Depending on the innovation and the situation, there is success with the other two styles.

Chapter 7—*How Does a Culture of Continuous Learning Support Implementation?*—addresses another important aspect of organizations—the overall feel, the shared values and assumptions; in other words, organization culture. In this chapter, a special type of culture, the *Professional Learning Community (PLC),* is examined. In organizations where there is a shared expectation that everyone should be learning, and that the organization itself should be learning, there will be more success with implementing change.

Chapter 8—*What Can Be Done to Understand a Part of the Change Process That Is Not Controlled by the Leaders or the Followers?*—introduces a hidden element of life in organizations. There is a category of interventions that the leaders do not initiate. Nor do all leaders and participants sense their existence. This hidden species of interventions is called *Intervention Mushrooms.* Just as the name implies, they grow in the dark, they can be nutritious or poisonous, and they are fed with "fertilizer."

The East Lake School District stories that accompany each chapter illustrate various ways that the chapter's construct and tools can come alive. You will find that in these stories the frame is that of a whole organization. At the same time, each story builds on our understanding of how implementing change is experienced by leaders and implementers.

CHAPTER 6

HOW DO LEADERS MAKE A DIFFERENCE IN IMPLEMENTATION SUCCESS?

Change Facilitator Styles

She knows what our school is to be about and where we are headed. She sees things that I didn't even know were out there. She always is thinking about how all the pieces can fit together. When there are decisions to be made, she meets with us teachers, and together we make the final decision.

—An Island Park teacher talking about Principal Inez Hernandez

He loves the challenges of getting the master schedule to work. When any of us teachers ask him about doing something, his first reactions will be to inquire if what we are proposing aligns with rules and procedures, and whether it is in the budget. Everything is well organized and gets done on time.

—Helen Morse, English Department Chair, talking about Principal Major, Mountain View High School

I have a hard time reading him. He says yes to everything. He listens to everything and acts on nothing. Wonderful man who does nothing. He wants everyone to get along.

—Bev White's observation of Principal Ray Raulson, River Run Elementary School

As these quotes illustrate, identifying characteristics of effective leaders is complex. Over the years there have been literally thousands of research studies that have examined characteristics and behaviors of leaders in a never-ending quest to answer the age-old question of how leaders can make a difference. In this chapter, we will consider leadership in a special context: *implementing change.* We examine recent studies that have focused on leadership during change processes and describe how different approaches relate to implementation success. By the end of this chapter, you will have a set of tools to assess yourself and leaders you have known. You also will have some clues about how to work with and influence different types of leaders.

LEARNING OUTCOMES

After reading this chapter, the learner should be able to:

1. Describe how leader behaviors relate to style.
2. Name and describe three different Change Facilitator Styles.
3. Describe implications of different styles of leadership for implementation success and outcomes such as student learning.
4. Identify effective approaches for working with different leader styles.
5. Describe differences in leadership teams in relation to the different styles of leaders.
6. Identify aspects of your leader style, and consider areas where you might want to change your style.

Each of us has our favorite stories about leaders who were great to work for, the ones who respected our skills and potential, who let us take on extra responsibilities, and who helped us to grow professionally and personally. We also have stories about the leaders who did not trust us, who maintained control over the smallest details, and who would not give genuine consideration to our ideas. And then, there are those leaders who were very friendly, who always had time to chat, and who verbally encouraged us to try anything, but in hindsight we can see that they never made a definite decision and that each attempt at change seemed to fall apart during implementation.

These types of experiences with leaders are typical rather than atypical. There are varied approaches to leadership, and different people lead in different ways. Further, there are patterns and similarities among those leaders who do make a difference and among those who do not. Depending on how the leader leads, the followers and the organization will have very different change process experiences, and the ultimate results of the change effort will differ as well.

We have identified different approaches to leadership that we call **Change Facilitator (CF) Styles**. Each style is defined by what the leaders do and their different perspectives about how to support change processes. Depending on their style, leaders send different signals to their staff and spend their time doing different things. For example, some leaders are never seen. They are in their office or out of the building attending some sort of meeting. Other leaders are ubiquitous! They seem to always be present and know about everything that is going on. The effects of these different styles can be observed in the amount and degree of success that the followers have in implementing and using innovations. Also, in our most recent research we are finding significant differences in test scores that are associated with school principal leadership.

Although the focus of our research has been on the formal heads of organizations—namely school principals—keep in mind that leadership in change efforts is not something that is done only by the designated administrator(s) at the top. As we will emphasize further in Chapter 11, *everyone who is engaged in change has a responsibility to assist in facilitating the process.* In addition, everyone will have a particular style. In other words, although most of the research presented in this chapter was done with school principals, the findings have implications for all who are participating in implementing change.

Two sets of implications of this work on CF Style must be kept in mind: First, the formally designated leaders of the change process will have their own CF Style. (How can you best work with each?) Second, regardless of your position in an organization, you have a potential role to play in helping to facilitate the change process, and in doing this you will have your own CF Style. (What will it be?) As you read this chapter, in addition to thinking about leaders you know, be sure to consider how each style may affect change success and outcomes.

Pothole Warning

Leading change processes is not simple or easy, so do not expect the leader to be able to do it alone.

Pothole Repair

All of the members of an organization have a responsibility to help the leader in achieving implementation success.

THE HISTORY OF RESEARCH ON LEADERS AND LEADERSHIP

> *Which way did they go?*
> *How many of them were there?*
> *I must find them!*
> *I am their leader!*

This oft-cited refrain summarizes much about leadership in general and especially as it relates to leadership in change. Too often, leaders don't lead until they figure out which way the troops are moving. The refrain is used here to introduce you to a number of important questions: In what ways do you see that leaders make a difference? What do you believe are the important characteristics of "good" leaders? What kind of leader do you like to work with? And how do you lead?

The metaphor of a dog-sled team is another way to begin thinking about some of the important differences in the way that leaders lead. Some leaders are like the lead dog. They like to be at the front, checking out the view ahead and breaking trail for those behind them. Others like to lead from within the team. They are not comfortable with the visibility that comes with being at the front, whereas those who like the front position point out that the view is always the same for those behind. Still other leaders stay at the back of the sled, like the driver, riding the rails of the sled, pushing the sled, and barking out commands to those on the team who are not pulling hard enough. Other leaders seem to be more like the spectators and race officials. They watch from the sidelines while the team, sled, and driver travel by. They are ready to evaluate, and occasionally cheer, the performance of the team and driver, but they do not enter the race themselves. So again, which kind of leader do you like to be with? How do you lead? And which type do you think makes the biggest difference?

The Legacy of Research on Leadership

Leaders and leadership have been the subject of study and theorizing for most of the twentieth and early twenty-first century. In fact, so much has been written about these subjects that there are major anthologies just to summarize the history of study and examination of leaders and leadership (see, for example, Bass & Bass, 2008; Northouse, 2007). Some of the earliest studies of leaders examined particular traits, such as height and eye color. Over the course of the twentieth century many models of leadership were proposed, such as the important work by Fiedler (1978) suggesting that the style of effective leaders is contingency dependent—in other words, a different style of leader is needed for different situations.

Many have proposed models of leadership suggesting that how a leader leads must be considered across two dimensions: a **task** dimension and a people, or **relationship,** dimension (see, for example, Blake & Mouton, 1964). According to some, the "best" leaders are those who exhibit high levels of both task and relationship behaviors. Others advocate shifting the balance of task and relationship behaviors depending on the "maturity" of the followers (see, for example, Hersey, Blanchard, & Johnson, 2000).

This long and extensive legacy of research, theory, and model building about leaders and leadership has focused primarily on business and industry contexts. In recent years, there have been an increasing number of studies on principal leadership (see, for example, English, 2004; Hallinger & Heck, 2011; Leithwood, Louis, Anderson, & Wahlstrom, 2004; Marzano, Waters, & McNulty, 2005).

Discovering in an Implementation Study That School Leaders Were Making the Difference

Nearly all of the research and models about leaders and leadership had their beginnings in studies of individuals in leadership positions or in theorizing about what people in leadership positions should be like. By contrast, our research on leaders and leadership had a very different beginning. Rather than starting with an agenda to look at change leaders, we stumbled onto the need to look at leaders because of some research findings about teacher success, and lack of success, in implementing change. In other words, our deciding to study change leadership emerged from our working directly with teachers and hearing about their experiences.

Implementation Data That Were a Mystery. As a research team, we were analyzing a very extensive set of data about teachers' Stages of Concern (SoC; see Chapter 4), Levels of Use (LoU; see Chapter 5), and Innovation Configurations (IC; see Chapter 3). We had just completed a two-year study of teachers' implementation of a very innovative science curriculum in a large (80 schools) suburban school district. All of the teachers had participated in carefully designed workshops that were presented by lead teachers. SoC, LoU, and IC map data had been collected twice a year, and the district office Change Facilitators had devoted themselves to coaching teachers. So we expected that at the end of two years, all of the teachers in all of the schools would be at the same point in terms of implementation. Wrong!

In the SoC, LoU, and IC Map data, we found very distinct variations that appeared to represent school-by-school differences. We were able to sort the schools into three groups according to how the implementation data differed. To use the SoC data as an illustration, in Group A, a few schools exhibited a gradual lowering of Self and Task concerns and an arousal of Stage 4 Consequence concerns. This is the profile we expected for all schools. But there were two other groups, each of which had more schools. In Group B, schools revealed generally flat concerns profiles that were low on all stages. In Group C, we found schools whose teachers had the "Big W" concerns profile; in other words, they had high Stage 1 Informational concerns, high Stage 3 Management concerns, and a serious "tailing up" on Stage 6 Refocusing concerns. These teachers were not pleased with having unresolved Task concerns and had some very strong ideas about what should be done to make things better. (A version of these SoC profiles were presented in Figure 4.6.)

What Would Explain the Differences?   We were puzzled about how to explain these data. All the teachers received the same district workshops and the same curriculum materials. The schools were generally alike in terms of student socioeconomic status and the like, and they all had had two years to implement the new curriculum. So we decided to present the three lists of school names to our district Change Facilitator colleagues and ask how they would explain the clustering of the schools. With little hesitation, one colleague summarized everybody's conclusions: "It's the principals! In the schools in Group A, the principals are very active and supportive of teachers using the new curriculum. In Group B, the principals are well organized, but they don't push their teachers to go beyond the minimum. In Group C schools, the principals don't help their teachers. They talk a good game, but they don't follow through."

Principal Leadership Is the Key.   The outcome of these discussions with our school-based colleagues was a set of in-depth studies to document and analyze the intervention behaviors of school principals to see if, indeed, what they did as school leaders could be correlated with the extent of teacher implementation success (Hall, Hord, & Griffin, 1980). From these and the earlier studies of teachers engaged in change processes, the concept of CF Style emerged. These studies did not originate with some a priori model of leadership or theories about what good leaders do. As with other Concerns-Based Adoption Model (CBAM) studies, the work on CF Style came out of what happens to real people living and working to implement change.

 REFLECTION QUESTION
What have you seen leaders do that made a difference in change process success?

THE CONCEPT OF CHANGE FACILITATOR STYLE

Interestingly, as obvious as it is, many school district leaders, staff developers, and researchers miss the fact that *all principals are not the same.* They continue to treat all principals in the same way while advocating for individualization of professional development for teachers. In reality, each principal views his or her role and priorities differently, and individuals in this position operationally define their roles differently in terms of what they actually do each day. One implication of this fact was that in studying principals as Change Facilitators we needed to construct samples of schools so that we had representations of different ways in which principals lead change efforts. Our emerging concept of CF Style provided the means for doing this. We could select study schools using the descriptions of principal leadership that had been discovered when comparing schools in Groups A, B, and C.

Style Versus Behavior

Note that so far we have been referring to *style*. For the rest of this chapter, it is important to understand that there is a big difference between the concept of *style* and the idea of *leader behaviors*. Style represents the overall tone and pattern of a leader's approach. Behaviors are a leader's individual moment-to-moment actions, such as talking to a teacher in the corridor, chairing a staff meeting, approving a budget request, talking on the telephone, and sending an e-mail. The overall accumulated pattern and tone of these behaviors form a person's style. Interestingly, more-effective leaders understand that each of their individual behaviors is important in and of itself as well as a sign of their overall style.

Pothole Warning

To assume that all leaders will fully and actively support implementation of a change is very risky.

Pothole Repair

Different leaders will have different views about the innovation and will approach their role in facilitating implementation in different ways. The views, styles, and behaviors of individual leaders should be understood, and system support strategies should take these differences into account.

Three Change Facilitator Styles

Through our studies of principal leadership we have identified three distinct Change Facilitator Styles: the Initiator, the Manager, and the Responder. We know that these three styles do not represent all possible styles, but they do represent three contrasting approaches that are regularly seen in change processes. In this section, each of these CF Styles is described. To make the descriptions come alive, we have included some of our favorite examples and anecdotes from the studies. Formal definitions of each CF Style are presented in Table 6.1.

While reading these descriptions, keep these questions in mind:

1. How well do these descriptions match with leaders you have experienced?
2. Which CF Style do you think is most highly correlated with greater teacher success in implementing changes?
3. Which CF Style do you use?

Initiator Change Facilitators. Initiators have clear and strongly held visions about what their school should be like. They have a passion for the school. They are motivators who are continually articulating what the school can become. When decision issues come up, they listen to all sides and quickly make decisions based on what they think will be best for students and what will move the school closer to their vision. Initiators set high expectations for teachers, they expect loyalty, and they push. They expect teachers to be engaged in teaching, supporting students, and contributing to the effort to continually improve the whole school. For example, one elementary school had a goal for children to write every week. To encourage teachers and students in this effort, the Initiator principal asked teachers to give him samples

TABLE 6.1   Descriptions of Three Change Facilitator Styles

Initiators have clear, decisive, long-range policies and goals that transcend, but include, implementation of the current innovation. They tend to have strong beliefs about what good schools and teaching should be like, and they work intensely to attain this vision. Decisions are made in relation to their goals for the school and in terms of what they believe to be best for students, which is based on current knowledge of classroom practices. Initiators have strong expectations for students, teachers, and themselves. They convey and monitor these expectations through frequent contacts with teachers and by setting clear expectations of how the school is to operate and how teachers are to teach. When they feel it is in the best interest of their school, particularly the students, Initiators will seek changes in district programs or policies, or will reinterpret them to suit the needs of the school. Initiators will be adamant but not unkind; they will solicit input from staff, and then decisions will be made in terms of the goals of the school, even if some staff members are ruffled by the directness and high expectations of the Initiators.

Managers place heavy emphasis on organization and control of budgets, resources, and the correct applications of rules, procedures, and policies. They demonstrate responsive behaviors in addressing situations and people, and they initiate actions in support of change efforts. The variations in their behaviors are based on the use of resources and procedures to control people and change processes. Initially, new implementation efforts may be delayed because they see that their staff are already busy and that the innovation will require more funds, time, and/or new resources. Once implementation begins, Managers work without fanfare to provide basic support to facilitate teachers' use of the innovation. They keep teachers informed about decisions and are sensitive to excessive demands. When they learn that the central office wants something to happen in their school, their first concerns are about resources: Will there be enough budget, time, and staffing to accomplish the change? Once these issues are resolved, they then support their teachers in making it happen. As implementation unfolds, Managers do not typically initiate attempts to move beyond the basics of what is required.

Responders place heavy emphasis on perception checking and listening to people's feelings and concerns. They allow teachers and others the opportunity to take the lead with change efforts. They believe their primary role is to maintain a smoothly running school by being friendly and personable. Responders want their staff to be happy, to get along with each other, and to treat students well. They tend to see their school as already doing everything that is expected and not needing major changes. They view their teachers as strong professionals who are able to carry out their instructional role with little guidance. Responders emphasize the personal side of their relationships with teachers and others. They make decisions one at a time, based on input from their various discussions with individuals. Most are seen as friendly and always having time to talk.

of all students' writing each Friday morning. He then displayed the samples around the school halls and common areas.

Initiators push teachers, students, parents, and personnel in the district office to support the things they believe will help students learn, teachers teach, and the school to move forward. They are the ones that implicitly, and sometimes explicitly, say "Lead, follow, or get out of the way." Sometimes they push too hard, which makes some feel pressured and uncomfortable. They also are knowledgeable about policies, rules, and procedures, but on occasion they will work with the philosophy that "It is easier to seek forgiveness than to seek prior approval." For example, if several budgets have specific rules about how the funds can be spent, they will still commingle the funds so that a combined activity can take place.

Initiators consciously question and analyze what they and others do. They reflect on what others have told them, on what issues may be emerging, and on how well tasks are being accomplished. They listen to teachers and students. They not only make decisions but consciously work to make sure that all decisions and actions move people and the school in the desired direction. They are focused on assessment, instruction, and curriculum. Initiators also have a great deal of passion. They care deeply about their students, teachers, and the school. Their pushing, monitoring, and bending of the rules are done to support everyone in doing his or her best. They also have what we call **strategic sense,** which means that they do not lose sight of the big picture while they are doing the day-to-day activities. They anticipate what might happen and envision alternative responses that they may need to employ.

Manager Change Facilitators.   Managers approach the leadership of change efforts with a different set of behaviors, expectations, and emphases. They are organized and get things done efficiently. They are skilled at making their school run like a well-oiled machine. They focus first on what the formal policies, rules, and procedures say. Then they focus on resources, budgets, schedules, and logistics. The bells ring on time, everyone knows the procedures for getting supplies, schedules are planned well in advance, and the various forms are filled out correctly and processed promptly. There are procedures for everything, including lesson plan format, teacher duty assignments, and procedures for students to move along the corridors. (In one school, there was even a rule for how far student shoulders should be from the walls—18 inches.)

As proposals for change are made by teachers or those outside the school, Managers do not rush in. When asked by an external facilitator or district administrator to try something different, their first response will likely be, "Well, that is an interesting idea, but my teachers are real busy right now." Managers buy time, which they use to study and to learn more about the change and to consider whether they should have the school engage with it.

When a change is proposed, Managers are quick to ask about the need for resources; for example, "Well, we can't do this unless I have more budget or another staff line. Is there a grant for doing this?" An important consequence of this tactic is that teachers and the school are protected to some extent from random changes. This dampening of the initiation of change also buys time for the principal and teachers to learn about the proposed change and to prepare for an efficient implementation. As a result, when changes are implemented, they tend to proceed smoothly and to acceptable levels.

Manager CF Style leaders also try to do many things themselves rather than delegate to others. They arrive at school early in the morning, stay late in the evening, and return on the weekends to do more of the administrative tasks. They work hard at having things organized and providing resources for the staff. In many ways, they demand more of themselves than they do of others. When one principal was asked about why she had written the School Improvement Plan (SIP) rather than ask the assistant principal or SIP Team leader to do it, she replied, "Well, it is easier for me to do it right the first time than to have someone else do it and then I have to fix it."

Responder Change Facilitators.   Responders approach leadership with a primary focus on what is happening now. They do not have many ideas about what the school should be like in the future or where education is going. Instead their attention is on everyone's current concerns, feelings, and perceptions. When they do One-Legged Interviews with teachers and others, their purpose is to discover concerns and perceptions about current topics and issues. Responders also spend time on the phone and e-mail checking with other principals about their perceptions of what the assistant superintendent was talking about in the last principals' meeting (e.g., "When she said . . ."). They engage in the same sort of discussions with parents, community members, and students. The pattern to their talk is chatty, social, and always willing to listen to concerns.

Responders are most willing for others to take the lead. For example, if a teacher wants to try a different curriculum approach, the Responder principal will say, "Go ahead. You know we always like to be innovative in this school." If someone from the district office or a nearby university wants to start a new project in the school, the Responder will welcome that person as part of the overall goal of trying to keep everyone happy. As a result, many disparate projects and activities can be going on in different parts of the school.

In contrast to Initiators, Responders delay making decisions. First, they want to hear from everyone about their concerns and perceptions. When they do have to make a major decision such as cutting a staff position or reassigning a classroom, they struggle and in the end tend to make the decision at or shortly after the deadline. And the decision will be most heavily influenced by the last person with whom they talked. Thus, it is possible for a teacher or someone else to influence a decision right up to the last moment.

Another part of the Responder CF pattern is the tendency to minimize the size and significance of proposed changes. They often feel that a change proposal is not as needed as its advocates claim. A Responder may say, "So what's the big deal? We have been doing most of this already—you just have a different name for it." Also, Responders tend to hire strong and independent teachers because a Responder's thought is, "They know more about teaching than I do. It is my job to work with the community and do the other things so that they can teach." Another theme with Responder CF Style leaders is their wish for everyone to get along and be happy.

 REFLECTION QUESTIONS

Which of these CF Styles have you experienced? What was it like to work with each? Which one do you prefer to have as your supervisor?

DISCUSSION AND IMPLICATIONS OF CHANGE FACILITATOR STYLE

Now that the different CF Styles have been introduced, it is important to think about some of the implications and related issues. The different CF Styles described here do not represent all principals, nor do all principals fit perfectly into one of these styles. However, they do appear to represent three more commonly found approaches to change leadership. If the CF Style descriptors offer nothing else, they can help you think in some different ways about leaders and change leadership. You also can think about your CF Style.

INDICATORS OF CHANGE FACILITATOR STYLE

1. CF Style is the overall pattern that is derived from accumulated observations of individual leader behaviors.
2. Managers emphasize following rules and procedures.
3. Initiators focus on doing what will be best in the long term for students and the school.
4. Responders want people to get along and be happy.
5. Schools with Manager leaders attain implementation success. However, little effort is made to move beyond the acceptable minimums.
6. Responders ask about concerns, but are less active in attempting to resolve them and in facilitating change.
7. Influencing leaders with different CF Styles requires customized approaches.
8. Responders place trust in others. Managers try to do most of the tasks themselves. Initiators push for ever-increasing success.

A Continuum of Change Facilitator Styles

One way to think about the relationship of one CF Style to the others is to place them on a 100-point number line (see Figure 6.1). The stereotypic Responder is positioned at point 30, the stereotypic Manager at point 60, and the Initiator at point 90. Then, by using the paragraph definitions (Table 6.1), it is possible to envision what persons who are combinations of the three styles would be like. For example, one principal might behave somewhat like a Responder, but overall tend to be more of a Manager. That person could be placed around point 50 on the number line. A leader who is developing a clearer vision about the school and is sometimes thinking of more long-term goals might be somewhere between the Manager and Initiator CF Styles, maybe around point 75.

Other CF Styles can be imagined by envisioning what people would be like at the extreme ends of the continuum. For example, a leader who scores above 100 would be a *despot* who does not listen and just decrees, whereas a person at the 0 end would display an extremely laissez-faire approach, neither taking a position nor helping with the change. Off the chart, far to the left, would be the *covert saboteur* who works behind the scenes to scuttle the change effort.

FIGURE 6.1   A Continuum of Change Facilitator Styles

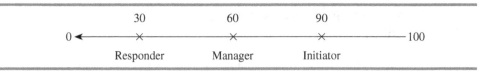

Metaphors for Change Facilitator Styles

Metaphors can be a useful way to summarize a great deal of information and ideas. A metaphor that should help in thinking about the totality of each CF Style is that of a game. What type of game would you see symbolizing each CF Style?

The Initiator is a chess player. Just as chess has many pieces, each with its own rules for being moved, the Initiator sees the individual differences in the school's people and activities. And just as good chess players use strategies and anticipate many moves ahead, Initiators not only engage in doing the day-to-day activities of change leadership, but are also constantly thinking about what needs to be done next. Initiators have several alternative strategies in mind in anticipation of possible scenarios that could unfold.

Manager leaders play a board game, too, but it is a simpler one—checkers. There are pieces and rules of movement, but a less complicated view of the organization. All the pieces look and move the same. There are tactics and strategies, but they are simpler. Still, in checkers, as in chess, the actions have a sustained purpose.

The game metaphor for Responders is that of flipping coins. Each flip of the coin is an act that is independent of the one that came before and the one that will follow. To a surprising degree, this is the case for the intervention behaviors of Responders. Each action tends to be taken independently. Much less consideration is given to stringing together such actions as individual One-Legged Interviews, faculty meetings, announcements, and e-mail notes to teachers to build toward a vision. For example, in one school a teacher was told at the beginning of the school year that she was responsible for maintaining the materials closet. As the year unfolded, the materials became increasingly disorganized and many were lost. The Responder principal did not monitor to see if the teacher was doing the task, or if anything needed to be adjusted. When asked, the principal responded, "I wouldn't check on her; she would think that I didn't trust her." One result of this disconnectedness is that the many small interventions do not accumulate to make tactics and strategies or to develop coherent themes that teachers can see.

Leader Succession.   Another potential application of the CF Styles construct is as a framework for thinking about leadership changes. As is illustrated in the following East Lake School District story, changing school principals requires careful thought. The three CF Styles provide a framework for assessing the situation in terms of the style of the exiting principal and what will be the desired style of the new leader. The CF Styles construct can also be of help in anticipating how the new leader will be received by the school's staff.

EAST LAKE SCHOOL DISTRICT'S STORY: ANTICIPATING LEADER SUCCESSION

Change in administrator assignments happens regularly in school districts and other organizations. However, there are some significant differences in how the process works. Quite often in businesses, the outgoing administrator has major input into setting criteria and expectations about the type of expertise that is desired in his/her successor. In the public sector, this is rarely the case. Typically, outgoing school district superintendents, university deans and presidents, and school principals have little opportunity to contribute to the succession process. One frequent result is hiring someone who is not at all like the departing administrator. This leads to less continuity in strategic directions. The CF Style ideas could provide a framework for thinking through some of the needs and expectations when there is leader succession.

In the East Lake School District, several principals have announced that they will be retiring. Using the CF Styles as a beginning framework, Superintendent Johnson and Assistant Superintendent Leslie Hanson have started talking informally about the needs of the schools. Some of the

(continued)

EAST LAKE SCHOOL DISTRICT'S STORY (CONTINUED)

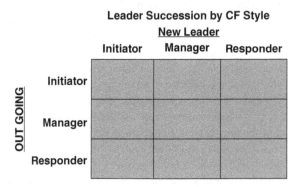

FIGURE 6.2 Leader Succession by CF Style

conversations have been about whether to move current principals. Another topic has been about whether to promote one or two assistant principals, or to hire from outside. Since they are conversant with the Change Facilitator Styles, they started to use these constructs in their discussions.

One of their discussion topics dealt with considering the CF Style of the current administrators. Then they started talking about the effects of different succession possibilities. Did they think that a certain school would benefit from now having a certain CF Style principal? This led them to start thinking about the dynamics in leader succession. For example, what happens when a Manager follows a Responder, or an Initiator follows a Responder? Various scenarios are possible. In fact there are nine possible successions, which can be placed in the Leader Succession by CF Style matrix (see Figure 6.2).

LEADER SUCCESSION MATRIX

Note that this analysis could be done from other perspectives as well. For example, if you have accepted the position of principal, you should be interested in finding out about the CF Style of your predecessor. Or, you could be interested in this analysis if you are a teacher in a school that is going through a change in principal. Another important application would be for the members of a hiring committee to consider the CF Style of the outgoing administrator and what implications could be drawn about what is desirable with the next leader. Interview questions could be designed to seek indicators of CF Style.

The Leader Succession by CF Style matrix also could be used not only to think about the kind of leader the school needs next, but to anticipate what some of the problems might be in the transition. Superintendent Johnson and Assistant Superintendent Hanson continued their discussion by using the matrix to imagine what some of the transitions could be like.

WHEN AN INITIATOR FOLLOWS A RESPONDER

In their discussion, they thought closely about the current state of River Run Elementary School. Leslie observed, "A lot of people like Ray, but I just don't see the teachers making good progress." Mike reflected, "I get complaints from some parents, and there is no growth in test scores." This discussion could lead to the frequently observed step of having an Initiator replace a Responder.

Consider the setting that the newly assigned Initiator will enter. To begin with, Responder-led schools are characterized by the "Big W" concerns profile (see Figure 4.3). Teachers are not happy about their continually having high Stage 3 Management concerns, which is reflected in the

EAST LAKE SCHOOL DISTRICT'S STORY (CONTINUED)

"tailing up" on Stage 6 Refocusing. They have some very strong ideas about how things ought to be different. Remember too that a Responder principal does not make clear and final decisions. We also know that in a Responder school, a small clique of teachers will have more control over what happens and that a large number of teachers will have little say. In addition, each teacher tends to be strong and independent because the Responder's view has been "I hire strong teachers who know more about teaching than I do." The result is that the teachers rarely agree on anything, ranging from how to do formative assessments to where to place the coffeepot.

Leslie reminded Mike of the time two years ago when Eva (a well-known Initiator) agreed to take over Moon Brook School and "turn it around." She was known for having a strong focus on student success and insisting that all the teachers work toward the betterment of the school. Leslie said, "Remember when we visited the school that first fall? Eva had said 'My expectation is that they should get on board, or move.'" "Yea," Mike replied. "I didn't think she would make it. Some of those teachers were complaining to me and to the school board all year."

One of Eva's opening steps was to study closely the achievement data of students and the records of the teachers. She came up with a set of key themes including "Be the best you can be" and "Treat students as you want to be treated."

"Remember Bill? He sure was a Responder." "Yes, even the distribution of paper was unequal. Some of the teachers hid most of it in their classrooms, and the other teachers got very little." "Eva expected that resources would be distributed evenly and without favoritism." "She also pressed the teachers to use evidence-based instructional practices and start implementing the new standards."

Mike and Leslie then identified what they judged to be the CF Style of each of the retiring principals. They used the Continuum of Change Facilitator Styles (Figure 6.1) so as to not too narrowly compartmentalize anyone. They then thought about what each school was like and what type of leader was needed. They turned back to issues that could be anticipated during succession. No matter which cell in the Leader Succession matrix was picked, there would be a need for them to keep sensing how it was going and coach the new principals.

Obviously, there is more to this story that could be told. The purpose here is to briefly introduce the strategy of using CF Style concepts to examine transitions in school principals. In thinking about leader successions, it is important to consider the CF Style of the departing administrator as well as the incoming leader. It is also necessary to understand what the school has been like and what the new principal will expect it to become. Remember also that teachers, parents, district office administrators, and students may perceive and value aspects of the principals' CF Style differently.

CRITIQUE QUESTIONS OF THE EAST LAKE STORY

1. What do you see as being the critical characteristics of the Responder and the Initiator in this case? How did the leaders differ in what they considered to be important? What should the district administrators have done to monitor and support the transition from Bill to Eva?
2. Consider some of the other possible transitions in the CF Style Succession matrix. What about Manager CF Style transitions? What will be the likely issues with these?
3. Which leader transitions have you experienced? What went well, and what were the challenges?

Additional Research and Support for Change Facilitator Styles

One could question whether these different CF Styles actually exist. How can we be assured that they are not just figments of the authors' imaginations? Also, do we know anything about the relationship of these CF Styles to teacher success in change or, even more importantly, student learning? Addressing these questions is one of the important purposes of research. This is also one reason we took the time at the beginning of this chapter to introduce the background studies that led to the hypothesis that there are different CF Styles. In this section, some of the related and more recent research studies are summarized.

Research Findings (Phase IA): Documenting Intervention Behaviors of Each Change Facilitator Style.   The first research study on CF Styles was the Principal/Teacher Inter-action (PTI) Study (Hord & Huling-Austin, 1986). In this study, full-time ethnographers systematically documented the interventions of nine elementary school principals (three in each of three districts in different states) for an entire school year. What they said in staff meetings, their One-Legged Interviews, their memos, and their time in classrooms were documented and described. Implementation was assessed by measuring teachers' SoC, LoU, and IC.

Statistically significant differences were found in the quantity and quality of the principals' interventions. For example, the interventions most related to innovation implementation took place in the Initiator schools, whereas the fewest occurred in the schools with Responder principals. Although the total number of interventions made by all facilitators was observed in schools with Initiator principals, Manager CF Style principals did the most interventions themselves (Hall & Hord, 1987; Hall, Rutherford, Hall, & Huling, 1984).

Since that first study, a number of other researchers in the United States have independently confirmed that principal intervention behaviors can be clustered according to these three styles (see, for example, Entrekin, 1991; Hougen, 1984; Trohoski, 1984). In addition, studies have been done in Belgium (Vandenberghe, 1988) and in Australia (Schiller, 1991) with similar results. In a major test of the cross-cultural generalizability of the three CF Styles, Shieh (1996) documented the intervention behaviors of six elementary school principals in Taiwan and observed the same differences in style and surprisingly similar anecdotal examples of perspectives and approaches to change leadership. Jehue (2000) found similar patterns in his study of military leaders' CF Styles. Although they certainly do not represent all possibilities, these three CF Styles do have a basis in systematic studies in a number of settings and do offer a way to think more holistically about change leadership.

Research Findings (Phase IB): There Can Be Other Change Facilitator Roles.   Further analyses of the data from the nine minicase studies provided important documentation about others who provide change facilitating interventions. In each of the nine schools, there was a *Second Change Facilitator* actively engaged in facilitating implementation. In most schools a well-regarded teacher was given assigned time to lead training sessions and to coach fellow teachers. Rarely is the Second CF the assistant principal; instead, the role is often assumed by a teacher who is recognized for having innovation expertise.

The Second CF has a more informal relationship with the principal. They frequently share ideas and notes about how teachers are doing and what is needed next. This confidant role is why we also have called the Second CF a *consigliere*. They work closely with teachers and with the principal, but do not have a personnel evaluation responsibility.

In most change efforts there will be one or more persons from outside the school, such as the district curriculum coordinator, providing change facilitating interventions. In other

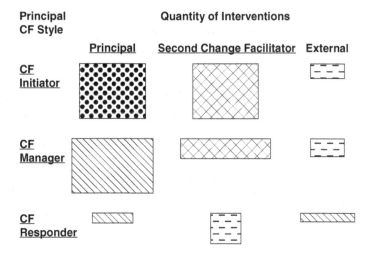

FIGURE 6.3   Comparison of the quantity and balance of interventions for Change Facilitator Teams with different principal Change Facilitator Styles.

projects, two to three master teachers were given special assignments to facilitate implementation across all the schools. They were housed in the district office, conducted workshops, answered teacher and principal questions, and did on-site coaching. We have named these external implementation supporters the *Third Change Facilitator.*

We also examined the relationships between the principal's CF Style and the count of interventions by the Second and Third CFs. A graphic representation of the findings is presented in Figure 6.3. One of the key themes reflected in this figure is that the Manager CF principals did the most innovation-related interventions. However, across the *Change Facilitator Team*, the most interventions occur in the Initiator CF schools. Another important finding is that significantly fewer interventions are done by the Second CF in Responder schools. They are assigned the role, but not given the support to do much with it. One consequence of this is that the External/Third CF has to do different things in Responder schools. The Third CF has to pick up on communications and structural problems, such as scheduling time for observations and coaching, that Manager and Initiator principals routinely handle.

As is illustrated in Figure 6.3, there are different relationships and amounts of intervention activity across the three Change Facilitator Teams. In the Initiator school, there is a complementarity of effort between the principal and the Second CF. Both are active across the school. In the Manager CF schools, the principal tends to supervise the Second CF ("We will meet Friday at 9:15 to review what you have been doing and to plan what you will do next week."). In the Responder schools, there is less communication and coordination ("I shouldn't check on her; she won't think that I trust her.").

Research Findings (Phase II): Relating Change Facilitator Style to Teacher Success in Implementing Innovations.   The early studies of CF Style focused on documenting the quantity and quality of change facilitating interventions. The next era of studies entailed examinations of relationships between principal CF Style and teacher success in implementation. The CBAM diagnostic dimensions of SoC, LoU, and IC provided very useful benchmarks for assessing the degree of implementation. The basic research question was, Is there a relationship between the principal's CF Style and how far and fast teachers move across the Implementation Bridge? Teachers who move to higher Levels of Use, with higher fidelity Configurations, and with reduction of Self and Task concerns and arousal of Impact concerns would be considered to have had greater implementation success. In other words, they have moved farther across the Implementation Bridge.

In these studies, the degree of implementation success was compared with the intervention behaviors of their principals and the principals' CF Styles. In most of the studies cited above, this comparison was made. In the original PTI Study, a correlation of 0.74 was found between CF Style and teacher implementation success. In other studies (for example, Schiller, 1991, 2002, 2003; Shieh, 1996; Vandenberghe, 1988), similar patterns have been observed. As is described in Chapter 12, more recent studies have further documented these relationships.

The general finding has been that teachers with Initiator principals have the highest levels of implementation success. Teachers with Manager principals are successful too, but not to the same extent as teachers in Initiator schools. Teachers with Responder principals are rated a distant third in terms of implementation success. As is summarized in Figure 6.4, these

FIGURE 6.4 Summary Characteristics of Three Change Facilitator Styles

Initiators: *Make it happen*

- Vision
- Passion
- Push
- Consistent decision making
- Always thinking ahead
- *Strategic sense; always thinking ahead*

Managers: *Help it happen*

- Efficient
- Follow the rules
- Organized
- Focus on use of budgets and resources
- Protect their staff
- *Try to do it all themselves*

Responders: *Let it happen*

- Concern for feelings and perceptions
- Most friendly, some more reclusive
- Listen to all
- Let others take the lead
- Delay making decisions
- *Want everyone to be happy and get along*

Implementation Success

findings suggest that Initiator principals "make it happen." They have the vision, passion, and push to help things move in the desired direction. They make decisions quickly and with consistency. Manager principals "help it happen." They see that things are well organized. They protect their teachers at the beginning. When implementation becomes an objective, it is accomplished efficiently. However, unlike the Initiators, they tend to accept minimal implementations and do not push to do more.

The conditions in schools led by Responder principals are quite different. These leaders "let it happen." Yes, they do listen to perceptions and concerns, but they seldom resolve issues with certainty. They continue to be open to new input and, as a result, do not bring closure. They can hear another piece of information and change their minds "again." Statistically, they are significantly less active in terms of the number of change-related interventions they make. The result for teachers is less implementation success and a tendency to have "Big W" SoC profiles (see Figure 4.3). Shieh (1996) observed that in the first months of implementation, teachers in Responder schools tend to use more of the less desirable Configurations of the innovation, whereas teachers in Initiator schools tend to use more of the desirable Configurations.

Research Findings (Phase III): Relationships of Principal Change Facilitator Style to Student Learning.   As interesting and useful as the CF Style idea might be, the bottom-line question remains: Are there any relationships between CF Style and student outcomes? The first major study that addressed this question was done in 27 elementary schools in an urban school district in Connecticut (Hall, Negroni, & George, 2008; Hall, George, & Negroni,

TABLE 6.2   Relationships Between Principal's Change Facilitator Style and Student Test Scores: Findings From the First Study

1. Students in schools with "Manager" CF Style principals did significantly better on the fifth-grade math test than those in schools with either Initiator or Responder CF Style principals.

2. Students in schools with Initiator CF Style principals did significantly better on the fifth-grade reading comprehension test than those in schools with either Manager or Responder CF Style principals.

3. The predicted average Direct Assessment of Writing Scores, based on fourth-grade scores, was highest in Initiator-led schools, lower in Manager-led schools, and lowest in Responder-led schools. Overall, these differences were not statistically significant; that is, the estimated probability that differences of this size or larger could be observed using these sample sizes, and given the variance in scores, was not less than 5%. It is very close, however, at 6.2%. Pair-wise comparisons reveal there was a statistically significant difference between the students' scores in Initiator-led schools over the Responder-led schools.

4. Students in schools with Initiator CF Style principals did significantly better on the fifth-grade editing and revising test than those in schools led by Responder CF Style principals.

5. Also, students in schools with Manager CF Style principals had higher predicted 2006 math test scores than students in schools with Responder CF Style principals; however, this difference was not statistically significant.

Source: Hall, Negroni, & George (2013).

2013). Principal CF Style was determined, and growth in fourth-grade students' test scores was analyzed for writing, editing, reading comprehension, and mathematics. The researchers found significant differences for three of the four subject areas. Students in schools with a principal who was seen to be an Initiator or a Manager had significantly higher test scores, with Initiator schools being highest in writing and reading. Students in schools with Manager CF Style principals scored highest in mathematics. Students in schools with Responder CF Style principals scored significantly lower for all subjects. An overall summary of findings from this study is presented in Table 6.2. Similar findings have been reported in two more recent studies, one in elementary schools (Lewis, 2011) and one in middle schools (Stewart, 2012).

REFLECTION QUESTIONS

What do you make of the idea that the CF Style of the principal is related to teacher success in implementing change and also related to student learning? What is it that principals do that makes these differences? What are implications for you as a leader?

UNDERLYING DIMENSIONS AND MEASUREMENT OF CHANGE FACILITATOR STYLE

So far our descriptions of CF Style have been as a gestalt—that is, a holistic view of what leaders do. In this section we take the whole apart by offering a *multidimensional* approach to CF Style. In our research, we have identified six underlying dimensions. Each dimension, individually, represents an important component of leadership. In combination, the Six Dimensions represent important depth to the overall gestalt of CF Style. In addition, a research instrument, *The Change Facilitator Style Questionnaire,* has been developed to measure each of these dimensions (Hall & George, 1999).

Six Dimensions of Change Facilitator Style

A combination of data from studies and years of observing principals contributed to the development of an expanded framework for describing and assessing leadership. In much of the traditional literature, leadership is represented with two constructs (task and relationship), with each typically being scaled from 1 to 10. In the Change Facilitator Style framework, three major components, or *clusters*, of leadership behaviors have been identified, with each being composed of two scales or *dimensions* (Hall & George, 1988, 1999; Vandenberghe, 1988). The full definitions of the three clusters and Six Dimensions are presented in Appendix 6A. An abbreviated description of each is presented in Table 6.3.

Concern for People.   This cluster addresses the personal aspects of leadership and change. This grouping in many ways is addressing the Relationship dimension of the traditional leadership models described at the beginning of this chapter. As was emphasized in Chapter 4, there is a personal side to facilitating change processes. Different styles of leaders spend more or less time addressing people's work efforts and their personal feelings and perceptions.

TABLE 6.3 Six Dimensions of Change Facilitator Style with Examples

I. CONCERN FOR PEOPLE

Social/Informal

- Sees the school as a family
- Begins staff meetings with celebrations
- Joins in attending ball game or concert
- Very sensitive to staff's and student's individual needs
- Shows empathy through listening skills

Formal Meaningful

- Checks on how implementation is going
- Uses data to guide actions
- Focus is on the work and tasks
- Explains what is needed
- Provides needed resources without fanfare

II. ORGANIZATIONAL EFFICIENCY

Trust in Others

- Lets others take the lead
- Does not have to control everything
- Development of new rules is done slowly

Administrative Efficiency

- Schedules are established and clear
- Attends to procedures
- Keeps policies, budgets, and requirements at the forefront
- Paperwork gets done on time and correctly

III. STRATEGIC SENSE

Day to Day

- Focus is on now
- Today's problem is the one attended to
- Limited, or little, view of the future

Vision and Planning

- Long-term vision
- Depth of knowledge about what is needed
- Anticipates possible future effects of today's interventions
- Maintains a systemic view

Social/Informal. Some leaders spend a great deal of time chatting informally with staff, visitors to the school, colleagues, and district office personnel. The talk topics are not about work, or any specific change initiative; they are social and personable. "How's it going with your new car?" "I think the Red Sox will go all the way this year."

Formal Meaningful.   Having many One-Legged Interviews that are task related is important. Our studies document that in schools with more of these small "incident" interventions, teachers have more implementation success. This dimension doesn't always mean direct talk. For example, one principal overheard a teacher saying that she did not have enough microscopes to do a particular lesson. The next day five additional microscopes appeared on the teacher's desk. These are the types of interventions made by effective mentors and coaches. They offer brief tips and suggestions related to particular concerns of the moment of individuals and groups. The tips can be of the how-to-do-it type for those with Task concerns, or suggestions to read an interesting article or to check out a certain Web site for those with Impact concerns.

Organizational Efficiency.   This second cluster of CF Style dimensions addresses the task or structure dimension of the traditional leadership models. The work has to be organized. Schedules, budgets, and paperwork have to be done.

Trust in Others.   Some leaders prefer to do all of the administrative tasks themselves; others delegate. Different CF Style leaders balance these two ends of a continuum differently. Managers tend to hang on to most, if not all, of the authority and responsibility. Initiators will delegate tasks and responsibilities *to those they trust* to get the job done. Responders and their staff are less clear about who has responsibility for any particular item: them or someone else.

For example, some principals expect teachers to take care of discipline in their classrooms. Some principals empower departments, grade-level teams, and committees to make decisions and implement action steps. Other administrators hold all final decisions close to their vests.

Administrative Efficiency.   Some leaders see their primary task being to manage tasks such as reports, teacher evaluations, ordering supplies, and making schedules. These tasks are lower priority for others. Another indicator of this dimension is how clearly tasks and responsibilities are assigned. For example, is everyone clear about how to obtain extra instructional supplies or to request a leave day?

Strategic Sense.   This third cluster focuses on the degree to which there are long-term goals and vision, or the primary focus is mainly on what happens daily. This set of dimensions is not found in the traditional literature, but is of critical importance to defining Change Facilitator Styles.

Day to Day.   Some leaders are consumed with what is happening right now. The next issue that pops up is the one they deal with. They are not thinking much about the long term or how what they do now may affect what happens next week.

Vision and Planning.   Some leaders have in mind the long-term directions for what they want their organization to be like. They also have in mind the steps it will take to achieve the vision. As one teacher observed, "Ms. J's passion for education is felt by the high expectations she has set for herself, her staff, and the students." Another teacher in reflecting on her principal observed,

She is always talking about doing more and improving what is already being done. When we were designated a *flagship school,* she took time out to celebrate our achievement as a school. But, the next day she was talking about how we could increase community partnerships and use the expertise of teachers and staff to create a professional development school. She is not content with settling on what is happening day to day—she is more concerned with a more comprehensive understanding of the direction the school is going. (Paula Taylor, June 2009)

Measuring Change Facilitator Style with the Change Facilitator Style Questionnaire

Each of the dimensions of CF Style can be thought about and rated separately. Just think about a scale from 0 to 10 for each dimension. The more a particular leader exhibits that dimension, the higher their score. There also is an instrument for doing this task with more reliability and validity, *The Change Facilitator Style Questionnaire* (CFSQ) (Hall & George, 1999), provided in Appendix 6B, along with its Scoring Device as Appendix 6C.

Pothole Warning

Do not be casual about use of the Change Facilitator Style Questionnaire, or followers as well as leaders will become threatened.

Pothole Repair

The CFSQ is a very useful instrument for self-assessment. It also can be useful for coaching leaders, and as a valid measure in research studies. However, if it is perceived to be an evaluation of a person, then the CFSQ can be uncomfortable or even threatening for the leader (such as a principal), and for those (such as teachers) who are asked to fill it out.

The scores for a large sample principals on the six dimensions of the CFSQ have been analyzed and certain profiles have been identified as being characteristic of each CF Style. However, any comparisons must be done carefully and with caution. It can be all too easy to overgeneralize. The characteristic CFSQ profile for Manager principals is relatively flat and at the midlevel of each scale. Teachers see Manager principals as doing about the same amount of intervening relative to each of the six CFS dimensions. Initiator principals are scored high on the Social/Informal, Formal/Meaningful, Administrative Efficiency, and Vision and Planning dimensions. This profile fits with what would be expected from the earlier descriptions of Initiators, with the possible exception of being higher on the Social/Informal scale than might be expected. This finding from our research brought home an important point: Most Initiators have many One-Legged Interviews that not only are related to use of the change/innovation (Formal/Meaningful), but also deal with personal and general topics of discussion (Social/Informal). In other words, Initiators talk with teachers about how the change process is going and find some time for social chat, too.

The CFSQ profile for Responder principals is high on the dimensions of Trust in Others and Day to Day. Responders tend to focus neither on making the school run efficiently nor on engaging in long-term Vision and Planning. What is particularly interesting about this profile is the relatively low score on Social/Informal. Based on our earlier description of the Responder CF Style, one would expect that a Responder would be rated highly on informal, non-task-related talk and chat, but this is not how they are seen by their teachers. In a research

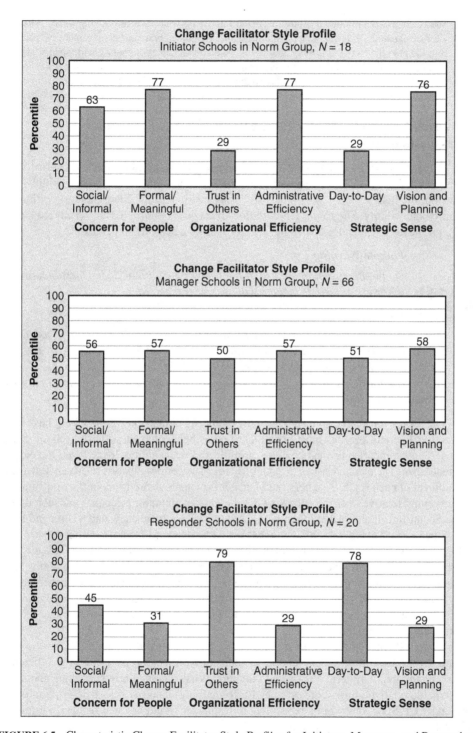

FIGURE 6.5 Characteristic Change Facilitator Style Profiles for Initiators, Managers, and Responders

finding that might be related, and as illustrated in Figure 6.3, we have found that Responder principals make fewer interventions related to a particular change process.

 REFLECTION QUESTIONS

How do you see yourself across the six CFS Dimensions? Which behaviors do you emphasize, and which behaviors are you less likely to exhibit?

IMPLICATIONS OF CHANGE FACILITATOR STYLE FOR CHANGE LEADERS AND FACILITATORS

Being successful and effective in working with different CF Style leaders can be interesting and rewarding. It also can be challenging. Each CF Style—Initiator, Manager, and Responder—brings with it certain advantages and disadvantages. Supervisors, coaches of leaders, and followers will find that success in working with each CF Style requires different strategies. The following scenarios provide illustrations of each CF Style and ways of working with them.

SUPERVISION AND COACHING DIFFERENT CF STYLES

Responders often do not understand the deeper reasons and nuances for change. They tend to focus more on the surface and count on their friendly, nonthreatening style to carry the day. At the same time, they have the potential to be busy behind the scenes, checking on gossip and rumors with their staff and their peers. Consequently, Responders will generally understand less and get less done, so closer supervision and more frequent contact will be necessary.

Managers focus heavily on staying within the rules, following all policies, and making sure the paperwork is done correctly. They also will press for more resources, no matter what the issue or opportunity. Some are fun to coach, especially those who are interested in becoming more effective as leaders. Their efficiency and organization skills can be very important to implementation success and organization effectiveness. A challenge for them can be in letting go and also in developing a clear long-term vision.

Initiators focus first on the production-related needs of clients/students and are continually looking for programs and strategies that can make a positive difference. One of the consequences for their supervisors and coaches is that they don't wait for you to come to them. They come to you! They will push for what they want for their unit. They also make their peers uncomfortable, since they will push and compete with them. As a result, one of the burdens for their supervisor is to spend time in resolving conflicts and perceptions of favoritism. Problems also can develop when Initiators "forget" about a rule or procedure and just go ahead and do what they think will be best for their unit.

SELECTING A SCHOOL FOR A PILOT/DEMONSTRATION PROJECT

Suppose there was a need to establish a demonstration site for an innovative program or some other new approach, such as a magnet school or piloting a new approach to serving ELL students. Which CF Style would be best, and why? Which will

(continued)

be most open to having such a project? Depending on CF Style, the questions and selling points will be different.

The *Initiator* will want to know how this new initiative aligns with current directions and attaining the future vision. If the Initiator sees how the new initiative will benefit his or her organization and its clients (students and/or teachers), there will be full support to go ahead. However, if the Initiator is not convinced that there are benefits for clients and the organization, then it will be a hard sell, and quite likely there will be little active support for the initiative. The Initiator will ask, "How will *my* unit and *our* clients benefit?"

The Manager will want to know about resources. "*I* will need another teacher to do this." One Manager, who one of the authors has worked with closely, will usually go further by stating an ultimatum based in the need for more resources: "If I don't get more resources, then *my* unit will have to stop what it is doing." The Responder will say, "Go ahead—*you* do it."

IDEAS, IMPLICATIONS, AND REFLECTIONS ABOUT CHANGE FACILITATOR STYLE

Of course, the three CF Styles of Initiator, Manager, and Responder do not represent all the possibilities. One must always be careful in applying any overly simplistic categorization. Still, the construct of CF Style along with the six CFS dimensions may be useful in a number of ways, some of which have been suggested above; others are introduced next.

Change Facilitator Style as a Heuristic

The construct of CF Style can serve as a heuristic for thinking about what we should do in leading change processes. The CFS construct can be used to ask ourselves questions such as:

1. What kind of CF Style do I want to have?
2. In the successful change processes of which I have been a part, what was the CF Style of the leader?
3. What are some implications for working successfully with different CFS leaders?
4. When I interview for a new position, what characteristics will I look for in my new supervisor?

Working with Different Change Facilitator Styles

CF Styles offer clues about why and how to be more influential with different leaders. Each CF Style leader by definition emphasizes particular aspects of the change process and elements of use of an innovation. They consider different factors when making decisions. For example, when teachers want their principal to make a decision in a particular direction, what they say to influence the decision making, and when and how they say it, will need to be adjusted to fit the principal's CF Style.

Working with Initiators.   Whatever the issue to be resolved, Initiators want to have reasons and evidence that explain how the decision will affect student success and advance the school. They expect teachers to have well-developed ideas and clear descriptions, supported by facts. Timing is important, since Initiators tend to think far ahead. They like to be able to anticipate what will work, as well as what might go wrong. Providing them with information early in the process is key. Once they hear the suggestions, they may need to consult with others, but they will make a decision fairly quickly.

Working with Responders.   In contrast, Responders will be less interested in hearing specifics and more likely to encourage proceeding without careful thought or fully understanding all that may follow. In their effort to be encouraging, they frequently will agree to two or more initiatives that overlap and may actually compete. In other words, do not count on continuity of support and follow-through. One piece of good news is that Responders will allow and even encourage an array of change initiatives. Don't forget, however, that if what is being asked involves a major decision or may create controversy, Responders will be very slow to agree. They will want plenty of time for talk, which may seem like a way to avoid making a decision. A good approach when dealing with a Responder is to begin with casual social chat and then raise the general topic. An important side strategy would be to regularly and continually monitor other related decisions that the Responder is making.

Working with Managers.   When making a request or a suggestion to Manager leaders, remember that they will want to hear about the time, logistics, related policies, and cost implications. Costs, structuring of work, and scheduling are important considerations for them. They will immediately think about related rules and policies that might block what is proposed. Be prepared to know what resources are needed and have suggestions about how your ideas can be managed. Managers can decide quickly if what is being asked is in line with initiatives that are already up and running. However, an entirely new proposal is likely to run into the dampening effect, which results from a combination of a Manager's desire to follow the rules, intention to protect and maintain stability around current efforts, and the need to first study and ponder.

SUMMARY

In this chapter, the focus has been on characteristics of those who lead change processes. The following talking points are summaries of key ideas.

1. There are important distinctions between a leader's individual behaviors and their overall style.
2. Three CF Styles have been proposed and confirmed through studies that documented the moment-to-moment and day-to-day intervention behaviors of principals.
3. The quantity and types of interventions by the different members of the Change Facilitator Team will vary with the CF Style of the principal.
4. *Everyone* who is part of a change process has the opportunity, and some responsibility, to help lead.
5. The CF Style of principals has been correlated with teacher implementation success.
6. The CF Style of principals is being related to student test scores.

DISCUSSION QUESTIONS

1. The research findings presented in this chapter describe a strong correlation between teacher success in implementation of educational innovations and the CF Style of the principal. What is it about the different CF Styles that makes for more, and less, implementation success?

2. Use the CF Style construct to analyze a leader you know well, such as a principal, district superintendent, college president, dean, or department chair. You also could use a state or national leader, such as a governor or U.S. president. What indicators of CFS do you have in mind? Where would you place the person on the CF Style continuum presented in Figure 6.1?

3. In your experience with supervisors, which CF Style do you prefer? Why?

4. If you were on the interview committee for selecting the next principal/superintendent, what types of questions could you ask to determine the candidate's CF Style?

5. What has been your experience in working with the three types of Change Facilitator Teams outlined in Figure 6.3? Do you agree with these patterns?

APPLYING CF STYLE IN FACILITATING IMPLEMENTATION

1. Use the six CF Style Dimensions to assess a leader you know well. Rate the person from low to high in terms of how much he/she exhibits behaviors on each dimension. How closely does this leader's CFS profile match one of the three presented in Figure 6.5?

2. Ask someone who has worked for a number of administrators to describe what it was like to interact with leaders with different CF Styles. Develop a report on the person's feelings and perceptions about working with the different styles. Also, be sure to ask about the extent to which change was more or less successful.

3. The primary theme in this chapter has been that a critical factor in change process success is the CF Style of the leader. If you were to interview prospective leaders of a change effort, what kinds of questions would you ask? Develop a list of the questions, and explain how you would expect the answers to differ depending on the person's CF Style. You could also use this activity when you are being interviewed for a new position. After all, the leadership style of your prospective supervisor will make a difference in how you answer the interview questions and, if hired, how successful you can be.

APPLYING CF STYLE IN RESEARCH AND PROGRAM EVALUATION STUDIES

1. One important direction is to conduct more studies of the possible relationships between principal CF Style and student test scores. In doing such studies, it will be important to keep in mind Hallinger and Heck's (2011) cautions about assuming direct effects between principal and student learning. After all, principals do not teach students; their effects are more indirect.

2. Studies that examine the interactions and intervention behaviors of the different members of the Change Facilitator Team (see Figure 6.2) would be informative. Study findings could be a guide to staffing of CF Teams and professional development for the different roles.

LEARNING MORE ABOUT CF STYLE

Summary of Findings from Principal Leadership Research: Sometimes scholars will review many of the published studies and report a summary of the common findings and emerging themes. One such review of the principal leadership research is Marzano, R. J., Waters, T., & McNulty, B. A. (2005). *School Leadership That Works: From Research to Results*. Alexandria, VA: ASCD.

Change Leadership is a good term to begin a Web search. You will find a never-ending list of books, principles, and experts providing perspectives and information about change and how to be an effective leader. Your challenge will be in filtering through the listings to find the most salient ideas.

CHAPTER 7

HOW DOES A CULTURE OF CONTINUOUS LEARNING SUPPORT IMPLEMENTATION?

I am so happy in my new job. I am part of the food purchasing team for our district. Our team meets to decide on purchases, pricing, and such. We know that we are successful because of our district's educators' and students' satisfaction and the balance sheet.

—Harold Washington, East Lake District's purchasing department

Our principal expects us to work together on instruction, but provides no time in our schedule to do so.

—Martha Robinson, fifth-grade teacher at River Run Elementary School

Can you believe it? The school board added several days to our contract year, and spread those days across the school year, so our middle school teachers have time to meet, share, and learn new instructional strategies.

—Ramone Gonzales, Middle school principal in East Lake District

Did you know? The faculty and administrators in my children's school get together regularly just like my medical doctors do to learn the latest and most effective ways to teach children, and to review individual student learning problems. Are we lucky in this district, or what?

—Parent, Island Park Elementary School

Our dean is encouraging faculty to meet, to assess how we are impacting our students, and to engage ourselves in learning new ways to enable all students to be successful.

—College history professor at East Lake's neighboring college

In Principle #1, in Chapter 1 of this book, we described how learning, change, and improved organizational effectiveness are related—therefore, the imperative to have an organization culture of continuous learning. Numerous researchers and practitioners agree: The culture in which organizations function, whether they are public sector schools, private corporate entities, or others, has a profound influence on the individual in the organization and on his or her individual and collective productivity. A growing literature has been developing as researchers and writers strive to understand this phenomenon, and to promote the

Professional Learning Community (PLC) as the ideal organization cultural context for learning. Is your organization's culture one of "continuous assessment," "continuous learning," "continuous improvement of effectiveness," or "laissez faire—we've done it this way for 40 years and it works." Hmm, does it work well? And, what exactly is *culture?*

Scholar/practitioner Edgar Schein (1992) maintains that

> *the culture of a group can now be defined as a pattern of shared basic assumptions that the group learned as it solved its problems . . . that has worked well enough to be considered valid and, therefore, to be taught to new members as the correct way to perceive, think, and feel in relation to those problems. (p. 12)*

In today's social, economic, and educational environments, it is difficult—nay, impossible—to ignore the assessment and consequent adjustment, modification, or change of one's organizational culture.

According to Trice and Beyer (1993), it is imperative for leaders of change efforts to be conscious of their organizations' cultures, to recognize dysfunctional elements, and to attempt to guide cultural evolution so that the organization can survive. Schein (1992) argues that leaders must manage cultures or "the cultures will manage them. . . . Cultural understanding is essential to leaders if they are to lead" (p. 15). Guiding, leading, or managing culture is not yet well understood, but much attention is being given to it. More research in today's schools begs to be done so that we might have a better understanding of it and how a PLC culture can be initiated, "managed," and assessed for continuous improvement in our schools.

LEARNING OUTCOMES

After reading this chapter, the learner should be able to:

1. Review the origins of planning for a learning organization or professional learning community (PLC) culture.
2. State a research-based definition of PLC.
3. Describe the values to be gained in a culture that is conducive to change and improvement.
4. Explain how the professionals, and all staff, interact in such a context.
5. Illustrate the leadership of a school where the focus is on the professional development of all, and the norm is continuous improvement in teaching and learning.
6. Visualize how the change process works in the PLC culture.

For a long time, organizational culture has been a subject of inquiry in the corporate world. Although schools have been likewise interested, educators have been late to give attention to this topic. To provide simplicity, and for purposes of this chapter, we offer this every-day, garden-variety definition of culture:

> *Culture **is the individually and socially constructed values, norms, and beliefs about an organization and how it should behave that can be measured only by observation of the setting using qualitative methods.***

Boyd (1992b) points out that the culture (people or human factors) and the situational variables (physical or structural factors) interact to make up the context, and that these two sets of variables are difficult to separate in terms of their individual and collective effects during the change process. Nonetheless, these concepts are important for understanding change in organizational settings. They can offer very important and useful additions to the change facilitator's portfolio of knowledge, skill, and understanding.

This chapter looks at the school organization's culture embedded in its context and how it interacts with the individuals engaged in the organization's work. We know that institutions, or organizations, do not change; individuals do. We know also that, although the individuals change the organization, the organization has a profound influence on its people.

You may also recall from Chapter 2 that one of the six strategies necessary for successful school change is "A Context Conducive to Change." We believe this context is well exemplified by professional learning communities.

 ### REFLECTION QUESTIONS

Think of the following three words: *professional, community, learning*. What kind of mental pictures does each stimulate for you? Describe your pictures.

ORIGINS OF ORGANIZATIONAL CULTURE AND PROFESSIONAL LEARNING COMMUNITY

Obviously, organizational productivity is affected by individual staff members' productivity. Consequently, most organizations are encouraged to remain open to the creative talents of their members and to the implementation of innovations and improvements that best serves their clients. These expectations are assumed to be true for schools as well as the corporate sector. Therefore, whether in the corporate world or in schools, attending to the staff's work-related needs is imperative. Those studying workplace cultures of both schools and businesses have identified important messages for school improvers.

Five Disciplines

Argyris (1982), Deal and Kennedy (1982), Likert (1967), McGregor (1960), Schein (1985), and others have analyzed and commented (sometimes profusely) about the organizational culture of corporations, and how people in particular settings can work more effectively. In addition, Deal and Peterson (1990), Boyd (1992b), and Boyd and Hord (1994) have identified factors that describe school organizational cultures that support the current, and likely the future, unprecedented demands on schools to change.

Senge's (1990) thinking about work in the corporate setting, reported in *The Fifth Discipline,* captured the attention of educational leaders struggling to persuade schools to become interested in change and improvement. Senge, looking to the work of Argyris (1982), identified factors that individuals and their organizations collectively need in order to establish a predisposition for change and to become a learning organization. Five disciplines, or ways of thinking and interacting in the organization, represent these factors.

The first discipline is *systems thinking* (discussed in Chapter 9), a consideration of the whole system that also recognizes the parts and their patterns and interrelationships. The systems approach makes it possible to structure interrelationships more effectively. This discipline integrates the other four, fusing them into a coherent body.

Building a shared vision, the second discipline, is the construction of compelling images shared by the organization's members and focused on what the organization wants to create. These shared pictures of the future foster genuine commitment.

Personal mastery, the third discipline, is the practice of continually clarifying and making personal vision more precise—identifying what each individual wants in his or her personal participation in the organization. Senge believes that unless all personal visions are included, there can be no shared vision.

The fourth discipline, the use of *mental models,* involves separating what has truly been observed from the assumptions and generalizations that people make based on their observations. Here, individuals reveal their assumptions for all to examine.

The final discipline, *team learning,* is the activity of coming together to discuss and to learn with and from each other. Developing team-learning skills involves each individual balancing his or her own goals and advocacy to achieve collaborative decision making that serves the well-being of all.

INDICATORS OF A CONTEXT CONDUCIVE TO CHANGE

REDUCING ISOLATION

Schedules and structures that reduce isolation
Policies that foster collaboration
Policies that provide effective communication
Collegial relationships among teachers
A sense of community in the school

INCREASING STAFF CAPACITY

Policies that provide greater autonomy
Policies that provide staff development
Availability of resources
Norm of involvement in decision making

PROVIDING A CARING AND PRODUCTIVE ENVIRONMENT

Positive teacher attitudes toward schooling, students, and change
Students' heightened interest and engagement in learning
Positive, caring student–teacher–administrator relationships
Supportive community attitudes
Parents and community members as partners and allies

PROMOTING INCREASED QUALITY

Norm of continuous critical inquiry
Norm of continuous improvement
Widely shared vision or sense of purpose

FIGURE 7.1   Six Elements of Professional Learning Communities

Shared values and vision: The staff's unswerving commitment to students' learning, which is referenced for the staff's work

Intentional collective learning and application: The identification and implementation of staff's learning in order to more effectively address students' needs

Supportive and shared leadership: Jointly held power and authority that involve the staff in decision making

Structural conditions: Physical or structural factors that provide the when, where, and how that enable the community to meet

Relational conditions: Human capacities that promote trust and collaborative organizational relationships

Shared personal practice/Peer-to-peer support: Feedback and assistance from peers that support individual and community improvement

This description of the interactive, collegial, vision-, and decision-sharing learning organization can be found in the educational setting (Boyd & Hord, 1994), and it is this new and less than frequently found school culture that commands our attention and challenges our action.

Seventeen Factors

Boyd (1992a) reviewing a wide range of the literature on organizational context in the public and private sectors, identified 17 indicators that describe an educational context conducive to change.

These 17 factors were clustered into four functional groupings by Boyd and Hord (1994): (a) reducing isolation, seeking to bring staff together into closer proximity so that interacting and working together is supported; (b) increasing staff capacity, which uses professional development to increase the staff's knowledge and skills to work together collaboratively; (c) providing a caring, productive environment that addresses not only the factors that support productive work, but also the affective factors that contribute to the staff feeling valued and cared about; and (d) promoting increased quality, in which the staff members continuously assess their work in order to increase their own effectiveness and that of the school. Figure 7.1 shows how the 17 indicators relate to the functional groupings.

Organizations adopt change; individuals implement change, and the organizational culture influences the work of individuals. Therefore, organizations must value and support individuals in change efforts. Leadership for change facilitation is shared among all participants in such a context as a PLC. The unceasing quest for increased effectiveness drives this community of professional learners.

THE PLC CONTEXT AND CULTURE

Rosenholz (1989) first brought teachers' workplace factors into the discussion of teaching quality by maintaining that teachers who believed themselves to be supported in their own ongoing learning and classroom practice were more committed and effective than those who believed they were not supported. Such support was manifested as teachers worked together, sharing their craft and wisdom, learning from each other, and collaborating on problems and issues of concern to them. This support increased teacher efficacy, which meant that they gave more attention to students' needs and adopted new classroom behaviors more readily.

Darling-Hammond (1996), Lieberman (1995), Little (1982), and McLaughlin and Talbert (1993) agreed with Rosenholz, and have been increasingly clear and insistent about the need to provide teachers with a context that supports their professional endeavors and nurtures their collaborative efforts. Their research has revealed the influence of the workplace culture on teachers' practices and, consequently, on outcomes for students. Darling-Hammond observed that workplaces that are supportive of teachers are few and far between, and that attention must be focused on rethinking the organizational arrangements of the work setting.

Typically, school-wide change efforts have been short term and lacking in participation by the entire staff. Encouraging the staff's motivation to change so that improvement in the school is ongoing has been a formidable challenge to school change leaders. If the context of the school affects teachers' ability and inclination to change, what does the research tell us about such school settings?

Dimensions of a PLC

The PLC has become widely heralded as the way for professional staff of schools to work for student benefits. The norms of collaboration and democratic participation in decision making, as well as sharing power and authority, contribute to a culture in which the staff grows in professionalism and efficacy. This efficacy instills a confidence that each faculty member is influential in the learning process of his or her students, persuading faculty that each student can learn with the appropriate material and strategies. The PLC is one such approach to a school's culture. In a review of the research on this topic, Hord (2004) identified five dimensions of PLCs: (a) shared values and vision, (b) intentional collective learning and its application, (c) supportive and shared leadership, (d) supportive conditions, and (e) shared personal practice.

In more current work of studying the outcomes or results of PLC, not only on students but also on educators, Hord and Tobia (2012) observed that as these teachers grew in their confidence and trust of their PLC colleagues, they changed their behaviors. They grew in sharing ideas and became more comfortable in promoting newly gained concepts and thinking. In this PLC environment of trust and collegial learning, there was improvement in practices related to students' needs; the teachers' professional mind-set and their perspectives matured (Hord & Tobia, 2012; Tobia & Hord, June 2012). Their new voice and growth in increasing their knowledge base, their analysis skills for determining student needs, and their increased repertoire of instructional strategies produced an increasingly competent and confident educator—a true professional. Thus, Hord and Tobia separated the two factors of the Supportive Conditions so that six dimensions of effective PLCs are now articulated (Tobia & Hord, June 2012) (see Figure 7.1).

Shared Values and Vision.   In the schools where the professional staff—administrators and teachers—are organized in learning communities, staff shares an undeviating focus on student learning. The staff assumes that students are academically able, and they create visions of the learning environment that will enable each student to realize his or her potential. In this community, each individual member is responsible for his or her own actions, but the common good is uppermost. The relationships of the individuals are described as caring, and they are encouraged by open communication and trust. The vision of the PLC maintains a focus on quality in the work of the staff and the students.

Intentional, Collective Learning and Application.   In the PLC, individuals rigorously study student performance data from a wide variety of sources. They determine where students have succeeded and work together collaboratively to identify areas where students have not performed well. These areas become the focus of attention and exploration of new practices to address the students' learning needs. This approach requires the staff's engagement in intentional learning in how to use the new practices effectively. The conversations that staff has about students, learning, and teaching form the basis for decisions about what to learn and how to learn it, so that staff's learning addresses students' learning needs. As a result of these learning conversations and interactions, decisions are made collectively and new content and instructional strategies are used in classroom practice. The intentional collegial learning and widely shared decision making are in turn applied to action and new practice, thus expanding the repertoire of all. Schools where the staff is sharing, learning, and acting on its learning produce increased learning outcomes for students.

Supportive and Shared Leadership.   If a school staff is working collaboratively and making decisions, the role of the principal remains a highly significant one, with the principal participating with the staff as a learner and contributing democratically to decision making. This new relationship leads to a collegial leadership in which all staff members are growing and playing on the same team. Three factors are required of principals whose school staff is operating as a PLC: a need to share authority, the ability to facilitate the work of the staff, and the capacity to participate without dominating.

Supportive conditions provide the infrastructure and basic requirements of the when, where, and how the staff can collectively come together as a whole to learn, to make decisions, to do creative problem solving, and to implement new practices—actions that are characteristic of the PLC. Two types of conditions are necessary: (a) physical or structural conditions and (b) the relational conditions/human qualities or capacities of the people involved. Examples of each type follow.

Structural Conditions.   These factors include the time to meet and interact, the size of the school, and proximity of the staff to each other, communication procedures, and resources. Schedules and structures that reduce isolation of the staff are important so that they can come together. Policies that foster collaboration and provide for staff development should be in place. Time is a vital resource and the hardest to find. This factor is bedeviling and currently being explored so that more creative ways may be found to create time for staff to meet and to learn collaboratively.

Relational Conditions (People Capacities).   Positive teacher attitudes toward students, schooling, and change are found among staff in PLC arrangements. Staff's heightened interest in continuous learning and norms of critical inquiry and improvement are routinely in place. Staff's openness to feedback, which typically assumes trust among the individuals involved, must be developed for the PLC to operate optimally.

In one of the early schools that we discovered operating as a community of professional learners, multiple activities were created by the staff to support its learning and working together, along with social activities that allowed staff members to get to know each other and develop positive relationships and trust. One of these was a regular every-other Thursday volleyball game after school in the school's basement gymnasium. On the alternate week on Friday after school, the staff convened at the local ice cream parlor to share the week's successes and concerns. Not to create the staff's social agenda, but to provide a forum for interaction, food, and brother-/sisterhood, was a monthly potluck supper served on a rotating basis in a staff member's home. These venues made opportunities for getting acquainted, learning about each other, breaking the barriers of isolation, and promoting comfort with each other.

Shared Personal Practice.   In the PLC, teachers visit each other's classrooms to review their teaching behavior. This practice is in the spirit of peers supporting peers. In these visits, teachers observe, script notes, and discuss observations after the visit. Making time for these activities is difficult, but the process contributes to the individual's and the community's improvement. Mutual trust and respect are imperative. The staff must develop trust and caring relationships with each other. These relationships develop through both professional problem-solving activities and social interactions of the staff. As a result, the staff finds support for each other's triumphs and troubles.

In terms of the change process, when a school staff learns and works collaboratively in a PLC culture, the outcomes for the staff are significant (Hord, 2004; Hord & Tobia, 2012). Not only do teachers express more satisfaction and higher morale (school climate factors), but they also make teaching adaptations for students—and these changes are done more quickly than in traditional schools. In such a context, teachers make a commitment to making significant and lasting changes, and are more likely to undertake fundamental systemic change. In their work together, sharing and promoting their ideas, they expand their perspectives and express the characteristics of true professionals.

Structure of the PLC Dimensions

The result of the PLC dimensions is the intentional learning of the participants and their application of the learning in their classrooms or other organizational settings. These dimensions are interactive, and to identify one as more important than others is frustrating, as all serve to support and sustain the work of the PLC as it goes about its self-initiated work.

In Figure 7.2 (Hord & Hirsh, 2008), we see Shared Values and Vision, Shared and Supportive Leadership, Structural Conditions, Relational Conditions, and Peer-to-Peer Support (Shared Personal Practice) combined as a frame that encloses the heart and soul of the PLC, the learning of its participants. This collective learning, intentionally determined by the PLC members and based on their study of student performance data, contributes vitally and without ceasing to quality teaching and student learning. The frame of the five dimensions supports the PLC in its targeted sixth dimension: professional learning.

Who Is the Professional Learning Community?

As noted earlier in the discussion of the dimensions of a PLC, sharing of ideas and responsibilities is important. The bringing of ideas and taking responsibility are assumed by the

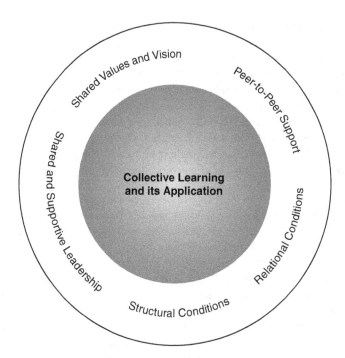

FIGURE 7.2   Two Dimensions of Professional Learning Communities

Source: From Corwin Press, *Sustaining Professional Learning Communities.* (2008). A. M. Blankstein, P. D. Houston, & R. W. Cole (Eds.), p. 35.

community of professionals in schools at the campus setting, or at the district level. Essentially, all professional staff—administrators, teachers, counselors, and others—are involved in reflecting on their practice and its benefits for their clients—in this case, students. They assess what they do for students and whether their various instructional practices result in desired effects. If not, they identify what they must learn to do differently in order to change so that their students are successful learners.

As noted in Figure 7.3, students are always at the heart of the community's conversation and efforts, but it is the campus professionals who have the responsibility and are accountable to serve students well. In addition to the professional community, increasing circles of individuals influence by their actions and policies (school board, parents, district office, community citizens) the work of the campus professionals. This structure is depicted in Figure 7.3.

Benefits of a Professional Learning Community

The research on PLCs reveals benefits that accrue to the staff and to students in a variety of settings and arrangements.

Schools.   Lee, Smith, and Croninger (1995) conducted an extensive study, sharing findings on 11,000 students enrolled in 820 secondary schools across the nation. In the schools

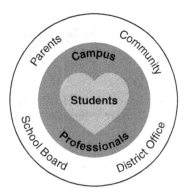

FIGURE 7.3   Who Is the Community?

Source: Achieving Learning Success for Each Student: Transforming Intentions into Reality. Northwest Regional Educational Laboratory for the Association Partnership including AASA, NAESP, NASSP, Portland, Oregon.

characterized as PLC, the staff worked together and changed its classroom pedagogy. As a result, students were engaged in high intellectual learning tasks, and they achieved greater academic gains in math, science, history, and reading than those in traditionally organized schools. In addition, the achievement gaps among students from different family backgrounds were smaller in these schools, students learned more, and, in the smaller high schools, learning was distributed more equitably.

The schools in the study were communally organized, and this arrangement promoted staff and students to commitment to the mission of the school; staff and students worked together to strengthen the mission. In these schools, teachers envisioned themselves as responsible for the total development of the students, and they shared a collective responsibility for the success of all students. In addition, the teachers and other staff expressed more satisfaction and higher morale, students cut fewer classes, and the dropout rate was lower. Both staff and students contributed to lower rates of absenteeism.

In a study by Bobbett, Ellett, Teddlie, Olivier, and Rugutt (2002), the researchers found in a study of Louisiana schools that a strong positive relationship existed between teachers' professional commitment found in the professional culture of the schools and school performance of the students. The school's professional culture was the strongest predictor of school performance in the elementary schools in the study. After statistically controlling for the effects of poverty, teachers' professional commitment and collegial teaching and learning in the school culture accounted for a large amount of the variation (23%) among schools in school effectiveness and outcomes (on school test scores).

Leadership Teams.   In an evaluation study in Louisiana, the external evaluator and external facilitators noted that in Louisiana Alliance schools, the principal, external facilitators, and leadership team supported the faculty's implementation of the Collaborative School Reform model. These leaders provided abundant guidance and assistance to the teachers in using the model. (For further discussion, see "Leadership and Interaction in a PLC.") In those schools where there was more support, and subsequently more frequent meetings of the teachers in subgroups, and the whole group engaged in community conversations, the degree of implementation of the process was greater. This higher level of implementation was associated with increased student gains on the state accountability measures (Rood & Hinson, 2002).

REFLECTION QUESTIONS

In which setting do you believe that the PLC could be most beneficial: schools, leadership teams, or universities? What is your rationale for your belief?

University.   In yet a different setting, Gonzalez, Resta, and De Hoyos (2005) looked at the barriers and facilitators related to the implementation of policy initiatives to transform the teaching–learning process in higher education. The transformation required a different approach to classroom instruction, and this was mandated by the highest level of the university's administration. After several years of staff development to support the faculty in changing their instructional practices and an effort to develop PLCs of the faculty, a study showed that faculty members who perceived they were part of a PLC expressed concerns about their impact on students. Those teachers who did not view themselves as having membership in a PLC expressed concerns for managing their classrooms and other time and logistical management issues. If these outcomes can be attributed to the presence of a PLC culture, what roles can leaders play, or what strategies do they employ to create and maintain a PLC?

LEADERSHIP AND INTERACTION IN A PLC

In a series of articles for the National Staff Development Council's journal, *Journal of Staff Development*, Hord traced the development of teachers' roles from that of individual entrepreneur to collaborator with other teachers in project work to participant in PLC decision making about adult learning necessary to support students' successful performance (Hord, 2007, 2008, 2009). For this latter role to become possible, school administrators and teachers experience a shift in their relationship so that they work on a more level plane in a more collegial environment. Although Hargreaves (1997) does not use the term *PLC,* he suggests that "the central task in creating cultures of educational change is to develop more collaborative working relationships between principals and teachers and among teachers themselves" (p. 2). According to Schmoker (1997), school personnel are being asked, many of them for the first time, to be "thinking contributors who can generate solutions to emergent problems and obstacles. This is something new . . . [to be] brought together—regularly—to be asked for their suggestions, to develop real solutions to the most pressing concerns students face" (p. 143). Similarly, Zmuda, Kuklis, and Kline (2004) maintained that a competent system necessitates several important changes that resonate here, "from an environment of isolation to one of collegiality . . . from individual autonomy to collective autonomy and collective accountability" (p. 1).

Collegial Learning

Collegial learning provides a means for enabling the culture of educational change. Thus, in their study of change, Caine and Caine (1997) quoted a teacher as saying that "actively processing in a social context is increasing my learning" (p. 197). And, in more poetic language, Wheatley and Kellner-Rogers (1996) exclaimed that "life leaps forward when it can share its learning" (p. 34). By supporting individual members, organizational learning can offer a very promising avenue to more successful change processes. This kind of organizational culture fosters mutual respect and regard, high levels of trust, and innovative solutions to problems. The faculty experiences the social and emotional support that these cultures produce. The staff is intellectually challenged by its peers and works and develops higher intellectual learning tasks for students. Teachers' conversations with other staff strengthen their content knowledge, broadening the repertoire of instructional strategies teachers bring to their students.

In schools where the staff exemplify the learning organization, the principal is not "the sage on stage," as some have suggested, but "the guide on the side." The requirement to understand and consider the implementer's concerns and evolving use of new practices does not diminish. And the leadership actions and strategies necessary to support implementation remain *de rigueur*. It is how the leadership role plays out that differs.

Sharing Responsibilities

In the learning organization context, all members of the staff share the leadership role, although the nominal leader remains the point person. Ultimate responsibility must not be abandoned, and the positional leader (principal, superintendent, etc.) assumes and maintains this responsibility—but operationally in a less visible and more democratic way. Everyone on the staff contributes ideas for change, and everyone contributes to the interventions or strategies needed for high-quality implementation (discussed in Chapter 2). The staff participates with peers in these strategies and facilitates implementation:

Developing a shared vision

Planning and providing resources

Investing in professional learning

Checking progress

Providing continuous assistance

Creating a context conducive to change

With the sharing of tasks, the obligation of any one individual is both lessened and strengthened. Each individual has the opportunity to be involved in a highly active and committed way. Over time, the opportunities are accepted, and expectations and norms are established for continuing this kind of behavior. The staff values its role of involvement as decision makers and facilitators of improvement. They experience a new dimension of their efficacy as professionals. In this way, the entire staff develops facilitating leadership that supports change. The first step in making such a support structure possible is for school and district leaders to declare high-quality professional learning for all faculty as part of the daily work. They make it a priority goal within their settings.

Using Conversations

It has been suggested that the PLC is a network of conversations. This being the case, the role of leaders is to support the conversations with the physical conditions necessary for the staff to meet: time, a location, and policies that support the time that the staff invests in its community of conversations. Change leaders must also attend to the emotional and interpersonal needs and skills of the participants. Thus, developing the skills of the staff in active listening, setting aside assumptions while in the conversation, and trying to understand each other's comments and making meaning of them are all necessary skills to be developed.

Additional attention must be given by leaders to enabling the community to articulate a shared system of beliefs, explanations, and values, which is continually sustained by further conversations (Capra, 1997). In a study that asked hundreds of executives and employees to describe the quality of conversations (as a Core Business Process) that had a powerful impact on them, Brown and Isaacs (1997, cited by Capra) reported about respondents' comments:

> There was a sense of mutual respect between us.
>
> We took the time to really talk and reflect about what we each thought was important.
>
> We listened to each other, even if there were differences.
>
> I was accepted and not judged by the others in the conversation.
>
> We explored questions that mattered.
>
> We developed a shared meaning that wasn't there when we began.

Types of Leadership

Capra (1997) clarified that two types of leadership are needed for conversation and community work. The first is the traditional idea of a *leader*—the person who is able to formulate the mission of the organization, to sustain it, and to communicate it well. The other kind of leadership is what facilitates the development and evolution of the community. This latter type is not limited to a single individual but is distributed, and its responsibility becomes a capacity of the whole. This means that the building up and nurturing of conversations occurs in a climate of warmth, mutual support, and trust, with continual questioning and rewarding of innovation. Thus, leadership means creating conditions, rather than giving directions, and includes the freedom to make mistakes. Although the spirit of disagreement and debate is present, these communities are caring communities as well as learning communities.

Other Leadership Ideas to Be Considered

Positional leaders model the democratic participation that they hope to engender in staff. They hire new staff with strong values of collaboration and collegiality, and they reward continuous learning among teachers. They identify and support the acquisition of additional skills and models that focus on resolving conflict, using data for decision making, using criteria for making selection of new practices, and using criteria for selecting research results to be used by the group in improving its practice.

In *Educational Leadership* (February 2009), Hord and Hirsh identified the approaches that principals use to support strong learning communities of professionals: emphasize to teachers that you know they can succeed together; expect teachers to keep knowledge fresh; guide the communities toward self-governance; make data accessible; teach discussion and

IMPLICATIONS OF PLC CULTURE FOR LEADERS FACILITATING CHANGE

1. The local board of education must support, encourage, and persuade the school staff to engage in collaborative work. They do this by providing districtwide time across all schools for the staff to meet as a community.
2. The board communicates to the district community the purpose and benefits to be derived for their children when the professional staff meet and work in this way.
3. The superintendent of a district and the principal of a school are key to the creation and maintenance of any culture; most certainly, this is true of PLCs. Therefore, these positional leaders must make certain that logistical and organizational arrangements are available to support the PLC.
4. Skills for operating as a PLC must be developed across the entire staff; otherwise, the PLC will not be productive. This suggests that the central office staff has roles to play in developing the capacity of campus-based administrators and teachers to work collaboratively.
5. An enduring focus provided by the school board should guide the PLC's work, and that focus is always on student results.
6. There should be accountability measures for the PLC's work (e.g., objectives that focus on outcomes for students, an agenda, activities to reach objectives, minutes of the meetings).
7. In collaborative learning school cultures, principals remain key to shaping the norms, values, and beliefs of the staff. Principals shape culture in the multiple daily interactions they have with the school community. Kent Peterson (Allen, 2003), who has studied and written about school culture for many years, has described the principal as a potter who builds culture through hiring, budget, and supervisory decisions; the principal is a poet whose written and oral messages can reinforce a healthy culture; the principal is an actor on all the stages of school events; and the principal is a healer who can help repair the culture when tragedy, conflict, or loss occurs.
8. Such actions by the principal and other leaders produce schools that are anchored in relationships and intellectual tasks that stimulate and challenge each member of the community to be his or her very best.

decision-making skills; share with teachers the research, and discuss how the results might be applied in their classrooms; and take time to build trust. Obviously, the principal must be current with regard to the research and up to date on data analysis skills. The administrator must also be required to share authority, power, and decision making; participate democratically in the learning community with the teachers; and help them develop discussion and decision-making skills.

 REFLECTION QUESTION
What are the most effective means for developing these skills and becoming effective in using the tools in the PLC membership?

EAST LAKE SCHOOL DISTRICT'S STORY

THE MATHEMATICS COMMON CORE FINDS EAST LAKE DISTRICT'S CLASSROOMS ...

Island Park Elementary School's senior secretary caught up with Principal Inez Hernandez on the way out of a classroom to report that Dr. Stephanie Struthers was telephoning to inquire if the principal was available for a moment. "Of course," Inez replied. "Tell her I'll return to my office and pick up my phone."

"Hello, Dr. Struthers, how are you, and the Office of Professional Learning?"

"I'm great, Inez. Could I have a visit with you after lunch today? I'm keen to chat about our Professional Learning Community effort, and how we are introducing Common Core for mathematics."

"How would 1:30 work, and could you come to Island Park? It would be good to include our instructional coach Beverly Denver and Joe Vance, the kindergarten teacher, each of whom is serving on the district's Game Plan Committee for Math. As you know, I'm working to develop and spread leadership opportunities across the staff roster, so it would be good to involve Beverly and Joe."

"Excellent idea ... I'll be there at 1:30."

By 1:45, greetings and inquiries about health and well-being had been accomplished, and Inez thanked Stephanie for arranging for six sessions, conducted across six weeks, that supported all of East Lake District's teachers in a review and study of data, and its interpretation for decision making and planning instruction for their students. Inez reported also that she had surveyed her faculty to inquire about their *concerns* as they prepared to move into the development of grade-level professional learning communities, now that they had developed their data-use skills. "So, now I'm ready to direct them to review their materials about PLC and move into action. It'll serve their instruction for students very well."

"Well," Stephanie responded, "I wonder if they are ready for that. Do they understand the connection between their developing data-use skills and participating in a PLC? I'm wondering what they understand a PLC to be, and if they see the value in it. The PLC is meant to provide its members opportunities to examine their students' data to identify where students are performing well and where they aren't, and then to determine what the community themselves will learn in order to teach more effectively, with the students' needs in mind. Does the staff really understand that the purpose of the PLC is the learning of the professionals—learning that is related to students' needs. I am hopeful that teachers across the district will determine that they need to address math for their students' improvement focus. We all, hopefully, know that mathematics achievement is at a disappointing level across the district, and that they'll take the Common Core math curriculum on board, but that will require some interactions with the teachers so that they understand what the Common Core standards involve.

"I seem to recall, Inez, that you are interested, along with Beverly and Joe, in developing a more collaborative leadership relationship with the staff. Now that you are well established here at Island Park, mmoving toward shared decision making in the PCs is a way of initiating collaborative leadershipwithbthe staff, and that you see PLC as a way of initiating that opportunity. I understand that the three of you have been reading some articles about how PLC gives teachers voice, and a collective responsibility for students' learning—a big change, and that way of working can lead teachers to becoming more invested, committed, and responsible for students learning.

"May I suggest a different approach to your initiating PLC, along with adopting the math Common Core ... Leslie Hanson and I will be discussing this approach at our principals' professional learning meeting next week ... This is what we're thinking as a result of visiting a district in the southern part of the state last week:

- The first step is engaging teachers in each of the buildings by grade levels or departments in examining their students' achievement data to identify where students are performing well and where their performance requires attention ... staffs are ready to do this since all schools have completed six weeks of study of student data, how to interpret it and use it for making

EAST LAKE SCHOOL DISTRICT'S STORY (CONTINUED)

decisions about instruction. All schools were rather dismayed to discover that students' math performance was dismal. Of course, you already knew that, for all our administrators have been studying the data along with central office staff, so

- the next step is having conversations with the groups of the teachers who have been studying the data; and supporting them in acknowledging the students' needs, and then
- engaging with the groups of teachers in a significant amount of time to study the mathematics common core curriculum that as a district, we think can solve the problem—resulting in the identification of specific new practices that teachers will adopt, commit to learn what the practices are, and how to use them effectively with students.

"We have not used the term *Professional Learning Community* because that would make teachers think that here comes another new thing to land on top of us. No, we should be using this data-driven and educator learning approach anyway; it's a newer kind of school improvement process. Essentially, a Professional Learning Community is a group of professionals coming together to assess their clients' needs (students in this case), determining new practices that will benefit the students and that they themselves will take on board and learn deeply about—what the new practices are, and how to use them for clients' benefit. The significant factors about a Professional Learning Community as a school improvement process are that the teachers are engaged in the data exploration, and in the decision and pursuit of new programs or practices that they will learn to use to provide students with more effective instruction.

Teachers don't have a totally blank check here, but they are involved in decisions (within realistic school and district policies and practices), which increases their interest in and commitment to the use of the innovation—the new "way" in which they will invest time and energy to learn how to do the new "way." All of these steps add up to creating a PLC (Professional Learning Community), and now we review with them what they have done, and pronounce them a PLC."

"Merciful heavens!" Inez exclaimed. "What an interesting approach of using data review to increase teachers making decisions."

"I just remembered," Stephanie said. "There are four teachers who teach Algebra and Geometry at Mountain View High and who have, as a result of their own work and learning together about Common Core, developed into a PLC. They are very energetic and enthusiastic about how they are learning and working together—and the results they are gaining with their students—from their focused learning about common core math, and using it to teach their students. I wonder: Would you and your staff be interested in a visit from them to share how they are working, and how they are progressing with Common Core?"

"Wow!" Inez exclaimed. "It sounds like that team has the tiger by the tail!"

Things are happening across the district in fits, and frenzy, in some cases. Nonetheless, by various means, Common Core is becoming known as an issue to which the schools will give attention. Island Park appears to be moving toward combining mathematics Common Core in tandem with creating PLCs—a significant challenge.

CRITIQUE QUESTIONS OF EAST LAKE'S STORY

1. Do you know of a school that exemplifies the kind of collaborative, PLC/staff learning culture, modestly described at Island Park? How did this culture develop at the school?
2. What is the role of the principal in the development and guidance of a school that operates collaboratively?
3. What are the advantages and disadvantages, in terms of change process, for schools that operate as a PLC does?

Pothole Warning

The ultimate and most important question for a PLC is how the culture or work ethic of a PLC affects student learning results. Beware of this focus becoming skewed and slipping.

Pothole Repair

One of the middle schools that we have studied uses a lens through which it examines every decision to be taken: "Is it good for students? If not, forget it."

TWO PRINCIPALS' STRATEGIES FOR FACILITATING PLC

Scenario 1

We know a retired high school principal and central office curriculum specialist, hired to "turn a poor performing high school around," who addressed his urban high school staff at its initial meeting in this way:

> This year . . . the conversation . . . will be about students . . . and learning . . . student learning and staff learning.
>   *Note:* The ellipses (. . .) indicate pauses.

This simple message was delivered in a clear, well-modulated voice, with a calm but smiling demeanor. This principal knew that a single statement would not gain desired results; therefore, this first pronouncement was followed by asking consistent questions, making comments, and having daily interactions with staff and students, in the hallways, in the cafeteria, and in the parking lot. In other words, One-Legged Interviews:

- Mrs. Falkland, what did you learn about John Smith's reading challenge?
- Mr. Kaiser, I've been reading this book on physics instruction and wondered if you've tried this strategy on page 46?
- Mary Alice, how is it going with the journalism course you're taking at the community college? Last week you shared with me about learning to create interest-piquing headlines.
- Josh, are you learning about colleges for a football scholarship that have a well-reputed engineering program that you're interested in?
- Mr. Albrecht, how is your algebra department's study of constructivist teaching and learning progressing? How can I help?

Scenario 2

Another high school principal in a rural area we know "snuck up on the blind side" of staff to initiate a PLC. Calling the staff together, he announced that the school board was asking the school to provide a recommendation on whether to require students to wear standard uniforms to school. Soliciting a discussion, the principal encouraged commentary. After lengthy sharing, the staff members volunteered that they were expressing their own points of view and that they recognized they didn't know enough about student uniforms to make a recommendation. After discussing this acknowledgment, the staff and principal determined that they needed to reorganize themselves into small teams to access more information from parents, students, the small business community, and any research studies that had investigated this matter. They agreed to meet in two weeks to share their learning.

When they met again and reported, they realized they had no solid knowledge about the expenses they would be imposing on parents. Thus, they reorganized to inquire of clothing suppliers and other schools that had experienced such a change. Staff members noted that they were surprised they did not have adequate knowledge to make an immediate decision. Not long thereafter, the staff agreed on a recommendation, sharing its sources of information used in the process. The principal noted that they had collaborated in identifying what they needed to know, and where to seek it in order to learn about required student uniforms. Further, he noted that in engaging in these activities, the staff members had engaged with each other as a PLC. Thus, he labeled their activities after they had experienced them—and strongly applauded their efforts. Before he adjourned this meeting, he announced that in two weeks they would meet for a half day to study their just-arrived student data so that they might celebrate those academic areas in which students had been successful learners and identify where focused attention was required. In this way, he was leading them to further exploration of students' needs—and what they would do about it.

REFLECTION QUESTIONS

Would one of these approaches work better for you? What would be a good alternative to launching staff into the work of a PLC?

We have seen a wide array of strategies and techniques that leaders may use to launch and develop a culture of collaboration. A final set of ideas, from Knapp, Copland, and Talbert (2003), contributes to the knowledge base of school leaders who build work cultures around learning:

- Create structures for regular staff interaction about learning and teaching.
- Set up cycles of school-wide inquiry into learning and teaching performance.
- Identify and address staff assumptions about norms, values, and beliefs related to learning.
- Recruit teachers who work from a values base consistent with the culture that leaders seek to develop.
- Create opportunities for staff to have a voice in decisions about issues related to teaching and learning.
- Celebrate accomplishments in student and teacher learning.

Clearly, there is much to be done to build a collaborative, continuously learning culture—that is, a PLC—that is focused on continuous improvement.

REFLECTION QUESTIONS

We have consistently promoted the idea of intentional collegial learning for the professionals in our schools and school systems. What could this look like, ideally, and how might you start to turn your mental image into reality?

OUR CLOSING PITCH

Joyce, Wolf, and Calhoun (1993) contend that the design and operation of the organization, rather than the staff, have been the major problems in improving schools. This idea can be inferred from our description of the PLC as a preferred arrangement. Further, they maintain that changing the organization will result in increased creativity and vitality of teachers and students. The challenge, then, is to create organizational settings (the school) that honor all individuals (children and adults) in a caring, productive environment that invites and sustains a continuous quest for improvement.

We, the authors, have lived and worked in a "learning organization" of the type that Senge (1990) has described; we have observed and studied schools that have the cultural attributes of a learning organization; and we profoundly believe that schools must develop this kind of context if real and continuous change and improvement are to occur. We see this as the educational challenge for the immediate future—and it is our own personal challenge as researchers and improvers. As Wheatley (1992) has suggested,

> We are beginning to look at the strong emotions that are part of being human, rather than . . . believing that we can confine workers into narrow roles, as though they were cogs in the machinery of production. . . . We are focusing on the deep longings we have for community, meaning, dignity, and love in our organizational lives. (p. 12)

SUMMARY

There is wide agreement that the professional culture described in this chapter—one with a competent, efficacious and caring staff, whose *heart* and *mind* are focused on children—is what is needed in schools today. Unfortunately, many educators work from a very simplistic model of professional culture.

Pothole Warning

Many school leaders assume that providing time for learning teams and the whole faculty learning community to meet will "do the trick." It just isn't so. Neither has the abundant emphasis that has been placed on collaborative work as the defining characteristic of the PLC been beneficial. Nor is electing to study and learn about the latest hot topic or innovation du jour a good idea.

Pothole Repair

If the construction of a PLC in your organization seems to be stuck and lacks direction, bring student performance data to a meeting. Ask the members to identify where students are performing well—then celebrate these results. But, also examine the data for areas where student results are not favorable. Focus on these data and use them to stimulate conversations and actions on what to do about the disappointing outcomes.

In this chapter, we have shared commentary from a wide array of school and organizational theorists and reformers, all of whom extol the virtues of paying attention to organizational culture in the workplace. We have promoted the concept of the PLC as an ideal form of culture in any workplace and in any context. (We have seen such a culture operating even in a context of authoritarian, hierarchical decision making—as a subculture that guided the norms and behaviors of a small group of staff members.) To share these ideas with others, the following talking points may be used:

1. Although time and a place for the community to meet is, obviously, vital, it is what goes on in the meeting of the PLC that is important.

2. To understand who and what the PLC is, consider the three words: *professional* refers to the certified or licensed staff in the school who have the responsibility and accountability for delivering an effective learning program for students; *community* indicates that these people come together in a group whose shared purpose is to *learn*—this adult learning is directly related to the learning needs of students.

3. The time and place is not for any activity but for the learning of the staff. Similarly, the PLC's purpose is not collaborative work per se, although working collaboratively should be an activity of interest. It is possible that collaborative work could produce learning results for the participants, but whether this by-product provides the learning necessary for the staff to become more effective with their students is problematic.

4. The PLC is defined by six dimensions, or ways of operating, as identified from the literature. These dimensions are shared values and vision, intentional collegial learning and its application, supportive and shared leadership, structural or physical conditions, relational conditions, and shared personal practice.

5. The PLC stimulates and generates values and benefits to both the organization's staff and to its clients (in the case of schools and districts, the clients are the students).

6. The role, strategies, and actions that leaders take to initiate, develop, and maintain a PLC are of prime importance. One set of those strategies must focus on supporting the staff members in transferring, or implementing, their learning into their classrooms. Learning how to teach in a constructivist mode is far easier learned in the community than is using these instructional practices in one's classroom when the door is closed. Thus, leaders must be conversant with change process tools and techniques—which, of course, is what the major part of this book is about.

So, back to our title at the beginning of this chapter: How Does a Culture of Continuous Learning Support Implementation?

The bottom line, as this book has maintained, is that improvement is based on changing what is not working for potential practices that will, and that such change is realized only through the learning of the implementers. This chapter has focused on and promoted the Professional Learning Community and its structures/strategies as the most promising culture of continuous learning, for that is the purpose and function of the PLC—the learning of educators, learning that is related to the needs of their students.

DISCUSSION QUESTIONS

1. Why would you want a school staff to be organized as a PLC?

2. What difference would it make to a school's change efforts if the school's culture were that of a PLC?

3. Discuss the "balance of power" in a staff organized as a PLC.

4. Describe key characteristics of the leadership needed for facilitating change in the learning organization school.

5. What functions does a context that supports change play? Explain why these functions are important.

APPLYING PLC IN FACILITATING IMPLEMENTATION

1. Identify a school that appears to be developing a PLC culture. Make an instrument of the 17 indicators (Boyd & Hord, 1994) by adding rating scales to each one. Administer the instrument to the school's leadership or management team. Lead a discussion with them of their results, focusing on where the school is strong and where attention is needed.

2. In the district or region, identify a low-performing and a high-performing school and conduct a qualitative (ethnographic) study that identifies elements of the culture in the organizations. Or conduct this study in your local fire department, tailor shop, or elsewhere, looking for descriptors or indicators of the culture of this workplace.

3. Find a school that has become a PLC. Interview longtime and new staff to solicit (a) current descriptions of the school, (b) descriptions of what the school was like before it changed, and (c) explanations of how it became a PLC.

4. Find a school that is amenable to becoming a PLC. Use interviews with several staff members to describe their vision of such an organization. Conduct a meeting with the school improvement council to plan strategies for recreating the school as a learning organization.

APPLYING PLC IN RESEARCH OR PROGRAM EVALUATION STUDIES

There is a need for additional rigorous research studies that will lead to understanding the contributions of PLC to the successful planning and implementation of change efforts. Consider one of these topics for study:

1. What skills must the community of professionals develop in order to learn and work together effectively? In addition, what skills are needed to support the community in implementing the most effective strategies and the highest quality instructional programs for students?

2. The most important question for continued study is this: How does the culture of a PLC affect student learning results?

LEARNING MORE ABOUT PROFESSIONAL LEARNING COMMUNITIES

Assessment Instrument

Of interest to many people who are working to maintain a PLC in their organizations, and to dissertation students who are studying the PLC in schools, is the School Staff as Professional Learning Communities instrument. This brief instrument uses the five dimensions of the PLC described in this chapter, and enables leaders to assess the degree to which the five dimensions are present in their organizations. For permission to use this copyrighted instrument, contact the Southwest Educational Development Laboratory, www.SEDL.org, (800) 476-6861.

Recent Books

Hipp, K. K., & Huffman, J. B. (Eds.). (2010). *Demystifying professional learning communities: School leadership at its best.* Lanham, MD: Rowan & Littlefield Education.

Hord, S. M., Roussin, J., & Sommers, W. A. (2010). *Guiding professional learning communities: Inspiration, challenge, surprise, and meaning.* Thousand Oaks, CA: Corwin Press.

Hord, S. M., & Sommers, W. A. (2008). *Leading professional learning communities: Voices from research and practice.* Thousand Oaks, CA: Corwin Press.

Hord, S. M., & Tobia, E. F. (2012). *Reclaiming our teaching profession: The power of educators learning in community.* New York, NY: Teachers College Press.

Huffman, J. B., & Hipp, K. K., with contributing authors A. M. Pankake, G. Moller, D. F. Olivier, & D. F. Cowan. (2004). *Reculturing schools as professional learning communities.* Lanham, MD: Scarecrow Education.

McLaughlin, M. W., & Talbert, J. E. (2006). *Building school-based teacher learning communities.* New York, NY: Teachers College Press.

Stoll, L., & Louis, K. S. (2007). *Professional learning communities: Divergence, depth and dilemmas.* Berkshire, UK: Open University Press.

CHAPTER 8

WHAT CAN BE DONE TO UNDERSTAND A PART OF THE CHANGE PROCESS THAT IS NOT CONTROLLED BY THE LEADERS OR THE FOLLOWERS?

Intervention Mushrooms

Two Schools: Two Views

River Run Elementary School

I was so surprised yesterday when Mr. Raulson stopped me in the hallway to ask about what I was doing with "DOK" [Depth of Knowledge] in math! He never asks me anything about what I am doing in the classroom. I wonder what he was really after.

—Betty Hollister, third-grade teacher

Well, I sure don't want him checking up on what I am doing all the time.

—Yvonne White, fourth-grade teacher

This whole thing takes too much time. I know what to do. Just leave me alone to do it. Did you hear that they now have another computer program they want us to use? There is just no end to the way they keep making busy work for us.

—Sara Johnson, fourth-grade teacher

Island Park Elementary School

Have you tried the Standards-Based Assessment Program yet?

—Mary Martin, third-grade teacher

Yeah! Doesn't it work great? It is saving time, and has really helped a couple of my kids who have been struggling the most. They are starting to assess where they are in relation to the standard and identify what they need to work on next!

—Kim White, fifth-grade teacher

Isn't it neat?! This is what Dr. Hanson said would happen. She really cares about
Learning-Centered Teaching and that our students are becoming problem solvers.

—Alberta Hood, third-grade teacher

Yes, it is the same points that she made at the districtwide meeting in the
beginning of the year. Best teaching practices and student success are
important priorities for her.

—Beverly Denver, Instructional Coach

Yes, it is so great to be in this school district.

—Mary Martin, third-grade teacher

The critical point that will be made repeatedly in this chapter is that it is not what you do that counts, but how other people perceive and interpret what you do. As the preceding quotes illustrate, participants in a change process develop a wide range of impressions and interpretations about what the change effort is about and what different Change Facilitators (CFs) intend. Just because the leaders of a change effort are well-intentioned does not mean that the participants will see them that way. Each participant individually, and each group of participants collectively, will construct their own understandings about what was intended and what it all means. Regardless of what was intended, Participant Interpretations will have an effect on implementing change. The construction of understanding represents a powerful and very different major category of interventions.

LEARNING OUTCOMES

After reading this chapter, the learner should be able to:

1. Explain how the interpretivist perspective is different from the more traditional positivist perspective.
2. Distinguish characteristics of Nutritious and Poisonous Intervention Mushrooms.
3. Describe the dynamics of individual and social construction of Intervention Mushrooms.
4. Identify keys to predicting and detecting Intervention Mushrooms.
5. Use examples to illustrate ways that construction of understanding is affected by different Stages of Concern (SoC), Levels of Use (LoU), and CF Styles.

A shift in perspective is important to understanding the kind of interventions that are introduced in this chapter. In all of the preceding chapters, the premise was explicit that leaders and others take actions to facilitate change efforts. An innovation was identified, implementers were engaged, and CFs and others were making interventions. In many ways, the thinking was that a change process can be successful if all the right steps are taken. The construct introduced in this chapter challenges that assumption. The leaders and facilitators do not control all that happens; there is another form of influence.

The key to understanding the ideas presented in this chapter is to make a shift in thinking. Instead of thinking only about the intentions behind the interventions that are made, thought has to be given to how the targets of those actions interpret what is being done to them. After reviewing an earlier version of the manuscript for this chapter, Carolee Hayes, codirector of the Center for Cognitive Coaching and former school district director of staff development, observed:

> This chapter represents a major shift in the book. Up to this point, the authors have taken a fairly left-brained approach to making sense of change. In this chapter, the reader will sense a shift to considering the uncontrollable, unpredictable factors in change and is drawn into a process of integrating the controllable, predictable factors with those that are controlled only by individual and shared interpretations. (Personal communication, 2005)

INTRODUCING MUSHROOMS: A UNIQUE FORM OF INTERVENTION

In Chapter 2, the topic was the different forms, sizes, and functions of interventions. In all those descriptions and analyses, with the different forms, sizes, and functions of interventions, the assumption was that CFs and others *initiated* the interventions—in other words, they *sponsored* the actions that were taken. In this chapter, we will describe a different form of change process intervention that is *unsponsored*. In fact, Change Facilitators have little control over this type of intervention, which we call **Mushrooms** (see Figure 8.1).

The metaphor of Mushrooms is particularly salient for describing this special "species" of interventions. Just as in nature mushrooms can be nutritious or poisonous, so can Intervention Mushrooms. Some help advance the change process, whereas others erode it. Just as mushroom plants come in many colors and shapes, Intervention Mushrooms in a change

FIGURE 8.1   Intervention Mushrooms Come in a Variety of Shapes and Sizes

process take different forms. There may be none, a few, or a great variety. Just as real mushrooms grow in the dark and are fed "manure," Intervention Mushrooms grow in the shadows of a change process and are fed by the actions of the CFs and other participants. Just as it takes an expert to identify and pick the nutritious, nontoxic mushrooms, some CFs are much more skilled at detecting and sorting Intervention Mushrooms—taking advantage of the Nutritious Mushrooms and discouraging the growth of Poisonous ones.

Two Ways of Knowing: Objectivist and Interpretivist

Before further explaining the construct of Intervention Mushrooms, it will be useful to review briefly two research traditions that have been very influential during the past 50 years. Each of these traditions has made significant contributions to our understanding of the change process. As is true in most fields, each of these traditions has a history of disagreement and competition among proponents. Interestingly, each tradition can be complementary of the other. In this chapter, these two research traditions will be used in combination to better explain and illustrate the concept and dynamics of Intervention Mushrooms (see Table 8.1).

The Objectivist Perspective of Change. From the 1950s to late in the 1980s, the dominant way of thinking about learning was labeled *positivist.* The focus in this approach is on objective analysis of observable behaviors. For example, classroom teachers were expected to describe student learning in terms of what the students could *do,* not what they "understood." Curriculum developers and teachers were trained and required to describe student learning using "behavioral objectives." The design of the research was influenced by the behaviorist perspective as well. Researchers focused on describing and counting the observable behaviors of teachers, such as the quantity of questions asked and the frequency of giving management directions. All were admonished never to use the word *understand,* because one cannot *see* "understanding." Instead, they were to deal only with behaviors that could be observed.

Since the primary emphasis in positivist research and practice was on being absolutely objective about what one did, the term *objectivist* was applied to this approach. The goal

TABLE 8.1 Two Ways of Thinking

OBJECTIVIST	INTERPRETIVIST
Quantity/counts	Qualitative/narratives
Careful observations	Documentation of constructions
Descriptions of researcher-observed behaviors	Description of Participant Interpretations
Taking into account of all possible variables	Rich description of thoughts and talks
Nonparticipant observation	Seen from the perspective of the participants
Rational explanation	Emergence of Themes
Observer independence	Immersion in the place

was to remove the biases and perspectives of the observers (i.e., researchers) by describing events in terms of cold, hard facts, or—in other words—objective descriptions of observed behaviors. This perspective dominated research on organizations throughout most of the 20th century.

The Interpretivist Perspective of Change.   As Kuhn (1970) so eloquently proposed, there comes a time in the study of any field of science when the regular way of thinking and working (i.e., the established paradigm) is challenged by a new model (i.e., a competing paradigm). When the established paradigm fails to explain some aspects of a phenomenon, a new, competing paradigm will be proposed. Such a "revolution" in the study of organizations, and in education research and theory, has been represented by the recent movement toward *constructivism*, which emphasizes how the learner develops, or "constructs," his or her own "understanding," or "interpretation," of reality. *Interpretivists* strive to analyze how understanding is developed by studying the ways people interpret and give meaning to events (e.g., look again at the quotes at the beginning of this chapter). Rather than simply dealing with observable behaviors, the interpretivist paradigm stresses unearthing and describing the interpretations and meaning that people attach to the actions.

Pothole Warning

Do not assume that everything about change is rational.

Pothole Repair

   As is suggested by introducing the interpretivist perspective, much about change is not subject to logical thinking and control. Intervention Mushrooms are not under the control of the leaders and CFs, but understanding them is critical to change success.

INTERVENTION MUSHROOMS ARE CONSTRUCTED

So what does this discussion of plants that grow in the dark, paradigms, behaviorism, and interpretivism mean for understanding the change process? Combining elements of the objectivist and interpretivist paradigms is very useful for explaining a very important, but little understood, component of change process dynamics, Intervention Mushrooms. To be sure, change processes are affected by the behaviors (interventions) of the CFs. But another category (dare we say species?) of interventions grows out of the participant's interpretations of what the actions of the CFs and others mean.

   In thinking about Intervention Mushrooms, Katrina Martinez, a first-grade teacher in Las Vegas, noted:

   – They represent the "fungus" that's found within all organizations.

   – They are found in various areas within and outside organizations.

   – This "fungus" doesn't go away, or may continually pop up again.

   – The big question is how to deal with them.

   There are observable behaviors associated with Intervention Mushrooms. For example, a teacher complains about having to go to a workshop. Both the teacher's complaint and the workshop are observable and describable change process–related actions, that is, interventions. Holding the workshop is a CF-*sponsored* intervention. But what about the teacher's complaint? It fits the definition of an intervention introduced in Chapter 2 in that it is an action or event that can influence the change process. The teacher is the Source. However, the action has the potential to become more.

Depending on how the complaint was stated and what the teacher does next, the complaint could be forgotten or start to grow into an Intervention Mushroom. If nothing more is heard, then the teacher's complaint disappears as an Isolated Incident. However, if the teacher complains repeatedly and perhaps involves others, then a *Theme* of "teachers complaining about having to attend the workshop" develops. One way to chart this Theme is presented in Table 8.2. Note that the Theme is constructed across the Individual Actions.

Recognizing the Theme of an Intervention Mushroom

The very first challenge with Intervention Mushrooms is for CFs and other leaders to recognize that a Theme is being constructed. If they only see each action individually, then it is unlikely that the developing Theme will be recognized and that it can continue to grow. For example, in Table 8.2 it would be very easy to simply react to Sarah's complaints, instead of connecting the dots across the set of actions. When thought is given to looking across the Individual Actions, it is possible to identify the developing Theme.

A next step is to think through what might be the reason for the interpretation. In the example of the teachers complaining about attending a workshop, a number of plausible interpretations can be imagined. For example, does the teacher see the workshop as useless in terms of content because she already knows the subject? Or is there a scheduling conflict because the teacher is committed to making an exploratory visit to a site where the innovation is in use? Or is she concerned that her lack of knowledge might be exposed, and that she could be embarrassed? Depending on the reason for the teacher's complaint, not wanting to attend the workshop could have very different implications for that teacher, other teachers, and the success of the change process. Note that we have not talked about the leader's reasons for offering the workshop; instead we are focusing on the views of some of the participants.

TABLE 8.2   Looking Across a Sequence of Individual Actions That Lead to a Constructed Theme

SEQUENCE OF EVENTS	INDIVIDUAL ACTIONS
Action 1	In a hallway conversation with Bill, Sarah complains about having to attend a workshop. "Why do I have to go to that?"
Action 2	Subsequently in the lunchroom, Sarah complains to a colleague (Judy) who does not want to attend the workshop either. "I don't have time for this."
Action 3	In the parking lot after school, Sarah and Judy again complain and plan to talk to their department chair.
Action 4	The next day during planning period, Sarah catches the department chair and complains about having to attend the workshop. "They are always demanding that we do these, and you know we never learn anything new."
Action 5	The department chair talks with the principal about the complaint.
The Theme	Some teachers are complaining about having to attend the workshop.

INDICATORS OF MUSHROOM INTERVENTIONS

1. Mushrooms grow out of interpretations of actions and events as a change process unfolds.
2. Mushrooms may be constructed by an individual or socially constructed by a group.
3. A critical aspect of understanding a Mushroom is to be able to see the overall pattern of actions that have contributed to growth of its Constructed Theme.
4. Mushrooms may be Nutritious or Poisonous to a change process.
5. In most cases, intervening in response to Individual Actions will not kill a Poisonous Mushroom, but instead will contribute to its further growth.
6. Contrary to what one might predict, both Positive and Negative Mushrooms can be constructed by people at each SoC and LoU.
7. To sustain or kill a Mushroom, interventions must be aimed at its Constructed Theme.

Being on the lookout for the construction of Themes is why the interpretivist perspective is so important to understanding the change process. Carolee Hayes has summarized nicely:

> The metaphor of mushrooms provides an image of fungi creeping into a system without any nurturing or intention on the part of the leadership. That is a powerful image, one which all leaders have experienced when best efforts become interpreted as something otherwise. It reminds us that being right or well-intentioned is only one perception of a situation. (Personal communication, 2005).

Mushroom Themes Are Like Rumors. You may have been thinking about this already. Rumors are pretty much the same thing as the Theme of Mushrooms. Rumors are the result of gossip, which entails a string of Individual Actions. The reason for the introduction of the idea of Mushrooms in this text is to go beyond the identification of rumors, also known as Themes. Here the aim is to introduce the idea of Mushrooms as a special class of interventions. Mushrooms affect change processes. Identifying the Theme, a rumor, is only one part of understanding the whole of Intervention Mushrooms. It is important to see the Theme and the Accumulated Effect, and to understand the interpretation and construction process. With these understandings, Change Facilitators may be able to intervene in ways that enhance or reduce the effects. Simply hearing about the rumors will not advance implementation.

 REFLECTION QUESTION

What are some examples of Intervention Mushroom Themes you have seen constructed in your work setting?

THE LIFE CYCLE OF INTERVENTION MUSHROOMS

Intervention Mushrooms are constructed out of the interpretations that each person makes of the unfolding actions and events in a change process. People look for ways to make sense of and to explain what is happening to them and around them, especially during a time of change. Each participant develops his or her own interpretation and understanding based on past experiences and what others say, as well as connecting to the normal Themes and patterns that are characteristic of his or her organization. Over time a Theme is constructed and used to provide meaning for subsequent actions. The challenge is to develop skill in detecting the gradual construction of Themes. Only when there is understanding of the whole Mushroom is it possible to do something about it. Responding to Individual Actions will not stop Theme construction; in many cases it will add to it.

The Birth of a Mushroom

Typically, Intervention Mushrooms begin in response to a single action or event. For example, something as simple as the superintendent's statement at a school board meeting that a curriculum director from the district office will be reporting on a new initiative at the next meeting could trigger the germination of an Intervention Mushroom, or there could be no reaction at all. If one or more persons think further, then "germination" may begin. For example, one principal who heard the superintendent's comment develops an "educated guess," based on extrapolations from past experience, that "a big change is coming." The principal's interpretation is his or her own (i.e., an individual construction) until he or she says to another principal, "Guess what I heard at the board meeting last night?" Then *social construction* begins. There is a high probability that this Intervention Mushroom will grow quickly, with the Constructed Theme being "The superintendent has another big change coming."

Consider another example of the birth of an Intervention Mushroom: If the principal always runs a staff meeting in a certain way, the staff comes to expect that this is the regular pattern. But if one day the principal changes the way the meeting is run—such as sitting at a different location or changing the sequence of agenda items—it may be seen as a sign of something. At first, what the "something" is will be uncertain. If the principal explains why the change occurred, this additional intervention will alter the potential for teachers to grow their own interpretations. If no explanation is offered as the meeting unfolds, some staff members will begin to develop their own explanations, or hypotheses, about what the change means.

Regardless of whether the principal explains the reason for the change or some staff members develop their own explanations, it is likely that some will exchange interpretations following the meeting. Then there will be gradual development of a shared interpretation of what the change means. The shared interpretation becomes the Constructed Theme of the Intervention Mushroom.

Charting Intervention Mushrooms

As you are beginning to see, there is a great deal of complexity to understanding the Intervention Mushroom idea. To help with understanding, we and our research colleagues developed a framework for charting Mushrooms. Tables 8.3 and 8.4 are examples of how Intervention Mushrooms are charted. The first step in charting is to note the **Sequence of Individual Actions**. In Table 8.3 the sponsored actions related to the principal are listed. In an objective sense, each of these actions may have nothing in common. However, if one or more participants begin to think there is a pattern, construction begins. In the example story introduced above about the principal's change in the meeting, one teacher thinks that the principal just forgot to do the usual routine. Another teacher thinks that the principal is using some new techniques that she picked up at a principals' conference last week. Two others believe that the change means that the principal is looking for a new job and is practicing a different leadership style. No one knows for sure what the principal is doing, but all have an individual *Participant Interpretation*. The mushroom begins to take shape and grow as participants share their interpretations. Arising out of the discussions a *Constructed Theme* is formed that "the principal is looking for another job"; "She has been here for five years; it's time." An Intervention Mushroom is born.

Two other columns of information important to charting mushrooms are *Change Facilitator's Isolated Responses* and *Accumulated Effects*. Quite often CFs will respond to some of the Individual Actions in isolation. They are not seeing an overall pattern and are just reacting to individual incidents. As the sequence of events unfolds, intervening on Individual Actions will likely contribute to further Mushroom growth instead of stopping it.

The bottom of an Intervention Mushroom Chart has a circle where the overall *Constructed Theme* is stated. The triangle is used to summarize the *Change Facilitator's Response to the Total Mushroom*. Often we find that there is no response to the overall Theme. In those cases, nothing is written in the triangle. The final box is for describing the *Accumulated Effect*. This is why Mushrooms are interventions; they "affect the change process." The Theme has its own effects, for better or worse.

The Growth of a Mushroom

Intervention Mushrooms can grow rapidly or very slowly. In some cases they don't grow; they just fade away. To further illustrate, we return to the principal meeting case and its chart in Table 8.3. Over the next 2 days, several new actions contributed to the growth of the Principal-Is-Leaving Mushroom. One teacher overheard the principal say to the assistant principal that she really is ready for a change. The teacher did not hear all of the conversation but is certain about what she did hear. Another teacher, who had been at the administration building to pick up a book, heard about an opening for a principal at the "head shed." Both of these individual events are shared and interpreted by all as further confirmation of the Principal-Is-Leaving Mushroom. Interpretations of new actions and events are shared. The Mushroom is growing and beginning to take on a life of its own. Note that the mapping of this Mushroom in Table 8.3 contains no principal responses since she is unaware that some are seeing a pattern across the various Individual Actions and have constructed a Theme.

The Maturing of a Mushroom

Many Mushrooms become well established and live on with occasional new actions to support them. The Principal-Is-Leaving Mushroom reaches maturity quickly. Over the next several weeks, other actions and events occur that, if the Mushroom did not exist, either would not have been noticed or would have been interpreted differently. However, with a rapidly growing Mushroom, many otherwise innocuous actions can be interpreted as support for the Mushroom's Theme and contribute to its continued and quick growth. For example, the superintendent's unannounced visit to the school and closed-door meeting with the principal further feeds the Principal-Is-Leaving Mushroom. Teachers begin comparing the frequency

TABLE 8.3 Mapping a Mushroom Intervention: Principal Changes Meeting Process

SEQUENCE OF EVENTS	INDIVIDUAL ACTIONS	PARTICIPANT INTERPRETATIONS	CHANGE FACILITATOR'S ISOLATED RESPONSES	ACCUMULATED EFFECT(S)
0	Principal changes meeting process.	Some notice, some don't, some are surprised.	Principal explains the change.	None observed
1	Teachers talk with each other about the change.	Some see it as no big deal; some think it means something.	—	Some energy going into examination of what the change means
2	More teacher dialogue occurs.	"The principal is looking for another position."	—	More energy going into constructing shared interpretation
3	Superintendent makes an unannounced visit.	"The principal is being checked out."	—	Increasing talk and distraction
4	Principal says to the secretary, "I am ready for a change."	"The principal is looking/leaving!"	—	More support for the Mushroom and less work activity
5	Principal closes the door to take phone call.	"The principal has a call about the new position."	—	More support for the Mushroom and less attention to teaching and learning

Constructed Theme
"The Principal is Leaving."

Change Facilitator's Responses to the Total Mushroom
None

Accumulated Effect(s)
Time and energy being drawn away from teaching and learning

of principal visits to the lounge with memories of her past behavior: "She is not in the lounge as much now." Something as simple as the principal closing the door to take a phone call adds further support to the Mushroom. Events and actions, many of which may in fact have nothing in common, are thus interpreted as being part of an overall pattern and Theme.

As can be seen in this very simple example, it is quite easy for a Mushroom to get started and for its growth not only to be assisted but to race ahead without any of the CFs being aware that it is happening. In this case, there was no recognition of the Constructed Theme and no Response taken against the Theme. There was an Accumulated Effect, however: Time and energy were drawn away from instruction.

Pothole Warning

Do not argue with the accuracy or correctness of an Intervention Mushroom's Constructed Theme.

Pothole Repair

Those who have constructed the Theme believe that it represents reality and it is as they see it. In most instances, arguing with the validity of a Theme will reinforce its construction. Instead, initiate actions that are targeted toward the Theme.

An important implication of Intervention Mushrooms is that the truth of the Theme is not easily questioned. For most, the constructed interpretation of the meaning for the actions is accepted as valid. With the case just described, whether or not the principal really is leaving is irrelevant to the ways that the Principal-Is-Leaving Mushroom is an intervention affecting the change process.

REFLECTION QUESTIONS

Think about an Intervention Mushroom that you have witnessed. What was the Constructed Theme? What were some of the actions and interpretations that contributed to its construction? Did anyone address the Constructed Theme?

KEYS TO THE CONSTRUCTION OF INTERVENTION MUSHROOMS

There are several ways to analyze Mushrooms. Some of the techniques can be used to anticipate the growth of new Mushrooms, and other approaches can help to explain those that already exist. Most of the constructs introduced in previous chapters are very powerful tools for understanding the different ways that Mushrooms can start, as well as the dynamics of their growth. Here, the constructs of Levels of Use (LoU), Stages of Concern (SoC), and Change Facilitator (CF) Styles are used to illustrate how Mushrooms are constructed and why they turn out to be Nutritious or Poisonous.

Stages of Concern as a Source of Mushrooms

SoC are a powerful catalyst for the development of Mushrooms. The perceptions and feelings that one has in relation to a change process are constantly in flux, and there is high sensitivity to everything related to the instability inherent to implementing change. Therefore, it is important not only to be assessing SoC for use in planning (sponsored) interventions, but also to use SoC to anticipate the potential for Mushrooms to germinate and to recognize developing Mushrooms. Here again, it is critical to keep in mind that Mushrooms can be either Nutritious or Poisonous, and can be constructed by one individual or be the product of a group.

Personal Concerns: A Significant Source of Negative Mushrooms.   Stage 2 Personal concerns represent a particularly sensitive time for individuals and groups. When Personal concerns are high, the antennae are up and looking for anything and everything that might represent a threat, real or imagined. By definition, an individual with high Personal concerns is interpreting actions and events chiefly in terms of what they might mean for him- or herself. There is less concern about what the change might mean for students or others; the concerns are centered on implications for oneself. Note that the real intentions of the CF are not at issue here, but rather how a person or persons with high Stage 2 Personal concerns might *perceive* and *interpret* actions and events.

Persons with high Stage 2 Personal concerns can easily interpret whatever occurs as an attempt to undercut or attack them. If this happens only once, there is no Mushroom. However, if over a few days or weeks the person *perceives* several events as suspicious, a poisonous individual Mushroom of insecurity and resistance will start to germinate: "The principal doesn't care what *I* think. He has his mind made up already." "I can't do this. I am just going to close my door and hope that nobody will see that I am not doing it." "You know the superintendent is all politics. She doesn't care at all about kids."

When two or more individuals who are growing such Insecurity Mushrooms talk to each other, the social construction process works overtime. "You are right. The superintendent doesn't care at all what we think or how hard we have to work." "Why, the last time we did this, do you remember how she went on and on about this being such a good thing? It turned out to be an absolute disaster." At this point the individual Insecurity Mushrooms have combined into one that is shared and is ready for rapid growth through continued group construction. If a SoC profile were made, it would likely show high Stage 2 Personal concerns as well as a "tailing up" on Stage 6 Refocusing. With this sort of concerns profile, the "here-we-go-again-I-don't-buy-this-one-either" Mushroom can grow faster and taller than Jack's beanstalk.

Intervening on Insecurity Mushrooms.   There are many wrong ways for leaders to respond to Insecurity Mushrooms. One very risky approach would be to say such things as "This really is different" or "Trust me. It will work well." "Trust-me" interventions usually accelerate the rate of growth of already rapidly expanding Poisonous Mushrooms: "Sure, I should trust him. He doesn't have to do it. What does he know?"

Another intervention that must only be used if carefully thought out is to put something in writing. Persons who have high Stage 2 Personal concerns and are cultivating a shared Insecurity Mushroom will be able to come up with interpretations of a written document that were never intended, or even imagined, by the author. No matter how well an e-mail is written, it can be perceived by those with high Stage 2 Personal concerns as further proof of the Theme of the Toxic Mushroom. "See, I told you so. She has no interest in what we think. She already has made the decision."

One potentially effective intervention would be to speak individually with people with high Stage 2 Personal concerns and present a positive, straightforward stance of interest in and support for them. Offering reassurances that the change process will work out well is useful. It is especially important for the leaders of the change process to continually act positively with such individuals. They also need to carefully monitor their own statements and actions for any that could be interpreted as negative or in some way doubtful of the chances for success. Those with supertuned Personal concerns antennae will pick up on any hints of doubt or uncertainty within the leaders.

Impact Concerns: A Significant Source of Positive Mushrooms.   Frequently overlooked in change processes are those people with various forms of Impact concerns. These are the people who have some combination of high concerns at Stage 4 Consequence, Stage 5 Collaboration, and Stage 6 Refocusing. All are concerned about the impact of the change on clients, especially students. Impact-concerned people are positive and enthusiastic and talk to each other about the strengths and successes they are experiencing in using the innovation. These are the people who naturally grow Positive Mushrooms within themselves and through dialogue with others.

The research and concepts related to organizational culture, such as those that were introduced in Chapter 7, are important to keep in mind in relation to the growth of Positive Mushrooms. A Professional Learning Community (PLC) is a culture of positive norms and Positive Mushroom Themes. When talking to each other about successes in teaching and student learning, teachers are growing Positive Mushrooms related to teacher collegiality with a shared focus on student learning. The chart for one Positive Mushroom is presented in Table 8.4.

Interestingly, as in Table 8.4, Positive Mushrooms are quickly claimed by the CFs: "I know that we are collegial in this school. I have been doing a number of things to help this happen." From a practical point of view, who gets credit for Positive Mushrooms is of little consequence. However, researchers as well as CFs need to understand when and how Positive Mushrooms develop, since by definition Mushrooms are not knowingly created by CFs. All Mushrooms begin their growth "in the dark"; it is the more finely attuned CF who detects the beginning of a Positive Mushroom and actively intervenes to nurture its further growth.

Levels of Use as a Guide for Understanding Mushrooms

LoU was introduced in Chapter 5 as a way to describe and understand a person's gradual development of skills and expertise in using a change/innovation. In that chapter, LoU was described in purely objectivist terminology. Very strong emphasis was placed on the fact that LoU is a behavioral Diagnostic Dimension. Further, LoU was defined in operational terms. The LoU Chart (see Appendix C) is composed of behavioral descriptions and indicators that are characteristic of each level. The method of assessing LoU is a special focused interview procedure that is based purely on soliciting and coding examples of the interviewee's innovation-related behaviors. Obviously, development of the LoU construct and its measurement relied heavily on the positivist research tradition.

TABLE 8.4 Chart of a Positive Mushroom for Teaching and Learning Science

SEQUENCE OF EVENTS	INDIVIDUAL ACTIONS	PARTICIPANT INTERPRETATIONS	CHANGE FACILITATOR'S RESPONSES	ACCUMULATED EFFECT(S)
0				
1	First workshop day before implementation	Maybe I can do this.	Reduced Task concerns at the beginning	We are ready to start teaching this.
2	District coordinators show their support.	We are being supported to do this.	Principal expresses support all the time.	It takes time and there is a lot of stuff, but it seems to be working.
3	Second workshop day halfway through the year	Now I know what to do with the next lessons and materials.	Principal expresses support all the time.	
4	Teacher needs extra materials.		Principal hears and provides materials.	We are succeeding.
5	Kids like science.	I need to keep trying.	Kids tell me they like science.	
6	Teachers talk with each other positively.	We are having successes.	Keep it going!	Others see school succeeding with new approach.
7	Parents are telling teachers and principal that their kids like science.	Everyone is liking science.	Our school is a winner.	

Constructed Theme
Enthusiasm for teaching and learning science

Change Facilitator's Responses to the Total Mushroom
Continuing to Encourage Use

Accumulated Effect(s)
All teachers teaching and all kids receiving science

195

Levels of Use From a Constructivist Perspective.   LoU also can be viewed and described in a constructivist tradition. Notice in particular the Knowledge Category in the operational definitions of LoU in Appendix C. If cognitive theory were applied to the LoU descriptions, the Knowledge column of this table would be seen as presenting snapshots of gradually increasing sophistication and complexity of "understanding" about how to use the innovation. Each Knowledge level represents a major step in the transition from nonuser to novice to expert. At the lowest levels, the schemas are very simplistic and incomplete. As one moves to higher LoU, they become more complex and multifaceted. In other words, although the early development and studies of LoU were based in the behaviorist paradigm, LoU can be explained in terms of the constructivist paradigm as well.

LoU-Based Mushrooms.   LoU can be a very useful tool for predicting and understanding Mushrooms. First of all, the types of Mushrooms that an individual constructs will be different depending on the person's level of understanding (i.e., his or her Knowledge Category rating). As obvious as this may seem, we frequently fail to recognize that there could be a number of potential Mushrooms growing in relation to a person's level of knowledge and understanding about what the innovation is and how it can be used. For example, a person at LoU I Orientation may have such limited knowledge that even when the innovation is described in minute detail, he or she cannot make the link back to how the change would work in his or her situation. As a result, the person might reject the innovation because it is perceived as being too complex, confusing, and unrelated to the immediate problem/need.

   This episode could be the beginning step in the growth of a Poisonous Mushroom. "That innovation won't work in my classroom." The Mushroom could disappear if the next facilitator intervention helps the person draw connections between his or her current understanding of the innovation and his or her needs. However, if the subsequent interventions are also detailed and intricate, they could reinforce the developing perception that this innovation is too complex and not relevant (see "Perceived Attributes of the Innovation" in Chapter 10). Then an individual Mushroom of resistance to the innovation could begin growing.

   The same intervention of providing minute detail about the innovation could easily lead to growth of a Positive Mushroom for a person who is at LoU IVB Refinement. He or she already has a full understanding of how the innovation works in the classroom, and how it can be fine-tuned for special needs. If this person were to meet and plan with another LoU IVB individual, they both could develop an interest in taking something new back to their classrooms. If these discussions were to happen several times, a Positive Mushroom related to collegiality and collaboration could begin growing. In this case, the movement toward LoU V Integration would be clearly indicated.

Pothole Warning

Leaders and other CFs frequently are not able to detect some Mushrooms.

Pothole Repair

   Often leaders must rely on knowledge from past experiences and key constructs such as LoU and SoC. They also must listen carefully and continually keep in mind the potential for emergence and possible existence of Mushrooms.

Change Facilitator Style and Mushrooms

Another frame to use in examining the growth of Mushrooms is the CF Style of the leader(s). The literature contains a long-running debate about the relationship of leader behaviors to style, and whether a leader can easily change his or her style. Our studies and those of our colleagues, as summarized in Chapter 6, lead us to conclude that leaders cannot easily or automatically change their overall style. Ideally, they will adapt or adjust their behaviors from situation to situation, but they do not readily change their overall style. Therefore, one source of continuity and predictability is the CF Style of the leader. Whether he or she is an Initiator, Manager, Responder, or something else, that style represents a pattern within which Individual Actions can be understood.

One of the generalized activities in which participants in a change process engage is constructing a shared description of the styles of the various leaders. The Individual Actions of the leader are interpreted within the constructed context of his or her overall style. As one veteran teacher said to a first-year teacher after the principal had growled at her, "Oh, don't worry about that. That is the way he always is. He doesn't mean anything by it." The principal had made a comment that by itself could be interpreted as demeaning of the new teacher. However, when it was interpreted by the veteran in the context of that principal's style, the meaning was mollified. *Once again, it isn't only what you do; it is how others interpret what you do.*

Different Change Facilitator Styles Have Different Meanings. An interesting example of the importance of understanding style is how the same action can have very different meanings depending on who does it. In other words, the same actions done by leaders with different CF Styles will have very different meanings for their followers.

Consider a simple CF action, a One-Legged Interview in the hallway as the principal stops and says to a teacher, "How's it going with your use of the new formative assessments?" This is a Simple Incident intervention that could be coded, using the objectivist paradigm outlined in Chapter 7, by Source (the principal), Target (a teacher), Location (the hallway), and so forth. If a number of these types of interventions were recorded, a quantitative analysis could be done, and different principals could be compared in terms of the frequencies of occurrence of different types of interventions and the difference that these made on teacher success in implementation. This is exactly what was done in the original Principal/Teacher Interaction Study and the subsequent studies that confirmed the three different CF Styles.

An analysis of the same One-Legged Interview using the interpretivist paradigm would be different. Instead of coding and counting the parts of the action, the analysis would focus on the interpretation of the action that a teacher constructs. In other words, what does the intervention *mean* to the teacher who receives it? Our hypothesis is that interpretation will depend on the CF Style of the principal.

Initiator Change Facilitator Style: The "Real" Meaning of a Question. An Initiator principal meets a teacher in the hallway and asks, "How's it going with your use of the new formative assessments?" What goes through the mind of the teacher? First, the teacher will place this Individual Action in the context of the CF Style of the principal. Given that this is an Initiator principal, the teacher will know that the principal is expecting several things of the teacher, including (a) that the teacher *is* using the new assessments, (b) descriptive information about what is happening with students, and (c) identification of any need or problem. Further, the teacher knows that if something needs to be done to support the teacher, the principal will see that it is done. Based on this interpretation, the teacher goes ahead and describes some "neat" things that are happening with students, which leads to a short dialogue and ends with a commitment by the principal to stop by to see the sixth-period class in action.

Manager Change Facilitator Style: The "Real" Meaning of a Question.   If a Manager CF Style principal met a teacher in the hallway and asked, "How's it going with your use of the new assessments?" the teacher's processing would lead to a different interpretation. The teacher would understand that this principal is interested in knowing whether (a) there are any logistical or mechanical problems, (b) the schedule is working, and (c) there are enough supplies. Of course, the principal is interested also in how the students are doing in a general sense. So the teacher responds that having some additional chairs or printer cartridges would help. The dialogue continues with discussion of the need for additional rules about student uses of computers outside of class time.

Responder Change Facilitator Style: The "Real" Meaning of a Question.   Interpretation of the same opening statement from a Responder principal would differ from that of either the Initiator or Manager principal. If a Responder principal stopped the teacher and asked, "How's it going with your use of the new formative assessments?" the teacher's first reaction would be to mask surprise and to try to recover from the shock of being asked at all. The normal style of the Responder principal is to chat in general about school topics or about some current issue in the community or in professional sports, not to ask directly about a specific initiative. The typical response of the teacher would be to offer some generalities, such as "Things are going well," and see what the principal says next.

The point here, as throughout this chapter, is not to present intricate depictions of the actions and interpretations of principals and teachers. Instead, the purpose is to use brief anecdotes to illustrate the Intervention Mushroom construct and to ask you to shift the way that you think about an important aspect of the change process. Rather than thinking solely in terms of what the CFs do, one action at a time, consideration needs to be given to the interpretations that the participants ascribe to the actions. Again, it is not only what you do but the meaning that others assign to what you do that counts. Further, there are both individual and group-constructed interpretations as well as interpretations of isolated events and of perceived patterns drawn across a number of events and experiences, all of which can result in Nutritious and/or Poisonous Intervention Mushrooms.

REFLECTION QUESTION
In your experience, how has the style of a leader contributed to the construction of a Positive Intervention Mushroom and a Negative Intervention Mushroom?

IMPLICATIONS OF INTERVENTION MUSHROOMS FOR CHANGE LEADERS AND FACILITATORS

There is no doubt that Intervention Mushrooms are part of all change processes. In most settings, there is the potential to have Nutritious and Toxic Mushrooms. The challenge for change leaders and facilitators is to appreciate their importance to success. However, nothing can be done about Mushrooms without understanding their overall design. The natural tendency is to respond to each action or comment as it occurs. "No, you didn't hear what I said." Doing so without seeing the overall construction typically contributes to further growth of the Mushroom. "I heard you, all right: 'No one will lose their job *at this time.*'"

Change leaders and facilitators need to be looking across the various Individual Actions and seeing if there is an overall pattern. In other words, they need to be attuned to when individual Participant Interpretations potentially might begin to accumulate into a Constructed Theme. It is the Constructed Theme that turns Individual Actions into an intervention with its own Accumulated Effect. Mentally, or on paper, charting what has been observed related to the various parts of Intervention Mushrooms can be quite useful in developing a full picture. Without the bird's-eye view, odds are high that leader interventions will miss the whole of the Constructed Theme.

DETECTING, ERADICATING, AND FACILITATING THE GROWTH OF INTERVENTION MUSHROOMS

As we stated at the beginning of this chapter, Intervention Mushrooms tend to grow in the dark. Still, their presence may be detected at any point in their growth, and responding interventions can occur. Once they are detected, deliberate efforts can be taken to nurture Positive Mushrooms and to weed out the Toxic ones. However, efforts to eradicate Poisonous Mushrooms are not easy or always successful.

Influencing growth and death of Intervention Mushrooms requires recognizing their totality. Targeting Individual Actions in isolation will only lead to more rapid growth, especially of Poisonous Mushrooms. As we have said repeatedly, unfortunately, leaders do not always see the overall pattern across the Individual Actions that contribute to the construction of a Theme.

It is critical for leaders and other CFs to become skilled at Mushroom detection. They must continually be looking for positive Themes arising out of Individual Actions, and strive to support their further growth. On the other side, they must be constantly on the lookout for the potential germination of Negative Mushrooms. Both start their growth in the dark at the edges of change processes. When a Negative Mushroom is detected, effort must be directed toward destroying its Constructed Theme, rather than responding independently to Individual Actions.

Keys to Detecting Mushrooms

The first key to detecting Intervention Mushrooms is to be continually looking for patterns in people's actions that might hint of a Theme under construction. As obvious as this recommendation may appear, it is not easy to do. In our experiences as coaches and researchers, we have regularly observed leaders and CFs miss major Mushrooms. They readily would tell us about some of the Individual Actions and how they reacted to each in isolation. They failed to see that there was an Accumulating Theme across the Individual Actions that *together* were affecting the change process.

A second key to Mushroom detection is to keep in mind constructs about change introduced in previous chapters. Each of these constructs can be used to anticipate possible Mushroom germination. For example, it is easy to predict that a staff that has had year-long unresolved Stage 3 Management concerns will have increasing frustration and dissatisfaction. There likely will be "tailing up" on Stage 6 Refocusing concerns. This is a fertile condition for birth of a Poisonous Mushroom. "The darn thing doesn't work and no one is fixing it." It is easy to imagine how two or three people sharing this concern can contribute to the construction of a Mushroom that will slow change process progress.

Positive Mushroom Growth Can Be Encouraged

Don't forget that Mushrooms can be Nutritious and a significant indicator of change success. Positive Mushrooms tend to be associated with more success with the innovation and/or the change process. For example, teachers who are excited and continuously chatting with other teachers about the helpful things that parents are doing in classrooms are Positive Mushrooms that should be nurtured. Taking advantage of Positive Mushrooms should be a straightforward process, assuming that the different Individual Actions are seen in the context of the larger pattern of each Mushroom's Constructed Theme.

Intervening on Positive Mushrooms.   A frequently observed problem is that CFs spend little or no time attending to Positive Mushrooms. In fact, they often fail to see their Constructed Themes. They may react to individual statements of enthusiasm but be slow to see the whole Theme. More deliberate efforts need to be made to recognize and support the Impact-concerned people and the Positive Mushrooms that they generate. Facilitators tend to be compulsive about attending to the persons with Self and Task concerns while failing to realize that people with Impact concerns like attention, too.

Frequently, all that is needed is to take the time to offer a compliment or a word of encouragement. Visiting a classroom and observing the innovation in use can be very supportive of the further growth of Positive Mushrooms. The facilitator can compliment the individual, and then share anecdotes about success with others. Another effective approach is to point out the existence of a Positive Mushroom. Once it has been identified, claim it as a strategy that all can nourish.

Mushroom Detection by Change Facilitator Style

Leaders and other CFs vary in their skill to detect, understand, and deal with Intervention Mushrooms. Some continually respond to the Individual Actions, and even when the Constructed Theme is pointed out, they fail to attack the whole. Others are highly skilled at early detection of emerging Mushrooms, and even anticipate the potential for certain ones to develop. Sometimes leaders and other facilitators unwittingly contribute to the growth of

EAST LAKE SCHOOL DISTRICT'S STORY: GROWING A NUTRITIOUS MUSHROOM

Poisonous Mushrooms are easy to find. We all have experienced them, and in many cases have helped to grow them. Nutritious Mushrooms are less well understood and rarely celebrated. There is something about the compulsive nature of educators that makes them overlook or discount the positive aspects of their work. The following is a short story about one Nutritious Mushroom. See Table 8.4 for a chart of this Intervention Mushroom.

This Nutritious Mushroom, which we shall call "enthusiasm for teaching and learning science," grew in Island Park Elementary School as the new science curriculum was being pilot-tested. Dr. Hanson (assistant superintendent) had decided that the year before the whole district would implement the new science program and the new national science standards, one school should take the lead with learning about it. The new program represented change, especially since up until then there had been little science teaching in elementary schools. "It isn't on the tests, so we have focused mainly on ELA and math."

The new science program contained the usual elements: manipulative materials, living organisms, cooperative groups, and field trips. The program also was based in the new standards, which address "crosscutting concepts" and "disciplinary core ideas." Probably the biggest difference was that there was no science textbook! One source of support for the pilot test was a set of professional development days for all Island Park teachers. The days were spread across the school year and designed to be Concerns Based by regularly assessing SoC and adjusting each day's sessions accordingly.

As the fall use of the program unfolded, teachers had the predictable array of Stage 3 Management concerns, such as "The daphnia are dying" and "The crickets escaped!" If not attended to, these Individual Actions could start the construction of Negative Mushrooms "about the time it takes, and all the work and mess."

Throughout the fall, the district science coordinator spent a lot of time at the school. As an experienced and respected science teacher, he was good at anticipating possible LoU III Mechanical Use problems (see Chapter 5). He helped prepare materials, reminded teachers of what was coming next, and suggested which pages in the Teacher's Guide had the how-to-do-it tips for the next lesson. "Don't forget to put the crickets in plastic containers. They will eat their way out of paper bags." As the fall months unfolded, the incipient Negative Mushrooms didn't continue to grow. Anticipating SoC Stage 3 Management concerns had resulted in these concerns staying low.

Also, it was clear that the principal, Inez Hernandez, was an Initiator (see Chapter 6). She was very supportive of the school being the one to pilot-test the new approach to teaching science. She advocated for the new approach with teachers, students, and parents. She also did the little things that signaled she was willing to help. She had attended the introductory workshop and closely monitored how implementation was going for teachers, students, and parents. She too made sure teachers had the necessary materials, and that schedules were supportive. In addition, she expected all teachers to use the new program. She regularly visited classrooms when science was being taught. "I also asked Bev (the instructional coach) to be sure to keep in close touch with all the teachers and to let me know about any concerns that were coming up. I sure want this pilot to go super-well and have Island Park Elementary School be seen as doing a great job with teaching science."

As implementation unfolded, teachers were discovering that their students liked the new approach. Several teachers reported, "My kids want science every day!" Parents began commenting about their children's enthusiasm for science. The district office science coordinator (Bryan Lincoln) was pleased with how implementation was progressing, and was telling other principals and teachers in other schools that the pilot at Island Park was going "super-well."

(continued)

EAST LAKE SCHOOL DISTRICT'S STORY (CONTINUED)

Further evidence of the growing positive Constructed Theme was that the early May SoC Questionnaire (see Chapter 4) profiles were much lower on Stage 1 Informational, Stage 2 Personal, and Stage 3 Management concerns. Further, there was a little increase in intensity of Stage 4 Consequence concerns.

All the actions and indicators document the spontaneous birth and growth of a Nutritious Mushroom. Everyone was talking positively about what was occurring around the use of the new approach. In February, when Dr. Hanson pointed out the emerging Nutritious Mushroom Theme to Ms. Hernandez, she said, "This has been part of my plan all along." However, we researchers have a different hypothesis: Ms. Hernandez's supportive actions and the early anticipation of potential Task Concerns resulted in teachers' Stage 3 Management concerns not becoming intense. Most certainly Ms. Hernandez reinforced and nurtured the growth of a Positive Mushroom. She and the science coordinator made every effort to reduce the potential arousal of Task Concerns and anticipated potential events that could contribute to the growth of a Poisonous Mushroom. The extent to which they knowingly engineered the construction of a Positive Mushroom could be debated. In some settings the very same interventions could have led to resistance and the growth of Toxic Mushrooms. As we keep saying, the leader's intentions behind interventions may not be what others interpret them to be. In this case, through accident or proactive principal and science coordinator leadership, the clear consequence was the construction of a dynamic and Positive Intervention Mushroom related to schoolwide implementation success. The Accumulated Effect was subsequent district adoption of the new science program.

CASE CRITIQUE QUESTIONS

1. What do you see as being key characteristics of the Individual Actions that contributed to the construction of this Nutritious Mushroom?
2. What type of action could lead to the death of this Positive Mushroom? How long would it take to kill it?
3. In this case, the principal claimed that the Nutritious Mushroom had been part of her plan from the very beginning. In what ways would this seem to be the case?
4. What was the science coordinator's role in the continued growth of this Nutritious Mushroom? How did the teachers contribute? Did the students also have a role?

---

a Mushroom. For example, a principal not attending a staff meeting may receive little attention. However, by the time the principal misses three meetings in a row and no explanation is provided, a Toxic Mushroom will likely be germinating.

Initiator Change Facilitator Style Leaders Are Early Detectors. Initiator CF Style leaders are good at Mushroom detection and disposal. They detect Positive Mushrooms almost as soon as they germinate. They take advantage of Nutritious Mushrooms by supporting and nourishing their further growth. They also are quick to claim Positive Mushrooms as something they caused to happen. Initiators cheer on individuals and teams to keep going. They will encourage spread of a Theme by linking Impact-concerned people with those who have Task and Self concerns. They will provide extra resources or offer a special award to keep a Positive Mushroom growing. They may make a special point to acknowledge a Positive Mushroom in a staff meeting and recruit others to do things that contribute to its development. On the other hand, Initiators are telepathic about sensing the emergence of Poisonous

Mushrooms and are quick to take actions to kill them, neutralize their toxicity, or turn them into Nutritious Mushrooms. In both cases, Initiators do not waste time on Individual Actions; they see the overall pattern, anticipate what is likely to happen next, and go right at the Constructed Theme.

Responder Change Facilitator Style Leaders Respond to Some of the Individual Actions. Responders tend not to see the overall Mushroom pattern and Theme, which means that when they do react, they tend to respond to some of the Individual Actions instead of the Constructed Theme. The result is a lot of flitting around from complaint to complaint in response to what was heard last. This approach reduces continuity and contributes to the growth of existing Negative Mushrooms and often fosters the development of new ones. Very few Positive Mushrooms seem to grow in Responder-led organizations, while Negative Mushrooms thrive.

Manager Change Facilitator Style Leaders Keep Things Evened Out.   Managers, as would be expected, primarily attend to the potential growth of Mushrooms related to resources, logistics, and following of all the rules and procedures. They are so efficient that, if it is within their control, Negative Mushrooms related to these issues will not grow. Although we do not have research related to the type and distribution of Mushrooms by CF Style of the leader, a working hypothesis is that there are fewer Mushrooms of either type with Manager CF Style leaders. Everyone is treated equally, resources are organized, external pressures are dampened, and rules and procedures are clear. Also, less proactive energy is likely to be directed toward the growth of Positive Mushrooms.

In the ideal setting, the most effective CFs are both objectivist and interpretivist. They observe behaviors, and they assess how things are going. They use these diagnostic data to anticipate likely interpretations that could be made, and they listen for individual and social construction of meaning. They check for understanding and map the overall pattern of Individual Actions that may combine and become a Mushroom. By keeping the big picture in mind, they are better able to respond to Individual Actions and events as they unfold. They then are prepared to sense the emergence of a Constructed Theme. With this approach, Mushrooms grow for a shorter period in the dark, and more of them can be put to positive use as the change process continues to unfold.

Pothole Warning

Some Intervention Mushrooms cannot be eliminated; they keep coming back.

Pothole Repair

Some Mushrooms won't die; they have to be tolerated, with occasional actions to keep them from flourishing. An important consideration is to reflect on how much effort to invest in restricting the growth of difficult-to-kill Poisonous Mushrooms. Too much time spent in this effort is time not spent on facilitating further implementation.

EVERGREEN MUSHROOMS

Some Mushrooms simply will not go away. No matter what is tried, they just keep coming back. We call them Evergreen Mushrooms. One example of an Evergreen Mushroom that we have experienced several times is the two-against-one Mushroom that grows in a school with three teachers at one grade level, or three teachers teaching the same subject. It also can happen among three or more department chairs or team leaders. Using the three-teacher example keeps the illustration of Evergreen Mushrooms relatively simple. A natural occurrence, due to the intensity of the work and the extensive time in the same work environment, will be an occasion for two of the three to become upset with the third. The two start having whispered conversations and leave out the third. After a while, work tasks are dropped ("That was Todd's responsibility") or a key piece of information is not communicated due to the unwillingness to talk with each other. An initial attempt to stop the growth of an Evergreen Mushroom is for the leader to talk to each teacher individually, and ask what can be done to resolve the issue. This seems to take care of the problem. The three return to working as a team.

However, within months, again two of the three are at odds with the third. It may be a different two, but the same scenario starts to unfold. Communications are dropped and certain tasks are not done. The two have whispered conversations about the third. The leader's first thought is something like "Here we go again." The response to the Theme this time could be to take all three to lunch and talk through the problem. Perhaps some tasks are restructured or schedules are changed. Following this response to the Constructed Theme, the three go back to being a team—for a while. However, no matter what interventions have been tried, in time this Evergreen Mushroom returns. Some Mushrooms cannot be killed; they just have to be tolerated.

Many other Evergreen Mushrooms could be discussed, such as the annual panic around creating the revised strategic improvement plan, the trauma surrounding yearly evaluations, and the disbelief over administering standardized achievement tests to all students at a late time of year such that by the time the results are returned they are of little use. These examples won't be mapped out here, but the key point to remember is that part of the wisdom of leading and facilitating change is to recognize when Mushrooms are not likely to go away. Some parts of the change process, such as Evergreen Mushrooms, need to be understood and then worked around.

As a check on your understanding, review the Indicators of Mushroom Interventions, introduced earlier in this chapter, for reminders of how to recognize and attempt to influence the growth of Intervention Mushrooms.

Sometimes Doing Nothing Is Best

The majority of the discussion up to this point has assumed that leaders and other CFs can take actions to accelerate growth or reduce the effects of Intervention Mushrooms. However, with some Mushrooms, no action is best. Sometimes any action taken just adds to Mushroom growth. For example, a mayor may make one small comment, such as "The police acted stupidly." The media and the mayor's political opponents then take the statement out of context and for days add their interpretations of its meaning, thereby growing a Mushroom. In an attempt to kill the Mushroom, the mayor says, "That is not what I said." This response just adds fertilizer. The next day he offers an expanded apology, and then invites the chief of police to lunch. Those growing the Negative Mushroom quickly label the apology as "incomplete" and the meeting as the "Lunch Summit." In this case, as well as with others, there are times when the best response is to do nothing and hope that with time the Mushroom will wither.

REFLECTION QUESTIONS
How good are you at detecting Intervention Mushrooms? What have you done to encourage the growth of a Mushroom? Have you ever tried to kill one? What happened?

SUMMARY

The success of any change effort is dependent not only on what the CFs do, but also on how the participants individually and collectively interpret and construct meaning for these actions and events. Here is a brief list of key talking points about Intervention Mushrooms.

1. Intervention Mushrooms are the result of individual and social construction.
2. Intervention Mushrooms provide a means for making sense within efforts to implement today's complex and sophisticated innovations.
3. Failing to understand the potential for growth of Intervention Mushrooms adds to the uncertainty and can extend the time it takes to move across the Implementation Bridge.
4. Success in facilitating change depends heavily on one's ability to detect Mushrooms early in their genesis.
5. More successful CFs are skilled at early detection and quick to see the overall pattern and Constructed Themes of both Positive and Negative Mushrooms.
6. Managing Mushroom Interventions requires taking actions that are aimed at their totality, the Constructed Theme, rather than just addressing some of the Individual Actions.

DISCUSSION QUESTIONS

1. Think about a Nutritious Mushroom that you have experienced. What name would you give it? What was done to keep it growing?

2. Describe and analyze a Poisonous Mushroom that you have seen. What name would you give it? What was done to kill it? What was done to sustain it?

3. What skills do you see being important to detecting Nutritious and Poisonous Mushrooms?

4. In your experience, what important ideas should you keep in mind when intervening on Positive and Negative Mushrooms?

5. For each SoC, predict likely Positive and Negative Mushrooms for a staff that has high concerns at each stage.

6. Describe experiences you have had or observed about the construction of Mushrooms with leaders using different CF Styles. Did they react to individual Incidents or to the totality of Mushrooms?

APPLYING INTERVENTION MUSHROOMS IN FACILITATING IMPLEMENTATION

1. Interview a CF about the degree to which he or she is sensitive to and watches for overall patterns in a change process. See if this person can describe examples of Positive and Negative Mushrooms he or she has experienced. What did he or she do to support or discourage the growth of particular Mushrooms? As was done in Tables 8.3 and 8.4, develop a chart for one of these Mushrooms to share in class. Estimate the person's CF Style and consider whether that style is related to his or her perception and handling of Mushrooms.

2. Follow the national news for several weeks and look for the growth of Mushrooms. Identify and chart the growth of one such Mushroom. List some of the Individual Actions. What is the Constructed Theme? After studying your Mushroom chart as a change process consultant, what would you advise the person(s) to do now?

APPLYING INTERVENTION MUSHROOMS IN RESEARCH AND PROGRAM EVALUATION STUDIES

1. Our understanding of Intervention Mushrooms is much more limited than for many of the other constructs introduced in this book. To understand more, systematic studies of the construction of Nutritious and Poisonous Mushrooms are needed. Better procedures for detecting Mushrooms would be of help in research and in developing change leaders. We also need many more examples of interventions targeted at Constructed Themes. Since Mushrooms are individual and social constructions, it is likely that more of the studies will use qualitative methods.

2. A working hypothesis, based on clinical experience with change processes, is that Initiators are quite good at detecting Mushrooms. Assuming this is the case, how do they do it? What are their clues? In several cases, we have observed that Initiators anticipate the birth of Mushrooms. What do they look for, and what frames of analysis are they employing?

3. Alternatively, it appears that organizations led by Responders have more Poisonous Mushrooms. If so, why is this the case? What could be done to reduce the potential for the occurrence of Poisonous Mushrooms? What drives their construction, especially when they hurt individuals and the organization as a whole?

LEARNING MORE ABOUT INTERVENTION MUSHROOMS

- A very useful approach to understanding Intervention Mushrooms is to learn about the meaning of symbols. An interesting approach to the meaning of symbols in organizations can be found in Bolman, L. G., & Deal, T. E. (2008). Part V: The Symbolic Frame. *Reframing organizations: artistry, choice, and leadership*. San Francisco, CA: Jossey-Bass.
- Another way to think about the Theme of Intervention Mushrooms is to recognize that they are similar to rumors. Stephen P. Robbins (2013) addresses this idea in Part IV, "The Truth About Communication," which includes "Truth 34: Hearing Isn't Listening," in *The Truth About Managing People* (3rd edition). Upper Saddle River, NJ: Pearson.
- As with any other topic, a lot can be learned related to Intervention Mushrooms by doing a web search. Type in "gossip and rumors in the workplace" and a long list of potentially interesting items will pop up.

DIFFERENT PERSPECTIVES FOR UNDERSTANDING THE BIG PICTURE OF CHANGE

Systems, Diffusion, and Organization Development

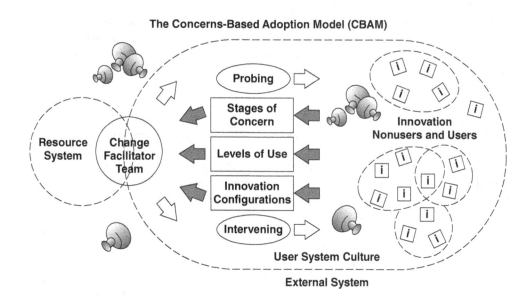

The Concerns-Based Adoption Model (CBAM)

207

Chapters 9, 10, and 11 provide macro perspectives for understanding change. The flow of the previous parts has been from the individual to views of how change processes unfold across whole organizations and agencies. Different elements of the Concerns Based Adoption Model (CBAM) have been highlighted to show where that part's content fits into a holistic view. However, there are other broad view perspectives for understanding, facilitating, and studying change processes. Each of these other perspectives has an extensive history of study and application. Each is widely applied and quoted. Each places heavy emphasis on certain constructs and ways of thinking.

In Chapter 9—How Can Systems Thinking Enhance the Success of Change Efforts?— introduces *systems*. In the systems perspective, the focus is on understanding the many sub-parts of an organization (or other agency) and how they interrelate. If one part, a *subsystem*, does something, other parts will be affected. This perspective places heavy emphasis on *systems thinking*. Leaders should be continuously thinking about the system as a whole, the various subsystems, and how actions and systemic reactions can unfold.

Chapter 10—How Do Communication Activities and Change Agents Affect Implementation?—introduces the most classic of change perspectives, *diffusion*. The rich history of studying change in this perspective was done in various social systems, rather than in formal organizations. An important premise is that the spread in the adoption of innovations takes place through communication—people talking to people. The study of the introduction of innovations to farmers and doctors, and across the members of a rural village, forms the historical foundation for the Diffusion perspective. Today, the constructs are used to study the spread of adoption of new technologies such as cell phones and apps. There are a number of important lessons for students of change, such as learning about the characteristics of people who are first, and last, to adopt an innovation.

Chapter 11—In What Ways Can Team Member Skills and Process Consultants Affect Implementation?—introduces another change perspective—*Organization Development (OD)*. This perspective also has a long and rich history of applications, especially in business settings. Key constructs in this perspective have to do with the *process skills* that teams develop. The focus is on training and consultation to help the working groups and whole organizations develop process skills that are generic. Once these skills are developed, the assumption is that the working groups and organizations will be equipped to address the job-based problems and planning processes that are regular aspects of the work.

The East Lake Story illustrates how elements of each chapter's change perspective might come alive. In reading each of the stories, pay particular attention to that story's focus. The story in each chapter deals with real-world scenarios, but how it is described and addressed is change-perspective dependent. The constructs, tools, and views for understanding and addressing the situations are completely different. Different Change Perspectives mean different ways of understanding and facilitating implementation. Important ways that these perspectives are reflected in the CBAM are highlighted in the following figure.

CHAPTER 9

HOW CAN SYSTEMS THINKING ENHANCE THE SUCCESS OF CHANGE EFFORTS?

Interconnections of Parts That Make a Whole

Now that we've aligned our curriculum and instruction with assessments and the state's standards, we are beginning to see some positive gains in our students' test scores.

—Mr. Major, Mountain View High School Principal

Well, what we have not yet done a good job of is coordinating and aligning our formative evaluation assessments with the standards and the K–12 curriculum.

—Director of Research & Evaluation, East Lake School District

I am working with the district budget people, Title I, the district calendar, and the union leadership to have a workable plan to provide PD and ongoing coaching for the first two years of implementation of the mathematics core curriculum across the district.

—Stephanie Struthers, Director of Professional Learning, East Lake School District

My child's school sent a letter to us explaining how the school is addressing our state's new curriculum standards, and how the administrators and teachers are learning to redesign their work with children to accommodate that. I don't quite understand all this, but I'm going to a meeting to learn how families can be part of this activity.

—Parent of an East Lake Middle School student

Construction is going well, but the increasing cost of cement, along with the shortage of plywood (due to the hurricanes) and not enough carpenters, could slow the completion of the new high school building and its technology lab designed for the new math curriculum.

—Manager of Facilities, East Lake School District

As each of these quotes illustrate, implementing change, any change, entails a complexity of people, processes, and things. There probably never was a time when one person or one organization could simply say "Do it." This most certainly isn't the case today. It seems as if everyone has a say, and there are all these rules, procedures, and authorities that have to sign off before something can be done. The change perspective that helps in understanding this morass is *Systems Theory and thinking systemically.*

To initiate this exploration of ways to understand systems and implications for facilitating change, we turn first to early theorists and school improvers to gain insights abut the evolution of "systems thinking." In addition, several current writers are bringing new insights and perspectives to the concept of systems change, which we welcome to the conversation.

For years, the profession, the press, and the public have been demanding school change and improvement to more effectively support students in their successful learning. Various approaches and strategies have been initiated but few, if any, have achieved broad-scale change. Examining these efforts has engaged the attention of numerous researchers and writers. For example, in 1992, Sashkin and Egermeier conducted an analysis of the history of policy approaches to school change and identified four strategies. The first was the "Fix the parts" approach that involved introducing and adopting specific innovations such as curricular programs and instructional practices. This approach viewed change as an exchange of new products (curriculum) or processes (instruction) for old. The national curriculum projects in the 1960s were a national effort to reform schools by fixing a part.

Sashkin and Egermeier termed the second approach "Fix the people." In this approach, training and development were provided to educational personnel to change their practices/behaviors, attitudes, values, and beliefs. The national personnel development initiatives of the 1970s used this approach.

In the third approach—"Fix the school"—the school (rather than programs or people) was seen as the unit to change. For example, a school improvement team would guide the school in needs analysis, solution identification, and plans for change. This approach underlies much of the Reform Movement, which was widely used throughout the 1990s (e.g., Effective Schools) and continues to be popular. A recent example of this approach was the Race to the Top requirement to restaff entire schools.

After analyzing these three approaches, Sashkin and Egermeier concluded that successful change had not been achieved but that a fourth approach, which they called "Fix the system," could do it. This meant giving attention to all parts of the system simultaneously, because changing one part of the system influences other parts. It is this whole system view that is the focus of this chapter, and we turn to the origins of systems thinking before moving to recent studies and implications for implementing change.

LEARNING OUTCOMES

After reading this chapter, the learner should be able to:

1. Explain what is meant by "systems thinking and using a systems approach" for implementing change.
2. Identify the critical pieces or parts of a system.

3. Justify the value of a systems approach and why thinking and working systemically should be considered.
4. Describe how the systems approach can be applied to implementing change in education.

INITIAL THOUGHTS ABOUT SYSTEMS THINKING

Systemic change, systems thinking, working systemically (not *systematically*), and a host of other similar labels have been bandied about for several decades. These labels have been sprinkled across the conversations of educators at the campus and district office levels. When asked what they mean in their use of such a term, many leaders tend to look askance, frown quizzically, and appear unable to provide a coherent response. Such reactions to the use of relatively new terms is not unusual. It seems that the nature of many executives and policy-makers is to hear a new idea, refer to it before fully learning about and understanding it, and then try to use it as an uninformed novice.

A useful beginning point for examining systems thinking and theory is *Designing Social Systems in a Changing World* by Bela H. Banathy (1996). Throughout his career, Banathy examined systems and was a student of the works of others. Banathy suggested that

> people . . . cannot give direction to their lives, they cannot forge their destiny, they cannot take charge of their future unless they also develop competence to take part directly and authentically in the design of the systems in which they live and work, and reclaim their right to do so. (p. vii)

Banathy further maintained that "this kind of empowerment when learned and exercised by families, groups, organizations, and social and societal systems of all kinds, is the only hope we have to give direction to our evolution, to create a democracy that truly represents the aspiration and will of people, and to create a society about which all of us can feel good" (1996, p. vii). Banathy expressed a grand challenge and a powerful goal.

Banathy's work was followed by Peter Senge (1990), who used systems thinking to articulate how organizations should be created and operate. Senge's *The Fifth Discipline* found its way from the corporate world to school trustees' boardrooms and served as a wake-up call for educators who were considering how best to design their systems for improved student outcomes.

Another classic volume that has been most helpful in understanding the complexity and interdependence of the parts of systems is *Systemic Change: Touchstones for the Future School,* edited by Patrick Jenlink (1995). Jenlink brought together the intellect, expertise, and advice of a score of writers to help us "get a handle" on systems in education.

Whereas Banathy first penned a book in 1973 about a systems view of education and others like Jenlink have followed, the current work of researchers, field practitioners in regional education development laboratories, faculty in higher education, and upper level school and district-level administrators of K–12 offer informative illustrations about the use of systems thinking in today's organizations. This chapter continues by sketching out what is now known about systems from the literature and how systems thinking is being used to define work, test its efficacy in practice, and make adaptations based on new learnings.

REFLECTION QUESTIONS

Banathy stated, "people . . . cannot give direction to their lives . . . unless they also develop competence to take part directly and authentically in the design of the systems in which they live and work." What is your reaction to this statement? What do you think influences your reaction?

EXAMINING A SYSTEMS VIEW

In early work, Ackoff and Emery (1972) characterized *social systems* as purposeful systems whose members intentionally and collectively formulate objectives. These social organizations are such that the state of the parts can be assessed only by reference to the state of the whole system. Further, change in one part of the system is influenced by changes in the system as a whole.

Argyris and Schon (1978) maintained that a social group is an organization when it designs decision-making procedures for the collectivity, giving to individuals the authority to act for the collective group and setting boundaries. Laszlo (1972) suggested that social systems are guided by values; thus, social systems are not concerned with physical needs but with values that depend on the beliefs and values that members have.

In 1995, Banathy explained a systems view of education. He noted that a systems view makes it possible to examine and describe the system and its setting, and also its components and parts. The systems view is a way of thinking that allows understanding and description of

- The qualities or descriptors of the amalgamated educational system operating at numerous interconnected levels (organizational, administrative, instructional)
- The relationships and interdependencies of the systems in operation at the levels
- The purposes and parameters of educational systems

INDICATORS OF SYSTEMIC THINKING

1. Any organization or system is made up of subsystems or components; these can be identified.
2. All parts or components of an organization or system are given attention when facilitating and evaluating change processes.
3. Most systems are organized in levels; these levels are recognized as well as the individuals within them.
4. For work in any system, identified competencies are required and are developed in the relevant individuals.
5. In systemic reform, as in any reform, certain actions and conditions facilitate and others impede; the wise leader plans for systems work with these in mind.
6. Because systems work is not without its shortcomings, leaders are aware and plan accordingly.
7. Doing systems work is juggling to keep all plates in the air at the same time, thus each "plate" is scrutinized continuously.

- The relationships and activities undertaken between the systems and their environment
- The dynamics of the actions, relationships, and designs of connectivity among the parts of the systems
- The characteristics of the whole system and the qualities that characterize various levels of the system as a result of systemic interaction and synthesis
- The behaviors and system changes and their environments that occur over time (p. 12)

Pothole Warning

The preceding introduction to systems thinking seems to make understanding change more difficult; there are so many systems, and each is so complex.

Pothole Repair

To develop deeper understanding, check out the statements that follow.

Perhaps a briefer and crisper articulation of systemic change offered by Jenlink, Reigeluth, Carr, and Nelson (1996) is helpful:

> Systemic change is an approach that [r]ecognizes the interrelationships and interdependencies among the parts of the educational system, with the consequence that desired changes in one part of the system are accompanied by changes in other parts that are necessary to reach an idealized vision of the whole, and [r]ecognizes the interrelationships and interdependencies between the educational system and its community, including parents, employers, social service agencies, religious organizations, and much more, with the consequence that all stakeholders are given active ownership of the change effort. (p. 2)

Obviously, a systems view examines the whole and relationships of its parts or subsystems. One could ask, What are these parts?

COMPONENTS OF THE EDUCATION SYSTEM

The components or parts of the education system have been hinted at by several authors cited previously. Other researchers and writers have further expanded identification of the parts or subsystems of an education system, specifically in the reform context.

Components of Systems in Change

Anderson (1993) identified the components of a system in change as vision, public and political support, networking and partnerships, teaching and learning changes, administrative roles and responsibilities, and policy alignment. Danek, Calbert, and Chubin (1994) stated that the essential components of systems reform are national standards for content, skills, and attitudes; learning, teaching, and assessing standards; ambitious learning expectations and outcomes for all students connected to a rigorous academic core program; examination of policies, practices, and behaviors, and their modification to remove barriers and achieve the standards; broad-based involvement in designing an action plan with autonomy in implementing the plan; outcomes that measure systemic change; a system for monitoring and evaluating progress and adjusting programs accordingly; and a timeline for delivering the outcomes.

IMPLICATIONS OF SYSTEMS THINKING FOR LEADERS AND FACILITATORS OF CHANGE

When working in any organization:

1. Leaders must understand their system, its parts, and its people. Typically, leaders tend to work more with one part of the system and give limited consideration to its connectedness to other parts and the mutual influence they may have—and then are surprised when things don't work as they had anticipated.
2. The major message for leaders planning for systemic work is that it is imperative to take into account the various subsystems and the system as a whole system plus the external factors that impinge on it.
3. Attention must also be directed to the interconnectedness of the subsystems. If the parts are not interconnected or are loosely coupled, then work must be initiated to enable interconnectedness and interrelationships to develop, because a loosely coupled organization will flounder.
4. The challenge is to see the interconnectedness between all the subsystems and the whole, not just some of the parts.
5. Acknowledging and attending to all people in the system is required. A culture of collaboration and interdependence is helpful (see Chapter 7). This means that people at all levels of the system (executive, administrative, and instructional if this is a school; sales or marketing or advertising if it is a business, support staff such as secretaries and custodian, etc.) must be involved.
6. There are tools for planning and implementing systems change. (These tools can be found in Part II.)
7. Systemic change, like any change, will not happen without consistent planning for implementation, taking action, and monitoring the results so that successive actions may be designed and taken. Short-term and long-range strategies will be necessary (see Chapter 2) and applied to a systemic effort.
8. A primary strategic action by leaders must be an articulation of the vision for change that leaves some space for others in the system to add to and shape or contribute to the vision. To fail to develop a shared vision and a plan for its articulation across the system dooms the reform's work to an early death.

Characteristics of Systemic Policy

Clune (1993) reported five characteristics of systemic policy: research-based goals in education practice and organization; models of new practice and knowledge; centralized/decentralized change process; regular assessment of inputs, outcomes, and process; and a coherent, sustained change-oriented political process. In the same year, the National Science Foundation noted the requirements of systemic reform: changes in financing, governance, management, content, and conduct of education (teacher preparation and enhancement, curricula and instruction, assessments), and all students learning science and math in a diverse educational system.

Elements of Systemic Reform

Smith and O'Day (1991) articulated three major elements for systemic reform. First was unifying the vision and goals of what schools should be like; second, establishing a coherent system of instructional guidance (knowledge, skills, capacities, curriculum, materials, professional development, accountability assessment) aligned with goals; and third, restructuring the governance system (state develops outcomes and accountability, schools determine means to achieve outcomes). An examination of Table 9.1 reveals wide disparity across the elements of attention in systemic change or reform, suggesting wide variance in what researchers and writers deemed important as components of the system.

REFLECTION QUESTIONS

Study Table 9.1 to organize the information shared in the sections on components, characteristics, and elements of systemic work. What, if any, items surprise you? Are there factors that you expected to find there that are absent?

TABLE 9.1   Components of Educational Systems

	ANDERSON (1993)	DANEK, CALBERT, & CHUBIN (1994)	CLUNE (1993)	NATIONAL SCIENCE FOUNDATION (1993)	SMITH & O'DAY (1991)
Vision	√				√
Public/political support	√		√		
Networking/partnerships	√	√			
Teaching-learning changes	√	√		√	√
Administrative roles/responsibilities	√			√	
Policy alignment	√	√			
National content standards		√			
Ambitious student learning outcomes		√	√	√	
Action plan/implementation		√			
Systemic change outcomes		√	√		
Monitoring/evaluating/adjusting		√	√	√	
Timeline for outcomes		√			
New models of practice			√		√
Centralized/decentralized change process			√		
Finance				√	√
Governance				√	
Teacher preparation				√	
Curriculum					√
Materials					√
Professional development					√
Accountability/assessment					√

WORKING SYSTEMICALLY IN SCHOOLS

In the early 2000s, as frustration grew over the single-shot, hit-and-run approaches to educational change and improvement, systemic change or systemic reform became more frequently considered as an alternative. Staff at one of the nation's regional educational laboratories, Southwest Educational Development Laboratory (SEDL), reviewed the literature and developed a scope of transformation work using a systems approach. The goal of this work was to transform low-performing schools into high-performing learning communities, with the work centering at both the district and school levels. This project's review and synthesis of the literature revealed three major parts of education systems that required reform and were incorporated into the laboratory's model: components, levels, and competencies (Herbert, Murphy, Ramos, Vaden-Kiernan, & Buttram, 2006).

Components

In systems thinking, all parts or components (also known as *subsystems*) of the system are inextricably linked. Support or pressure on one part exerts influence on others. This model gives attention to thinking and working across all the components listed as follows:

Standards: What students are expected to learn and be able to do

Curriculum: What the district expects students should know and be able to do

Instruction: The "how" of teaching and strategies used to deliver a curriculum

Assessment: Formal and informal procedures that provide a means for measuring student progress

Resources: Staffing, time, budget, facilities, equipment, and materials

Professional staff: Recruitment and retention of high-quality personnel, professional development, and appraisal

Policy and governance: Rules and procedures to be followed and how decisions are made to implement those rules and procedures

Family and community: Support systems that build positive connections among teachers, parents, schools, and the community

Again, keep in mind the interconnectedness of these many parts; none functions in isolation of the others. Quite obviously, curriculum and instruction are, or should be, tied directly to standards. Assessment must be closely related to the standards; thus, standards, curriculum and instruction, and assessment are aligned. Professional development must focus on the standards and on curriculum and instruction so that the staff is prepared to teach effectively what students must know and do. Resources must be allocated with the aforementioned components for all to function well. In working systemically—that is, *paying attention to all the parts*—all subsystems must be considered in the planning and implementation of new practices.

Levels

In addition to the components, working systemically requires that all organization levels of the system—state, district, school, and classroom—be given attention. These levels can be thought of as concentric circles, each providing expectations and demands that influence student achievement. The federal and state governments create policies and regulations that districts must implement; districts set rules and procedures to which all schools must adhere; schools provide the structures and immediate facilities in which classrooms operate; and all these impinge on classrooms and the teaching and learning that occur. In reform efforts, all levels of the system of public education must be kept in mind. A third part of the system focuses on competencies to be mastered by individuals involved in the effort.

Pothole Warning

Ah, all this information is like slugging along in soft sand and then hitting a hole. It all sounds quite befuddling.

Pothole Repair

Fear not. Clarification is next on the agenda. The competencies detailed next will be helpful and may well enable you to imagine mental pictures of what is happening in systemic work.

Competencies

In addition to components of the system and levels of the system that require attention, competencies for successful systemic work are needed and have been identified by Cowan, Joyner, and Beckwith (2008):

> *Creating coherence.* Creating coherence is making certain that the different parts of the system reflect the beliefs and values held by the organization and that they function together to accomplish the goals of the system. This approach ensures a shared understanding of the extent to which curriculum, instruction, and assessment are aligned to state standards and involves a coordinated effort to avoid competing priorities. Stakeholders at all levels engage in collaborative and purposeful work to improve teaching and learning—essential for creating a coherent instructional focus.
>
> *Collecting, interpreting, and using data.* Collecting, interpreting, and using data supports leaders in identifying underlying factors contributing to core issues and problems that need to be addressed. It entails collecting data from multiple sources, organizing the data in formats that help staff interpret and draw conclusions, and using information from the data to take appropriate action. It is essential to making sound decisions about improving schools and districts, and demands developing the capacities of school and district staff to collect, interpret, and use data effectively.
>
> *Ensuring continuous professional learning.* This competency ensures that all staff continuously develop their knowledge and skills that are most effective for helping students meet challenging standards. Further, it increases the probability that staff will become ever more effective in enabling all students to become successful learners. In these systems, principals participate directly in professional development sessions with staff in planning, conducting, implementing, and evaluating the effort. This process is long term and integrated into daily practice.
>
> *Building relationships.* District and school leaders create structures and processes that promote collaboration and collegiality so that all educators share their knowledge, ideas, and strategies. Mutual respect and trust are essential to building these professional relationships. In this environment, school, district, family, and community leaders work to define a common vision for improving schools. Time and settings to encourage positive interactions among all stakeholders must be provided to enable such relationships and their outcomes to develop.

Responding to changing conditions. Adapting to myriad demographic, societal, economic, and political changes is a reality in today's schools and districts. Changes that districts and schools typically confront include leadership transitions, resource allocation, availability of quality teaching staff, state and local politics, and state and national policy. Staffs are better equipped to face these pressures when the members are knowledgeable of appropriate solutions and the schools and districts promote continuous learning for adults as well as students. (pp. 9–13)

The Cube

Figure 9.1 graphically portrays "the cube" that contains the levels, components, and competencies of the SEDL's working systemically model. These three dimensions of the model are the focus of attention for work planned and carried out through district and school leadership teams. These teams have overlapping members. Early in the project, SEDL staff guided and directed work in the field sites with the district and schools teams, giving their attention to the levels of the larger system and their interrelationships. The SEDL staff planned for the sites' learning of the components that must be addressed in order to improve student achievement. Particular attention was given to the alignment of standards, curriculum, instruction, and assessment, along with coordinated professional development.

The competencies received much attention from the SEDL site staff who led the district and schools in identifying causes that could explain the areas of student achievement data that were of concern. Building the capacity of site educators was always the objective. This was done through well-organized staff-development sessions as well as through follow-up coaching and assistance. Multiple phone calls and e-mails supported the efforts between the

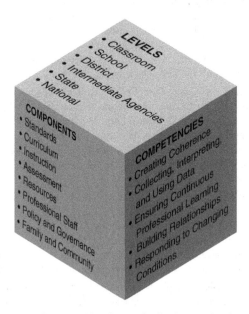

FIGURE 9.1   The Cube Model of the Working Systemically Approach

Source: From *Working Systemically in Action: A Guide for Facilitators* (Figure 1: Dimensions of the Working Systemically Approach, p. 5) by D. Cowan, S. Joyner, and S. Beckwith, 2008, Austing, TX: SEDL. Copyright (c) 2008 by SEDL. All rights reserved. Retrieved from http://www.sedl.org/ws/the works.html. Reprinted by Pearson with permission from SEDL.

twice-monthly visits by SEDL staff. When the teams were ready to provide more leadership, SEDL staff stepped back into a facilitating and supporting role.

Competencies from Other Writers

Other writers have addressed competencies needed for systemic work. For example, Floden, Goertz, and O'Day (1995) described strategies that are needed for capacity building in systemic reform: enhancing teacher capacity; providing vision and leadership; changing the organization or governance of schools; providing guidance on curricular content and instruction; establishing evaluation or accountability mechanisms; providing resources; and facilitating access to outside sources of support. These competencies resonate with some of those mentioned earlier by Stiegelbauer and colleagues. At the state level, Timar and Kirp (1989) noted the roles, and thus the capacities or competencies, required of state-level personnel. These are to establish professional standards and expectations, provide support, and nurture organizational characteristics that foster excellence.

EFFECTS OF WORKING SYSTEMICALLY

The SEDL staff used its cube model to conduct fieldwork (as described) in 16 districts in the five-state region served by SEDL (Arkansas, Louisiana, New Mexico, Oklahoma, and Texas). It has fine-tuned the model and developed more specificity and a sharper focus, particularly in the competencies needed by school and district leadership to do the work. SEDL staff members also have seen progress in field site participants' knowledge and understanding of systemic work, as measured by the Working Systemically Survey (created by SEDL's research team) and through semi-annual interviews conducted by the research team that followed the effort.

Outcomes for Educators

The survey and interview data suggest that educators (administrators and teachers) perceive that alignment of curriculum, instruction, and assessment has improved over time. Alignment of these important components of the system is essential for systemic work. The data also indicate positive changes in alignment between instruction and assessment, curriculum and standards, and vertical alignment. The educators also perceive that leaders' capacities to promote alignment in the district and schools has increased over time. Further, the educators indicate that describing and setting expectations, monitoring, classroom involvement, and understanding data and alignment are the top roles for leaders at the school and district levels. Responses to questions examining leadership roles suggested that leadership around alignment improved somewhat from the previous year. If some positive changes have been noted in educators' capacities and actions, what about student change?

REFLECTION QUESTIONS

When you have been involved in change initiatives, to what extent was systemic thinking included? Did you observe leadership that addressed the various components/parts/subsystems and results such as those reported above? Were some of the subsystems given too much or too little attention?

Results for Students

Student results in 13 of 16 SEDL schools were examined for the 2004 year-end report (Bond-Huie, Buttram, Deviney, Murphy, & Ramos, 2004). Student results in one or more grade levels showed decreases in the percentage of students categorized at the lowest performance categories. Out of 21 sets of test results in one of SEDL's states, 15 sets of results suggested a decrease of greater than 5% in the percentage of students categorized at the lowest performance levels on the state exam. Although there are positive trends in the data, three sets of test results indicated an increase in the percentage of students who were categorized at the lowest performance levels as defined by the state. SEDL has adjusted its approach so that its current work launches the model at the school unit, subsequently expanding participation across the district.

FACILITATORS AND BARRIERS TO WORKING SYSTEMICALLY: A CASE FROM MEXICO

At the same time that SEDL was working systemically in south-central United States, a large-scale systemic reform effort was underway in Mexico. The Instituto Tecnológico y de Estudios Superiores de Monterrey (ITESM), more familiarly known in the United States as the Monterrey Institute of Technology, had undertaken a major effort to transform the teaching–learning paradigm across its entire higher education institution of 33 campuses spread across Mexico. ITESM is among the first institutions of higher education to recognize the need for incorporating new learning approaches into classroom instruction throughout an entire multicampus system.

The mandated change resulted from a broad study conducted by the highest level of the university system to determine if the university was preparing its graduates for success in the twenty-first century knowledge-based, global economy. It was discovered that many graduates were lacking in nine key attributes necessary for today's high-performance jobs: leadership, teamwork, problem solving, time management, self-management, adaptability, analytical thinking, global consciousness, and basic communication skills. After considering this report, and further study of the university's classroom environments and pedagogical approaches, a new vision of the teaching–learning process for the university's classrooms was developed and prepared for launching. As can be imagined, a careful attempt was made to balance academic freedom and academic performance expectations—a journey into uncharted territory.

A top-down mandated strategy (note that in Chapter 1, Change Principle 9 indicates that mandated change can work) was employed that involved multiple aspects of support and assistance for faculty and administrators. Several years of intensive professional development were provided to enable faculty to use a more constructivist and technology-based approach to teaching and learning. The professional development focused on multiple levels of the university's system: executive, administrative, faculty, and support personnel. It affected resources and policy, and resulted in new ways of delivering professional development electronically. New capacities were developed throughout the staff to accommodate the implementation of the new model. So, what success was accomplished?

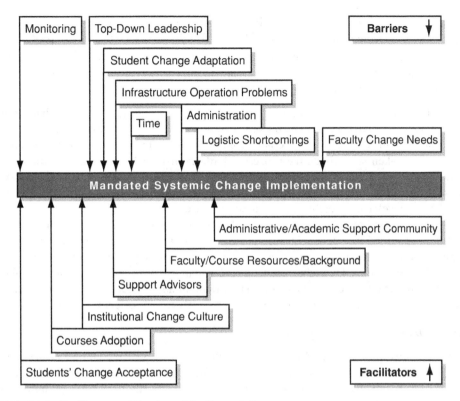

FIGURE 9.2   Facilitators and Barriers of the Systemic Process

Source: C. E. Gonzalez, P. E. Resta, and M. L. De Hoyos. Paper submitted for presentation at the annual meeting of the American Educational Research Association, 2005. Reprinted by permission of Carlos Enrique Gonzalez.

Facilitators of the Change

A study of one ITESM campus was undertaken to understand better how the change process was facilitated and what barriers hindered its progress (Gonzalez, Resta, & De Hoyos, 2005). The facilitators depicted in Figure 9.2 are a mix of people who provided interventions (support advisors and administrative and academic support) and conditions present in the university setting.

Their brief descriptions follow:

Students' acceptance of change: ITESM students' participation and acceptance of the change that included the use of technology aided the change process.

Adoption/adaptation of courses: The faculty had system-level, high-quality courses available for their adoption, or they could adapt existing courses for their use.

Institutional change culture: ITESM philosophy and values-based culture promoted innovation, change, and an entrepreneurial spirit.

Ongoing support and training: Support was provided by pedagogical and technological advisors from ITESM Learning Technology Centers.

Faculty academic background: Faculty members' individual academic discipline, years of teaching experience, and pedagogical skills supported the change process.

Professional Learning Community: Collegiate work in ITESM systemwide academies and local academic departments, and the appropriate organizational structure of the institution, enabled the change effort to make progress.

These strategic interventions were identified through a five-stage process. First, administrators were asked to generate a listing of interventions that they had done that they believed were helpful to the change effort. Second, faculty were invited to identify actions that administrators had taken to facilitate the process. Third, the lists of both the administrators and faculty were submitted to factor analysis. The results were then field-tested in the fourth step. These results were further analyzed in the fifth step and produced the six facilitating factors (described above) and the eight barriers (described next).

Keep in mind that this was a nationwide systemic effort and that the facilitators (i.e., strategies identified in Figure 9.2) were present across all campuses of the ITESM system. Support for implementation was provided at all levels of the system (executive, administrative, and instructional). The resources and policies at all campuses were coordinated to focus systemically across the entire university on curriculum and instructional processes and on professional development to support the change to a new teaching–learning model.

REFLECTION QUESTIONS

It was quite exciting for us to learn about this large-scale change effort across a large university system and to learn how it evolved. What is your take on the approach that was used by the executive level of the university system? How would this type of systemic change effort unfold across your state?

Barriers to the Change Process

Any change effort will be challenging. In the ITESM initiative eight barriers were identified:

Monitor implementation: This factor cited the lack of institutional evaluation of the implementation of the project and lack of classroom monitoring to improve.

Top-down leadership: ITESM's centralized decision-making process promotes upper-level decisions to the exclusion of a bottom-up effort.

Students' adaptation to change: There was a lack of students collaboratively developing new learning habits and adaptation to the work, and students showed apathy toward ITESM's new teaching–learning process (interestingly, students' acceptance appears to be both a facilitator and, when it is absent, a hindrance—easy enough to understand).

Infrastructure operational problems: This involved proper operation of technological platforms, computational servers, operational failures, and general maintenance of the infrastructure.

Time: This complaint is a typical one. In this case, the problem was lack of time for continuous improvement of courses and interaction with students, lack of time needed to fully understand the new approach, and lack of time to become involved in the change process and for feedback during the implementation process.

Administrative alignment and support: Academic units and administrative staff had different goals, and alignment of administrative processes with the change was somewhat lacking. In addition, academic administrators' understanding of the change was an issue.

Support shortcomings: Cited were support deficiencies during the implementation process as well as lack of support from technological and pedagogical advisors. (Here again is a contradiction of a factor that was a facilitator to some and a barrier to others, most likely stemming from participants' own personal experience with the change process.)

Faculty issues: Faculty skepticism arose about the effectiveness of the new approach, which required use of didactic methods in redesigned courses.

These barriers clearly reflect the systemic nature of change initiatives. There are no surprises in this list. All are regularly identified in change efforts. In hindsight, the ITESM effort could have thought more about working systemically so that all of the subsystems were kept in mind simultaneously.

For example, time is typically an implementation issue, and it seems reasonable that the executive and administrative layers of ITESM could have provided resources and developed policies to make time available at all campuses. In addition, policies could have addressed administrative alignment and support. More professional development for administrators would have clarified their understanding of the change so that monitoring implementation would occur more comprehensively and systemically.

The sheer scope or magnitude of conducting such a far-reaching change across 33 campuses of a very large university system challenges the intellect. What is useful here is the identification of what worked systemically to encourage implementation and the identification of factors that need to be addressed more directly in order for implementation to make additional progress across the entire system. Further, these findings represent useful ideas for the consideration and study by others who anticipate attempting large-scale systemic change efforts.

LIMITATIONS OF WORKING SYSTEMICALLY

If the definition and the expansive lists of components required for using a systemic approach to educational reform sound daunting, they are. Fullan (1993) identified two limitations of the systemic approach. First is that individuals and groups greatly underestimate the complexity of how systems operate and the daily dynamics that ensue, requiring large amounts of attention, energy, and resources. Second, it is not clear if the systemic approach or process can be extended to new situations. What is needed, Fullan suggested, is a new paradigm more in tune with the realities of systems and their dynamic complexity.

At this point, the reader may be haunted by the early work of Karl Weick (1976), who introduced the concept of *loose coupling*. Weick explained that in viewing an organization as a system, some elements will be tightly coupled, such as budgeting and spending. Other areas may have limited linkages, such as a nonspecific policy about how employees dress (i.e., loose coupling). Weick explained that the connections, links, or interdependence between any two entities will have a degree of coupling. More tightly coupled individuals, groups, and events will respond to each other. Also, the degree of coupling between two parts of a system depends on the amount of activity or strength of the variables or elements that the two share. If the two have few variables in common or share weak variables, they will be loosely coupled and more independent of each other.

For example, if budget decision making is closely held by the principal and not shared with teachers, then teachers and the principal can be assessed as being loosely coupled with regard to the budget. At the same time, if the principal is closely associated with teachers in instructional planning, then they are considered to be tightly coupled instructionally. Weick says, "Loose coupling simply connotes things, any things, that may be tied together either weakly or infrequently or slowly or with minimal interdependence" (1976, p. 5).

Pothole Warning

Although interconnectedness and interrelationships are required for success-ful systems work, be careful in making casual assumptions about the degree of interconnectedness and tight coupling of the system's parts.

Pothole Repair

As noted, some parts of the system will have tight coupling, and others will be loosely connected. Charting where connections are tight and loose, along with continuous observation and monitoring so that adjustments may be made, are wise strategies to consider.

Clearly, if the parts of a system are loosely coupled, developing change process–related integration and coordination will require more effort. However, Weick (1976) noted that if there are rules, regulations, or prerequisites for how the subparts of the system will inter-act and relate to each other, then the longer the list, the tighter the coupling. One might be reminded of the introduction of site-based management in the late 1980s. Schools were given unbridled authority to act, and soon in many districts the flotilla of schools was meandering in all directions and floundering on the shoals. For this, and other reasons, efforts have been made in many districts to tighten the coupling so that the district operation is better aligned with the schools and the system at large functions coherently. For systemic change to work, the components of the system must have sufficiently tight coupling so as to work with maxi-mum interdependence.

CURRENT RECOMMENDATIONS FOR DEVELOPING COMPETENCIES AND CAPACITIES

It is clear that early thinking and writing about systems work focused on identifying the parts of the system, their relationships, and impact on each other. Writers were explicit in identifying components, levels, and elements. Currently, the focus is on the competencies or *capacities* of people, subsystems, and systems as a whole. There are at least three different perspectives about capacity that are important to consider: Organization Consultation, the school board, and the superintendent.

From the Organization Consultant

Harsh (2014) advocated for a Multi-Dimension Approach (MDA) for understanding and build-ing capacity. Harsh identifies five types of capacity—Foundation, Enhanced, Proficiency, and

Higher Order, and Learning—each of which is increasingly more complex. Harsh is clear that building capacity requires change (moving to new ways of knowing and doing, or exchanging one skill set for another), and change requires learning—a thesis strongly proclaimed in this book.

Harsh shares twelve guides that undergird her multiple-dimension capacity-building model:

1 and 2: Any capacity-building effort must be grounded in a theory of action from the literature; and that theory must be put into operation. Thus, change agents must know how to integrate the theory into the change efforts of the organization.

3 and 4: Complex change initiatives, whether involving general or specific capacities can be the target of capacity building; but a simple solution will not adequately address the multiple dimensions of a complex issue. Instead, solutions should build the capacities needed to fully implement interventions or resolve the issue.

5 and 6: Capacity building should be considered at the individual, organizational unit, and system levels; and, should be guided by a clear process that increases the probability that the results desired are achieved.

7: The concerns of staff, and their lack of success in achieving improved performance, indicate a demand for capacity building.

8 and 9: Capacity building demands greater resources of time, attention, effort, and support than typical technical assistance; although, not all reform challenges require capacity building, and can be guided and supported by other efforts.

10: For success, change agents should have a repertoire of tools and processes to guide successful decision making.

11: Effective change agents, in addition to tools and processes (above), must acquire a wide range of analysis and support skills, as well as understanding.

12: Finally, Harsh maintains, that an "ah ha" from a staff member signals that the individual "got it."

One might question the "science" of the judgment in number 12, when there are tools and techniques to understand this moment more scientifically. Nonetheless, these principles articulated by Harsh prepare the student of capacity building with a frame for further learning.

From the School Board

Hirsh and Foster (2013), ex-school board members, directors of nonprofit organizations, and passionate about the work of school boards, agree that the selection of superintendents is the board's most important decision. Further, the qualities and characteristics the board looks for in candidates—along with the important role definition the board expects—drives this selection.

The search for a new superintendent is grounded in the board's description of the role of this school system leader, because it is the superintendent who is responsible for translating the board's vision and goals into the daily life of the school system. Their depiction of the superintendent's list of tasks and responsibilities is headed by teaching and learning. Further, Hirsh and Foster maintain that, in many communities, the schools are seen as a vital pathway to the increased effectiveness and productivity of the community and its citizens. These authors further maintain that the superintendent becomes the representative of their expectations for the future of their community.

They further caution that most boards will select a candidate who is able to improve the performance of the schools in the district without rocking the boat, or ruffling the feathers of the community's residents. And, there is no way to get improved student results without reviewing data to find the areas of greatest lack of student learning, and address that with new practices that have the potential to reach improved student learning outcomes. This means that up and down and across the system, leaders at all levels, and at most positions related to instruction, will require the capacities to introduce and to support new practice to its implementation in the classroom. Back to system-wide competencies and capacities, as suggested by Harsh (above)!

Hirsh and Foster's significant contribution to this newer way of thinking about system change is in the manner in which the competencies and capacities will be achieved by the system-wide range of leaders. They maintain, and certainly so, that professional development/professional learning will be the vehicle that carries the change leaders to their new knowledge, skills, and dispositions about their role in supporting change. Hirsh and Foster proclaim and advocate for high-quality professional learning that produces the competencies and capacities needed. This quality professional learning rides on the use of Standards for Professional Learning, identified and described in a variety of resources (Learning Forward, 2011; *Journal of Staff Development*, August, 2011; Hirsh & Hord, 2012).

These understandings and ideas take us to the ultimate system leader.

From the Superintendent

John Ash and John D'Auria have worked all over the map of schooling, and have spent many years collectively serving as the system's chief leader. A thread that is visible across the whole of their tapestry of comment in *School Systems That Learn*, the title of their new book (Ash & D'Auria, 2013), is what you would surmise from the title: All individuals in the system must be continuous learners in order for the system to serve students well. The bottom line is that there are, indeed, competencies and capacities at each level of the organization in order to make it work well—surprise! Back to capacities, and now a three-part chorus of champions for this requirement. Ash and D'Aurio's take is to introduce and explain four drivers of change that "will unleash teacher creativity to develop new educational solutions for all students" (p. 13).

The first of these is the *importance of trust*. If a family, a sports team, a school, or other organized group doesn't trust its members, there will be little interaction, collegiality, or collaboration, and thus, no learning with and from each other. Trust and trustworthiness are characterized by the members of a group by their respect, their regard for each other, and each person's competence—whether the competence is strong or weak, recognizing that individuals may be highly competent in one way, and not in another. Thus, each person is valued by his/her unique skill set and/or knowledge base.

Staying true to what one says she/he will do, and then following up by doing it, demonstrates integrity—another element of trust. Probably each of us has had the experience of an individual promising to take some action, and then the disappointment, and shaken belief and trust in the "promiser" when that individual fails to act.

A second driver identified by Ash and D'Aurio is that of *boundless collaboration*—that is, interacting interdependently vertically up and down the system and its levels, and horizontally across those positioned at the same or similar level. Collaboration occurs intra- and inter-school (*intra* means within the school; *inter* means across schools). These authors use the time-tested adage: none of us is as smart as all of us (p. 78) to illustrate their identification of collaboration as a powerful factor in the learning and growth, and the problem-solving results of a system's collaborating inhabitants.

For the third driver, our authors turn to *capacity building*, as a way to turn from the typical needs of professional development of the individual teacher, to professional learning for teachers whose students' performance reveals their needs for attention, thus, focusing teachers' learning on student needs. The hypothesis here is that as teachers direct their learning to the needs of students, their teaching quality increases for their students, and students subsequently gain. Thus, we understand the indirect, but significant, link between effective professional development and student performance.

And, the fourth driver is *leadership at all levels*. Ash and D'Auria identify six attributes required of leaders "who energize others to expand the school's capacity to educate all students at higher levels" (p. 125). These six skill sets (p. 126) required of such learning leaders are:

1. Act on their core values
2. Inspire confidence
3. Build an inclusive network
4. Build a positive school culture
5. Demonstrate sincere inquiry
6. Support risk taking

These two writers consistently push the premise that when school systems learn, professional practice improves and student achievement increases—assuming that the system is learning the "right stuff." For further information from two current writers, see Additional Readings/Resources, at the end of this chapter.

It is entirely clear that current writers promote capacity building and the increased quality of facilitation competencies as a means to address "spread" of new practice, so that the larger system (e.g., school district) benefits from specified innovations. These competencies are the focus of this book, and the capacity building of individuals is the goal.

We turn now to visit East Lake District to see if, and how, the personnel of the District is using, or planning to use, systems thinking to spread the mathematics core curriculum.

The following chapter in East Lake District's change story illustrates the system/capacity building perspective.

EAST LAKE SCHOOL DISTRICT'S CONTINUING STORY

Dr. Stephanie Struthers, Director of Professional Learning for the District, was very pleased with the successful progress made by the pilot test in the middle school of the new math standards and curriculum. Now, several other schools were interested and following the efforts of the middle school. Their principals were eager to learn about and involve their schools in the new math curriculum. Stephanie judged it was time to visit with Superintendent Mike.

"Mornin' Mike. Thanks for giving me a bit of time today. I want to talk with you about our pilot math initiative. It has progressed very well. The middle school with their math department has moved ahead in terms of growing into an effective learning community, thus, the teachers are very pleased. The kids think that they are kings of the mountain for doing this "different" way of studying math. They really like it, and the parents couldn't be more pleased.

(continued)

EAST LAKE SCHOOL DISTRICT'S CONTINUING STORY (CONTINUED)

"All the schools across the district have studied their student data and haven't been surprised to learn that math seems, consistently, to be the academic area of students' lowest performance. These data studies have really arrested the attention of the schools generally, although, as usual, there are a few that are not yet concerned about their students' progress. Inez shared a book with me last week about what's termed *thinking systemically* about change for improvement. It seems to me that the district might be ready for this approach, as our administrators generally see the value of undertaking the math change wholesale, with everyone plunging in! And, you'd be amazed that they remember that math was pulled up to be the focal point of school improvement efforts. So, the winds of change may be blowing on us, and perhaps we should think about getting ready to pursue the math goal."

"That is good news, Stephanie," Superintendent Mike responded. "As a matter of fact, at a church reception last week a number of our key school leaders, as well as our community constituents, expressed interest in the 'new' math program. Parents are wondering if, or how, it is different from how they experienced math instruction in their young school days. Perhaps we should call our Mathematics Game Plan Team together to update everyone and to plan for launching the mathematics core standards system-wide. Please contact Leslie, if you will, and schedule a meeting for next Tuesday at 2:00 p.m. That time shouldn't affect instruction in a difficult way. Oh, and ask everyone to bring their Game Plan strategies material with them."

"I will. The team as a whole has spent time learning about IC Maps, supported by Joe and Josh, but led in this professional learning by Leslie. They've been learning how to use this tool in a change initiative, and they're fired up about it, although feeling a bit shaky too—normal, of course."

"Maybe I'll serve some hot fudge sundaes to the group—to sweeten the conversation."

On the next Tuesday, the group met in the boardroom for their dessert and discussion. The math team from the middle school was there, as well as "systems" specialist Braun Lincoln from the regional service center. He had been in conversation with Stephanie, Leslie, and Mike to prepare for this meeting. After Mike called the meeting to order, he asked for commentary from the school and district staff. To a person there was genuine interest, although varying degrees of confidence in whether the district could manage this apparently large and entirely new math program. Mike asked Joe and Josh to report on what they had been learning in their three-week, twice a week, sessions.

"Well," Josh began, "we've focused on a tool called IC Maps, or Innovation Configurations . . . this tool helps people to see what a new school curriculum or new classroom practice looks like when it has been taken on board and put into place. It was a bit confusing at first to get the gist of it, but I think I have a pretty good handle on it now. It's really neat, because if we can create such a map for this new math curriculum, that'll be a great help, because the map gives a person a written down vision of what this new thing is, and what it should look like when we've put it in place in a high quality way. It gives us a mental image . . . does that make any sense? We actually made a first, crude start on a map for the new math."

"That's really great that you have a small group here that is learning about IC Maps," Braun said, "because they are multipurpose and can serve in a variety of ways to help implementers when they are adopting and implementing something new. I notice that you have your Game Plan Strategies with you—some of us call them the 'sacred six,' because they are basic to any change initiative. Perhaps Joe and Josh could lead us in a discussion of how we can use an IC map to help us with the strategies. Do you have a component mapped out yet?"

"No," Joe reported, "but we're struggling to get clear on how to do it. One of our resource people has an IC Map of CCSS Mathematics for the middle grades, so we've been looking into that. It's given us some good ideas, and we'll use it to get a start on depicting our math curriculum for all

**EAST LAKE SCHOOL DISTRICT'S CONTINUING
STORY (CONTINUED)**

levels, so that all teachers and administrators will have a common language of what we'll be doing. I've brought copies. Would you all like a copy?"

"Indeed, yes, we need all the help that we can get. We have asked Braun Lincoln to be with us today, and to help us get our heads around how we'll launch our math initiative so that we're doing this system-wide, and that's a significant challenge. The school board thought that it would be good to start everyone together so as not to show favoritism. We've committed a large investment in learning about school and system change and about the various tools and strategies that can be used. Now, we're ready to put that learning into practice," Superintendent Mike challenged everyone.

The Planning Team spent several hours considering just where and how to start, and determined that one group of constituents were parents, so they identified two people to start planning for that. A resource they thought they should look into was the math team at the high school that had been piloting the core math for the past year. The group assumed that this team would have much to share. They scheduled a next meeting with plans to include the Math Quartet.

Braun suggested that they study thoroughly the strategies paper in order to discuss that, and he shared with the group that the literature on systems change had, for the past number of years, been recommending strongly that to make a change system-wide would require many in leadership positions and beyond to become very competent in facilitating change, and that capacity building would be a large priority up and down the school system and across all the schools.

"Do you mean that we'll really use these strategies, and the Innovation Configuration Maps that we've been hearing and learning about . . . and how about the time we spent in understanding and practicing the one-legged conferences to gain information about our people's concerns—that should be a big item for such a big challenge as taking on core math across the system!" Mary exclaimed.

"That's right, Mary," Leslie remarked, "Now is when the rubber hits the road. But, as you can recall, we've been in preparation for developing facilitation and support competencies and there are other bodies of work that we've addressed that will support our capacity building as well."

"Oh, you mean that LoU stuff—er, I mean Levels of Use, where we practiced doing one-legged conferences to assess how people will be behaving with this new math program. . . did I get that straight?" Josh wanted to know.

"Ah," Braun chortled, "You have been really preparing for this big event. I am here to help you as will be several additional people and we will all convene and get into gear. It's great that you have developed these concepts and skills. How did that work?"

Leslie chimed in, "We used several small new instructional schema on which to practice so as to have a real-life experience, and it was interesting how much we learned, and how much our confidence grew. There were twenty or so additional school-based people who were learning with us. You know, maybe it would be interesting to collect data on ourselves relative to this new project—we could do that when we meet. What do you think of that?" On this jocular note, the group disbanded with reminders of their big planning date.

SUMMARY

Systems work, systems thinking, and *systemic change and reform* are terms that have been used for some years but seem only fairly recently to have concrete definition. The ideas have been in the literature for decades, but this perspective has only recently been espoused for application in schools and school districts.

The following talking points may be considered when communicating briefly with others about systemic change:

1. Consider all the parts of the system even when attempting to change only one or two elements.
2. Punching on one part of the system will cause something to pop up in another part. Thus, attention to all parts of the system seems highly realistic.
3. Interconnectedness and interrelationships must prosper for the system to operate effectively and efficiently; the systems approach requires consideration of all.
4. "Complexity in a system occurs from the interaction of system variables over time . . . meaning that it is difficult if not impossible for humans to comprehend—predict—phenomena under this condition" (Schneider & Somers, 2006).
5. In systems thinking, monitoring the process is of high importance in order to make corrections when data deem it necessary.
6. There are limitations to this approach in education and other organizational reforms.
7. Guiding and managing such efforts will require leaders who can take the balcony view (watching all elements of the system), who are conceptually and intellectually capable at a high level, who are quick witted and have the energy to act on short notice, and who continually care about the organization and its individuals.

REFLECTION QUESTIONS

What is the most compelling idea that you found in this chapter? Why did it grab your attention, or confirm your values or beliefs, or cause you to disagree strongly?

DISCUSSION QUESTIONS

1. Why would you want a school's administrators to think about their school's change efforts systemically?
2. What difference would it make to a district's or a state's change efforts if the effort were planned and executed with systems thinking?
3. Identify and discuss the key characteristics of highly effective leaders involved in systems work.
4. List and explain strategies that should be provided for a systemic reform to be successful.
5. For systems reform, hypothesize factors that could be considered to engage the participants in developing systems thinking.

APPLYING SYSTEMS THINKING IN FACILITATING IMPLEMENTATION

1. Do you know an organization that operates in a systemic way? If so, describe it. If not, what topics would you use to ascertain if it operated systemically?
2. Assume that an executive or superintendent asked you to identify any of her administrators who engage in systemic thinking. What characteristics would you look for?

3. Find a district, a school, a business, or another organization that has accomplished major change through a systems approach. Query the staff to learn (a) how it started, (b) who initiated the effort, (c) what parts of the system were key, and (d) how the staff knows it was successful or not successful.

APPLYING SYSTEMS THINKING IN RESEARCH AND PROGRAM EVALUATION STUDIES

1. Identify tools and interventions that are typically found in noncomprehensive or nonsystemic change. Compare these to the kinds of tools and applications that are made in planning and implementation of a systemic change effort. Observe and document the results, and compare them to results gained. Derive conclusions about the systems thinking, the use of tools and interventions in systemic processes.

2. We know little about the array of skills and knowledge that the facilitators of systemic change initiatives require. Design a descriptive study for identifying the skills, knowledge base, and qualities/characteristics of effective facilitators of systemic change.

LEARNING MORE ABOUT SYSTEMS AND SYSTEMS THINKING

Jenlink, P. M., Reigeluth, C. M., Carr, A. A., & Nelson, L. M. (1998). Guidelines for facilitating systemic change in school districts. *Systems Research and Behavioral Science, 15*, 217–233.

    This how-to-do-it monograph describes the characteristics and elements of a systemic change guidance system that builds on the principles of process facilitation and systems design. It examines the integral values or beliefs related to facilitation and systemic change, the types of events and activities typically needed, the processes that form the guidance system, and how to create the guidance system.

Joseph, R., Jenlink, P. M., Reigeluth, C. M., Carr-Chelman, A. A., & Nelson, L. M. (2002). Banathy's influence on the guidance system for transforming education. *World Futures, 58,* 379–394.

    This publication is a tribute to the work of Bela H. Banathy. The article identifies how Banathy has influenced the authors' work on systemic change in education, the crux of which is found in systems design. Systems design is a process that engages stakeholders in conversations about their visions, ideals, values, and aspirations with the goal of creating their ideal educational system. The authors identify the process values and the process activities that drive Banathy's theoretical framework and compare these to the values and activities that they have developed in their guidance system. The intention of the article, as noted in the title, is to demonstrate the extent to which Banathy's work has influenced the development of a guidance system for facilitating systemic change in public school districts.

CHAPTER 10

HOW DO COMMUNICATION ACTIVITIES AND CHANGE AGENTS AFFECT IMPLEMENTATION?

The Diffusion Perspective

Scene One: Mountain View High School Staff Lounge

These new standards are really a neat approach. I get a thrill out of seeing my students probe each other's thinking.

—Paul Jones, AP Social Studies

I think I will wait for a while on trying this. It could result in too many disruptions. Besides, some of the parents won't understand and will think that their kids are arguing back.

—Mary Thompson, Freshmen English and Yearbook

If Paul says it really works well, that's good enough for me. I am going to try what he is doing.

—José Garcia, Social Studies

Dr. Morse from the university seems to know what she is talking about. I understand what she is saying about why this is a better way.

—Greg Hanover, Chair, Social Studies Department

This is just another set of standards. I don't see what the big deal is.

—Katrina Romano, Volleyball Coach and Remedial Math

Scene Two: Introduction of a New Resource

Professor Connie Morse from Northland University is just back from attending a national conference where she learned about a new Web-based program for unpacking the Common Core Standards. The program links the standards to well-thought-out formative assessments and related lesson plans. She is now suggesting to Assistant Superintendent Leslie Hanson that East Lake District try this program.

If one approach to understanding change were to be selected as the grandparent of change models, the likely winner would be Diffusion. The groundwork for this perspective was established early in the 20th century. Now, there are more than 100 years of accumulated research findings and widespread applications of the many Diffusion constructs. The two scenes illustrate basic elements of the Diffusion Perspective. The first is the importance of person-to-person communication about new ideas. The second has to do with which people's ideas are respected and accepted by others.

LEARNING OUTCOMES

After reading this chapter, the learner should be able to:

1. Describe Characteristics of adopters that are associated with different Rates of innovation adoption.
2. Explain Characteristics of some adopters that increase their influence.
3. Describe elements of the communication process that affect making an Adoption Decision.
4. Provide examples of the ways that Perceptions of an innovation contribute to acceptance of an innovation.
5. Compare the role of a Change Agent to that of a Change Facilitator.
6. Chart how the rate of adoption relates to Characteristics of adopters.

THE LONG AND RICH HISTORY OF THE DIFFUSION PERSPECTIVE

Two key components of the Diffusion Perspective that will be reflected in the examples presented in this chapter are thinking about change as it takes place inside of *social systems* and the act of *communication*. In the Diffusion Perspective, information about a new idea becomes distributed throughout a social system by people talking to people. For example, farmers are members of their community, which is a social system. Any single farmer talks to some farmers a lot and to others very little or not at all. Their learning about and deciding to take on a new idea, such as hybrid corn seed, unfolds through personal communication.

Another important construct in the Diffusion Perspective is *adoption*. Rather than change being seen as a process that involves administrators, exploration of alternatives, and an extended implementation process as outlined in the Change Principles of Chapter 1, in the Diffusion Perspective the emphasis is on each individual making an *Adoption Decision*. Villagers in developing nations either boil water or they do not. Physicians either prescribe a new drug or they do not. Individual consumers decide to purchase a hybrid car or an iPad, or they do not. Potential adopters work their way through a decision-making process. In the end they either adopt the new idea or continue with their traditional practice.

Rich History of Research and Applications

One of the earliest contributors to what has become the Diffusion Perspective was French sociologist Gabriel Tarde (1903). As he reflected on change, one of his wonderments had to do with why so few innovations were actually used out of the hundreds that were conceived. Through his studies and writings he introduced many of the concepts that are still foundational to this perspective. For example, he concluded that an innovation that was similar to current practice would be adopted more quickly.

The studies of Ryan and Gross (1943) also were seminal. They examined the rate of adoption of hybrid corn seed in two communities in rural Iowa. Before the 1930s the source of corn seed available to farmers was the ears of corn that had been stored over the winter in a specially designed crib or shed. Researchers at Iowa State University (ISU) had been developing hybrid corn seed specifically grown to include various plant characteristics such as disease resistance, consistent height, and a standard number of ears per stalk. In 1928, hybrid corn seed became available to farmers through the ISU Agricultural Extension Service and seed companies.

Hybrid corn seed at that time was an innovation. It also represented a new cost for farmers. Instead of using the seed available for free in the crib from last year's crop, farmers had to buy hybrid corn seed. As would be expected, some farmers made the decision to adopt hybrid corn seed quickly while others delayed for years. In the early 1940s, Ryan and Gross reviewed the history of the adoptions in two communities by interviewing well over 300 farmers. Based on analyses of these interviews, they proposed many of the key Diffusion constructs that are used to this day.

The research methods and constructs of Ryan and Gross have been used ever since to study a wide range of innovations and adopters. The characteristics of physicians and their rate of adoption of new pharmaceuticals have been studied. The adoptions of boiling water and steel-tipped plows by rural villagers have been studied, as has been the spread of diseases such as AIDS. Diffusion constructs are regularly included in the training of sales representatives and applied to the introduction of new products (electric cars) and services (Web site development).

Over the last 60-plus years, the leading Diffusion scholar has been Everett Rogers. He contributed as a researcher, educator, and leading spokesperson for the Diffusion Perspective. His classic book *Diffusion of Innovations* (2003) continues to be a very informative and useful resource. Literally hundreds of studies and thousands of wide-ranging applications of Diffusion constructs have been made. More recent applications range from the appeal of shopping online (Blake et al., 2005), to wireless applications (Grantham & Tsekouras, 2005), to use of broadband Internet access in Korea (Park & Yoon, 2005).

Key constructs from the Diffusion Perspective will be introduced in this chapter along with illustrations of how they can be used to understand and facilitate implementation of change.

COMMUNICATION WITHIN THE LINES AND NETWORKS

Once stated, many of the findings from Diffusion research seem obvious. The immediate reaction can be "Well, of course, but I had not labeled it." No matter how obvious the findings may seem, they often are overlooked. The findings from studies related to lines of communication are like this. They seem to be more obvious in hindsight than appreciated as a change process is unfolding. For example, one basic finding is that communication about the innovation occurs along the established lines, or channels, of communication. But we regularly observe change initiatives where this idea has been ignored.

Components of Interpersonal Communication

Interpersonal sharing of information about an innovation is central to understanding change from the Diffusion Perspective. In a social system, the spread of adoptions is mainly driven by people communicating with others. Keep in mind that in a social system the distances may be large, and therefore the spread of information across the system will not be even. Face-to-face communication requires proximity, but distance is not a factor with electronic communication. Corporate and professional social systems are spread across states and nations that have near-instantaneous communication. Still, the type and layout of the lines of communication can enhance or inhibit the transmittal of information.

A wonderful illustration of the role of communication lines can be seen in a study by House, Steele, and Kerins (1971). In 1963, the state of Illinois established a grant program that provided state funds to school districts for gifted and talented student activities. The program was voluntary, but if school districts applied, they received funding. Each year, House and colleagues plotted the statewide distribution of school districts that received the grants (see Figure 10.1). This plot graphically illustrates two key points from the Diffusion Perspective.

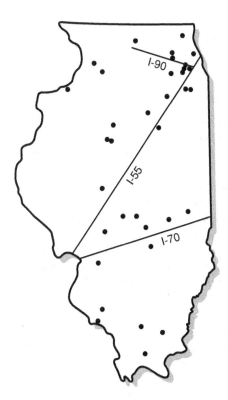

FIGURE 10.1 Spread of Gifted Programs in Illinois, 1964–1965

Source: Based on E. R. House, J. Steele, & C. T. Kerins. *The gifted classroom.* Urbana, IL: Center for Instructional Research and Curriculum Evaluation, University of Illinois, 1971.

First, the researchers found that there were more adoptions in those parts of the state with larger cities and where there were universities. (A criterion for receiving the grant was to partner with a university.) Do not miss the key point with this generalization. Yes, there are more schools and districts in cities. From the Diffusion Perspective the generalization is this: Where there are more people, there will be more and earlier adoptions since there is greater likelihood of adopters exchanging information about the innovation and perhaps seeing it in use.

The second finding, which is so well illustrated in Figure 10.1, is that adoption of innovations occurs along the lines of communication. The lines of communication in this case are the U.S. highways. In the 1960s, the network of U.S. highways was the main travel pattern within the state. Early adoptions of the gifted and talented grants occurred mainly along these highways. For adoption of innovations in other settings, think of the U.S. highways as a metaphor for the lines of communication. In other systems the lines of communication would not be highways per se, but the equivalent could be the regularly traveled corridors in a school or office building. They also could be the regularly traveled streets between headquarters and a satellite office. The easier it is to talk with another about the innovation or to "stop by" and see it in use, the more rapid will be adoption of the change. The same theme applies with electronic communication. E-mail, Facebook, and Twitter become sources of communication *if* one participates.

Pothole Warning

Do not assume that communication is always one-way and in a straight line and accurate.

Pothole Repair

Communication is often multidirectional, with one person sharing with several others. Also, the content of communication can be distorted when passed along, so repeating the original content and checking for distortions are important steps.

Understanding Communication Networks.   Another useful tool for understanding communication about an innovation is to analyze the social networks. Whether the system is a geographic region, a community, or a school, some people will be more closely connected to others, and some will have little or no connection with many others. Diffusion researchers will make charts of the connections each person has with others. They will identify the different cliques as well as the individuals who are more isolated socially. An example of this charting is presented in Figure 10.2. The data for this type of *sociogram* can be obtained by observing and asking about who talks to whom. Which people eat lunch together? Which departments/grade levels are more cohesive? Who never attends meetings? Who seems to be most aware of what is going on across the whole system? Who plays on the softball or bowling team or is part of the quilting group? Whose Twitter tweets or Facebook pages are monitored and talked about the most?

Charting the interpersonal networks is very useful for understanding to whom (which participants) information about an innovation will spread more quickly and who will have less opportunity to learn about the change. People with more connections to others will be in a better position to learn more and learn it earlier than those with fewer networks. The same people will be able to tell others and share more information because they have more contacts.

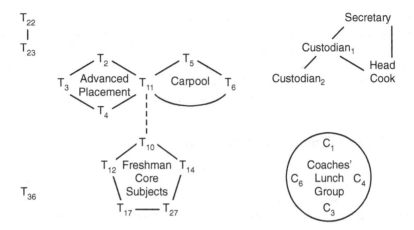

FIGURE 10.2   Social Networks in One High School

Implications of Communication Networks for Facilitating Change.   Failure to attend to the lines or channels of communication is regularly observed in change efforts. Instead of thinking of a state as the social system, as was the case in Figure 10.2, think about the geography of a school campus. What are the lines of communication in this case? If an innovation is to be introduced through a pilot or demonstration site, which classroom should be selected? Do not select a classroom that is far off the "highway" that prospective adopters rarely travel. Instead of having the pilot done in a remote portable classroom, select a classroom that is on the direct route to the staff parking lot or on the way to the office or the staff lounge.

Once a sociogram has been developed, use it. From the Diffusion Perspective, working with T36 (in Figure 10.2) makes no sense. Apparently, this teacher does not associate with any others. Therefore, he or she will have little communication with others about the innovation. The most obvious candidate to persuade to become involved early is T11. This person is interconnected with three groups. Whatever T11 says and does has the potential of being shared with 10 colleagues. If T11 likes the innovation, then a number of other prospective adopters are likely to hear about it. The corollary is also true. If T11 does not like the innovation, a number of other prospective adopters are likely to hear about that. Also, the Coaches' Lunch Group will need to be targeted specifically, since it appears that it has minimal lines of communication with other groups.

REFLECTION QUESTIONS
Take another look at Figure 10.2. Who would be the primary target for communication within the support staff clique? Why?

Communication of Innovations: Who Is Doing What?

In the Diffusion Perspective, change is seen first and foremost as a process of communication. Initially, a new idea is introduced to a few members of a social system. Through various means of communication, word of the new idea is passed to other members. Over time, most members become aware of the innovation and may adopt it. Therefore, understanding communication processes is a core component of the Diffusion Perspective. Knowing who is talking with whom and what is being said about the innovation is important. Identifying the paths along which information is communicated and charting the interpersonal linkages are other important tools. Keep in mind that the medium that is used can include more than talk. Texting, television, e-mail, YouTube, and the Web are other important sources for learning about an innovation.

Elements Within Communication: Note Taking

An often overlooked, and certainly underappreciated, element of change is the talk that occurs among the various members of a social system. This is one reason we have placed so much emphasis on One-Legged Interviews in other chapters. The Diffusion Perspective places high priority on the importance of these actions. Consider each of the following quite typical interactions:

- In the monthly principal meeting, the superintendent describes an approach that she has heard about at the last state superintendent meeting.
- Two teachers talk about how things are going with their students' efforts to incorporate digital photos into their reports.
- A farmer goes to the Web to find information about the best interval to use between each planting. The farmer then shares the information with a neighbor when they meet at the corner cafe.
- A teacher shares her excitement for a lesson on Facebook.

It is easy to see how each of these actions could be especially important to the adoption of an innovation. In any change effort, hundreds of these types of interactions take place. At a minimum, change leaders and researchers need to be fully aware that there is a lot of communication going on.

Sometimes it can be useful to develop a record and count of the various communications that are taking place. A simple, but useful, note-taking form for doing this is presented in Figure 10.3. As is described in Chapters 2 and 6, this basic form has been used to count and categorize interventions in several year-long research studies. The following note-taking categories can be useful to have in mind:

1. **Source.** Communication begins with someone initiating action. The person's name can be inserted on the form, or a code list of potential sources can be established, for example: P = Principal, AP = Assistant Principal, T1 for the teacher Greg, and so on. This set of codes could be adjusted and expanded to name any who initiate communication. If a careful record is kept for 1 or 2 weeks, or for months, the frequency count can be quite informative. For example, these data would provide direct evidence about who is initiating the most communication, as well as who may not be communicating with anyone. This basic approach is how we were able to report that Responder Change Facilitator Style principals make significantly fewer interventions.

2. **Target.** Communication efforts will be directed toward one or more persons. The list of codes that is developed for *Sources* generally will work for *Targets*. Knowing the frequency with which each person is targeted provides an indication of how well-informed he or she may be.

FIGURE 10.3   Note-Taking Form for Documenting One-on-One Communication (i.e., One-Legged Interview)

NOTES: Communications (One-Legged Interviews)

Date ___/___/___   Location_____

I. Source _____ II. Target _____ III. Location _____ IV. Medium _____

V. Topic/Purpose:

VI. Follow-up (if any)

---

3. *Location.* Sometimes knowing where most of the communication takes place can be useful. For example, in one of our studies in California, four teachers carpooled for one hour to and from school each day. There was bound to be school talk during those long rides.

4. *Medium.* Another useful item to have on the form is notes about the medium that is used for communication. In some settings, e-mail is used more than face-to-face communication. One of the authors talks via cell phone with a colleague two to four times a day. Texting is frequent with another colleague. In these instances, placing memos in mailboxes would result in little communication and would not be timely.

5. *Purpose.* Tracking the topics and what is discussed is of obvious importance. Is the communication related to the innovation, or just social chat? Is the exchange about making a decision to adopt the innovation or reject it?

6. *Follow-up.* Often one exchange leads to another. Sometimes a leader can contribute to progress by initiating action. For example, if the principal happens to overhear the teachers talking in the introduction to this chapter, she or he could follow up with encouraging comments and perhaps by observing student talk in classrooms.

Implications of Noting One-on-One Interactions for Facilitating Change.   As obvious as each of the findings from Diffusion research may be, it is surprising how frequently most of these findings are ignored when change is being implemented. In some cases, actions are taken that are exactly opposite to what the coding of actions should suggest. For example, keeping track of the most active sources of communication provides clues as to whom to target to help with sharing additional information. Asking someone who does not initiate many communication actions to tell others about the innovation is not likely to result in information being spread rapidly.

REFLECTION QUESTIONS

Pick a change effort in which you are an active participant. From which Source do you receive the most communication? Which Targets do you communicate with most frequently? Why do you emphasize these particular Targets?

CHARACTERISTICS OF ADOPTERS

Probably the most widely studied and shared ideas from Diffusion research are those related to the characteristics of adopters. Remember the early Diffusion research question of Gabriel Tarde? Why do some people adopt an innovation quickly and others take longer? Even when

IMPLICATIONS OF THE DIFFUSION PERSPECTIVE FOR CHANGE LEADERS AND FACILITATORS

1. Keep in mind that communication is never done. Making an announcement in a staff meeting or sending everyone an e-mail does not mean that everyone "received" the message. It is very important to repeat messages and to use a variety of media to say the same thing. Off-site opportunities to communicate are important, too. Carpools, meetings at the district office or headquarters, and train and plane time are important opportunities during which to share information.

2. The metaphor of the U.S. highway system representing the lines of communication can easily be applied in organizational settings. Teachers, or other employees, travel certain routes as they come in from the parking lot, as they pick up mail, and as they go to the cafeteria. Amazingly, many change efforts do not take advantage of this phenomenon. Use it! Set up the demonstration classroom, the innovation exhibit, and examples of students' work along the lines of communication.

3. The importance of Opinion Leadership and Opinion Leaders cannot be underestimated. One of the early activities in any change effort needs to be to identify the Opinion Leaders. These individuals need to be courted and sold on the importance of the innovation. If they adopt the new idea, then others will follow. If they resist, then others will follow.

4. If the Adopter Category studies are accepted, then early in a change effort there is little reason to engage with the Late Majority and Laggards. However, there are some exceptions. For example, if an individual with many of the characteristics of the Late Majority or Laggards is a leader of a key unit, then that person must be courted. With that person's understanding and support, the rate of adoption will be much faster.

5. An external change agent needs to build linkages with the Opinion Leader(s). There is a personal side to this process, which may mean talking about hobbies, playing golf, or joining in some other, more social, activities. Most change agents are not seen as all business.

6. Be alert to the interpersonal connections. Sociograms become a very useful tool for charting relationships. Members of one group will have similar levels of knowledge about the innovation. Knowing which individuals participate in multiple groups is important, since they can pass information across groups.

there are obvious advantages, some people take longer to make the adoption decision. Literally thousands of studies have examined the characteristics of adopters. A major part of the Ryan and Gross (1943) study of farmers adopting hybrid corn seed addressed this question. Many studies have been done in developing nations as various technological innovations have been introduced. Out of all the studies, a general set of Adopter Categories has been agreed upon, and extensive descriptions of the characteristics of each have been established. Use of these categories is widespread in business and technology transfer. However, keep in mind that each of these categories is a composite and that, depending on the change, real people will vary from these archetypes.

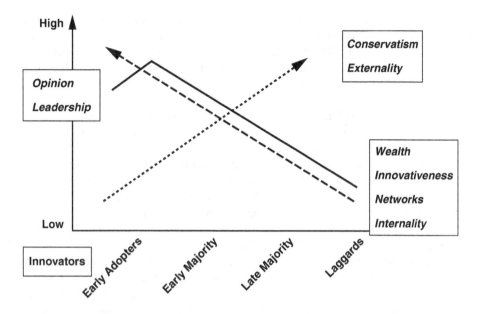

FIGURE 10.4   Distribution of Characteristics Across Adopter Categories

Adapted from Figure 5-3, p. 190, E. M. Rogers & F. F. Shoemaker (1971). *Communication of Innovations: A Cross Cultural Approach* (2nd ed.). New York, NY: Free Press.

Five Adopter Categories

A number of variations on the names and number of categories of adopters have been proposed. There is general consensus around five categories: Innovators, Early Adopters, Early Majority, Late Majority, and Laggards. Curiously, these categories and their associated characteristics tend to hold up across innovations and cultures. An overall summary of Adopter Categories is presented in Figure 10.4.

Innovators Are Excited About Trying Something New.   The very first people to adopt an innovation are the Innovators. Rogers (2003) calls them "venturesome." They enjoy change for the sake of change. They are always looking for new ideas and are ready to try them. Innovators tend to be more cosmopolitan and have more extensive networks. In schools, these are the teachers who are very active in their profession regionally and perhaps nationally. Through their more extensive networks, Innovators are likely to hear about new ideas first and bring them back to the local setting. In business and agriculture, the Innovators tend to be wealthier. Their companies have larger budgets, and the farms have more acreage. This means that trying a new idea on a few acres doesn't equate to "betting the whole farm." There is less risk if an adoption fails. Innovators also tend to see themselves as having control over their destiny (internality), rather than being the victims of circumstances (externality). At the same time, they may not be respected as much at home. "They are always trying something different."

Early Adopters Think Before Adopting.   Early Adopters adopt new ideas quite quickly, but only after reasoned consideration. They are respected locally and tend to have been in place for an extended time. Their focus is local and they are seen by their colleagues as solid, sensible decision makers. Others turn to them to learn what they think. Once they adopt an innovation, because they are highly respected, others will look more favorably on it.

Early Majority Are Careful.   Whereas the Innovators and Early Adopters are fairly quick to adopt, the Early Majority are more deliberate. They take more time and give more consideration in making the adoption decision. They are connected to others but less likely to have positions of influence, as is characteristic of Early Adopters. The Early Majority represent a large proportion of the potential adopters. Rogers (2003) estimates that 34% of the potential adopters will have characteristics of the Early Majority. This makes them an important Target for those who want to see an innovation adopted by many individuals.

Late Majority Are Cautious.   The Late Majority are slow to adopt and tend to do so only when there is pressure from others or the need becomes very strong. They need more pressure to make the change. For example, if they are losing market share or can no longer afford to compete against the success of those who have already adopted, they will move toward making the change. Peer pressure can also influence their decision making. They approach change with doubts and caution. Rogers (2003) estimates that in the typical population, the Late Majority represent about 34%. They tend to want to avoid risk because the cost of failure will be much higher for them.

Laggards Resist the New.   This label brings with it an unfortunate negative connotation. However, as the name implies, Laggards are very slow, and even resistant, to the adoption of new ideas. They are more conservative, more provincial or isolated, with less education and more limited resources. They are traditional in outlook and take a very long time to make an adoption decision. In other words, they are resistant to change. As one of our colleagues once observed, "They would complain if you hung them with a new rope." Laggards are a cause and a victim of their circumstances. Since, in general, they are less well educated, more conservative, and less wealthy, change presents more risk. Since Laggards have fewer connections to others, they also will likely have less information and understanding about the potential benefits of the innovation and fewer resources to invest in making an adoption successful. The consequence of these characteristics and conditions is that Laggards are more likely to be trapped in place.

Pothole Warning

Do not assume that all Laggards can be ignored until they see the need to adopt the innovation.

Pothole Repair

Often persons with the characteristics of Laggards will have a responsible position and can undercut adoption by others. A regularly observed possibility is for some Laggards to become excited about the innovation. In one major change project, the most visible Laggard was put in charge of making the change successful, and it was.

THE FLOW OF INFORMATION ACROSS ADOPTER CATEGORIES

As already stated, the primary theme in the Diffusion Perspective is communication. Close attention is placed on understanding the ways and the means of communication. Examining who communicates and how their communications are interpreted is important for change leaders to understand. These understandings can then be used to increase the rate of adoption. One important characteristic of some adopters is that they are *Opinion Leaders.* Another important concept is understanding the way *communication flows* across the five Adopter Categories.

Opinion Leaders

In any social system or organization, some people will be seen as the solid citizens. They are well respected locally and turned to when expert advice is needed. They are the trusted colleagues. In other words, they are the Opinion Leaders. These individuals have extra influence, although they tend to be more low profile. They probably have been in the system for quite some time, are successful in their own practices, and have had some leadership roles. At the same time, they tend to not be flashy and not be apt to engage in change for the sake of change. When it is important to obtain sound insight or advice about what is happening in a particular situation, the Opinion Leaders are the ones who are sought out.

Opinion Leadership varies across the Adopter Categories. Innovators have some influence at home, but in many ways they are seen as the ones who are always ready to try crazy ideas. They are not always trusted to have the best advice. The Early Adopters are the strongest in Opinion Leadership. They are the ones whom the other members of the system respect and to whom they turn. If they adopt an innovation and have favorable ideas about it, others will look more favorably on making the adoption decision. Innovators may be the first to try a new idea, but it is the Opinion Leadership of the Early Adopters that others follow.

Opinion Leaders in Opposition

The above description of Opinion Leaders assumes that they are in favor of the innovation. This is not always the case. Quite often, important Opinion Leaders will be opposed to the change. In these situations their strengths and influences will be working against the adoption decision. A readily available situation for observing oppositional Opinion Leaders is most political bodies. Any decision in front of a school board, a legislature, or Congress will have not only those leaders who are supporting the impending decision, but also those who are actively opposing it. Each side has Opinion Leaders who are striving to influence the direction of the decision. All the followers have to listen and then decide which way they will vote.

Communicating Across Adopter Categories

A related insight from Diffusion research is the general pattern of flow of communication across the Adopter Categories. This can be thought about in terms of where people are most likely to get their information. (This is another way to think about Sources and Targets.) The Innovators obtain a lot of their information through their extensive external networks, whereas the Laggards have very limited sources of information. In between are the other Adopter Categories.

Each Adopter Category has more communication with its adjacent Adopter Categories than with those farther away. There also is a directionality to the flow of communication that parallels the time of adoption. For example, the Early Majority learns from the Early Adopters. As adoptions spread within the Early Majority cohort, the Late Majority is learning from them. In other words, there is a general flow of communication, as well as adoptions, across the Adopter Categories from Innovator to Early Adopter, to Early Majority, to Late Majority, and finally to Laggards.

The Rate of Innovation Adoptions

Another theme within the Diffusion Perspective has to do with how quickly the adoption of an innovation spreads across a social system. We know of many innovations, such as all-day kindergarten, that have taken more than a century to be adopted by most states and schools. Other innovations, such as cell phones, seem to have been adopted by everyone within months. Studies of the rate of adoption document these differences. For example, Mort (1953) charted the adoption of kindergartens beginning in the early 1900s and found that it had taken 50 years for most states and school districts to adopt kindergartens. It should be noted that even now, another 50 years later, some states, such as Nevada, still do not require all-day kindergarten for all children.

Technology innovations seem to be adopted at ever-faster rates. Compare the rate of adoption of kindergarten with technologies such as cell phones or flat-screen TVs. The first cell phones were bigger than a book and only worked in certain areas. Business executives were the first to adopt mobile phones back in the 1980s when the phones were provided by their companies. As cell phones become smaller and had service over wider geographic areas, there were more adoptions. Today in some social systems, such as Hong Kong and Finland, the adoption rate can be over 100% due to some adopters having more than one phone, which has led to worldwide adoption within 30 years!

A related factor that can affect the rate of adoption is refinements in the innovation and increasing capabilities. Think about how rapidly cell phone technology has moved beyond making calls to taking pictures and accessing the Web, and with each new app, it becomes an even more useful device. Adopting these changes and "improvements" can easily be related to the Adopter Categories.

REFLECTION QUESTIONS

Which Adopter Category best matches you in relation to your adoption of the many innovations now available for cell phones? To find out about the latest apps, which Opinion Leaders, sources, and networks do you turn to?

The S Curve Explains It All

Another of the many contributions of Ryan and Gross (1943) was the introduction of the S curve as a way to graphically chart the rate of adoption. Figure 10.5 is an example of the S

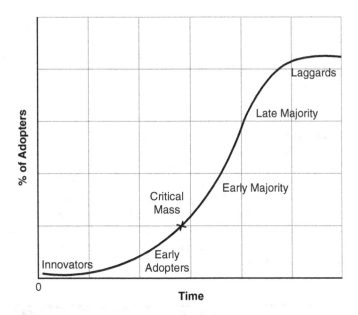

FIGURE 10.5   The S Curve for Rate of Adoption by Adopter Categories

curve and includes the typical distribution of adopters by category. Nearly all studies of the rate of adoption result in a curve of this shape. The difference from innovation to innovation will be in the steepness of the curve. In other words, as with the examples of kindergartens and cell phones, the rate of adoption across time can be charted as an S curve, but the amount of time can vary dramatically.

As the S curve illustrates, adoption of an innovation starts very slowly and then gradually picks up speed. The curve then progresses upward until nearly all of the potential adopters have adopted the innovation. As adoptions near 100%, the rate slows down significantly. The overall timeline for moving from few to most having adopted an innovation can vary from a few months to years, to decades, to hundreds of years, if ever.

The other concept addressed in Figure 10.5 is the relationship between Adopter Categories and the rate of adoption. The Innovators are few (typically, 2%–3% of a population), so the rate of adoption doesn't begin to accelerate until the Early Adopters accept the innovation. This is followed by periods of steady growth as the Early Majority and then the Late Majority adopt the innovation. As the S curve approaches 100%, the rate of adoption slows, with gradual acceptance of the innovation by Laggards.

Critical Mass Signifies an Important Point.   One of the themes of the Diffusion Perspective is that communication about and adoption of an innovation flows across the Adopter Categories. A related assumption is that at a certain point, activity and rate of adoption are sufficient so that the process will become self-sustaining. In other words, the process will reach *critical mass*. Just as the atomic reaction in a nuclear bomb becomes self-sustaining at a certain point, Diffusion theorists see a similar phenomenon happening with the adoption of an innovation. There is a point when enough adoptions have taken place and awareness of the innovation has spread far enough that further adoptions will occur without outside pressures. The actual point along the S curve at which critical mass occurs seems to range from 16% to 40%. Given the complexity of the change process in any system, it makes sense that the actual point of critical mass would vary. The key idea being introduced here is that at some point, according to Diffusion theorists, the continued adoption of an innovation within a social system should become self-sustaining.

Implications of Adopter Categories for Facilitating Change.   Social systems and organizations will have individuals that represent each of the Adopter Categories. The meaning of wealth may differ. For example, the wealth of farmers might be indicated by the quantity of acreage they own, whereas wealth for a sales representative could be the quantity of technology (e.g., laptops, GPS systems, Web connections) used to reach potential customers. Still, Change Facilitators can use the Adopter Categories and identification of Opinion Leaders to think about which individuals are most likely to be first, second, or later to make an adoption decision. They also should realize that the rate of adoption will start slowly and, with time, increase, as illustrated in the S curve.

EAST LAKE SCHOOL DISTRICT'S STORY: WORD SPREADS FAST, OR "HERE WE GO AGAIN!"

When Sara Johnson returned to River Run Elementary School from her meeting at the district office with other building union representatives, she couldn't wait to spread the word. At the meeting she immediately talked with her close colleague, Dave Johnson from Mountain View High School, who also was very active in the union. "The assistant superintendent (Leslie Hanson) has had some sort of meeting with Connie Morse from the college. Now the district is buying a new program that has something to do with the new standards, and soon teachers will be receiving special training."

Sara did not see any reason why the district should be spending money on another program when teachers needed a raise. "Those new standards aren't that different. Besides," said Sara, "today's kids just don't study. If they spoke English and did their homework, we wouldn't even be talking about changing the curriculum."

Sara did not hear that the just-announced Standards-Support Program would help teachers match formative assessments to the learning needs of at-risk students, and save teachers time in lesson planning. All Sara heard was that teachers were going to have to change their teaching "one more time." Her primary concern had to do with whether or not teachers would be paid for the time spent in training. Having been a teacher in the district for 27 years, she was "fed up" with having to do things without real compensation.

Bev White, the literacy coordinator, had attended the same meeting and was very excited about the new program. She saw it as a real possibility for helping at-risk kids succeed. She also liked that the plan included regular visits by the professor and her graduate students to help teachers adopt the Standards-Support Program. Bev immediately scheduled a meeting with the district literacy committee, which included teacher representatives from each building. Her first call was to Paul Borchardt at Mountain View High School, who is an outstanding literacy teacher in one of the most poverty-stricken parts of town. He listened carefully, asked a few questions, and agreed that this sounded like a good opportunity. Paul said that he would e-mail three of his fellow committee members and would tell several colleagues in his school over lunch.

EAST LAKE SCHOOL DISTRICT'S STORY (CONTINUED)

AN ANALYSIS WITH NEXT STEPS

At this point this story is unfolding in typical fashion. News about a meeting, a decision, and a new initiative is beginning to be communicated across a "user system." Different versions and different perceptions are being shared. Constructs from the Diffusion Perspective can be used to diagnose the current situation and in planning next steps.

The Change Agent in this case is Connie Morse, the university professor, and her graduate students. In some ways, Bev White is an "internal" Change Agent, although she is more of a Change Facilitator in CBAM parlance. Bev will have day-to-day responsibility for districtwide implementation of the change. But she also has to learn about it and how to use it. The Adopter Categories can be applied—but carefully. In some ways the categories are too simplistic and it is too easy to label someone. Still, it sounds like Sara has some of the characteristics of Laggards. She and Bev have different perceptions of the innovation. Sara does not see anything wrong with current practice (Relative Advantage) and believes funds should be spent on teacher salaries instead of another new program (Compatibility).

Paul seems to be an Early Adopter. Bev turns to him first, which suggests he has strength as an Opinion Leader, but Paul is careful (although positive) and ready to communicate with others. A beginning sociogram would have Sara and her fellow building union representatives in one group, with Paul and the other literacy-building representatives in another group.

The Diffusion Perspective can help formulate some questions at this point, too. Bev is connected to the district literacy committee, but what are her committee members' connections to their building union's representative members? To what extent do Paul and his building representatives belong to overlapping networks? What about Sara and the literacy-building representative in her school? Do they share views?

A lot of positive and timely communication to all teachers is needed. Bev needs to get ahead of Sara's message to all teachers. This is assuming that she knows about Sara's agenda, or is anticipating that someone will likely be initiating Sara's role. Immediate communication with the principals also is needed. The communication channels depend on what is available. Maybe there is a listserv for teachers. Hopefully a principal meeting is taking place very soon during which Assistant Superintendent Leslie Hanson can explain her vision and agenda. It would help to have Connie Morse from the university there, too. She is well respected. Of course, these messages will need to be repeated and sent via multiple media. For example, Bev could prepare a one-page handout of "talking points" that principals would share with their teachers. A short e-mail could be sent to all teachers and administrators.

The constructs of Observability and Trialability would be useful to consider. Perhaps classrooms in one or two schools could pilot the program. Other teachers could then see the program in action. Of course, the highways metaphor is an important consideration here. Paul's classroom would be a logical one to choose, but we don't know if he is on the "highway" or off the beaten path.

Identifying Early Adopters and getting them ready to consider and adopt the new approach will be another important part of the effort. Bev should be able to assume that the teachers on the district literacy committee will be excited about the new program. Bev should ask them to start communicating back in their buildings about the importance of this opportunity, and to show that they personally are supportive.

(continued)

EAST LAKE SCHOOL DISTRICT'S STORY (CONTINUED)

From here out, communication must continue, and as adoption begins, it will be important that the early implementers have success. They will be communicating to the Early Majority and, in time, the Late Majority.

CRITIQUE QUESTIONS

1. In this story, as with most school district adoptions, there is an expectation that use of the change will happen at the same time for everyone. The Diffusion Perspective assumes that individuals make the adoption decision at different times. What do you see happening in East Lake School District to accommodate this tension?

2. To what extent should constructs from the Diffusion Perspective be shared? Should Bev tell members of her committee that these constructs are being used? For example, sociograms could be constructed and used to plan communication activity. Who should see these? Also, in the case of sociograms, which individuals and groupings would you want to see charted?

3. In many ways, Laggard is a pejorative term. Still, the construct seems to be real. How can it be used in positive ways? In this case, Sara cannot be ignored, so what should be done?

4. Given your developing understanding of Diffusion constructs and your knowledge of the three principals (Inez Hernandez, Island Park Elementary School; Ray Raulson, River Run Elementary School; and Michael Major, Mountain View High School), how should Bev approach each of them with the adoption of the new Standards-Support Program?

PERCEPTIONS OF THE INNOVATION

Another important idea from the Diffusion Perspective is how the change is defined. In Chapter 3, when Innovation Configurations were discussed, the change was defined in terms of its operational form. What would you see when the innovation was in use? What would people be doing? In the Diffusion Perspective, the innovation is defined differently. Rather than being defined operationally, the emphasis is on understanding how the innovation may be viewed by prospective adopters and others in a social system.

Perceived Attributes of the Innovation

Instead of defining an innovation in terms of its function, or its pieces, or its intents, in the Diffusion Perspective the innovation is considered in terms of how it is *perceived*. Regardless of whether the perceptions are accurate or inaccurate, understanding how the innovation may be viewed by adopters is important to understand. In many ways, perception is reality. If an innovation is perceived to have certain attributes, then those perceptions must be considered as real and need to be addressed. There is general acceptance in the Diffusion Perspective of the following five Perceived Attributes of innovations.

Relative Advantage.   One obvious comparison prospective adopters make is to appraise the potential of the innovation in regard to it having an advantage over current practice. When there is a perception that the innovation will have greater outcomes, profits, or consequences when compared to what is being done currently, it will be adopted more quickly.

For example, a Web-based system for managing each student's test scores could be perceived as being more useful when compared to the current paper–pencil notetaking. Farmers would see a particular hybrid wheat seed that is disease resistant to be advantageous. Teachers could perceive that a particular set of curriculum materials will lead to higher student test scores. Each of these examples is based on the perception of the innovation having an advantage over current practice. This does not mean that in an absolute reality the perceptions are fully valid. Also, relative advantage could be related to other factors besides effects. For example, the innovation may be cheaper to use in terms of money or time, or the innovation may present a potential increase in status. Perceptions that are favorable will tend to increase the rate of adoption. Inversely, the adoption rate will be lowered if the innovation is perceived as not being as good in some way as what is currently being done.

Compatibility.   The degree to which the innovation is perceived to be compatible with the adopter's values, needs, and concerns influences the adoption decision. Prospective adopters weigh the innovation in terms of how well it matches with what they see as important values and cultural norms. In some groups, driving a big SUV is still "in," whereas in others it would be seen as unacceptable. These are values-based decisions. Higher compatibility will increase the chances of an affirmative adoption decision, whereas perceptions of incompatibility will decrease the rate of adoption. One of the authors of this book had a Taiwanese graduate student drop his course on change "because the course was not taught by lecture." In hindsight, given the student's cultural background, it is easy to understand how he could have had the perception of incompatibility.

Complexity.   The importance of this Perceived Attribute is obvious. Innovations that are perceived to be very complex are likely to be adopted more slowly. Innovations that are perceived to be simple to implement and use will be more readily adopted. Technological innovations are an easy example to use to illustrate complexity. The earliest VCRs were complicated to use. A dozen steps were required to record a program, and failing to do any of the steps would mean that the desired program would not be recorded. Today's recording devices automatically analyze the programs watched and then record similar programs in the future. Potential adopters like to hear from someone that "it is easy to use."

Complexity misperception is a serious problem for educational innovations. All too often policy makers, education experts, and parents will perceive that a particular educational innovation is simple and will be easy to implement. However, teachers will perceive the same innovation as complex and difficult to use in the classroom. These types of misperceptions make for interesting case studies of change attempts.

Pothole Warning
It is all too easy for policy makers and leaders at the top of organizations to perceive that a particular innovation is uncomplicated, while those who have to implement it perceive that it is very complicated.

Pothole Repair
Policy makers and leaders need to think more about how an innovation will be perceived. It might in fact be simple, but if it is perceived as complex, this perception will need to be addressed. If it really is complex, more will need to be done to facilitate implementation.

Trialability.   Innovations that are easy to try out have an increased adoption potential—in other words, trialability. Test-driving a hybrid car provides useful information. It is much more difficult to try out a new assembly line process or a year-long science curriculum. To address this potential limitation, many innovation developers create samplers and trial activities. With other innovations, it may be possible to test it in a limited way before making a 100% commitment. This happens when a farmer plants one field with new seed and the rest of the fields with regular seed. In schools, textbook adoption processes frequently include opportunities for some teachers to try out sample units. Being able to sample a component and experience success positively affects the adoption decision.

Observability.   When the innovation can be seen in use, a favorable adoption decision is more likely. Some innovations are easy to see. A drive through the Midwest in summer presents an easy-to-see example of observability. Driving along a rural road, you will see miles of corn. Occasionally there will be several rows of corn that have posts with signs shaped like corn ears. If you look more closely, you will see a number on each of the signs, such as "DeKalb A6746," and each sign has a different number. The numbers designate the particular hybrid that has been planted in that row. As farmers drive by, they can stop, look over each row of corn, and see for themselves what each type of seed produces. The farmer is then in a better position to decide which seed to purchase for next year. This is a classic example of observability. It is also a classic example of how the findings from Diffusion research can be used to increase the rate of adoption.

Addressing Perceived Attributes of the Innovation

One of the generalizations derived from the Diffusion Perspective is that the more positive the perceptions of the innovation, the more likely the chances are of having a favorable adoption decision. Keep in mind that we are talking about perceptions, not objective reality. If the perception is there, then it is a reality that should be considered. Each of the Perceived Attributes represents an area that can be anticipated and that can be addressed. To the extent perceptions are addressed, adoptions should be higher.

THE ROLE OF CHANGE AGENTS

A very important role in the Diffusion Perspective is that of a Change Agent. Unlike the Change Facilitators we have described in previous chapters who tend to be local leaders, by definition most Change Agents are external innovation experts. Their job is to engage with the user system and prospective adopters to introduce and encourage adoption of the innovation. Change Agents have expert knowledge about the innovation and its use. The Change Agent also needs to be expert in understanding how the Diffusion process works.

A good and very effective example of a Change Agent is the agricultural extension agent, who typically is part of the state university that has an agricultural research station and related academic programs. These agents also staff county extension offices. Extension agents learn from university researchers and then travel around the state and introduce farmers to the latest findings and ideas about best practices. Pharmaceutical sales representatives serve in

INDICATORS OF THE DIFFUSION PERSPECTIVE

1. The Diffusion Perspective applies to all types of systems, including businesses, and communities. A social system may be more local, such as the farmers in a geographic region or the employees in a school. A social system may be geographically dispersed, such as the participants in a Web chat room.
2. The amount of communication and the number of people engaged in making and receiving communications are key to adoption rates. More communication with more people will have a positive effect. Those with fewer connections and involvement will be slower to adopt.
3. Innovators are the first to adopt new ideas; however, they are less influential as Opinion Leaders. They certainly are Opinion Leaders, but the Early Adopters are the most influential.
4. Perceptions of the innovation influence the rate of adoption. Innovations that are seen as having an advantage over current practice, not being complicated, being able to be sampled, and matching well with current values are more likely to be adopted.
5. Early Adopters are highest in Opinion Leadership. Their views and adoption decisions influence many others.
6. Lines or channels of communication become important because those who have more access will have more and earlier information about the innovation.
7. Information about an innovation will travel fastest when there are more lines or channels of communication and more people. This is true within a building as well as across a region.

the same way with physicians. They are the *linking agents* who provide a personal connection between the researchers and the adopters. They are skilled at translating and applying what the researchers have been studying.

In addition to expert knowledge about the innovation and its use, Change Agents possess appropriate interpersonal skills for interacting with clients. When potential adopters perceive a commonality with a Change Agent, the potential for a favorable adoption decision increases. The mode of attire, the kind of car, and even whether one smokes or drinks can make a difference in Change Agent effectiveness. Change Agents may be more effective with some clients and have more difficulty in matching up with the values and interests of others. Patience and the skill to listen are other important characteristics.

Frequency of contact also becomes an important indicator of Change Agent effectiveness. More frequent contact should be associated with increases in adoption rates. However, it is possible to wear out one's welcome. Here again, becoming an effective Change Agent requires being sensitive to people and their needs, as well as being expert with the innovation.

 ### REFLECTION QUESTIONS

In your work life, who are the Change Agents? How closely do they fit the description presented in this chapter?

SUMMARY

The Diffusion Perspective has a long and rich tradition of research and widespread application. Many of the constructs have become standard content in the training of sales representatives and others who have Change Agent roles. In the Diffusion Perspective:

1. Change is viewed as a communication process.
2. Networks and lines of communication are important to increasing the rate of adoptions.
3. Five Adopter Categories have been identified and examined in detail.
4. Some adopters have greater Opinion Leadership.
5. Innovations are defined in terms of five Perceived Attributes.
6. Change Agents bring expert knowledge about the innovation and its use to the adoption decision.

DISCUSSION QUESTIONS

1. Use the Diffusion constructs introduced in this chapter to analyze the quotes that were introduced at the beginning of this chapter. Which Adopter Categories are represented? What should a Change Agent do after hearing each?

2. Choose an innovation that you, or others, are currently considering or have recently adopted. Which of the Perceived Attributes were most important in making the decision to adopt the change?

3. Think about a Change Agent you have experienced. Was this person housed inside or outside? What was the person's level of expertise with the innovation? What were the person's interpersonal strengths?

4. Think about a social system you know well, such as a church, family, community, school, or business. In that setting, who is an Opinion Leader? What characteristics are key to this person being an Opinion Leader? Which side of an adoption decision did he or she represent?

5. In the Diffusion Perspective, adoption of an innovation is typically seen as a decision that an individual makes. Farmers decide which corn seed to plant. It is an individual decision whether to buy a hybrid or an SUV. In organization settings, the adoption of a new idea is not an individual decision. To what extent do you think the organization context reduces the usefulness of Diffusion constructs, or does it?

APPLYING THE DIFFUSION PERSPECTIVE IN FACILITATING IMPLEMENTATION

1. Sociograms are fun to construct and a very useful tool for Change Agents. For a system where you have access, develop a sociogram of the interpersonal connections. Who sits together in meetings and at lunch? Who does the most text messaging? Which people are members of the same team or department? Which people seem to be isolated? If you were a Change Agent and wanted to begin implementation of a particular innovation, which people would you want to target first, second, and last?

2. For a system where you have more knowledge, identify a person who is an Opinion Leader. Interview that person about how he or she sees his or her role in the school. Also interview two or three other people about this person as an Opinion Leader. First, ask them whom they turn to when they want to know what is going on (keep in mind that they may identify someone else). Then explore what they see as the key characteristics of the identified Opinion Leader(s) that make him or her or them a trusted source.

3. For a change effort that you are part of, use the five Perceived Attributes to analyze the innovation. Which attributes have favored adoption, and which have discouraged it? To what extent have the Change Agent(s) addressed these attributes?

APPLYING THE DIFFUSION PERSPECTIVE IN RESEARCH AND PROGRAM EVALUATION STUDIES

1. Although there has been extensive study of the characteristics of the different Adopter Categories, less has been done in schools and higher education settings. These settings are different from a social system of farmers in that the leader(s) quite often make the adoption decision. All members of the school then are expected to implement the innovation. An interesting study would be to explore more closely the characteristics of teachers as adopters. What are the characteristics of those who implement early as contrasted against those who implement later?

2. Understanding and using the lines of communication is another important Diffusion construct. For a school or district where an innovation is being (or was) pilot-tested in several sites, map the location of the demonstration classroom at each site. Are the placements of the pilot classrooms aligned with the lines of communication? Does there appear to be a relationship between placement and the adoption decision?

LEARNING MORE ABOUT DIFFUSION

Rogers, E. M. (2003). *Diffusion of innovations* (5th ed.). New York, NY: Free Press.

Although older, this book continues to be the definitive resource for learning more about the Diffusion Perspective. All of the constructs and themes of Diffusion are described. Each chapter includes interesting examples of how each construct has been studied and applied. The rich history of Diffusion is reviewed. The last chapter explores the important topic of the potential for good as well as bad consequences of change efforts.

CHAPTER 11

IN WHAT WAYS CAN TEAM MEMBER SKILLS AND PROCESS CONSULTANTS AFFECT IMPLEMENTATION?

Organization Development (OD)

Our school leadership committee is really good at solving problems. We don't jump to conclusions and always begin with examining the symptoms.

—Inez Hernandez, Principal, Island Park Elementary School

We never make a decision. The meetings don't start on time. There is a lot of side-talk and the meetings go on, and on, and on. There never is closure.

—Mary Sawyer, Instructional Coach, River Run Elementary School

As a committee chair, she listens closely to what each member says and makes sure that everyone's views are heard. She never has a hidden agenda.

—Bev White, K-12 Literacy Coordinator, observation of how the Assistant Superintendent, Dr. Hanson, chairs district committees.

I like the way she (Judy Robinson, Director of Personnel Services) restates what someone has said and makes sure that we understand what the person meant.

—Fred Johnson (Director of Transportation), reflection about a team member's skill.

This consultant comes in every month and leads training sessions. We don't deal directly with our work, but what we learn can be applied.

—View of the role of a process consultant and team training experiences

In our school everyone has the opportunity to present his or her view, but once we have consensus, everyone supports it. All team members have responsibilities for what happens after a decision is made.

—Martin Chin, Instructional Coach, Mountain View High School

A regular activity in all organizations is people working with others. Meetings, committees, and teams are important ways to organize tasks, assign responsibilities, and produce services and products. When these group efforts work well, a significant amount can be accomplished efficiently and effectively. Each member feels that their ideas are heard, agreements are made, and participants are satisfied with the results. In effective group work, tasks are clear, little time is wasted, and most of the time the best ideas are agreed upon.

Unfortunately, frustration is often greater than satisfaction in group work. A lot of talk and not much listening happens, with the same points repeated and few agreements finalized. Discussion making turns into debates, with each person arguing his or her point of view in an attempt to win the argument. The alternative to never ending debate is having a dialogue where there is give and take along with an effort to develop mutual understanding. Unfortunately, group work often entails long meetings, repeated debates, little or no dialogue, and few decisions that are final.

In this chapter, the Organization Development (OD) perspective is introduced as a way of understanding the interpersonal processes and skills that can help group work be effective. OD is represented as a change model where the focus is on the processes of working together. OD is not intended to provide solutions to technical problems; instead, it is about building the capacity to solve problems. Over the years, OD experts have developed a variety of methods and tools for assessing, intervening, and growing healthy processes, especially in teamwork. The proponents of OD view it as the major approach for making long-term change in organizations.

LEARNING OUTCOMES

After reading this chapter, the learner should be able to:

1. Describe key assumptions and the overall emphases of the Organization Development perspective.
2. Identify and name characteristic group skills of effective teams.
3. Identify and name characteristic skills of effective team members.
4. Explain similarities and differences between organizational climate and culture.
5. Describe strengths and weaknesses inherent in the OD Consultant role.

WHAT IS ORGANIZATION DEVELOPMENT?

The OD perspective focuses on the interactive *processes* of people in doing their work rather than on the technical substance of the work. The primary assumption about change in this perspective is that if the members of an organization develop process skills, then the organization will be more successful in its core work. To accomplish tasks in most organizations requires teamwork. Understanding and improving the processes that teams use to solve problems and make decisions is a primary focus of OD. Another important emphasis is on the facilitating skills that each individual brings to teamwork.

Understanding and becoming expert in the use of group and individual skill processes can be very helpful for those engaged in implementing change whether they are department chairs, principals, district office administrators, team leaders, team members, committee chairs, or consultants. Today, OD strategies and consulting processes are applied widely in business and industry, in government, and in the military. Little has been done directly with OD in schools since the 1980s (see Fullan, Miles, & Taylor, 1980). However, as you will see in reading this chapter, use of many of the processes have become routine in schools.

The Beginnings of OD

The foundations of the OD perspective can be traced back to World War II and the efforts to prepare teams of military personnel to accomplish various tasks and objectives. Psychologists identified the kinds of interpersonal skills that more effective teams used. They also identified skills of individual members that contributed to overall team effectiveness. Following the war, attention was given to how these types of analyses and skills could be used for personal growth and to improve teamwork in businesses. Over time, these initiatives devolved into OD and the Human Relations movement.

The emphases within the OD perspective have varied over time, but the primary goal has continued to be to help the members of a system/organization develop expertise and the capacity to use group and individual process skills to handle whatever changes come their way. Addressing this goal now includes cross-organization processes as well. One important caveat is that in the OD perspective, the various process skills and change foci are viewed as generic. The assumption is that individuals, teams, and organizations/systems will be better able to solve their specific problems when they have developed expertise in using generalized process skills. In contrast to the Diffusion Change Agent (remember the agriculture extension agent), OD Consultants do not introduce solutions to particular problems and needs. Instead, their focus is on helping the members of the organization/system develop process skills that can be used again and again as specific problems and needs arise.

OD Definitions across the Decades

Throughout the 1950s and 1960s, development of OD was parallel to development of the human potential movement. In both cases, psychologists focused on the human side of change. In OD, the subjects were employees in organizations with an interest in improving performance; in the human potential movement, subjects were people interested in personal growth. Both movements used similar approaches. For example, rather than working with clients individually, trainers and psychologists worked with them in groups. Various types of "exercises" were created with the aim of developing group and individual skills. Each facilitated learning new skills and gathering insight into the causes of resistance to change.

Training and Planning.   The earliest methods employed to improve organization effectiveness were (a) personnel training and (b) long-range organization planning (French, 1971; McGill, 1977). The training method that emerged as most important was the *basic skill training group,* also known as the *T-group,* laboratory training, and sensitivity training. The training design typically had participants engaging in group work with artificial (rather than job-specific) tasks. The training process emphasized collecting data and receiving feedback about one's own behavior and the behavior of the group. The training approach also emphasized using the feedback to better understand oneself and others. It was believed that feedback about participants' interactions in the laboratory setting provided rich personal learning experiences that could then be applied in the workplace and/or life. The training did not directly address the workplace; rather, it was assumed that the participants could make the job-related transfer.

The emergence of systems theory (see Chapter 9) in the 1950s brought a new cornerstone to OD. In systems theory, the members of one department in an organization are seen as one of many interconnected subsystems. Each of these subsystems affects others and is affected by others. An assumption in the OD perspective is that improving the knowledge and skill of a subsystem will lead to overall improvement in the organization. In other words, training that leads to behavioral change and improvements in the members of one part of an organization will lead to overall improvement across the whole organization.

Changing OD Definitions.   As Hall and Shieh (1998) observed, one of the challenges in developing a clear definition of OD is that across the decades the definition has evolved. Definitions also vary from author to author. For example, Beckhard (1969) emphasized OD being "planned" and "organization-wide" (p. 9). Kimberly and Nielsen (1975) saw OD as a "philosophy" and a "pastiche of techniques" (p. 191). Dick Schmuck, an OD specialist who worked with schools, emphasized having "change in both formal and informal norms" (1987, pp. 1–2). More recently, Cummings and Worley (2008) talk about the "systemwide application and transfer of behavioral science knowledge" (pp. 1–2).

One trend in the definition of OD across the decades has been the shift from focusing on teams to addressing whole organizations. In recent years, the general practice is to apply OD approaches to all parts and to facilitate more long-term products, such as the development of strategic plans; at the same time, the basic themes of training in and applying process skills, data and feedback, and not solving specific technical problems have been maintained. Although different in vocabulary and emphasis, each definition and approach reflects the importance of personal and interpersonal relationships, process skill development, and having the purpose of increasing organization health and effectiveness. For those interested in implementing change, the understandings, techniques, and strategies offered through the OD perspective can be very helpful as sources of interventions, even if the total perspective is not used in a particular setting.

 REFLECTION QUESTION

Think about your experiences in being part of a committee or team. What did people do that made positive and negative differences in the group's effectiveness?

TEAM/GROUP PROCESS SKILLS

Although the overall perspective of OD is about developing the capacity for change in whole organizations, the contributions have been particularly strong in bringing about change through the identification of process skills and training of teams. In most organizations, much of the work is accomplished through people meeting with others. There are departments, teams, task forces, the ubiquitous committees, and other group-like arrangements. With the advent of such innovations as total quality management, site-based decision making, and school improvement, not only is more work being done in groups, but the groups are also expected to make group decisions. This can be a very frustrating and inefficient experience unless the members have developed skill in working as a team.

TABLE 11.1 Characteristics of Effective Teams

- Most of the talk is related to the task
- The task/purpose is understood and accepted by all
- Nearly everyone participates
- Members listen to each other
- The climate is comfortable and somewhat informal
- There are moments of humor and laughter
- There are disagreements
- Criticisms are offered and accepted
- Feelings are expressed as well as ideas
- The team leader does not dominate
- Most decisions are the result of consensus

Team Process Skills

Simply assigning people to a committee does not necessarily lead to productive results. A number of important group skills and processes have been identified; if teams use these skills and processes, the result will be more effective work. Training teams in understanding and applying these skills is a particular strength of OD. The following are some of the core skills of effective teams, some of which you will be familiar with.

Ideal Teams.   Over the years, many of the characteristics of effective teams have been identified. A sampling of these is presented in Table 11.1. In reviewing the list, you can easily compare your experiences with teams to what the ideal can be. The challenge for each group and its members is to develop the skills to perform according to these ideals.

Team Decision Making.   A key premise in the OD perspective is that, on average, groups will make better decisions than individuals. This is a disturbing idea for some, especially those who like working alone. Also, those who are more comfortable with the traditional chain of command and organizational chart perspective can be less amenable to teamwork. In many ways it is easier if the "top" make the decisions and those below follow orders. However, in most of today's organizations nearly all members are expected to contribute to making decisions.

Developing Consensus.   Proponents of OD place major emphasis on groups achieving consensus in decision making. Reaching a decision by consensus does not mean that everyone's position will be supported; however, each position is to be heard and respected. Through discussion, a decision direction emerges that has wide support within the group. As this decision takes shape, an expectation is that, in the end, those whose points of view have received less support will still accept the agreed-on decision of the group. Voting and decisions being made by the formal leader are seen as last resorts.

Data and Feedback.   In OD, the data are information about how well the group is functioning, not data about the organization's work. Surveys of participants are done regularly.

TABLE 11.2   Rules for Brainstorming

1. Set a time limit (e.g., 10 minutes)

2. Seek a large number of ideas

3. Be rapid-fire

4. Accept all ideas (in other words, no judging of quality)

5. Building on earlier ideas is expected

6. Have someone record the items

7. As a variation, try

   - Writing ideas on sticky notes and posting them

   - Sharing the sticky notes with another and adding on

   - Giving each person tokens that set the number of ideas he or she can offer

In some way, participants are asked such questions as: How did you feel the meeting went today? What could be done to make our teamwork go better? The OD process consultant/ advisor will also lead debriefing discussions and offer critiques about how the teamwork is going. Often, there will be feedback about the functioning of the team as a whole, and also feedback to the individual members about their performance. The aim of all is focused on how to further improve the team's effectiveness.

Brainstorming.   Often a team will too quickly focus in on a particular problem or solution. Alternatives and different ideas do not get mentioned or someone will quickly discredit another's idea: "We tried that once; it didn't work." This is where the team skill of *brainstorming* becomes important. Rather than leaping to a conclusion, effective groups first work through a process of generating alternative ideas, some of which may represent out-of-the-box thinking. As with other OD skills, brainstorming has a set of rules, some of which are summarized in Table 11.2.

Pothole Warning

An important skill in brainstorming is for all participants not to indicate judgment or valuing of ideas by voice or nonverbal reaction. Such evaluative behaviors inhibit others from introducing ideas that might stretch the thinking.

Pothole Repair

Begin a brainstorming activity by reminding participants of the rules. List the rules on a slide or handout. If, during brainstorming, someone violates the rules, all participants should be reminded of the rules.

Force-Field Analysis.   With the force-field analysis technique, two columns are presented on chart paper or with digital projection. In one column, participants list those forces that will be supportive of a certain action or solution; in the other column, forces that will inhibit implementation are listed. The next part of the problem-solving process entails selecting a solution (hopefully through consensus) and developing a plan to take advantage of the supportive forces and tactics for offsetting the potential effects of the inhibiting forces.

TABLE 11.3   Elements of Well-Run Meetings

1. The agenda is posted in advance (several days)

2. The purpose is clear

3. Time and place are appropriate

4. All key participants attend

5. Limited time on communicating information

6. Starts on time

7. Decisions are made

8. Next steps and timeline are assigned

9. There are surveys and feedback about meeting effectiveness

10. Minutes/notes are kept and posted (within 24 hours)

11. There is follow-up

Meeting Skills.   So much time in organizations is spent in meetings that one would expect that there should be ideas about better ways to run them. Skills and procedures for making meetings more efficient and effective have been identified. A sampling of the important elements necessary for conducting well-run meetings is presented in Table 11.3. Important additional recommendations from the OD perspective would be to have assigned roles for a Facilitator, Notetaker, Timekeeper, and Process Observer. Each of these roles provides a resource for assessing and further developing the processes that result in well-run meetings.

Team/Group Process Strategies

The above descriptions were of some of the process skills that effective teams learn and apply. Another set of processes are the larger strategies that groups use to solve a particular prob-

---

IMPLICATIONS OF OD FOR CHANGE LEADERS AND FACILITATORS

1. Everyone—consultants, leaders, and followers—will be more effective as they come to understand and develop skill in using OD processes.
2. The many methods, exercises, and survey feedback techniques of OD can be applied on a small scale as well as in sustained, whole-organization, planned change efforts.
3. Developing the skills of problem solving can be very useful because so many people jump to solutions without first identifying the facts/symptoms and describing the problem.
4. OD exercises and methods for analyzing and improving group decision making can be used by any team/department/unit.
5. The OD perspective addresses conflict resolution through a variety of strategies as well as the role of the consultant. The strategies can help organizations reduce conflict and/or develop positive ways of dealing with conflict.
6. OD is an excellent source of interventions for facilitating change, even when OD itself is not being used as the change model.

lem, develop long-range plans, and accomplish other major tasks; for example, most schools develop School Improvement Plans and most districts develop District Improvement Plans, and universities and many businesses develop Strategic Plans. In each case, individuals will be assigned to a committee with the assignment to develop the plan. The following are some of the strategies that can be used in accomplishing these major missions.

Problem Solving.   A very important set of group process skills is related to *problem solving*. When a problem is introduced in a work setting, individuals and groups have a strong tendency to leap immediately to offering solutions. In the OD perspective, solving a problem begins with first asking questions about the facts and then defining the problem. There is a careful avoidance of jumping to solutions. A number of steps to the problem-solving process have been identified, and many training exercises have been developed to help teams become better at problem solving. Figure 11.1 portrays some of the steps that can be included in problem solving. Note that problem solving is represented as a cycle; usually, solving one problem leads to new problems, so the steps may need to be repeated.

A number of training exercises may be used to facilitate a group in becoming more skilled in applying each of the steps in problem solving. For example, identifying symptoms and distinguishing these from solutions is an important early step. However, many symptoms are causes of other symptoms. This analysis could lead to the discovery that what initially was assumed to be one problem is in fact a chain of problems. Every identified problem in the chain is not of equal importance; the key is to select one of the problems that will make the biggest difference and to focus on fixing it.

Action Research.   Another useful strategy for engaging teams in learning more about their work is *action research* (Mills, 2010; Mertler, 2012). This strategy begins with an individual

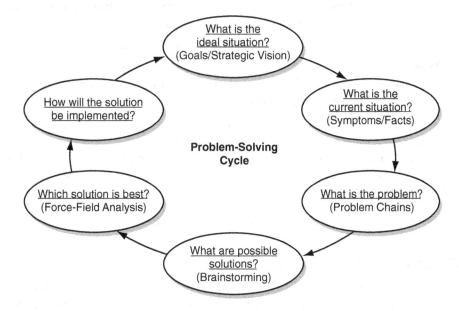

FIGURE 11.1   Problem-Solving Cycle

or team identifying a question or problem about their practice for which they would like to understand more. It could be teachers wondering if a certain instructional approach is serving English language learners or administrators questioning the effectiveness of a particular schedule. In action research, a team of implementers is established and asked to study the problem. Often, an outside expert or researcher will be available as a technical resource. However, this person is not there to make decisions for the team.

An important beginning task is coming to a consensus on the question to be studied. The next step is to identify the type of data that will be collected to answer the question. The team then collects data (in their own setting/classroom), analyzes the data, and shares the findings with colleagues. This strategy reflects many of the attributes of OD. The purpose is to examine current practice by collecting data and then having a team work on the problem. Once the skills of teamwork and data analysis are applied, the findings are then used to increase effectiveness.

Strategic Planning.   Strategic planning has become a very comprehensive and extended process used regularly by businesses, institutions of higher education, school districts, and governments. The goals are to envision the ideal future for the organization and to identify the strategies and steps for achieving the vision. School improvement processes and plans are an example of strategic planning. Developing a full strategic plan can take several years. Once developed, it must be reviewed regularly and updated as progress is made or the situation changes. Typical process steps and products are presented in Table 11.4.

"SWOT."   You may have wondered "What in the world is *SWOT*?" You know about swatting flies. Actually, SWOT represents a very useful framework that is used in strategic planning and other problem analysis efforts. Each of the letters represents a key component of what a team needs to address in developing a strategic plan:

Strengths—An organization has current strengths. What are they?

Weaknesses—An organization has weaknesses. What are they?

Opportunities—Where are there underserved needs, or emerging niches?

Threats—What forces and factors could endanger the future?

Effective teams use the group process skills such as those introduced above in their conducting a SWOT analysis. For example, brainstorming would be a useful way to begin addressing each question, and could be especially useful when exploring weaknesses. There may be discomfort in pointing out areas where things are not going well. Having the rule of not evaluating ideas during brainstorming sessions will allow for some of the not-often-talked-about issues to be named. Ideally, deciding on which items to include in the official statement of the strategic plan should be accomplished through consensus.

Making Strategic Planning Real

When a strategic planning process is introduced, the first response of many is, "So what?" These people might attend the planning retreats and offer cursory feedback about the drafts but make no real commitment to the plan. For many, a strategic plan does not become real

TABLE 11.4   Strategic Planning Process Steps and Components

COMPONENTS OF THE PROCESS

- A process consultant
- A designated leader or coordinator
- A strategic planning committee
- Retreats and workshops, including process training
- Surveys of organization members, customers, clients, consumers, and policymakers
- Top-down and bottom-up contributions
- All the organization unit's activities and aspirations nested inside the organization's plan
- Championing of the plan by the top executive leaders and governing board
- Multiyear timeline

COMPONENTS OF THE PLAN

- *Beliefs:* Statements of core values and assumptions about the organization, its members, its clients, and how things work
- *Vision Statement:* A sentence or single paragraph that describes an ideal view of the world that the organization serves (in some cases, this will be the organization's ideal view)
- *Goals:* General statements of the desired accomplishments for the organization over the next 6 months to 5 years
- *Mission statement:* An outline of the purposes and products/services of this organization that will contribute to achieving the vision
- *SWOT Analysis*: Description of Strengths, Weaknesses, Opportunities, and Threats
- *Strategies:* A set of plans, resources, and activities are described that will be used in combination with others to accomplish each goal
- *Action plan:* The specific objectives, tasks, activities, assignments, and timeline for the work that will be done
- *Indicators:* Areas of evidence that could be used to benchmark progress toward accomplishing objectives, strategies, and goals
- *Measures:* The specific pieces of data that will be collected and used to make judgments about progress
- *Cost–benefit analysis:* An analysis of the direct cost (time, dollars, and other resources) to do a task, which is compared to the potential gains (tangible and intangible) and can be used to judge the potential "return on investment"
- *Opportunity cost:* An examination of the other tasks, activities, and accomplishments that will not be done, or done with less priority, in order that those identified in the plan can be done

until the time when "real" decisions are made based on the plan. For example, if the decision on next year's department budget is heavily influenced by how well the department's proposed activities are in line with the plan, then the following year, all departments will take the strategic planning process more seriously. If the plan is used only as a public relations document, then it will have little effect on changing the organization.

Obtaining Evidence: Indicators and Measures.   Two components of strategic planning that have become increasingly important are the *indicators and measures.* In the past, clarifying assumptions and developing a vision statement had the most emphasis. There also tended to be a lot of discussion about the differences between *vision* (the ideal situation) and the *mission* (steps for moving toward the ideal). More recently, the plan for action and the timeline have been key topics in the planning process. Now the key focus is on what evidence has been and will be collected to indicate that there was change and, it is hoped, improvement.

Actually, quite a lot of hard thinking goes into deciding on what evidence is most important. The first step is identifying possible indicators that are associated with the desired improvements. For example, in a school improvement plan, there could be an objective to increase student learning in a particular subject, such as mathematics. There then must be identification of indicators related to learning mathematics, such as knowing the multiplication tables or solving quadratic equations. Once the indicators have been agreed on, the measure(s) must be determined—in other words, what data will be collected as evidence? It could be teacher-assigned grades, a standardized test score, or evaluation of student homework.

Pothole Warning

Frequently, strategic planning processes get drawn out to the point that some of the participants become very frustrated. Intervention Mushrooms (see Chapter 8) may start growing with such themes as, "This is a waste of time," and "Every meeting is the same stuff."

Pothole Repair

Leaders must continually monitor the pace of the planning process and anticipate the possible growth of themes of frustration. Also, tension may develop between the slower pace desired by the OD Consultant and the participants who desire to "get on with it."

INDIVIDUAL TEAM MEMBER PROCESS SKILLS

Consideration of individual member skills is reflective of another OD value, shared leadership (i.e., *followership*). The designated leader of a team is expected to have certain skills. In addition, the OD perspective places expectations on the "followers." Rather than the leader being solely responsible for leading, there are expectations that all members of the group will facilitate the team's work. Team leadership is seen as a shared responsibility. A number of process skills have been identified that each member of a group can use to increase team effectiveness. Some of these skills are described in Table 11.5.

Today's OD experts have refined the descriptions and use of individual team member skills. They also have created new training materials that help individuals and teams increase their effectiveness. For example, Garmston and Wellman (2008) provide training and consultation to school districts all around the United States. Their materials provide detail about the reasoning behind each skill and offer examples of ways to say things (Table 11.6). Learning and practicing these skills can be done every time you are a member of a committee or a participant in a meeting.

TABLE 11.5   Individual Skills for Increasing Group/Team Effectiveness

Encouraging: Asking another to say more, participate, elaborate, and/or lead by being warm toward and accepting of their contributions.

Clarifying: Saying an idea or point in a new way and asking, "Is this what you mean?"

Consensus testing: Asking for an indication of where each member of the group is positioned at this time. This does not mean that it is his or her final position—it is just a check on where each person is right now.

Compromising: Offering a new position that takes into account points of disagreement and suggests a middle ground.

Gatekeeping: Inviting someone to contribute. This may be someone who has not said much or a person with relevant information.

Information seeking: Asking for information about the topic or a member's concerns.

Listening: Paying attention and carefully following a discussion.

Opinion giving: Presenting one's own position or feelings.

Paraphrasing: Restating what someone has said in order to be sure that there is shared understanding.

Perception checking: Asking a person if what you think he or she said is what the person intended to say.

Seeking opinion: Directly asking for an opinion.

Summarizing: At various points in a discussion, briefly reviewing the points that have been made so far and the flow of topics.

TABLE 11.6   Advocacy Skill Steps and Examples

Make Your Thinking and Reasoning Visible

State your assumptions. "Here's what I believe about . . ."

Describe your reasoning. "I came to this conclusion because . . ."

Describe your feelings. "I feel _____ about this."

Distinguish data from interpretation. "These are the data I have as objectively as I can state them. Now here is what I think the data mean."

Reveal your perspective. "I'm seeing this from the viewpoint of _____ or _____ or _____."

Frame the wider context that surrounds this issue. "Several groups would be affected by what I propose . . ."

Give concrete examples. "To get a clear picture, imagine that you are in school X, . . ."

Test Your Assumptions and Conclusions

Encourage others to explore your model, assumptions, and data. "What do you think about what I just said? Do you see any flaws in my reasoning? What can you add?"

Reveal where you are least clear. "Here's one area you might help me think through . . ."

Stay open. Encourage others to provide different views: "Do you see it differently?"

Search for distortions, deletions, and generalizations. "In what I've presented, do you believe I might have overgeneralized, or left out data, or reported data incorrectly?"

Source: Garmston, Robert, & Wellman, Bruce. (2000). The Adaptive School Developing and Facilitating Collaborative Groups (4th ed.). Sacramento, CA 95762. Center for Adaptive Schools, www.adaptiveschools.com. Reprinted by permission.

REFLECTION QUESTIONS

Have you thought about your skill as a follower? Which skills do you use regularly in meetings?

Learning OD Tools and Techniques

The OD approach employs a number of methods for developing process skills in individuals, groups, and organizations. In many ways, these techniques and tools provide an operational definition for OD. When used well, these become powerful interventions. When used poorly, resistance develops, and OD as a change approach loses its credibility.

Survey Feedback.   An important theme in the OD perspective is collecting performance data and providing feedback to the participants—in other words, *survey feedback.* Floyd Mann, at the University of Michigan, is credited with developing this strategy (Mann & Likert, 1952). The main functions of survey feedback are to collect information about members' attitudes and opinions, to provide survey information to organization units as feedback, and to design corrective actions based on the feedback information. Various forms and formats can be used to collect the data, with questionnaires probably being the most frequently used. The regular use today of a continuum to rate each item on a questionnaire (i.e., *Likert scales*) is a direct descendant of the early survey efforts. Interviews, telephone surveys, and data about customer satisfaction or student performance are other examples of information sources. In the OD perspective, feedback of the survey data typically will be provided by an external consultant. The consultant will guide the participants in constructing an analysis and interpretation of the data. Following feedback, the consultant assists organization members in identifying steps that can be taken to improve their functioning—in other words, OD.

Exercises.   The *exercise* is the training situation that has been used for more than 50 years in OD for development of new skills, as well as in creating opportunities for reflection on current practice. It will range in length from half an hour to several days. Each exercise is designed to help participants, individually and as groups, learn new skills and reflect on their learning. Standard components of each exercise include an introduction that poses a problem; then the participants will engage in a set of activities, such as building a tower using paper and masking tape, or developing a consensus set of rankings concerning a question or topic. At one or more points during an exercise, there will be an assessment of the participants' knowledge and skill in relation to the exercise's process objective. Once the group work is completed, a debriefing and critique will focus on how the *process*—not the product—of the exercise unfolded and what was learned. Often there will be no "right" answer to the exercise; the focus will always be on the participants' process skill development and reflections about how their work in this context-free situation transfers back to their work setting.

Building Consensus.   Making decisions in teams is one of the traditional OD skills. As we said earlier, the preference is for the group to come to a "consensus" through dialogue that has all members understanding and supporting the decision. An expectation inherent in consensus

TABLE 11.7   Problem Sheet for the Exercise *Lost on the Moon*

LOST ON THE MOON: PROBLEM SHEET

You are a member of a space crew originally scheduled to rendezvous with a mother ship on the lighted surface of the moon. Mechanical difficulties, however, have forced your ship to crash-land at a spot some 200 miles from the rendezvous point. The rough landing damaged much of the on-board equipment. Because survival depends on reaching the mother ship, the most critical items available must be chosen for the 200-mile trip. The following list contains the 15 items left intact after landing. Your task is to rank them in terms of their importance to your crew in its attempt to reach the rendezvous point. Place number 1 by the most important item, number 2 by the second most important, and so on through number 15 (the least important).

_____ Box of matches

_____ Food concentrate

_____ Fifty feet of nylon rope

_____ Parachute silk

_____ Solar-powered portable heating unit

_____ Two .45-caliber pistols

_____ One case of dehydrated milk

_____ Two 100-pound tanks of oxygen

_____ Stellar map (of the moon's constellation)

_____ Self-inflating life raft

_____ Magnetic compass

_____ Five gallons of water

_____ Signal flares

_____ First-aid kit containing injection needles

_____ Solar-powered FM receiver/transmitter

Source: Based on J. Hall, "Decisions, Decisions, Decisions," *Psychology Today,* 5 (1971): pp. 51–54, 86, 88. For a full description of this exercise, consult a resource such as R. A. Schmuck & P. J. Runkel, *The Handbook of Organization Development in Schools and Colleges* (Prospect Heights, IL: Waveland Press, 1994).

decision making is that those who would have preferred a different decision still will support the one that has been agreed on. Voting is discouraged. It is seen as reducing consensus and encouraging a minority view that may be unsupportive of the majority's decision.

A classic OD training exercise for developing skill in consensus decision making is called *Lost on the Moon* (Hall, 1971). The session begins with setting the situation of a space crew having crash-landed on the moon. Each group is given a handout with a list of fifteen items that could be used in making their way back to the mother ship (Table 11.7). The first activity is for each member to make their own ranking. Then, each group is asked to develop a consensus ranking of the items. The group's ranking is then compared with the ranking developed by NASA. Usually, the group's ranking will be more closely aligned than the average of the individual rankings. In this case, there is a more valid ranking, but this is secondary to learning more about group decision making. This type of exercise is based in the OD assumption that teams make better decisions than individuals.

Team Functioning.   Another area of skill development has to do with how well each member of a team understands the task and how they contribute to the effort of the whole. Ideally, team members do not divorce themselves from the task by not contributing (or texting under the table). More effective team members strive to recognize the problems that other team members may be having. An exercise classic for learning about team functioning is *Five Squares*. In 1950, Bavelas introduced the idea, and over time it has been adapted by many consultants and presenters, including Schmuck and Runkel (1994).

With the Five Square exercise, participants are organized so that each group has five members seated at a table and one or two others are designated as observers. Each participant at a table receives an envelope with several cardboard pieces that are different in size and shape from what other participants have in their envelopes. The task of the group is to pass pieces to each other so that when the activity is completed, each participant will have assembled in front of them a square. Several important process rules must be followed: (a) Participants may not talk or gesture; (b) participants may only pass pieces to others—they cannot take pieces; and (c) the activity is concluded only when all of the assembled squares are of the same size.

The Five Squares exercise has several process objectives. Participants certainly discover the importance of talking and taking, because they are not permitted to do either in this exercise. Participants often become frustrated at not being able to talk. When several groups are doing the activity, a sense of competition develops between the groups, which adds tension. Often, one of the participants will pass all of his or her pieces to the other members and then sit back with folded arms. The group experiences added difficulty in completing the task when one member does this. The process observers will be taking notes throughout the activity, which often takes more than 30 minutes.

After the activity is completed, a debriefing about what has happened takes place. Participants are asked about their feelings and what the keys to success were. The experience will then be used as a metaphor to talk about how the members share and help each other in their workplace. For example, the observers or the OD Consultant will ask about the person who withdrew: "Does this happen at work?" "How does this affect the ability of the team/department to accomplish its tasks?"

Pothole Warning

Using an OD exercise as an intervention simply because it is interesting has the potential to cause harm.

Pothole Repair

Individual OD exercises can be used as interventions; however, the reason for the use and how it is applied must be carefully thought out and explained to the participants.

OD Exercises Are Job-Context Free.   As has been pointed out, typically, OD exercises will not directly address job-specific tasks or problems. As with the two classics described here, exercises are designed using unfamiliar contexts and with materials and activities that are job neutral. The expressed intent is to remove the job-setting context so that it does not interfere with learning new skills. The explicit assumption is that once a process skill is learned, the participants can make the transfer back to the work setting.

Finding and Sharing OD Exercises.   Many sources and types of OD exercises are available. One of the traditional strengths and significant norms of OD experts is their willingness to share exercises and to encourage others to add to the quality of each. Excellent beginning sources are the earlier publications of such experts as J. William Pfeiffer and John E. Jones in business, and Richard A. Schmuck and Matthew B. Miles in education. The Web is a very useful resource for finding exercises and learning about their applications. Reflecting the evolution in definition of OD, contemporary sources have a more holistic view of OD with more reliance on case studies; see, for example, *Organization Development: The Process of Leading Organizational Change* (Anderson, 2010).

REFLECTION QUESTIONS

Have you ever participated in an OD exercise? What did you learn from the experience? Will learning more about OD make a difference in your approach to participating in the future?

USING OD TO CHANGE WHOLE ORGANIZATIONS

As the OD field has evolved over the past 50 to 60 years, one of the trends has been toward more systematic strategies for changing whole organizations. In its early days, *planned change* was a key purpose (e.g., see Lippitt, Watson, & Westley, 1958). Proponents believed that organization change could be more successful when various processes were internalized as the regular way of working. Over time, the processes for organization change have become more complex and the view of the organization more holistic. Today, especially in business and industry, the range of models and strategies is quite wide. Still, core strategies continue to include addressing climate/culture, strategic planning, and process consultation. However, there have been significant increases in complexity and sophistication, as well as more rigorous research about their effectiveness.

Assessing and Developing Climate/Culture

Organizational climate is an important topic for survey feedback. Over the years, many questionnaires have been developed for surveying elements of climate. For example, questionnaires can be used to measure the values and norms organization members hold about such constructs as autonomy, reward orientation, the amount of communication, and feelings about colleagues ("We trust each other") and their clients ("*Those* kids can't learn this"). The OD Consultant can then work with the organization to help it become clear about its explicit and implicit assumptions. Targets can be set and action plans developed for improving one or more aspects of climate as measured with the survey.

Pothole Warning

Many climate questionnaires have little or no indications of statistical quality. If used, the resultant findings from data analyses may be misleading.

Pothole Repair

It is best to obtain information about reliability and validity of any climate questionnaire before deciding to use it. If a questionnaire with uncertain psychometric qualities is used, be sure to provide caveats of caution in drawing inferences from data analyses.

Organizational Climate Defined. The earlier efforts to define and measure organizational climate became quite confused. Many climate surveys were developed, but few had systematic estimates of reliability and validity. Often there would be little obvious connection between the survey items and the construct being measured. For example, measuring the average size of offices might be associated with a scale called *task specialization.* Quite literally, consultants would create climate surveys on the plane and apply them the next day. Very little research documented that the various climate measures did measure elements of climate (i.e., validity) and that the measures did this consistently (i.e., reliability).

A very important conceptual and empirical analysis of the early climate measures was reported by James and Jones (1974). In the introduction to their article, they observed, "Organizational climate research occupies a popular position in current industrial and organizational psychology. However, conceptual and operational definitions, measurement techniques, and ensuing results are highly diverse, and even contradictory" (p. 1096). Actually, given the state of practice at that time, James and Jones were kind in their appraisal of the state of climate measurement.

The first need was for clarity in definition of what was being measured. James and Jones proposed that three separate constructs were being addressed under the organizational climate umbrella:

1. *Situational variables* are attributes of the organization that are relatively stable over time and that represent an objective view. Such factors as size, organization structures, goals, and the degree of specialization influence the behavior of individuals and are true for the organization as a whole. Situational variables can be measured objectively, almost as if they were facts about a particular organization.
2. *Psychological climate* is an individual's perceptions of characteristics of the organization. Each person will have his or her own view of the organization. The factual situation may be different from an individual's perceptions, but the individual's perceptions are reality for him or her.
3. *Organizational climate* is the summary of the individual perceptions of particular characteristics of the organization. At its simplest, organizational climate is the average of all the psychological climate scores.

As useful as the James and Jones (1974) definitions are, they also raise questions. For example, when there is wide variation in individuals' perceptions, what is the true picture of organizational climate? Still, the definitions continue to be useful in clarifying designs and uses of climate surveys and related feedback activities.

Climate versus Culture. As the 1990s were unfolding, a new term, *culture,* became popular to use in survey feedback. This trend was taking place at the same time as the rise in use of qualitative research methods. Both trends were foreshadowed by the writings of Schein (1985) and others. Qualitative research methods emphasize the importance of in-depth observations in the field, developing rich narrative descriptions, and then looking for patterns and themes. These are the preferred methods for studying the culture of an organization.

A problem with climate surveys is that a standard set of items is used across organizations and an established a priori scoring procedure is used to determine scale/construct scores. Organization culture proponents assume that each setting will be unique in some ways and that a standardized questionnaire will miss some of the important local themes. There also is a risk that, as a consequence of a climate survey including a standard set of scales, one or another of the scale constructs could receive emphasis in a feedback session when it really is of minor relevance to a particular organization.

Assessing Organization Culture.   Being able to describe an organization's culture requires extensive time inside the organization. It also requires being especially observant and sensitive to how participants interpret symbols and ascribe meaning to actions and events. There is a delicate balancing task for the culture observer. He or she must enter the setting and be able to distinguish between seeing things as they are in some sort of objective view and learning how members of the organization interpret the same phenomenon. The culture observer also has to be able to understand the biases the participants bring to the setting. Many observers fall into the trap of interpreting things from their experiences, rather than hearing the meanings and interpretations constructed by the organization members.

Interviews are one of the key tools for assessing organization culture. Special interview questions must be developed. These will be open ended and address key elements such as the role of the leader(s), the perceptions of colleagues, and the explanations for how things are accomplished. This is what Spradley (1979) calls an *ethnographic* interview.

Examples of Organization Culture.   A wonderful example for studying organization culture was developed by a research team in Belgium under the leadership of Roland Vandenberghe. They developed a set of questions that are both open-ended and good at drawing out culture themes (Staessens, 1993). A sampling of their questions is presented in Table 11.8. The findings from their research clearly illustrate that *organization culture is a social construction.* The type of culture and its shape are the result of individual and interactive interpretation and construction of meaning. This research team identified three culture types:

1. *The Family-School:* There is an informal culture of congeniality, with an aversion to official and structural matters. The basic assumption is, "We are a great group with good intentions. We can trust the spontaneous development of matters." Teachers don't talk about their classroom work or subject matter, or visit each other's classrooms. The principal can be characterized as a *grandfather figure:* "If you have problems, you can call on me."
2. *The School as a Professional Organization:* Teachers are expected to be part of the team. There is a basic philosophy about teaching and learning that is pervasive. "We devote our heart and soul to our work." It is taken for granted that by working hard together, a great deal can be achieved. Teachers characterize the principal as an architect. Teachers can always call on the principal for help with their professional problems, and the principal puts forward his/her own ideas. "The school is his hobby."
3. *The Living-Apart-Together School:* "A ship without a compass." Teachers lack a vision about the future and speak in individual terms rather than as *we.* The principal is often not present at school or functions in an invisible way. Teachers say, "Whether the principal is present or not, it really doesn't matter much."

As these examples of organization culture imply, leadership, teacher consensus about school goals, and the shared values and norms can be quite different.

TABLE 11.8 Example Organization Culture Interview Questions

HOW TEACHERS PERCEIVE THEIR PRINCIPAL

- Do you have many contacts with your principal? What do you talk about?
- Can you tell me what is of great importance to your principal?
- To which matters does your principal pay little or no attention?
- What does your principal expect from you as a teacher?
- What does your principal expect from you as a member of the team?

DISCOVERING THE EXISTENCE OF A SHARED VISION

- What does the staff consider as very important in this school?
- Why is this considered important?
- Does everyone in the school consider this matter as important, or is this only true for a few teachers?
- How would you characterize your school during a conversation with parents?
- What exactly makes your school different from other schools?
- What are some of the stories, expressions, or slogans that are used to express what is considered as very important?

DISCOVERING THE VALUES AND NORMS AMONG TEACHERS

- How often is there a staff meeting in your school? What themes are discussed at these meetings?
- During lunch and at other times, what do you talk about?
- Do you ever look in on a colleague's classroom? How often does that happen? What makes you do that? Do you discuss it afterward?
- When you think over all the contacts with colleagues you have just described, can you say which contacts are most precious to you? Why?
- Are there things in this school that you are not able to talk about?
- Are there ever conflicts between staff members? What are they about?

Adapted from: Staessens, K. (1990). *De Professionele Cultuur van Basisscholen in Vernieuwing: Een Empirisch Onderzoek in V.L.O.-Scholen* [The professional culture of innovating primary schools: An empirical study of R.P.S.-Schools]. Unpublished doctoral dissertation, University of Leuven, Leuven, Belgium. For more information, see Staessens, K. (1993). Identification and description of professional culture in innovating schools. *Qualitative Studies in Education, 6,* 2, 111–128.

Comparing Measurement of Climate and Culture. As with other OD tools and strategies, potential strengths and weaknesses are inherent in choosing to apply a climate survey or to do the more in-depth fieldwork that is required to develop a picture of organization culture. Climate surveys are economical to use, and the resultant information can be informative. The feedback session could include each respondent receiving feedback about his or her scores (psychological climate). The individual scores could then be compared to the average for all respondents (organizational climate). This type of process can reveal to the individual how closely his or her perceptions are in agreement with those of others and provide everyone with information about the shared perceptions.

Assessing organization culture begins with extensive observation, interviews, and analysis of documents and artifacts. The resultant identification of themes will be rich and

---

INDICATORS OF OD

1. The processes of OD can be observed whenever there is a meeting of a committee, team, department, or some other group.
2. In effective teams, all members contribute to discussions and understand the importance of consensus decision making.
3. Individuals' use of process skills such as perception checking and gatekeeping are indicators of positive followership.
4. The individual skills of OD can be applied to conflict resolution.
5. Effective meetings have a posted agenda, available minutes from past meetings, and discussions that mainly stay on the subject.
6. OD Consultants observe and provide feedback about group and individual process skills. They do not advise about technical core problems.
7. Caution is advised in using climate surveys because they may emphasize characteristics that are less central to any particular organization.
8. OD Consultants expect to have a longer-term relationship.

---

grounded in the uniqueness of the particular organization. The feedback process requires special skills and should come from a consultant who is trusted. In the feedback process the resultant themes are introduced along with examples of evidence that illustrates how the themes were identified. Some of the themes would likely overlap some organizational climate survey scales, whereas others would be unique to that organization.

 REFLECTION QUESTIONS

Consider the culture in your organization. What themes are repeated frequently? What themes/issues are not talked about?

ORGANIZATION DEVELOPMENT PROCESS CONSULTANTS

Introducing an organization to OD and assisting members in developing skills to move through a multiyear process, such as is required for strategic planning, is the job of the OD Consultant. Most OD Consultants come from outside the client organization, and they have a wide range of expertise. They must be expert in consultation and training, and they must be able to diagnose problem areas and avoid inserting their own agendas. Particularly important is having good interpersonal skills. An OD Consultant's continued credibility is dependent on how well they can communicate with and be seen as supportive by all members of the organization. To be effective, they must be equally comfortable and eloquent in communicating with managers and workers. Because they are introducing processes and skills rather than dealing directly with the production of the organization, they must be able to help members understand why skills and understandings of processes are important.

OD Consultants at Work

OD Consultants bring to the organization a repertoire of process skills and understanding of interpersonal dynamics. They understand goal setting, communication, problem solving, decision making, conflict resolution, and the skills that groups and individuals need to function effectively. They also bring with them a set of interventions, including feedback surveys, exercises, training protocols, and skills in coaching individuals and groups at all levels of the organization.

Planned Change Steps.   In its totality, OD is viewed as a way of accomplishing *planned change.* In the OD perspective, a set of process steps are identified for improving an organization's capacity to change. There is a sequence to how change works, and with each step the consultant provides relevant process training and consultation. The external OD Consultant serves as coach, guide, and trainer to the organization as it addresses a need and moves through the steps entailed in changing.

From the consultant's view, accomplishing OD work goes through several phases, each laying the foundation for the next:

1. *The Beginning:* In many ways, beginning a relationship involves a courtship. The prospective client is in need of some type of help. The client is reading the interpersonal style of the consultant closely and carefully. The consultant also is engaged in an early assessment of the organization. Both are asking questions: "Can I trust and work with this person?" "Do I have the right resources to offer?" "Can we work together to address the problem?" Several contacts will be made before an agreement is struck, which will likely cover the first steps. Long-term commitment must be earned.

2. *Introductions:* Meeting key members of the organization must be done carefully. There will be uncertainty and "Self" concerns about who this outsider is. At the same time, the consultant must be a fast learner. There are bound to be mixed signals and individual perceptions that represent only part of the picture. All actions of the consultant are watched closely. Keys to success include identifying shared values, recognizing that the consultant has expertise, and seeing the consultant becoming sensitive to organization politics and building linkages with key Opinion Leaders.

3. *Assessment and feedback:* Obtaining systematic information about the current situation is important. Before deciding on a course of action, the consultant and client must share an evidence-based understanding of where things are now. As important as gathering information is, giving feedback is even more critical. The feedback must be based in the assessment and presented in ways that are seen as accurate.

4. *Stating the Problem:* The resultant dialogue leads to consensus about the problem and identification of the process strategies that will be developed. The initial assessment, the statement of the problem, and the identified strategies also provide the baseline for future measurement of change.

5. *Action planning:* To accomplish change, actions must be taken. The process of developing the action plan should include as many of the members of the organization as

possible. What will be done and the timeline should be clear. The plan must be affordable, doable, and supported by top executives.

6. *Interventions:* To accomplish the change, interventions likely will be needed at three levels: whole organization, groups, and individuals. Whole organization interventions might include training in strategic planning, a reorganization of production tasks, or a change in the reward system. Group and team interventions could include exercises in interpersonal communication, decision making, and team skills in meeting roles and responsibilities. Addressing how individuals work in organizations could be done through self-study and reflection as well as interpersonal process skill development.

7. *Evaluation:* Collecting and using evidence is a continuing part of the OD process. Each intervention activity can be evaluated and used to refine the next steps. Evaluations should be done across time so that there are regular snapshots for viewing progress and identifying emerging areas of need. Evidence should be collected at the end to judge how successful the process has been.

8. *Sustaining:* Only after outcomes become a staple in group work and are ingrained in the organization culture does it mean that the organization has changed permanently. Another indicator is that the new ways continue when there are changes in key personnel and the client is no longer dependent on the presence of the OD Consultant. This does not mean a rigid adherence to a certain way of doing things, however.

9. *Separation:* The consultant is no longer needed for the change to be sustained, or the consultant role is reduced to occasional appraiser of continuation of the change.

OD Consultant Issues.   As with all change perspectives, OD presents a number of issues and potential problems. One is the extent of knowledge and skill required of the OD Consultant. For example, each of the OD processes and related intervention exercises is interesting. However, processing the exercise sessions is a delicate matter and requires a high level of skill. Consultants also must be skilled at working with all levels of an organization. The consultant is likely to be contracted by a top-level executive (e.g., the district superintendent), but he or she must also be able to work with principals, teachers, and perhaps bus drivers. This requires flexibility and genuine comfort in working with diversity.

Because OD Consultants come from outside, they must earn their continuing involvement. Their contract can be terminated at any time. They must work well with the executives. They also should continually remind themselves that their primary client is the organization, not just the top executive(s). They must do all of this while maintaining confidentialities with everyone. Consultants will have knowledge of impending strategic decisions and various employee personal problems. They must be responsible to the people, the organization, and the planned change effort.

REFLECTION QUESTIONS

What are your thoughts about you serving as an OD Consultant? Which of the skills do you already possess? Where would you have the most difficulty in being effective?

EAST LAKE SCHOOL DISTRICT'S STORY: ANOTHER DYSFUNCTIONAL MEETING

A ONE-LEGGED INTERVIEW

"We just won the basketball game by ten! We're going to Regionals!" These were the thoughts of Mountain View High School Principal Michael Major as he saw Superintendent Johnson approaching.

"Congratulations! This year's Mountain View team sure works well together."

"Yea! I sure wish the school's Administrator Council worked as well."

Superintendent Johnson inquired, "What's wrong?"

"All of them are good professionals. It's just frustrating that every time we have a meeting, everyone doesn't get there on time. If he comes, Bob Smith (Athletic Director) always arrives late. Then he and Helen Morse (Chair of the English Department) continue to snipe at each other. It's hard to get agreement and a decision made. Then at the next meeting, someone who wasn't there will question what we decided at the last meeting."

"Sounds like you need a coach to build a team."

"Boy, that's right. Maybe I should have Paul (the basketball coach) reassigned—after we win state."

"You know Judy Robinson (District Director of Personnel Services)? She's been doing some work with the board. She might be of help. Why don't I ask her to sit in on one of your meetings?"

SCHOOL ADMINISTRATOR COUNCIL MEETING

Two weeks later was the regularly scheduled meeting of the Mountain View High School Administrator Council. Judy had talked with Mr. Major beforehand and they agreed that she should sit in as a *meeting process observer*. The meeting unfolded as usual. Mr. Major had listed the meeting topics on the white board. Coach Smith arrived 12 minutes late and sat across from Helen Morse. Within minutes, in a snide way, he had questioned Helen's suggestion. Their back and forth ran the discussion of topic. Two of the others were texting most of the time. Nothing was decided. It was not a collegial or effective gathering.

PRINCIPAL AND PROFESSIONAL LEARNING DIRECTOR DEBRIEF

"You were right. The meeting unfolded as you had expected." Continuing, Judy suggested several steps and changes that will sound familiar to those who know about OD:

1. Post the agenda for each meeting two days ahead of time.
2. Begin each meeting on time (regardless of who is not there).
3. Assign seats (just like managing unruly students in class).
4. Begin the next several meetings with a meeting skill activity (so that all can learn more about their responsibilities as followers).
   a. Let's start with an exercise called "Five Squares" that will help them learn about providing information to others.
   b. At the next meeting, we can work on consensus decision making using another exercise called "Lost on the Moon."
   c. To balance talk time, we can give each person four tokens.
   d. We also can work on the rules of brainstorming.
5. Let's establish some new roles—timekeeper, note taker, and facilitator.
6. And, let's disseminate the minutes of each meeting, with decisions highlighted, within 24 hours.

EAST LAKE SCHOOL DISTRICT'S STORY (CONTINUED)

DEVELOPING TEAM MEETING SKILLS

Judy agreed to serve as the Process Facilitator for the next several meetings. At each meeting, she provided survey summaries about how the "team" was working. She served as the OD Consultant in leading and reflecting on the "Meeting Skills Activities," which were now an expected part of each meeting. As was hoped, being late was no longer a problem and the meetings were gradually becoming more productive, and sometimes even "fun." Posting meeting minutes with an emphasis on decisions made had nearly eliminated the second-guessing.

CRITIQUE QUESTIONS

1. What relationships do you see between how the administrator meetings were functioning and the OD exercise suggested by Judy?
2. If you were the OD Consultant in this case, which group (Table 11.3) and individual process skills (Tables 11.5 and 11.6) would you want to see developed first?
3. What characteristics and style would Judy have to possess in order to be credible as meeting facilitator? After all, she is a district office administrator.
4. At what point would you decide that Judy was no longer needed at the meetings?

SUMMARY

OD represents a different perspective for understanding and implementing change. Key themes in this perspective are:

1. The role of the external process consultant and the planned change steps represent a systematic approach to change.
2. The OD perspective does not focus directly on the core technology of the organization or implementation of a particular innovation.
3. Change is addressed through development of group and individual process skills such as team building and problem solving.
4. Providing feedback from surveys, climate measures, and observations are fundamental interventions for organization development.

DISCUSSION QUESTIONS

1. Have you ever participated in an OD planned change effort? What was it like? What processes were used?

2. Have you ever participated in an OD training exercise? What skills were being developed? Did you find that you were able to bring the skill back to your work setting? Why or why not?

3. Planned change efforts using strategies such as strategic planning and school improvement are designed to involve everyone in reviewing the current situation and setting an agenda for the future. As a leader, how would you see using OD concepts and methods to involve everyone?

4. Participants in OD are often slow to see any connection between the time spent in doing exercises and doing their job. What do you think about the OD reasoning of not using the work context in process skill development? What would be gained or lost from embedding the training in the work context?

5. The OD Consultant represents himself or herself as not bringing a solution to any particular problem and not representing a certain direction for the organization. By comparison, the Change Agent in the Diffusion Perspective openly represents and advocates for adoption of a specific innovation. In many ways, OD and the OD Consultant are innovations that must be adopted. To what extent do you think that OD and the OD Consultant are innovations? With OD, what is the innovation(s)?

APPLYING ORGANIZATIONAL DEVELOPMENT IN FACILITATING IMPLEMENTATION

1. Observe several meetings of a group. This could be a committee, a department, a team, or a complete staff. Use the skills list presented in Table 11.5 and 11.6 to observe the group's process. Which skills do individual members of the group apply? How are decisions made? Does the leader make them, or are they made by consensus or voting? Would other skills, if used, help the group in accomplishing its tasks?

2. Go to the Web or consult one of the suggested readings and select a training exercise that you could process for a group. Work closely with a colleague or your instructor on all that is entailed in serving as the process consultant for the selected exercise. Develop a feedback form to evaluate your role in leading the exercise and your skill as the consultant. Select a group of colleagues or fellow students and try leading an OD exercise. At the end, be sure to critique the exercise and your role as the process consultant.

3. For at least one week, see how many of the skills listed in Tables 11.5 and 11.6 you can use. You can apply them as the follower and/or as the leader of a group or committee. You also can use them in One-Legged Interviews. Take down some reflective notes about your skill and the effects of your efforts.

APPLYING ORGANIZATIONAL DEVELOPMENT IN RESEARCH AND EVALUATION STUDIES

1. Many interesting and useful action research studies can be imagined. For example, if a particular team or committee wanted to improve its functioning, a study could be made of the process skills currently used. With agreement to do action research, the list of individual process skills outlined in Tables 11.5 and 11.6 could be used to develop a checklist. Then a colleague who is not a member of the group could observe several meetings and use the checklist to tally skills use. Subsequent analysis and discussion of the checklist data could be used to identify skills that are frequently used and some for which an OD exercise might provide useful training.

2. OD theory, constructs, and tools could be used to study planning processes. For example, each year, most schools and districts must complete an improvement plan. Studies could be done of the extent to which different OD constructs, skills, and tools are used. A major source of variation is the extent to which the once developed improvement plan is used to make decisions throughout the year. Examining differences among schools or districts that are associated with higher/lower OD skill expertise, and more/less implementation of the plan, could be informative.

LEARNING MORE ABOUT ORGANIZATIONAL DEVELOPMENT

Books about OD

There are many books related to OD, especially related to its applications in business settings. Some texts relate more to schools and education settings.

Anderson, D. L. (2012). *Organization development: The process of leading organizational change*. Thousand Oaks, CA: Sage.

> The historical background of OD provides the basis for describing the role of the consultant and the processes of OD. An elementary school case is used to illustrate how OD can work.

Brown, D. R. (2011). *An experiential approach to organization development* (8th ed.) Upper Saddle River, NJ: Pearson.

> The emphasis is on learning OD through experience. OD concepts and theories are related to techniques, exercises, and behavioral simulations.

French, W. L., & Bell, C. H. (1998). *Organization development: Behavioral science interventions for organization improvement* (6th ed.). Upper Saddle River, NJ: Prentice-Hall.

> For a traditional view of OD, how it works, and keys to its success, this is the book. The authors are long-time scholars and practitioners in the field of OD. The history, current practices, and examples of efforts to make long-range change in organization culture and social processes are described. In many ways, this book reflects the dynamic and evolving nature of OD, from its earlier human potential days to today's context of globalization and contemporary innovations such as total quality management.

Gallos, J. V., & Schein, E. H. (Eds.) (2006). *Organization development: A Jossey-Bass reader*. San Francisco, CA: Jossey-Bass.

> The authors for each chapter in this book of readings, and the editors, are major names in the field. The early chapters present the history of OD. There are readings that describe various theories and others that explore interventions. Separate readings explore intervening with small and large groups. Other readings address intervening on whole organizations.

Learning More about OD Online

Searching for OD on the Web is like most other topics. There are many sites and potential resources, as well as much that is worthless. Using the search term "OD" yields some 2 billion possible sites! Attempts to narrow the search with phrases such as "organization development, exercises for schools" don't narrow the list. Web searching will just take time, which is why accessing one or more of the books and references suggested in this chapter will most likely be more useful.

PART V

COMBINING VIEWS

Perspectives, Constructs, Tools, Applications, and Implications

The Concerns-Based Adoption Model (CBAM)

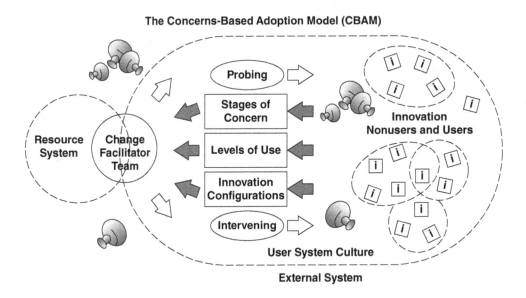

The previous 11 chapters have introduced different ways of understanding and facilitating change processes. Chapter 1 introduced a set of *Change Principles* that we see as givens. There is no need to debate any of them. Chapter 2 addressed *Interventions*, the actions that are taken to facilitate implementation of the change. The change itself is the *Innovation*, which must be implemented by users before we can say that the organization has changed.

Chapters 2 through 9 flow from understanding implementation at the individual implementer level (Part II) to ways of understanding and facilitating change across organizations (Part III) to different perspectives for understanding and facilitating change at the macro level (Part IV).

In this final chapter, we delve into ways to apply different combinations of the constructs and perspectives that have been introduced in the preceding chapters. Examples of findings from research and suggestions for needed research are presented. Studies of program evaluation are sampled to point out implications for future studies and for facilitating change efforts. There also are descriptions of several conceptual extensions that go beyond what we currently know from research.

In all, in this last part, the intent is to provide examples and illustrations of how the various constructs and tools have been, and could be, applied to facilitating and studying change processes. It is hoped that some of these examples and stories will lead to you, the reader, having better ideas and ways for facilitating and/or evaluating and/or studying change processes.

Once again, here is the graphic of the Concerns Based Adoption Model (CBAM). However, this time no particular elements are highlighted; instead, the whole of the Concerns Based perspective is displayed. In this perspective, there are three *Diagnostic Dimensions* (Stages of Concern, Levels of Use, and Innovation Configurations). *Change Facilitators* and researchers/evaluators must be continually *probing* (using measures such as *One-Legged Interviews*) to determine the current status of SoC, LoU, and IC of the various *individuals* and *groupings*. These diagnostic data are then used to make *Interventions* that facilitate movement across *The Implementation Bridge*

Change Facilitator Styles becomes important, as does understanding *Organization Culture*—especially having a Personal Learning Community (PLC). Also, there will be various nutritious and toxic *Intervention Mushrooms* that must be understood. Also, any organization or *User System* is part of, affects, and is affected by its *External System* context.

In a *Systems View* for understanding and facilitating implementing change, the many constructs identified in CBAM are moving at the same time. This means that there must be continual assessing of the current state of individuals, the innovation, and the user system. More effective change leaders and scholars do this naturally. To address this dynamic, reality in research and modeling requires delving into *Adaptive Systems Theory*, but that is the topic for another text.

An important caveat that ranges across all that has been introduced is the *ethics of change agentry*. Each of the constructs and tools can be used for better or worse. There are no formal ways of monitoring or appraising what you, the reader, and others do with these resources. It is very important that before, during, and after use of any of the constructs and tools that users should reflect thoughtfully on the following question:

"Is what I am doing responsible and being done for the right reasons?"

■ ■ ■ ■ ■ ▬▬▬▬▬▬▬▬▬▬▬▬▬▬▬▬▬▬▬▬▬▬▬▬▬▬▬▬▬▬▬▬

CHAPTER 12

HOW CAN CHANGE CONSTRUCTS BE COMBINED TO UNDERSTAND, ASSESS, AND LEAD EFFORTS TO IMPLEMENT CHANGE?

We have so many programs and initiatives going on! How are we supposed to know what is worth keeping?

—Michael Johnson, Superintendent, East Lake School District

You know, I think there are some important relationships among SoC, LoU, and IC that we now need to understand.

—Dr. Leslie Hanson, Assistant Superintendent, East Lake School District

I see such basic differences in how principals lead. I think what they do, and don't do, affects more than teacher success in implementing new programs.

—Bev White, K-12 Director of Literacy, East Lake School District

There is a larger system view that we need to keep in mind. For example, some organizations, such as districts and some schools, are more ready for change. They have the capacity to accomplish more.

—Hillarie Martinez, State Superintendent of Public Instruction

The objective of this chapter is addressing the questions and different views introduced in these quotes. Preceding chapters introduced a rich set of principles, constructs, tools, and perspectives. Each can be of assistance in understanding, facilitating, evaluating, and researching change efforts. Across the chapters, the unit of change—that is, the *implementer*—ranges from the individual(s) to groups, to whole organizations, to considerations of change across large social systems. Also, facilitating change has different scope and depth depending on the size and type of change unit. Implementing a change with a few individuals is vastly different from accomplishing a companywide change or changing a state or nation.

The change perspective that served as the foundation for all chapters is the *Concerns Based Adoption Model (CBAM)*, first proposed by Hall, Wallace, and Dossett (1973). A significant characteristic of the constructs and tools presented in this text is that all are *evidence-based*. The information and ideas introduced in each chapter are not groundless generalities and platitudes, but have been conceived through research and deal with the realities of implementing change on the ground. Each chapter makes reference to some of the extensive research verifying and supporting the introduced constructs and their applications. Each chapter provides illustrations of how each construct and its tools can be used to increase change process success.

In this chapter, we describe how the various constructs and tools can be used *in combination*. Also, success entails more than having implementers move across the Implementation Bridge; the ultimate purpose of a change initiative is to *increase outcomes*. In this chapter, we present research examples and issues related to linking extent of implementation to outcomes. The final, and not to be underrated, topic is *ethics of change agentry*. All of the constructs, tools, and applications introduced in this text can be picked up and used in responsible or malevolent ways. Users and recipients of use of these constructs and tools must continually reflect on the question, "Is this an appropriate action to take?"

LEARNING OUTCOMES

After reading this chapter, the learner should be able to:

1. Describe combined applications of SoC, LoU, and IC for measuring the extent of implementation in program evaluation and research studies.
2. Reflect on issues related to assessing implementation of multiple innovations.
3. Examine relationships between core change constructs.
4. Identify issues and implications related to sustaining change.
5. Describe emerging relationships between Change Facilitator Style and outcomes.
6. Understand the importance of being sensitive to and reflective about responsible use of evidence-based change constructs and tools.

ASSESSING IMPLEMENTATION IN PROGRAM EVALUATION AND RESEARCH STUDIES

In the first decade of this twenty-first century, the phenomenon of implementation and its related challenges became a major focus of attention for policymakers and scholars. For a long time, practitioners on the ground have been engaged with increasingly complex innovations and experiencing the many real world challenges of implementing change. Until very recently researchers were confident that random assignments and experimental study designs accounted for differences in implementation qualities. Policymakers, who had been through the struggles to get new policies approved, tended to move on to the next agenda. Few wanted to hear about the complexities, which would mean longer time periods before other changes could be launched, more costs, and delays in obtaining the desired outcomes.

This all changed in the first decade of the twenty-first century. Researchers, program evaluators, policymakers, and change leaders were in agreement that the phenomenon of implementation had to be addressed and that the issues are complex. A new discipline was established: "Implementation Science." Indicators of this emerging discipline and widespread interest include such items as a 2005 literature review that cut across the social sciences (Fixsen et al., 2005), and in 2013, a two day panel entitled "Investing in what works: Supporting the implementation and evaluation of evidence-based programs for children, youth, and families" was organized by the American Institute of Research for the Department of Health.

Now, it is more important than ever that evidence-based tools be applied to assess implementation in program evaluation and research studies. The constructs and tools introduced in the preceding chapters provide strong examples of ways to assess implementation, draw connections between the extent of implementation and outcomes, and identify emerging questions. For example, what should be the unit of analysis?

Units of Change: Systems, Organizations, Groups, Individuals

An important question to answer early in a change effort is this: What is the unit of change? Is it an entire system or organization, certain departments, or particular individuals? The answer to this question tells a lot about what should be the primary unit of analysis in studies, as well as the target(s) of interventions. Regardless of the answer, without exception some individuals will be expected to implement change. Systems and organizations may adopt change, but individuals implement it. There are four basic units of change that must be kept in mind: the individual, a group or team, an entire organization, and large systems (see Figure 12.1).

The System as the Unit of Change.   Often, large systems such as the farmers in Iowa (Chapter 10), a national company, the statewide delivery of a service, or a school district are

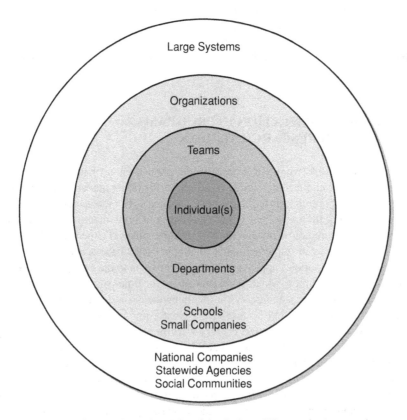

FIGURE 12.1   Units of Change: Potential Units of Analysis and Targets for Interventions

targeted for change. For example, many school districts are engaged with implementing the Common Core State Standards. All states and districts have implemented some approach to *Response to Intervention (RTI)*. As another example, many states and school districts are implementing new teacher/administrator evaluation programs that are closely connected to student outcomes. Each of these initiatives includes the expectation that the "smaller" units will be implementing the change. If they do not, there will not be system-wide change.

The assumption is often made in large-scale change initiatives that all parts of the system must do the same thing and at the same time. For example, federal education mandates often require all states, school districts, and schools to do the same thing. In this "one size fits all" approach, all subparts or subsystems of the system are given the same directives, rules and regulations, and consequences. In terms of implementation research, it is obvious that different subsystems will implement at different rates and with different degrees of fidelity.

A systems approach should build in adjustments in anticipation that there will be variations. With education policies, for example, adjustments could be based on the proportion of English Language Learners, the extent of teacher professional development, and the extent of state-required testing already in place. These differences in implementation context become important to document in evaluation and research studies.

Pothole Warning

Many policymakers, organization leaders, and researchers assume that proc-lamations and directives will accomplish uniform change across all parts of a system.

Pothole Repair

Regardless of the intent, there will likely be important differences in implementation across subunits and individuals that must be documented, understood, and addressed.

An Organization as the Unit of Change.   An organization as the unit of change could be a particular business site, such as the local fast-food restaurant or a specified school within a district. Each of these units does not operate independently of the system of which it is a part, but each organization has its own change context. For example, some changes are initiated from outside, others are launched by the organization, and some start from lower levels within the organization. Another element of the context is that the leader of the organization (e.g., the school principal, the plant manager) has a particular CF Style (Chapter 6). The organization leader has an important role to "rally the troops" and convince them that the change is important and beneficial; however, each does it in their own way. The overall plan for implementing change, and any evaluation or research study, should take these characteristics into consideration.

Teams or Divisions as the Unit of Change.   A smaller intervention unit is that of teams and departments. This unit is important to consider in studies and most certainly is an important target for interventions. As stated previously, even when a whole organization or system is implementing change, some customized intervening must be done for each team/group. The OD perspective (Chapter 11) represents a resource for process skill development interventions to help these units develop problem-solving and group-work process skills. Customizing support as well as documenting differences in capacity are important. For example, the marketing division will need support and assistance that differ from the sales division. The district office curriculum department staff will need different interventions than will the accountability department.

The Individual as the Unit of Change.   Regardless of the overall scale of change, in the end, implementation of the innovation is accomplished at the individual level. In some way, each change perspective addresses the role of the individual in implementing change. The Diffusion perspective identifies five Adopter Categories. The OD perspective emphasizes process skills, whereas the cornerstone of the Concerns Based model is the three Diagnostic Dimensions (SoC, LoU, and IC). Nearly all—if not all—change initiatives should take into account the role of the individual. As has been emphasized at several points in this text, change is not accomplished until each person implements the innovation.

CBAM Begins With the Individual.   As the name implies, the CBAM perspective begins with emphasizing the importance of understanding and addressing the personal side of change. Each person may differ measurably in terms of their understanding and skill to implement a particular change (LoU), willingness to change (SoC), and achieving fidelity to the developer's vision (IC). Some will change readily, others will come to understanding and be willing to implement a change over time, and some will never reach full acceptance. Some will become confident and competent users of ideal Configurations quite quickly. Others will struggle. Understanding and addressing these differences are important to overall implementation success. Regardless of how big or small the overall unit of change, the three Diagnostic Dimensions of the CBAM perspective can be used to account for and address individual differences. The individual data can be aggregated to assess teams, whole organizations, and/or systems.

REFLECTION QUESTIONS
In your experience, which units of change have you seen emphasized? Which should have received more/less emphasis?

Evaluating and Facilitating Implementation of Single Initiatives

Most change initiatives are about a particular innovation or innovation bundle. The resources, technical assistance, and/or study are aimed at seeing the change fully implemented and the associated outputs happening. The three CBAM Diagnostic Dimensions can be used alone or in combination to assess and facilitate these initiatives. With each construct, the initial measurement is of individuals. The individual data can be aggregated to see how larger units of change are doing.

Stages of Concern: Whole Group Profiles

In the CBAM perspective, diagnostic information about individuals can be aggregated for teams, departments, whole organizations, and across large systems. For example, in most projects the individual SoC profiles will be combined to develop a group SoC profile. With a large sample of respondents, subgroup SoC profiles can be identified as well.

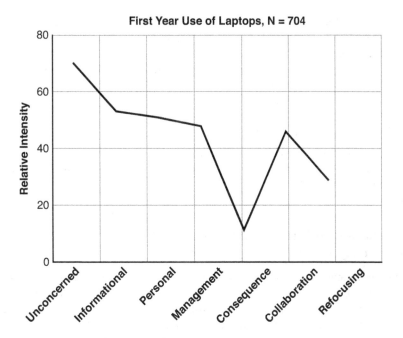

FIGURE 12.2   Group SoC Profile for Teachers in the First Year Implementation of Laptops

SoC Whole Group Profiles (an example): Laptop Computers for Teachers.   In Victoria, Australia, the Ministry of Education decided to provide each teacher with a laptop compu- ter. As part of the initiative, an evaluation team was contracted to monitor implementation (Matthews, Marshall, & Milne, 2000). One of the assessment measures was the SoC Ques- tionnaire (SoCQ). Figure 12.2 is the SoC group profile for the study sample of 704 teachers.

   This profile compares well with the theoretical SoC Wave Motion (see Figure 4.1) that depicts the flow of concerns as implementers move from nonuse to early implementation. The group laptop SoC profile indicates a combination of Self and Task concerns being intense, which reflects what the researchers had been finding through interviews. Some teachers were still not doing much and uncomfortable about what they should be doing (Stage 1 Informa- tional and Stage 2 Personal), while others had concerns about how to be efficient and to pri- oritize trying out the many programs and potential uses (Stage 3 Management).

   An atypical point on the group SoC profile is the higher Stage 5 Collaboration con- cerns. On further investigation, this was explained by the fact that for 6 years the state depart- ment of education "has encouraged teachers to work together and to support one another" (Matthews & Hall, 1999, p. 3). There had been several years of system support for teacher collaboration.

SoC Subgroup Profiles.   With a large sample of individual data, it can be important to search for subgroups of individual SoC profiles that have common characteristics. For exam- ple, in the laptop study, six subgroups were identified. Each fit within the overall Self–Task early implementation theme but varied in which SoC were most intense. Some were very high on Stage 1 Informational, while another subgroup had very intense Stage 2 Personal concerns. Two of the subgroups had "tailing up" on Stage 6 Refocusing.

All these data reflect the importance of understanding the current status of individual implementers and aggregating to assess the overall status of groups and the whole system. With this diagnostic information, interventions can be prepared that are customized for each subgroup as well as for the whole.

 ### REFLECTION QUESTION

Given the information from the Australian SoC implementation assessment of teachers using laptops, what would you recommend be included in the next phase of change facilitating interventions?

The Implementation Bridge: Using LoU and IC to Assess Change Progress

Collecting implementation data at any point in time represents a snapshot of current status. One-time data collection does not tell us what the situation was in the past, or what it might be like in the future. Information from a snapshot most certainly can be used as diagnostic information for planning next steps. Ideally, multiple snapshots will be accrued across time. Then movement across the Implementation Bridge can be charted. The following example comes from a study where LoU and IC were measured at the end of the first and second years of implementation.

A School District Superintendent Wants to Know.   One school system with a history of making concerted efforts to improve schooling and to evaluate the results is the U.S. Department of Defense Dependents Schools (DoDDS). This is the system of school districts spread around the world to provide schooling for the children of members of the U.S. military. In one of the DoDDS school districts in Germany, the superintendent made a concerted effort to support the implementation of a dramatically different approach to teaching mathematics. The curriculum innovation was based on the standards for teaching and learning developed by the National Council for the Teaching of Mathematics (NCTM). The approach required teachers to make a dramatic change in their teaching. Rather than teaching rules for computation, the new teaching strategy was constructivist: Teachers should pose mathematical problems, and the students should construct answers using their own approaches. Rather than the teacher explaining the one correct way, students must explain their reasoning and how they got their answers.

This approach represented a major change for many veteran teachers. Understanding this, the superintendent developed an Intervention Game Plan (Chapter 2) centered on employing three master teachers as district-wide specialists. These change facilitators designed workshops, presented demonstration lessons, consulted with teachers, and paced the implementation effort. In addition, the superintendent understood that change is a process, not an event (Change Principle 2), so the commitment to having three math specialists, as well as other resource and training supports, was kept in place for 3 years (Johnson, 2000).

The size and seriousness of the investment plus the political risk (because focusing on mathematics for 3 years meant that a number of other areas were not as high on the priority list) led the superintendent to ask the question: "How can I know if this investment is making any difference?"

Assessing Extent of Implementation (Levels of Use and Innovation Configurations).
The Implementation Bridge metaphor made sense to the superintendent and the other district leaders. The decision was made to assess the extent to which teachers were moving across the bridge by measuring each teacher's LoU (see Chapter 5) and for each classroom completing an Innovation Configuration (IC) Map (see Chapter 3).

Action Research Can Happen.   An added dimension to this effort was that the change process researchers and the school district staff collaborated in design and conduct of the study. School district administrators and lead teachers were engaged in data collection, data analysis, interpretation of findings, and report writing. It was a true example of action research (Stringer, 2013). The research questions were developed by the district, and researchers and practitioners collaborated in conducting all aspects of the study. In addition, the data about implementation were used as diagnostic information for further facilitating implementation, as well as for answering the superintendent's question.

Two Snapshots Are Better than One.   To document change, extent of implementation must be measured a minimum of two times. In the districtwide mathematics implementation project, extent of implementation was measured at the end of the first and second years of the effort. The school district staff, including the superintendent, were trained to research criterion in conducting and rating LoU Interviews. Each year they, along with the researchers, collected data on more than 100 teachers representing all schools and across grades K–8 (Thornton & West, 1999).

LoU across Two Years.   The LoU data for the first 2 years of the implementation effort are summarized in Figure 12.3. Three key findings were as follows:

1. Each year, all teachers sampled were users at some level of the new approach. No teachers were rated at LoU 0 Nonuse, I Orientation, or II Preparation.
2. The year 2 pattern of an increasing proportion of teachers being at LoU IVA Routine Use or higher was a clear indication that teachers were moving further across the Implementation Bridge.
3. Even after 2 years of systematic support, one third of the teachers were still at LoU III Mechanical Use.

Assessing Fidelity of Implementation (Innovation Configurations).   The LoU data documented that teachers were engaged with using the innovation, but these data do not inform about the pieces, features, and functions of the innovation that were being used. Answering this question is the purpose of Innovation Configuration Mapping (see Chapter 3). For the math study, an IC Map was developed. A component of this map was presented as Figure 3.4. The IC Map was used to observe and document classroom practices as well

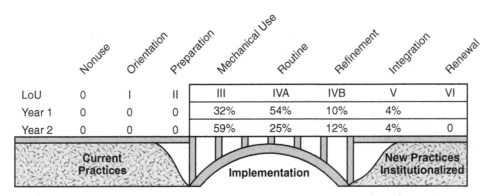

LoU	Nonuse	Orientation	Preparation	Mechanical Use	Routine	Refinement	Integration	Renewal
	0	I	II	III	IVA	IVB	V	VI
Year 1	0	0	0	32%	54%	10%	4%	
Year 2	0	0	0	59%	25%	12%	4%	0

FIGURE 12.3 Percentage of Teachers at Each Level of Use (LoU) of a Standards-Based Mathematics Program

as a guide for targeting teacher training, coaching, and professional development (Alquist & Hendrickson, 1999).

Pothole Warning

Do not trust what an implementer says he or she is doing with an innovation, including responses on paper-and-pencil or Web-based surveys.

Pothole Repair

Determining what actually is being implemented must be checked through direct observations, review of artifacts, and carefully constructed interview questions.

Fidelity of Implementation.   As described in Chapter 3, in an IC Map, the critical operational *Components* of the innovation are identified. For each Component, the different ways it could be made operational, the *Variations,* are described. The *a* variation presents a word–picture description of best practice; the *b* variation is slightly less ideal; the *c* variation is acceptable but not exciting; and the *d, e,* and *f* variations describe practices that are different from what is expected as part of the innovation—in this case, traditional practice. Based on classroom observation and interviewing, the appropriate Variation of each Component is circled on the IC Map.

Computer clustering procedures can be used to group classrooms according to the extent of fidelity of implementation. IC Maps that have more *a* variations circled represent high fidelity, whereas those with many *d, e,* and *f* variations represent limited fidelity and/or use of something other than the innovation. When IC Map data are placed on the Implementation Bridge (see Figure 12.4), those configurations of practice that include more *a* and *b* variations are placed farther across the bridge.

Fidelity of Implementation of a Mathematics Innovation.   The analysis of the IC Map data for the mathematics study revealed a wide range of configurations, including some classrooms that were all *a*'s and *b*'s, and other classrooms with more *c*'s and *d*'s. In the *d/e* classrooms, many of the ratings of IC Map Components indicated that traditional practices were still prevalent. One overall finding was that at the end of two years of implementation effort,

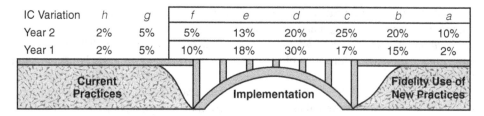

IC Variation	h	g	f	e	d	c	b	a
Year 2	2%	5%	5%	13%	20%	25%	20%	10%
Year 1	2%	5%	10%	18%	30%	17%	15%	2%

FIGURE 12.4   IC Map Data for the First 2 Years of Implementation of a Standards-Based Mathematics Program

fewer than one third of the classrooms exhibited implementation with high fidelity. This is not an unusual finding and should again remind leaders and evaluators that implementing complex innovations takes time and extended support.

REFLECTION QUESTION

There are three ways to assess implementation (SoC, LoU, and IC). Which would you want to use in your next change initiative?

Three Major Questions Related to Assessing and Facilitating Implementation

The three CBAM Diagnostic Dimensions provide evidence-based tools for assessing the extent and quality of implementation. These constructs and the Implementation Bridge metaphor provide the basis for considering three now important challenges: (1) *sustaining* change, (2) *implementing multiple innovations* at the same time, and (3) *thinking through* outputs and outcomes.

IMPLICATIONS OF USING COMBINATIONS OF CHANGE CONSTRUCTS BY EVALUATORS, RESEARCHERS, AND LEADERS FACILITATING CHANGE

1. The unit of change can range from large social systems to individuals. Some interventions are needed that address each unit of change. Assessing implementation must begin with measuring at the individual level.
2. In the CBAM, systemic thinking is used as change facilitators regularly assess SoC, LoU, and IC, and then to provide relevant interventions to individuals, subgroups, and the whole system.
3. When Self concerns are high, any indications of uncertainty and/or misleading information contribute to the rapid germination and growth of Toxic Mushrooms.
4. The design of evaluation and research studies should not implicitly assume use and nonuse; this must be checked at the individual level in *both* treatment and comparison groups.
5. Studies of outputs and outcomes should incorporate assessment of extent of implementation in treatment as well as any comparison groups.
6. Studies of outcomes should include more than the aggregation of effects of individual implementers; they should also address cross-innovation interactions as well as the role and potential for effects of the leaders.

Sustaining Change Represents Different Challenges.   As described throughout this text—we know a lot about *creating* innovations and *adopting* change, and we know a lot about *implementing* change. However, we know little about *sustaining* change. There are far too many examples of major efforts to implement exciting innovations only to find little remaining after the funding ended or a key leader moved on. There are too many examples of attempts at bottom-up change where a few individuals invested several years in creating and implementing an exciting new way, but found no real support from their organization to keep it going.

One indication of the developing awareness of the challenge of sustainability was that there were sufficient papers and analyses for the U.S. Education Department to able to commission a report, *Reading First Sustainability Literature Review* (RMC, 2009). The report offers a definition:

> Sustainability is the ability of a program to operate on its core beliefs and values (its reading culture) and use them to guide essential and inevitable program adaptations over time while maintaining improved outcomes. (Adapted from Century & Levy, 2002, As quoted in the RMC report, page 4)

In this report, as well as others, key structures and processes that are associated with sustaining change are being identified. For example, in a study of one medium-size school district, Hall and Robison (2009) identified key factors and strategies that were related to 10-plus years of effort to dramatically increase test scores. Another initiative where sustainability has been addressed is a statewide 5-plus year project to implement Instructional Consultation Teams (Rosenfield & Gravois, 1996) in schools and districts (Nevada IC Teams, 2010). The project team developed a framework and checklist of factors that must be addressed in order to have sustainability. Based on these reports and our field experiences, Table 12.1 is a listing

TABLE 12.1   Themes, Strategies, and Structures Related to Sustaining Change

Themes—To what extent is there	Strategies and Structures—To what extent are the following in place?
Shared strategic vision	District personnel have assigned authority, responsibility, and time to support continued use.
Sustained focus on improving learning (of students *and* adults)	Policies have been added and/or adjusted to accommodate continued use.
Problem ownership by all	Budgets have line items for innovation-related continuing costs.
Assessment thinking	Board agenda regularly contains information about use and effects of the innovation.
Accountability based in user-friendly data	Superintendent "champions" the innovation inside the school system and in public.
Continuity in leadership from top to bottom	Leader succession planning includes expectations related to the innovation.
Construction of a professional learning community	Leader evaluation includes elements related to innovation use.
Trust and sharing of successes and failures	Implementer evaluation includes elements of innovation use.
Continuing refinement and adaptation while keeping the ultimate outcome in mind	Data related to use are systematically collected, shared, and considered.
	Professional development of new employees includes innovation expectations.

TABLE 12.2   **Stages of Concern (Feelings/Perceptions)**

	TIME	SELF	TASK	IMPACT
Innovation 1	October	60%	30%	10%
	April	30%	60%	10%
Innovation 2	October	80%	10%	
	April	85%	10%	
Innovation 3	October	30%	60%	10%
	April	10%	50%	30%

of factors and strategies related to sustaining change in school districts. It appears that nearly all of these items must be addressed to sustain use.

Implementing Multiple Innovations at the Same Time Is Reality.   Some years ago, we suggested names for some commonly observed change strategies such as "The Pennsylvania Contingent" and "Rent a Martyr" (Hall & Hord, 1987). Another frequently observed strategy is the Multiple Adoption Design (MAD). In most settings, there is not just one change, but several. Each innovation has its own implementation requirements, champion, and expectations for implementers and others. Most change managers and evaluators focus on their one, and give little consideration to the others.

Assessing MAD Strategies.   When multiple changes are being implemented at the same time it is like having two, three, or more bridges in parallel. There is not a linear sequence to the bridges; the expectation is that they all are to be crossed at the same time. This is not only a challenge for the implementers; it makes program evaluation and research studies much more complicated.

As an illustration, Tables 12.2 through 12.4 are snapshots of a likely scenario when three innovations are being implemented at the same time. Consider the implementation assessment data. Which innovation is making progress? Which is not making progress? Which is ready for summative evaluation? What should the change leaders do from this point forward?

TABLE 12.3   **Levels of Use (Nonuse–Novice–Expert)**

	TIME	NONUSERS (LoU 0, I, & II)	MECHANICAL (LoU III)	ROUTINE (LoU IVA)	INTEGRATION (LoU V)
Innovation 1	October	75%	15%		
	April	20%	65%		10%
Innovation 2	October	85%	10%		
	April	90%	10%		
Innovation 3	October	30%	50%	15%	5%
	April	10%	40%	30%	20%

TABLE 12.4   Innovation Configurations (Fidelity of Implementation)

	TIME	TRADITIONAL PRACTICES	LOW *d*	MED *c*	HIGH *a* & *b*
Innovation 1	October	80%	15%	5%	0%
	April	15%	20%	60%	5%
Innovation 2	October	90%			
	April	88%	10%		
Innovation 3	October	30%	40%		8%
	April	10%	30%	45%	15%

MAD Thinking as Braiding.   In addition to all of the variables and effects related to implementation of each innovation singularly, there are interactions between change initiatives. Some factors may be mutually supportive; there may be interferences; and in some instances, conflicts are created. For example, there are limits on resources such as time for training and schedules for use. Implementers cannot be in two places at the same time. Leaders and evaluators must be taking greater account of the interactions between multiple innovation implementations. Osher (2013) suggested that rather than viewing each innovation independently, facilitators and program evaluators must think in terms of *braiding* (see Figure 12.5). Implementation support must be integrated, and in addition to the outputs of each innovation separately, there will be cross-initiative interactions and combined effects that should be addressed.

Outputs and Outcomes Are Different

In program evaluation studies, an important distinction can be made between outputs and outcomes. *Outputs* are those changes in practice and results that are directly associated with full use of the innovation. *Outcomes* are the indirect and more long-term effects of implementation of the innovation. For example, an evidence-based reading program promises 6-month gains in test scores, which is an output. A related outcome could be increased teacher skill in formative assessment that is applied in other subject areas.

As important as facilitating implementation and assessing the extent of implementation are, the ultimate purpose must be thought through. Is the change effort only about the promised output of increased test scores, or is there thought about how the initiative(s) also will contribute to improvements in other ways? Think back to our discussion in Chapter 9 about capacity. As Wandersman et al. (2008; 2012) point out in their Interactive Systems Model, communities and organizations have a certain level of capacity at the beginning of a change initiative. Ideally, a component of outcomes should be increased capacity. This should especially be the case when the MAD change strategy has been in place. In schools, one capacity-related outcome from changes in curriculum, instruction, and school reforms could be increases in the continued construction of a Professional Learning Community. In communities, a particular program's output could be

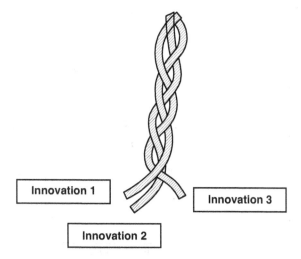

Innovation 1

Innovation 3

Innovation 2

FIGURE 12.5   Facilitating Implementation and Evaluating Multiple Innovations Is Best Accomplished When There Is Braiding

reduction in the teen pregnancy rate. The program also could contribute to the outcome of improved health.

CONCEPTUAL AND OPERATIONAL INTERRELATIONSHIPS AMONG SoC, LoU, AND IC

Stages of Concern, Levels of Use, and Innovation Configurations are three independent constructs, each of which addresses a different aspect of implementation. Each has a purpose-built methodology for measurement. Each is used in program evaluation and research studies, and each provides diagnostic information for facilitating change. In nearly all of the preceding descriptions, the three CBAM Diagnostic Dimensions have been applied singularly. However, there are some obvious logical relationships. For example, the *Stages of Concern* and *Levels of Use* sound a lot alike, except one dimension deals with feelings and the other deals with behaviors. Also, in his review of applications of SoC in Canada, Anderson (1997) pointed out the need for more "theoretically motivated—not just applied—research." Some of the possible relationships and some suggested implications for theory, research, and practice have been explored and are discussed next (Hall, 2013).

SoC × LoU

The most logical way to think about the relationships between use and concerns would be a one-to-one correspondence represented by the diagonal dash line in Figure 12.6. The SoC and LoU labels even sound a lot alike (e.g., Task Concerns, Mechanical Use). However, it turns out that the SoC × LoU relationships are not that simple.

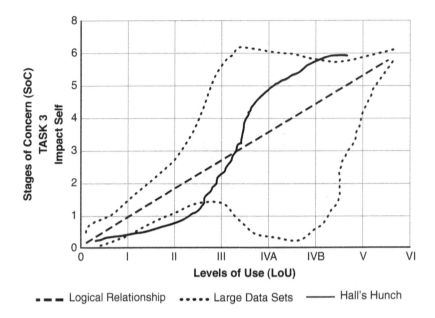

FIGURE 12.6   Possible Relationships Between Stages of Concern and Levels of Use

To explore what might be the best fit, our methodologist, Dr. Archie George, pulled some large data sets where we had both SoC and LoU data. Most of these data sets were of cross-sectional samples in terms of years/cycles of experience with various innovations. The samples included large numbers of nonusers too. The pattern that emerged is represented with the dotted lines in Figure 12.6. At the ends, SoC and LoU could be predicted one from the other. However, at LoU IVA Routine, it was not possible to predict SoC from LoU, or LoU from SoC.

This finding makes sense. First, we find that in stratified samples based on years of use of an innovation that approximately 50% of the users will be at LoU IVA Routine. Some of these users will have just made it beyond LoU III Mechanical Use and be "recovering"; some will be reviewing and thinking about making some sort of change in order to increase outcomes. At the next measurement time, many of these people will likely be at LoU IVB Refinement. Then there is the third set of LoU IVA users who are what a British colleague referred as the *settlers*. They have their routines in place and have no interest in making any changes. Each of these LoU IVA subgroups are users, they have routines, and are not making any changes in their use—but their concerns will be quite different.

The solid line in Figure 12.6 is the current hypothesis about what happens longitudinally. This is a much more nuanced view of the possible relationships between SoC and LoU. We don't have data on this one. Keeping in mind Frances Fuller's idea that there are differences in the types of interventions that lead to arousal of a concern versus what it takes to resolve a concern, we now think the following:

At the beginning of a change process, before people are on the bridge and for those who are out on the bridge, the actions of Levels of Use trigger the arousal of Stages of

Concern. For example, it is the introduction of the idea of the innovation that arouses Stage 1 Informational concerns. A clearer case is the relationship between Task concerns and LoU III Mechanical Use. Stage 3 Management concerns are not aroused until *after* people are on the bridge. Even days before first use, Task concerns are not as intense as they are 3 weeks into implementation. One implication of this for change facilitating interventions is the timing of the how-to-do-it workshop. Typically, as a new program is launched, there will be a session(s) on how to use the new way. With teachers, this "training" takes place in August, before school begins. However, based on the hypothesis that early implementation use arouses Management concerns, that how-to session would be seen as more useful if done at the end of September after first use has taken place. It is being out on the bridge that heightens Task concerns.

For the other half of Figure 12.6, the hypothesis is that the arousal of Impact concerns leads to higher Levels of Use. For example, a concern about some students not doing as well (Stage 4 Consequence) leads to adapting the innovation by adding another tool such as a computer study program (LoU IVB Refinement). Once an implementer is across the bridge, any further adaptations and refinements are likely triggered by Impact concerns: "What can I do to further increase student learning?"

Pothole Warning

Assuming that no nonusers are in randomly assigned treatment groups and no users are in randomly assigned control groups is a mistake.

Pothole Repair

Use/nonuse and fidelity must be documented at the individual unit level within both the treatment and control groups.

LoU × IC

Based on limited data and extended thinking, the probable relationships between Levels of Use and Innovation Configurations are presented in Figure 12.7. The lower left box represents people who are at LoU 0, I, or II—in other words, nonusers. In terms of IC, people in this box are using *e–g* configurations, which in most IC Maps are descriptions of traditional practices (i.e., the "old" way). People in this box are clearly nonusers. They are using configurations that are not representative of the innovation, and they are not engaging in implementing the new way. The people in this box are the only true control/comparison group.

The upper left part of Figure 12.7 represents an especially interesting condition. These are people who are not users in terms of LoU. They are not looking for information or considering using *the* Innovation. However, when an IC Map is used to observe classroom practices, it turns out they are doing the same things that *the* Innovation prescribes. They may—or they may not—call it the same thing; but the performance and functions are the same. Without having checked closely, it is quite likely that representatives of this group are in most control/comparison groups. This will happen especially when there is random assignment without checking. It also is the case when the only check is a self-report reply to the question, "Do you use The Innovation?" "No."

The lower right box in Figure 12.7 represents people who claim to be users of the innovation, but their Configurations are not even low fidelity. We often find this pattern with people who are engaged in their first attempts to use the innovation. They will be at LoU III

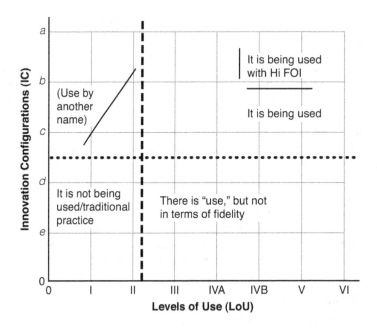

FIGURE 12.7   Possible Relationships Between Levels of Use and Innovation Configurations

Mechanical Use and caught between trying to use Components of the new way while hanging on to what they had been doing in the past. They see themselves as "users" and their behaviors are at LoU III, but the Configurations are not in the ballpark. This is a profile where coaching, developing additional how-to knowledge and skill, and leadership are particularly important. Although people in this box may be high on Levels of Use, there is no fidelity, which means they should not be in the treatment group or the summative evaluation study.

The upper right part of Figure 12.7 represents implementers who are users of acceptable Configurations. These are the people to have in the treatment groups and summative evaluation studies. However, based on the few data sets we have to this point, it appears that true High Fidelity implementation occurs only when the implementer's Level of Use is higher than LoU IVA Routine. Also, we have never had a case of a high-fidelity configuration with LoU III Mechanical Use. If this theme holds, then more thought needs to be given to the time it takes to achieve high FOI. It is not likely to be observed until after 3 to 5 years/cycles of use.

IC × SoC

The relationship between Innovation Configurations and Stages of Concern is less easy to chart. The relationships are more idiosyncratic and complex. For example, if the innovation is perceived to represent a big change, then Self concerns will be more intense and likely sustained for a longer period of time. If a critical component of the innovation can be easily plugged into current practice, then it may be seen as addressing an Impact concern about increasing student learning. Many other scenarios seem possible. At this point, we don't see a predominant set of relationships between IC and SoC.

There Is More to It than SoC, LoU, and IC

There are studies that have included two or three of the dimensions and acknowledged that there are more factors to consider. For example, Park (2012) was the first to apply CBAM constructs in a study of teachers in Bangladesh. Although mainly qualitative, he applied all three Diagnostic Dimensions to explore relationships between teacher implementation efforts and the need for professional development. Yung (2010) used SoC, IC, and LoU in a 2-year case study of an experienced mathematics teacher in Hong Kong who was implementing alternative assessments. Her study describes well the difficulties experienced teachers have in trying to change practices in an "examination driven competitive system" (p. 281). These two studies bring forth another major aspect of the change process—external and internal system pressures. To paraphrase Hill and Crevola (1999), it seems likely that success with implementing an innovation is closely tied to beliefs and understandings—in other words, organization culture. We must think a lot more about the social construction of culture and its relationship to leadership as well as implementation success.

In the future, we need studies that look systemically at all that is involved in having successful change processes. SoC, LoU, and IC provide constructs and measures for benchmarking change process progress. Other elements of CBAM, as well as other constructs, can help in framing more holistic views. For example, Intervention Mushrooms seem to be similar to norms of organization culture (Hall & Hord, 2011). The next phase in developing understanding about change processes needs to build on what we already know, and it should be more multivariate, systemic, and longitudinal.

THE IMPORTANCE OF LEADERSHIP

Leaders and actions to facilitate change are other critical factors. As was described in Chapter 6, the Change Facilitator Style of the leader is correlated with implementation success. In Chapter 2, the importance of interventions, the actions taken to facilitate change, was addressed. The difference between interventions and innovations, the change being implemented, was made clear in Chapter 3. Each of the other chapters provide another evidence-based construct for understanding, facilitating and/or evaluating change. All these resources are available to be used responsibly or in wrong ways. In this final section of the last chapter, we offer a few final ideas, findings from research, and our current questions. The final topic is the reminder to continually reflect on the ethics of what you are doing.

Relationships Between Principal CF Style and Student Outcomes

In Chapter 6, three different behavioral profiles of leaders—CF Styles—were described. *Initiators* have a vision; they push and have passion for their school. *Managers* focus on following the rules, having clear procedures, and controlling budgets. Most *Responders* are friendly, and all want everyone to get along. Chapter 6 presented research findings about the relationships between principal CF Style and teacher implementation success. Three additional themes about the importance of leadership are (a) the relationship of leadership to student outcomes, (b) relationships to organization culture, and (c) themes to consider when there is leader succession. We discuss each in turn next.

The Possibility of Principal Effects on Test Scores. There is a rich history of research and evaluation studies that draw causal connections between what teachers do and how much students learn. There also have been a variety of studies about the effects of principals. In their literature reviews, Hallinger and Heck (2011) offer cautions and make a very strong case that the effects of principal leadership on student learning are indirect. Principals rarely teach students; therefore, their effects will be *indirect*. Still, as head of the organization unit, it seems possible that there is some sort of pass-through relationship. We know that there are significant relationships between principal CF Style and teacher implementation success. What could be the relationships between principal leadership and student learning? Or are all of the outputs dependent directly on what individual teachers do? We now have three studies that explore the relationships between principal CF Style and test scores.

Principal CF Style and Student Test Scores, Study Findings. The first study, described in Chapter 6, was of 27 elementary school principals in one urban school district. Their CF Style was assessed, and fourth-grade student test scores on the Connecticut Mastery Tests (CMT) for Direct Assessment of Writing, Editing and Revising, Reading Comprehension, and Mathematics were used as the indicators of student outcomes. Students' CMT scores from fourth grade were compared with the scores they obtained near the end of fifth grade (Hall, Negroni, & George, 2008; 2013). Statistically significant relationships were found between the principal's CF Style ratings and student achievement on three of the four tests. In each case, students in schools with Responder CF Style principals had significantly lower growth in test scores. Schools with Initiator CF Style principals had significantly higher test scores in writing, editing, and reading comprehension. Test scores in mathematics (both computational and conceptual) were highest in schools with Manager CF Style principals.

In a study of nine elementary schools in a large urban district, Lewis (2002) found a similar pattern—students in schools with Responder CF Style principals scored significantly lower than those students whose schools were led by Initiator principals. Stewart (2012) had similar findings in his study of middle schools. Principal effects may be indirect in the sense that they are not teaching the students directly, but it certainly appears that in some ways they have systematic cross-school effects. In addition, the effects are differential based on principal CF Style. In future studies, more must be learned about the ways that leadership, indirectly and directly, affects outputs and outcomes.

One Way to Summarize Effects of Principal Leadership. Figure 12.8 is a graphic summary of what has been found about the relationships among the extent of implementation, leadership, and outcomes. There are some gaps that can be filled in through new studies; there also are some areas where the findings, so far, have been consistent. For example, most studies document that higher outcomes are observed with those implementers who are farther across the bridge. Another pattern is that leadership is significantly correlated with extent of implementation. In addition, it appears that there are emerging patterns of relationships between leadership and school-wide outcomes. All are important areas for further study.

Principal CF Style and School Organization Culture

As described in Chapters 7 and 8, the participants in an organization share their beliefs, views, and interpretations of events and actions. One result is the Constructed Themes of Intervention

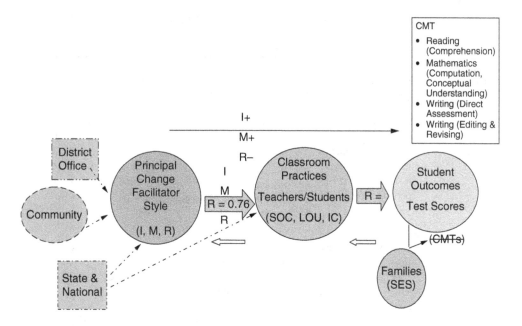

FIGURE 12.8   Summary View of Emerging Relationships Between Leadership, Extent of Implementation, and Student Outcomes

Mushrooms; another is identification of what is important. Still another is the implicit rules about how things really get done within the organization. In many ways these themes and elements are the characterization of the organization's culture. Further, it appears that particular organization cultures are associated with each CF Style.

Three CF Styles, Three Organization Cultures.   More recently, some of our graduate students and colleagues have helped us develop a set of characteristics of organization culture that are associated with each CF Style (Table 12.5). As can be inferred from these descriptions, the themes, what is valued, and how things work within each of these cultures differ dramatically. In the Responder CF Style school, the culture is *balkanized*, meaning that a small group of teachers runs the school. These teachers have all the supplies and control the agenda. The teachers who are not members of the controlling clique are left out: "Where did you get that paper? There is none in the supply closet." The Manager CF Style school culture is *organized and efficient*: "Everyone will have the same amount of supplies."

In the Initiator CF Style school, the culture is based in *vision and function*. For example, distribution of resources is based on function and need: "Because she is teaching ESL, she should have the white board, while math teachers need document projectors."

CF Style, Organization Culture, and Leader Succession

An additional application for this framework about the relationship of CF Style to organization culture is in considering factors related to leader succession. Interesting predictions can

TABLE 12.5 **Indicators and Relationships Between Principal CF Style and Organization Culture**

	CF STYLE		
ELEMENTS OF CULTURE	**RESPONDER**	**MANAGER**	**INITIATOR**
Culture Name	*Balkanized*	*Efficient*	*Strategic*
Indicators of Culture	Individuals are isolated, with a clique running the school. Principal decision making is influenced most through personal contact.	Schedules, procedures, and tasks are clearly spelled out. Principal controls through literal interpretation of rules and procedures and allocation of resources.	Efforts are integrated from top to bottom with clear connections between day-to-day activities and principal's vision. Leadership is shared with those who support the vision.
Myths and Stories	Gossip about adults. Frustrations and complaining about what students (and parents) don't do.	Stories about obtaining and using resources and when someone did not follow the rules	Student and adult successes, sharing resources, and exchange of ideas about instruction
Symbols	Adult centered; some have a lot, others little.	Published rules and procedures; forms, plenty of supplies	Data walls; celebrations of student and adult learning
Center of Action	*Taking care* of me *Protecting* one's classroom	*Controlling* tasks, schedules, and resources *Following* rules and procedures	*Everyone learning*, *everyone* pulling together *Collective* effort and continuing improvements
Who gets what	First come, first served: attending to the loudest voices	Equality: All receive the same.	Equity: Each receives what he or she needs based on job tasks.
Themes	"We are one big happy family." "Us. vs. Them" A few have everything; others have what's left.	"We are very busy." More resources will be needed to do more things.	"We are a team." All continually working to improve learning for all students.

be made about what will happen when a particular leader leaves and is replaced by another. For example, when an Initiator replaces a Responder, the clique that had been getting its way will no longer be able to do so. The Initiator takes control of resource allocations, schedules, and school priorities. The clique no longer can run the school. The clique's typical reaction is to complain to parents, district administrators, and maybe members of the school board about how bad the new principal is doing. The first year or two can be rough as new norms and procedures are established. Similar scenarios can be envisioned for other combinations of leader successions.

INDICATORS OF USING COMBINATIONS OF CHANGE CONSTRUCTS

1. Impact concerns (Stage 4 Consequence, Stage 5 Collaboration, and Stage 6 Refocusing) will be found regularly in organizations that have a PLC type of organization culture. In these settings, there will be fewer Toxic Intervention Mushrooms.
2. In nearly all settings, the Multiple Adoption Design (MAD) strategy will be in place.
3. Achieving high-fidelity implementation requires implementers to be across the Implementation Bridge.
4. Ethical leaders regularly ask themselves, "Is this the right thing to do?"
5. Sustaining use of innovations requires structural changes and continued leadership from the top.
6. System change requires continuing leadership at all levels and support for implementation that addresses Stages of Concern, Levels of Use, and monitoring of Innovation Configurations.

REFLECTION QUESTIONS

What kinds of changes in organization culture have you observed when there was a change in the leader? What was the CF Style of the departing leader, and what was the CF Style of the incoming leader?

FINAL REFLECTIONS ABOUT IMPLEMENTING CHANGE

As this final chapter comes to a close, we offer several points of reflection. Some relate to facilitating change, others to studying change processes, and some hint at current dilemmas the authors face.

Ethical Issues in Facilitating Change

As architects and creators of the CBAM model, and as researchers and writers about PLCs and systemic change, we worry about how the constructs, measures, and ideas described in this text will be used. We have no doubts that you, the reader, are well-meaning, but to what extent do you and others really understand the constructs? Do you and others have sufficiently adequate skills to interpret results from use of the measures, and will interventions be valid and appropriate? These concerns speak to ethics.

Understanding the Constructs.   We receive frequent phone calls from individuals who have modest knowledge of SoC, LoU, IC, CF Styles, and/or PLCs. One frequent clue is when they ask for information about *levels* of concern. They tend to have high levels of enthusiasm and want permission to use one or more of the constructs and related measures. It is worrisome to us that some of these people are trying to use these tools without sufficient understanding. We worry about how they will use these measures and the results that they will yield based on their limited knowledge and skill. We ask them to obtain and study the technical manuals. We encourage them to talk with us again about their interests in using the ideas for facilitation change, and/or for research and evaluation. We also encourage participating in training workshops and becoming certified.

Responsible Use.   It is even more troubling to receive phone calls of inquiry from people who have administered the SoCQ, or one of the other measures, and don't know how to score it or interpret the results. It is important, we believe, to be sure the various instruments and techniques are used responsibly. But the flip side—one that is more troubling—is not knowing about the many others who have not contacted us or accessed the technical resources. On the surface, constructs such as SoC and PLC appear deceptively simple, but, in truth, they are quite complex. The ethical dilemma for us, and the construct/measure users, is how to determine and ensure that each has sufficient knowledge and skill to use the constructs and measures responsibly.

Support at All Levels of the Organization.   Many change efforts fail because facilitation and assistance are not provided to all members of the organization, whether they are in executive, management, or staff positions. Support must come from the top of the organization to the middle managers as well as to the front-line implementers. In the case of educational change, this means that principals of the schools expected to change will need professional development, including coaching, in order to exercise well their facilitation role. All too frequently, principals and other middle managers are left alone in that space between the executive or policy level that requests change and the level of staff who need to implement the change. Frequently, these leaders are without the tools or skills to do the job of supporting and assisting the staff well. Promoters of change should pay closer attention to the need to develop and support the middle managers who are the key to implementation success.

What about the Ethics of Change Agentry?   This is a question that we always raise with our students and clients. One way we phrase it is to ask, "When does change facilitation become manipulation?" After all, we are talking about tools and techniques to get people to change. Unfortunately, little has been said or written about this important issue. Early in our work, we asked the late Matt Miles (1979) to write a paper and provide us with a seminar on ethics. His thoughts and wise counsel have stayed with us. For example, in reflecting on OD consultants, he pointed out critical issues related to the accountability of OD change agents:

> To whom are OD change agents accountable? At one level, as Bermant and Warwick (1978) point out, they are personally accountable for their actions, like any person in society. They should not lie, cheat, steal, or engage in similar socially reprehensible actions. And they are legally accountable in a very general sense, not only for misdemeanors and felonies, but for items like breach of contract. However, I have never heard of malpractice litigations being threatened against an OD practitioner (though it has occurred for encounter group leaders).
>
> In any case, litigation is a gross tool for insuring ethical behavior by practitioners. The most central form of accountability is that which OD consultants have toward their sponsors, who are paying the bill, in several senses. Sponsors can terminate contracts, or at least revise them, if the program is not functioning as intended. ... Finally, there is professional accountability for OD practitioners, for which at present there are no formal structural supports comparable to those in medicine, law, accounting, and psychology. (Miles, 1979, pp. 8–9)

Matt Miles wrote these words 35 years ago. Unfortunately, the situation remains the same today. Maintaining ethical behavior is still mainly a personal responsibility.

Ethical Behavior from a Concerns Based Perspective.   In the Concerns Based perspective, *good* and *bad* are primarily defined in terms of what Change Facilitators do and do not do in relation to the present state of their clients. It is neither good nor bad for individuals to have certain concerns profiles, LoU, or IC. What *is* good or bad is the types of interventions that are made in response to each diagnostic profile. All interventions must be *Concerns Based.* They must be related to each client's current concerns and extent of use, not the Change Facilitators.

Wrong Interventions.   As a simple example, consider a teacher with high Stage 2 Personal concerns. We have heard administrators and others say to these individuals something like, "You should be concerned about students, not yourself." This is a wrong intervention from a Concerns Based perspective, because its single effect will be to further raise the teacher's Personal concerns. "Good" interventions acknowledge the Personal concerns, attempt to provide additional information to increase understanding, and are supportive by providing stability.

Deliberate Manipulation.   At many points in this text, the authors have emphasized the importance of being Concerns Based. Still, there will be times when inappropriate interventions are made out of either ignorance or innocence or, in some cases, malevolence. Unfortunately, there are many examples of deliberate efforts to mislead. Further, it seems that the larger the system, the easier it is to manipulate its members.

A classic example unfolded in the summer of 2009 around President Obama and Congress' efforts to change health insurance law. Over the congressional summer recess, public forums were held around the country. This intervention strategy was intended as a way to hear from voters and to explain elements of the draft bills. Keep in mind the context at that time: It was the low point of the Great Recession, the stock market had plunged, and many people had lost their jobs. Stage 2 Personal concerns were high.

The public forums turned into orchestrated shouting matches, and code words such as *death panels* were used to misrepresent the real wording in what has now become known as "Obamacare." In a few weeks, Toxic Mushrooms were seeded and grew large across the nation. This anecdote is offered here as another ethical reminder: The use of disinformation and taking advantage of personal fears in times of uncertainty cannot be tolerated.

Continue to Ask the Ethics Question.   Our point here is that the leaders and other facilitators bear major responsibility for everyone achieving implementation success. In the Japanese management model, if an employee is not doing well, the manager has failed. Failure in a change effort is mainly in the hands of the leaders. Making Concerns Based interventions increases the likelihood of success for the implementers and the facilitators. The question we frequently ask our students bears repeating: "When does change facilitation become manipulation?"

The responsible change facilitator frequently asks:

"Is what I am doing right and best for everyone?"

SUMMARY

In this text, we have presented key constructs, research findings, and insights about implementing change. We have continually related the ideas to what happens to the people who are living with implementing change and how the process unfolds in organizational settings. Many additional ideas, research findings, and stories could be discussed, but it is time for you, the reader, to use what you have learned. Whether you are a potential user of an innovation, a key Change Facilitator, a leader, a program evaluator, or a researcher, the constructs and tools presented here should be of help. We offer one brief caveat and one of our favorite phrases in the way of conclusion.

The Caveat

We touched on the ethics of being a Change Facilitator. Here we offer a different emphasis. As dramatic as it may sound, the information presented in this and similar texts can be used in very inappropriate and inexcusable ways. In fact, the tools and findings from research in the social sciences are in many ways far more dangerous than what the physicists were doing underneath the football stadium at the University of Chicago in 1940, because social scientists are talking about how to change people, organizations, and social systems. In addition, there are no rules of use. Anyone can choose any idea out of this text, some questionnaire, or any other piece of work, and do with it what he or she pleases. No codes of conduct are in place; no security clearances. What happens from here depends on the integrity and professionalism of the user. We ask that you think often about whether you are being responsible in what you do.

Fortunately, the first concerns that are aroused when there is change are Self concerns. To a large extent, people begin a change process by protecting themselves. Only when the innovation and change facilitators are perceived to be safe will people move to implement the change. Your job is to make sure that Self concerns are respected and that the abusive intentions and actions of others are challenged. Change success is achieved when Self and Task concerns are resolved and, ideally, when Impact concerns are aroused.

A Final Phrase

An important perspective to keep in mind when engaged in the change process is summarized in one phrase:

The road to success is always under construction.

DISCUSSION QUESTIONS

1. What has been your experience with moving across two or three Implementation Bridges at the same time? Were all the bridges the same or did they vary in size and length? Were there interactions between the change initiatives?

2. Do you think the gold standard (randomly assigned treatment and control groups) research design should be required in evaluation studies? Why or why not?

3. The importance of leadership to success in implementing changes has been emphasized again in this chapter. How do you think leaders affect outputs such as test scores across the whole organization such as a school?

4. This chapter concluded with a discussion of ethics in change agentry. What do you see being critical to change leaders being ethical?

5. In the next change initiative in which you are a participant, which constructs and tools will you want to be sure to incorporate? In what ways will you use each?

APPLYING COMBINATIONS OF CHANGE CONSTRUCTS IN FACILITATING IMPLEMENTATION

1. Examine a recent program evaluation or research report to see how implementation was addressed. What was the research design? Was the extent of implementation documented? Was there an assumption that implementation was dichotomous (use/nonuse), or was there a view similar to having an Implementation Bridge?

2. Use a combination of change constructs such as SoC and CFS to examine a current change initiative in an organization or a larger social system. Develop an estimate of how far across the Implementation Bridge the effort has progressed. What is the current status of the effort in terms of obtaining the desired outputs and outcomes? What are the key strategies and themes that are contributing to success (or failure)? Are all the leaders and Change Facilitators performing in ethical ways? Based on your analysis, what would you recommend that leaders and facilitators do next?

APPLYING COMBINATIONS OF CHANGE CONSTRUCTS IN RESEARCH AND PROGRAM EVALUATION STUDIES

1. Design a program evaluation study that goes beyond assessing extent of implementation and examines what is entailed in sustaining change. Use one, two, or all three of the CBAM Diagnostic Dimensions (i.e., SoC, LoU, and IC). Be sure to keep in mind that the leaders and facilitators of the change effort will be very interested in having access to the information. They need all sorts of ideas about how best to facilitate further movement across the Implementation Bridge and how to sustain its use. Be sure to plan for confidentiality and providing implementation assessment information in understandable ways.

2. Studies that address outputs and outcomes should take into account extent of implementation by individuals. In addition, research reported in this chapter suggests that studies must take into account the role and style of the leaders. We need more studies in schools—and in other types of organizations—that explore relationships among the style of the leader, the extent of implementation, and outputs and outcomes.

LEARNING MORE ABOUT USING COMBINATIONS OF CONSTRUCTS TO ASSESS IMPLEMENTATION

Bolman, L. G., & Deal, T. E. (2008). *Reframing organizations: Artistry, choice and leadership* (4th ed.). San Francisco, CA: Jossey-Bass.

This text is a useful primer for learning more about organizations as context, and about leaders and leadership. The extensive literature of research and theory about organizations, leaders, and leadership is organized around four frames: Structural, Human Resource, Symbolic, and Political. Each frame is described and illustrated with interesting anecdotes and examples from businesses and other types of organizations.

McDavid, J. C., Huse, I., & Hawthorn, L. R. L. (2013). *Program Evaluation and Performance Measurement: An introduction to practice* (2nd ed.). Thousand Oaks, CA: Sage.

Many texts address the theories and practices of program evaluation. This text introduces the key questions, steps, and components that should be part of evaluation studies. The authors also emphasize the importance of professional judgment in conducting and review of program evaluation studies.

■ ■ ■ ■ ■ ▬▬▬▬▬▬▬▬▬▬▬▬▬▬▬▬▬▬▬▬▬▬▬▬▬▬

STAGES OF CONCERN QUESTIONNAIRE (SoCQ)

Three technical manuals are available for use in measuring Stages of Concern. The appropriate manual should be studied before any efforts to assess Stages of Concern. Each of these manuals is available from the Southwest Educational Development Laboratory (SEDL) in Austin, Texas, http://www.sedl.org.

STAGES OF CONCERN QUESTIONNAIRE SoCQ (FORM 075)

George, A. A., Hall, G. E., & Stiegelbauer, S. M. (2006). *Measuring implementation in schools: The Stages of Concern Questionnaire.* Austin, TX: Southwest Educational Development Laboratory.

CHANGE FACILITATOR STAGES OF CONCERN QUESTIONNAIRE CFSoCQ

Hall, G. E., Newlove, B. W., George, A. A., Rutherford, W. L., & Hord, S. M. (1991). *Measuring change facilitator stages of concern: A manual for use of the CFSoC Questionnaire.* Austin, TX: Southwest Educational Development Laboratory.

OPEN-ENDED CONCERNS STATEMENTS

Newlove, B. W., & Hall, G. E. (1976). *A manual for assessing open-ended statements of concern about the innovation* (Report No. 3029). Austin: The University of Texas at Austin, Research and Development Center for Teacher Education. (ERIC Document Reproduction Service No. ED 144 207).

> **CAUTION:** The corresponding technical manual for assessing Stages of Concern should be obtained and studied before applying any of the three measures.

Stages of Concern Questionnaire

Name (optional): _____

The purpose of this questionnaire is to determine what people who are using or thinking about using various programs are concerned about at various times during the adoption process.

The items were developed from typical responses of school and college teachers who ranged from no knowledge at all about various programs to many years' experience using them. Therefore, **many of the items on this questionnaire may appear to be of little relevance or irrelevant to you at this time.** For the completely irrelevant items, please circle "0" on the scale. Other items will represent those concerns you do have, in varying degrees of intensity, and should be marked higher on the scale.

For example:

This statement is very true of me at this time.	0	1	2	3	4	5	6	(7)
This statement is somewhat true of me now.	0	1	2	3	(4)	5	6	7
This statement is not at all true of me at this time.	0	(1)	2	3	4	5	6	7
This statement seems irrelevant to me.	(0)	1	2	3	4	5	6	7

Please respond to the items in terms of **your present concerns,** or how you feel about your involvement with _____. We do not hold to any one definition of the innovation so please think of it in terms of your own perception of what it involves. Phrases such as "this approach" and "the new system" all refer to the same innovation. Remember to respond to each item in terms of your present concerns about your involvement or potential involvement with the innovation.

Thank you for taking time to complete this task.

0	1	2	3	4	5	6	7
Irrelevant		Not true of me now		Somewhat true of me now			Very true of me now

Circle One Number For Each Item

	0 1 2 3 4 5 6 7
1. I am concerned about students' attitudes toward the innovation.	0 1 2 3 4 5 6 7
2. I now know of some other approaches that might work better.	0 1 2 3 4 5 6 7
3. I am more concerned about another innovation.	0 1 2 3 4 5 6 7
4. I am concerned about not having enough time to organize myself each day.	0 1 2 3 4 5 6 7
5. I would like to help other faculty in their use of the innovation.	0 1 2 3 4 5 6 7
6. I have a very limited knowledge of the innovation.	0 1 2 3 4 5 6 7
7. I would like to know the effect of reorganization on my professional status.	0 1 2 3 4 5 6 7
8. I am concerned about conflict between my interests and my responsibilities.	0 1 2 3 4 5 6 7
9. I am concerned about revising my use of the innovation.	0 1 2 3 4 5 6 7
10. I would like to develop working relationships with both our faculty and outside faculty using this innovation.	0 1 2 3 4 5 6 7
11. I am concerned about how the innovation affects students.	0 1 2 3 4 5 6 7
12. I am not concerned about the innovation at this time.	0 1 2 3 4 5 6 7
13. I would like to know who will make the decisions in the new system.	0 1 2 3 4 5 6 7
14. I would like to discuss the possibility of using the innovation.	0 1 2 3 4 5 6 7
15. I would like to know what resources are available if we decide to adopt the innovation	0 1 2 3 4 5 6 7
16. I am concerned about my inability to manage all that the innovation requires.	0 1 2 3 4 5 6 7
17. I would like to know how my teaching or administration is supposed to change.	0 1 2 3 4 5 6 7
18. I would like to familiarize other departments or persons with the progress of this new approach.	0 1 2 3 4 5 6 7

0	1	2	3	4	5	6	7
Irrelevant		Not true of me now		Somewhat true of me now			Very true of me now

Circle One Number For Each Item

19. I am concerned about evaluating my impact on students.	0 1 2 3 4 5 6 7
20. I would like to revise the innovation's approach.	0 1 2 3 4 5 6 7
21. I am preoccupied with things other than the innovation.	0 1 2 3 4 5 6 7
22. I would like to modify our use of the innovation based on the experiences of our students.	0 1 2 3 4 5 6 7
23. I spend little time thinking about the innovation.	0 1 2 3 4 5 6 7
24. I would like to excite my students about their part in this approach.	0 1 2 3 4 5 6 7
25. I am concerned about time spent working with nonacademic problems related to the innovation.	0 1 2 3 4 5 6 7
26. I would like to know what the use of the innovation will require in the immediate future.	0 1 2 3 4 5 6 7
27. I would like to coordinate my efforts with others to maximize the innovation's effects.	0 1 2 3 4 5 6 7
28. I would like to have more information on time and energy commitments required by the innovation.	0 1 2 3 4 5 6 7
29. I would like to know what other faculty are doing in this area.	0 1 2 3 4 5 6 7
30. Currently, other priorities prevent me from focusing my attention on the innovation.	0 1 2 3 4 5 6 7
31. I would like to determine how to supplement, enhance, or replace the innovation.	0 1 2 3 4 5 6 7
32. I would like to use feedback from students to change the program.	0 1 2 3 4 5 6 7
33. I would like to know how my role will change when I am using the innovation.	0 1 2 3 4 5 6 7
34. Coordination of tasks and people is taking too much of my time.	0 1 2 3 4 5 6 7
35. I would like to know how the innovation is better than what we have now.	0 1 2 3 4 5 6 7

STAGES OF CONCERN QUESTIONNAIRE (SoCQ) SCORING DEVICE

Stages of Concern Quick Scoring Device

The Quick Scoring Device can be used to hand score the Stages of Concern Questionnaire (SoCQ) responses and to plot an individual profile. It is especially useful when only a small number of questionnaires need to be processed or when computer processing is not available. By following the step-by-step instructions, the SoCQ responses are transferred to the device, entered into seven scales, and each scale is totaled. Then the seven raw scale score totals are translated into percentile scores and plotted on a grid to produce the individual's SoCQ profile.

Instructions

1. In the box labeled A, fill in the identifying information taken from the cover sheet of the SoCQ.

2. In the table labeled B on the Scoring Device, transcribe each of the 35 SoCQ circled responses from the questionnaire (raw data). Note that the numbered blanks are not in consecutive order.

3. Row C contains the Raw Scale Score Total for each stage (0–6). Take each of the seven columns (0–6) in Table B, add the numbers within each column, and enter the sum of each column (0–6) in the appropriate blank in Row C. Each of these seven Raw Scale Score totals is a number between 0 and 35.

4. Table D contains the percentile scores for each Stage of Concern. For example, find the Raw Scale Score Total for Stage 0 from Row C ("12" from the example) in the left-hand column in Table D, then look in the Stage 0 column to the right in Table D and circle that percentile rank ("69" in the example). Take the raw score for Stage 1 ("31" in the example) to Table D and locate that numeral in the left-hand Raw Score Total column. Move across in the percentile table to the Stage 1 column and circle the percentile value ("98" in the example). Do the same for Stages 2 through 6.

5. Transcribe the circled percentile scores for each stage (0–6) from Table D to Box E. Box E now contains seven numbers between 0 and 99.

6. Box F contains the SoCQ grid. From Box E, take the percentile score for Stage 0 ("69" in the example) and mark that point with a dot on the Stage 0 vertical line of the SoCQ grid. Do the same for Stages 1–6. Connect the points to form the SoCQ profile.

You can now check your own scoring by using the blank profile sheet (see Appendix C). You will want to make copies of the blank scoring device before writing on it. Reproduce the data in the example by recording the original data from the completed SoCQ.

Stages of Concern Quick Scoring Device

A

Date: _____

Site: _____ SS#: _____

Innovation: _____

B

Individual Item responses (fill in the blanks with average of other item on that scale)

Stage	0	1	2	3	4	5	6
	3 ___	6 ___	7 ___	4 ___	1 ___	5 ___	2 ___
	12 ___	14 ___	13 ___	8 ___	11 ___	10 ___	9 ___
	21 ___	15 ___	17 ___	16 ___	19 ___	18 ___	20 ___
	23 ___	26 ___	28 ___	25 ___	24 ___	27 ___	22 ___
	30 ___	35 ___	33 ___	34 ___	32 ___	29 ___	31 ___

C Raw Score Totals   ___   ___   ___   ___   ___   ___   ___

E Percentile Scores   ___   ___   ___   ___   ___   ___   ___

F

RELATIVE INTENSITY — SoC Stages

UNCONCERNED (0) · INFORMATION (1) · PERSONAL (2) · MANAGEMENT (3) · CONSEQUENCE (4) · COLLABORATION (5) · REFOCUSING (6)

D

Percentiles

Raw Scale Score	Stage 0	Stage 1	Stage 2	Stage 3	Stage 4	Stage 5	Stage 6
0	0	5	2	2	1	1	1
1	1	12	12	5	1	2	2
2	2	16	14	7	1	3	2
3	4	19	17	9	2	3	5
4	7	23	21	11	2	4	6
5	14	27	25	15	3	5	9
6	22	30	28	18	3	5	11
7	31	34	31	23	4	7	14
8	40	37	35	27	5	10	17
9	48	40	39	30	5	12	20
10	55	43	41	34	7	14	22
11	61	45	45	39	8	16	26
12	69	48	48	43	9	19	30
13	75	51	52	47	11	22	34
14	81	54	55	52	13	25	38
15	87	57	57	56	16	28	42
16	91	60	59	60	19	31	47
17	94	63	63	65	21	36	52
18	96	66	67	69	24	40	57
19	97	69	70	73	27	44	60
20	98	72	72	77	30	48	65
21	99	75	76	80	33	52	69
22	99	80	78	83	38	55	73
23	99	84	80	85	43	59	77
24	99	88	83	88	48	64	81
25	99	90	85	90	54	68	84
26	99	91	87	92	59	72	87
27	99	93	89	94	63	76	90
28	99	95	91	95	66	80	92
29	99	96	92	97	71	84	94
30	99	97	94	97	76	88	96
31	99	98	95	98	82	91	97
32	99	99	96	98	86	93	98
33	99	99	96	99	90	95	99
34	99	99	97	99	92	95	99
35	99	99	99	99	97	98	99

Concerns Based Systems International

LEVELS OF USE OF THE INNOVATION (OPERATIONAL DEFINITIONS)

Two technical manuals have been prepared to assist in becoming prepared to conduct Levels of Use (LoU) Interviews. No one should assume that they have become reliable and valid LoU Interviewers from studying only these manuals. For research and evaluation studies, only certified LoU Interviewers should be used. These individuals have been through the established training program that was presented by a trainer approved by one of this text's authors. Also, it is not possible to measure LoU with questionnaires and online surveys. The only two methodologies are ethnographic observation and the established LoU Interview protocol.

Each of these manuals is available from the Southwest Educational Development Laboratory in Austin, Texas, http://www.sedl.org.

LEVELS OF USE TECHNICAL MANUALS

Hall, G. E., Dirksen, D. J., & George, A. A. (2000). *Measuring implementation in schools: Levels of use.* Austin, TX: Southwest Educational Development Laboratory.

Loucks, S. F., Newlove, B. W., & Hall, G. E. (1975). *Measuring levels of use of the innovation: A manual for trainers, interviewers, and raters.* Austin: The University of Texas at Austin, Research and Development Center for Teacher Education. Available from the Southwest Educational Development Laboratory, Austin, TX.

CATEGORIES

SCALE POINT DEFINITIONS OF THE LEVELS OF USE OF THE INNOVATION	KNOWLEDGE	ACQUIRING INFORMATION	SHARING
Levels of Use are distinct states that represent observably different types of behavior and patterns of innovation use as exhibited by individuals and groups. These levels characterize a user's development in acquiring new skills and varying use of the innovation. Each level encompasses a range of behaviors, but is limited by a set of identifiable Decision Points. For descriptive purposes, each level is defined by seven categories.	That which the user knows about characteristics of the innovation, how to use it, and consequences of its use. This is cognitive knowledge related to using an innovation, not feelings or attitudes.	Solicits information about the innovation in a variety of ways, including questioning resources persons, corresponding with resources agencies, reviewing printed materials, and making visits.	Discusses the innovation with others. Shares plans, ideas, resources, outcomes, and problems related to use of the innovation.

LEVEL 0 NON-USE

State in which the user has little or no knowledge of the innovation, no involvement with the innovation, and is doing nothing toward becoming involved.	Knows nothing about this or similar innovations or has only very limited general knowledge of efforts to develop innovations in the area.	Takes little or no action to solicit information beyond reviewing descriptive information about this or similar innovations when it happens to come to personal attention.	Is not communicating with others about innovation beyond possibly acknowledging that the innovation exists.
	0	0	0

DECISION POINT A   *Takes action to learn more detailed information about the innovation.*

LEVEL 1 ORIENTATION:

State in which the user has acquired or is acquiring information about the innovation and/or has explored or is exploring its value orientation and its demands upon user and user system.	Knows general information about the innovation such as origin, characteristics, and, implementation requirements.	Seeks descriptive material about the innovation. Seeks opinions and knowledge of others through discussions, visits or workshops.	Discusses resources needed in general terms and/or exchanges descriptive information, materials, or ideas about the innovation and possible implications of its use.
	I	I	I

DECISION POINT B   *Makes a decision to use the innovation by establishing a time to begin.*

LEVEL II PREPARATION

State in which the user is preparing for first use of the innovation.	Knows logistical requirements, necessary resources and timing for initial use of the innovation, and details of initial experiences for clients.	Seeks information and resources specifically related to preparation for use of the innovation in own setting.	Discusses resources needed for initial use of the innovation. Joins others in pre-use training, and in planning for resources, logistics, schedules, etc., in preparation for first use.
	II	II	II

DECISION POINT C   *Changes, if any, and use are dominated by user needs. Clients may be valued, however management, time, or limited*

LEVEL III MECHANICAL USE   **KNOWLEDGE**   **ACQUIRING INFORMATION**   **SHARING**

State in which the user focuses most effort on the short-term, day-to-day use of the innovation with little time for reflection. Changes in use are made more to meet user needs than client needs. The user is primarily engaged in a stepwise attempt to master the tasks required to use the innovation, often resulting in disjointed and superficial use.	Knows on a day-to-day basis the requirements for using the innovation, is more knowledgeable on short-term activities and effects than long-range activities and effects, of use of the innovation.	Solicits management information about such things as logistics, scheduling techniques, and ideas for reducing amount of time and work required of user.	Discusses management and logistical issues related to use of the innovation. Resources and materials are shared for purposes of reducing management, flow and logistical problems related to use of the innovation.
	III	III	III

DECISION POINT D-1   *A routine pattern of use is established. Changes for clients may be made routinely, but there are no recent changes outside*

LEVEL IV A ROUTINE

Use of the innovation is stabilized. Few if any changes are being made in ongoing use. Little preparation or thought is being given to improving innovation use or its consequences.	Knows both short- and long-term requirements for use and how to use the innovation with minimum effort or stress.	Makes no special efforts to seek information as a part of ongoing use of the innovation.	Describes current use of the innovation with little or no reference to ways of changing use.
	IVA	IVA	IVA

DECISIONS POINT D-2   *Changes use of the innovation based on formal or informal evaluation in order to increase client outcomes. They must be recent*

LEVEL IV B REFINEMENT

State in which the user varies the use of the innovation to increase the impact on clients within his/her immediate sphere of influence. Variations are based on knowledge of both short- and long-term consequences of client.	Knows cognitive and affective effects of the innovation on clients and ways for increasing impact on clients.	Solicits information and materials that focus specifically on changing use of the innovation to affect client outcomes.	Discusses own methods of modifying use of the innovation to change client outcomes.
	IVB	IVB	IVB

DECISION POINT E   *Initiates changes in use of innovation based on input of and in coordination with what colleagues are doing.*

LEVEL V INTEGRATION

State in which the user is combining own efforts to use the innovation with related activities of colleagues to achieve a collective impact on clients within their sphere of influence.	Knows how to coordinate own use of the innovation with colleagues to provide a collective impact on clients.	Solicits information and opinions for the purpose of collaborating with others in use of the innovation.	Discusses efforts to increase client impact through collaboration with others on personal use of the innovation.
	V	V	V

DECISION POINT F   *Begins exploring alternatives to or major modifications of the innovation presently in use.*

LEVEL VI RENEWAL

State in which the user reevaluates the quality of use of the innovation, seeks major modifications of or alternatives to present innovation to achieve increased impact on clients, examines new developments in the field, and explores new goals for self and the system.	Knows of alternatives that could be used to change or replace the present innovation that would improve the quality of outcomes of its use.	Seeks information and materials about others innovations as alternatives to the present innovation or for making major adaptations in the innovation.	Focuses discussions on identification of major alternatives or replacements for the current innovation.
	VI	VI	VI

Procedures for Adopting Educational Innovations Project. Research and Development Center for Teacher Education, University of Texas at Austin, 1975, N.I.E. Contract No. NIE-74-0087.

CATEGORIES

ASSESSING	PLANNING	STATUS REPORTING	PERFORMING
Examines the potential or actual use of the innovation or some aspect of it. This can be a mental assessment or can involve actual collection and analysis of data.	Designs and outlines short- and/or long-range steps to be taken during process of innovation adoption, i.e., aligns resources, schedules activities, meets with others to organize and/or coordinate use of the innovation.	Describes personal stand at the present time in relation to use of the innovation.	Carries out the actions and activities entailed in operationalizing the innovation.
Takes no action to analyze the innovation, its characteristics, possible use, or consequences of use.	Schedules no time and specifies no steps for the study or use of the innovation.	Reports little or no personal involvement with the innovation.	Takes no discernible action toward learning about or using the innovation. The innovation and/or its accouterments are not present or in use.
0	0	0	0
Analyzes and compares materials, content, requirements for use, evaluation reports, potential outcomes, strengths and weaknesses for purpose of making a decision about use of the innovation.	Plans to gather necessary information and resources as needed to make a decision for or against use of the innovation.	Reports presently orienting self to what the innovation is and is not.	Explores the innovation and requirements for its use by talking to others about it, reviewing descriptive information and sample materials, attending orientation sessions, and observing others using it.
I	I	I	I
Analyzes detailed requirements and available resources for initial use of the innovation.	Identifies steps and procedures entailed in obtaining resources and organizing activities and events or initial use of the innovation.	Reports preparing self for initial use of the innovation.	Studies reference materials in depth, organizes resources and logistics, schedules and receives skill training in preparation for initial use.
II	II	II	II

experimental knowledge dictate what the user does.

ASSESSING	PLANNING	STATUS REPORTING	PERFORMING
Examines own use of the innovation with respect to problems of logistics, management, time schedules, resources and general reactions of clients.	Plans for organizing and managing resources, activities, and events related primarily to immediate ongoing use of the innovation. Planned-for changes address managerial or logistical issues with a short-term perspective.	Reports that logistics, time, management, resource organizations, etc., are the focus of most personal efforts to use the innovation.	Manages innovation with varying degrees of efficiency. Often lacks anticipation of immediate consequences. The flow of actions in the user and clients is often disjointed, uneven and uncertain. When changes are made, they are primarily in response to logistical and organizational problems.
III	III	III	III

the pattern.

ASSESSING	PLANNING	STATUS REPORTING	PERFORMING
Limits evaluation activities to those administratively required, with little attention paid to findings for the purpose of changing use.	Plans intermediate and long-range actions with little projected variation in how the innovation will be used. Planning focuses on routine use of resources, personnel, etc.	Reports that personal use of the innovation is going along satisfactorily with few if any problems.	Uses the innovation smoothly with minimal management problems; over time, there is little variation in pattern of use.
IVA	IVA	IVA	IVA
Assesses use of the innovation for the purpose of changing current practices to improve client outcomes.	Develops intermediate and long-range plans that anticipate possible and needed steps, resources, and events designed to enhance client outcomes.	Reports varying use of the innovation in order to change client outcomes.	Explores and experiments with alternative combinations of the innovation with existing practices to maximize client involvement and to optimize client outcomes.
IVB	IVB	IVB	IVB
Appraises collaborative use of the innovation in terms of client outcomes and strengths and weaknesses of the integrated effort.	Plans specific actions to coordinate own use of the innovation with others to achieve increased impact on clients.	Reports spending time and energy collaborating with others about integrating own use of the innovation.	Collaborates with others in use of the innovation as a means of expanding the innovation's impact on clients. Changes in use are made in coordination with others.
V	V	V	V
Analyzes advantages and disadvantages of major modifications or alternatives to the present innovation.	Plans activities that involve pursuit of alternatives to enhance or replace the innovation.	Reports considering major modifications to present use of the innovation.	Explores other innovations that could be used in combination with or in place of the present innovation in an attempt to develop more effective means of achieving client outcomes.
VI	VI	VI	VI

Reprinted from Hall, G.E., Loucks, S.F., Rutherford, W.L. & Newlove, B.W. Levels of Use of the Innovation: A framework for analyzing innovation adoption. *The Journal of Teacher Education.* 1975. 26(1), 52–56

SIX DIMENSIONS OF CHANGE
FACILITATOR STYLE

Cluster I: Concern for People

The first cluster of CF Style behaviors deals with how the principal, as the change facilitator, addresses the personal side of change. People have feelings and attitudes about their work and about how a change process is going. They have personal needs, too. Day to day, facilitators can monitor, attend to, and affect these concerns and needs in different ways and with different emphases. For example, it is possible to spend little time directly addressing the feelings of others or to become preoccupied with listening and responding to each concern that is expressed. The emphasis can also be on attending to individual concerns as they are expressed daily or on focusing on the more long-term needs of all staff, with attention to individual concerns on an as-needed basis.

The Concern for People cluster is composed of two dimensions that weigh the degree to which the moment-to-moment and daily behaviors of a facilitator emphasize *social/informal* and *formal/meaningful* interactions with teachers. The Social/Informal dimension addresses the extent to which the facilitator engages in informal social discussions with teachers.

Social/Informal   This dimension addresses the frequency and character of the facilitator's informal social discussions with teachers and other staff. Many of these discussions may not be even remotely related to the work of the school or a specific innovation. Facilitators who emphasize this cluster engage in frequent social interactions. They attend to feelings and perceptions by emphasizing listening, understanding, and acknowledging immediate concerns, rather than providing answers or anticipating long-range consequences. There is a personable, friendly, almost chatty tone to the interactions. When concerns are addressed, it is done in ways that are responsive rather than anticipatory.

Formal/Meaningful   This dimension addresses brief, task-oriented interactions that deal with specific aspects of the work and the details of the innovation implementation. Facilitators are centered on school tasks, priorities, and directions. Discussions and interactions are focused on teaching, learning, and other substantive issues directly related to use of the innovation. Interactions are primarily intended to support teachers in their school-related duties, and the facilitator is almost always looking for solutions that are lasting. The interactions and emphases are not overly influenced by superficial and short-lived feelings and needs. Teaching and learning activities and issues directly related to use of the innovation are emphasized.

Cluster II: Organizational Efficiency

The work of the organization can be facilitated with varying degrees of emphasis on obtaining resources, increasing efficiency, and consolidating or sharing responsibilities and authority. Principals can try to do almost everything themselves, or they can delegate responsibility to others. System procedures, role clarity, and work priorities can be made more or less clear, and resources can be organized in ways that increase or decrease availability and effectiveness. In this cluster the principal's administrative focus is examined along two dimensions— *trust in others* and *administrative efficiency.*

Trust in Others   This dimension examines the extent to which the facilitator assigns others tasks of locating resources, establishing procedures, and managing schedules and time. When there is delay in making decisions, administrative systems and procedures are allowed to evolve in response to needs expressed by staff and to external pressures. The assumption is that teachers know how to accomplish their jobs and that they need a minimum of structuring and monitoring from the principal. As needs for additions or changes in structures, rules, and procedures emerge, they are gradually acknowledged and introduced as suggestions and guidelines rather than being directly established. Formalizing procedural and policy change is left to others and to time.

Administrative Efficiency   This dimension addresses the extent to which establishing clear and smoothly running procedures and resource systems to help teachers and others do their jobs efficiently is a priority. Administration, scheduling, and production tasks are clearly described, understood, and used by all members of the organization. Emphasis is placed on having a high level of organizational efficiency so teachers can do their jobs better. As needs for new structures and procedures emerge, they are formally established.

Cluster III: Strategic Sense

To varying degrees, principals are aware of the relationship between the long-term goals and their own monthly, weekly, daily, and moment-to-moment activities and those of their school. Some principals are more "now" oriented and treat each event in isolation from its part in the grand scheme, while others think and act with a vivid mental image of how today's actions contribute to accomplishing long-range aspirations. Some reflect about what they are doing and how all of their activities can add up, while others focus on the moment. Principals also vary in the degree to which they encourage or discourage the participation of external facilitators and in how they prescribe their role in the schools. This cluster examines the principal's strategic sense according to two dimensions: *day-to-day* and *vision and planning.*

Day-to-Day   At the high end of this dimension, there is little anticipation of future developments, needs, successes, or failures. Interventions are made in response to issues and needs as they arise. Knowledge of the details of the innovation is limited, and the amount of intervention with teachers is restricted to responding to questions and gradually completing routine steps. Images of how things could be improved and how more rapid gains could be made are incomplete, limited in scope, and lacking in imagination. There is little anticipation of longer term patterns or consequences. External facilitators come and go as they wish and spend an extraordinary amount of effort advising the principal.

Vision and Planning   The facilitator with a high emphasis on this dimension has a long-term vision that is integrated with an understanding of the day-to-day activities as the means to achieve the desired end. The facilitating activity is intense, with a high degree of interaction related to the work at hand. There is depth of knowledge about teaching and learning. Teachers and others are pushed to accomplish all that they can. Assertive leadership, continual monitoring, supportive actions, and creative interpretations of policy and use of resources to reach long-term goals are clear indicators of this dimension. Also present is the ability to anticipate the possible systemic effects of interventions and the broader consequences of day-to-day actions. Effects are accurately predicted, and interventions are made in anticipation of likely trends. Moment-to-moment interactions with staff and external facilitators are centered on the present work within a context of the long-range aspirations. The focus is on completing tasks, accomplishing school objectives, and making progress. External facilitators are encouraged to be involved in the school according to the principal's perception of their expertise and value.

For additional information, see G. E. Hall and A. A. George, "The Impact of Principal Change Facilitator Style on School and Classroom Culture," in H. Jerome Freiberg (Ed.), *School Climate: Measuring, Improving and Sustaining Healthy Learning Environments* (Philadelphia and London: Falmer Press, 1999), pp. 165–185.

CHANGE FACILITATOR STYLE QUESTIONNAIRE (CFSQ)

An important resource related to use of the Change Facilitator Style Questionnaire is Hall, G. E., & George, A. A. (1999). The impact of principal Change Facilitator Style on school and classroom culture. In H. J. Freiberg (Ed.), *School climate: Measuring, improving and sustaining healthy learning environments.* Philadelphia: Falmer Press.

> **CAUTION:** The CFSQ has strong psychometric qualities. However, great caution needs to be taken in using it, since it can be perceived as some sort of personnel evaluation. The CFSQ is not intended for personnel evaluation.

School: _____   **Date:** __/__/__

Change Facilitator Style Questionnaire
(CFSQ)

On the following page is a list of short phrases that describe different activities, goals, and emphases that leaders can exhibit. Studies have shown that different people place different emphases on each of these behaviors and that an overall pattern or style is unique to each.

This questionnaire is a way to estimate the emphasis that is given to different leadership activities. One of the key uses of this questionnaire is to help leaders analyze and reflect on what they are doing. There is no right or wrong way; rather, there are variations in emphases and patterns that may be worth considering.

In this instance, consider the leadership/facilitating activities of your principal.

Note that some of the items in this questionnaire refer to how this person is working in relation to a particular program or innovation. For these items, please think about *your principal's role with facilitating change in the school.*

Also, some of the items are similar to other items. This is done deliberately in a questionnaire of this type. By having similar items, each item can be less complex, and it is possible to complete the questionnaire in a minimum amount of time.

Having each item rated on a continuum is important, too. For most facilitators/leaders, most items will apply; what constitutes the difference is the amount of emphasis or de-emphasis a particular leader gives to each type of activity.

Please read each phrase and use the following scale points to rate the degree of emphasis given to each by your principal.

1	2	3	4	5	6
Never True Not True	Rarely True	Seldom True	Sometimes True	Often True	Always or Very True

Change Facilitator Style Questionnaire

Please indicate how accurately each statement describes your principal:

1 Never True Not True	2 Rarely True	3 Seldom True	4 Sometimes True	5 Often True		6 Always or Very True		
1. Is friendly when we talk to him or her				1	2	3	4	5	6
2. Knows a lot about teaching and curriculum				1	2	3	4	5	6
3. Procedures and rules are clearly spelled out				1	2	3	4	5	6
4. Discusses school problems in a productive way				1	2	3	4	5	6
5. Seems to be disorganized at times				1	2	3	4	5	6
6. Shares many ideas for improving teaching and learning				1	2	3	4	5	6
7. Plans and procedures are introduced at the last moment				1	2	3	4	5	6
8. Keeps everyone informed about procedures				1	2	3	4	5	6
9. He or she is heavily involved in what is happening with teachers and students				1	2	3	4	5	6
10. Proposes loosely defined solutions				1	2	3	4	5	6
11. Is primarily concerned about how teachers feel				1	2	3	4	5	6
12. Asks questions about what teachers are doing in their classrooms				1	2	3	4	5	6
13. Has few concrete ideas for improvement				1	2	3	4	5	6
14. Provides guidelines for efficient operation of the school				1	2	3	4	5	6
15. Supports his or her teachers when it really counts				1	2	3	4	5	6
16. Allocation of resources is disorganized				1	2	3	4	5	6
17. Efficient and smooth running of the school is his or her priority				1	2	3	4	5	6
18. Uses many sources to learn more about the new program or innovation				1	2	3	4	5	6
19. Being accepted by teachers is important to him/her				1	2	3	4	5	6
20. He or she sees the connection between the day-to-day activities and moving toward a longer term goal				1	2	3	4	5	6
21. Knows very little about programs and innovations				1	2	3	4	5	6
22. Is skilled at organizing resources and schedules				1	2	3	4	5	6
23. Has an incomplete view about the future of his or her school				1	2	3	4	5	6
24. Attending to feelings and perceptions is his or her first priority				1	2	3	4	5	6
25. Explores issues in a loosely structured way				1	2	3	4	5	6
26. Chats socially with teachers				1	2	3	4	5	6
27. Delays making decisions to the last possible moment				1	2	3	4	5	6
28. Focuses on issues of limited importance				1	2	3	4	5	6
29. Takes the lead when problems must be solved				1	2	3	4	5	6
30. Has a clear picture of where the school is going				1	2	3	4	5	6

CHANGE FACILITATOR STYLE
QUESTIONNAIRE (CFSQ) SCORING DEVICE

The responses for an individual can be scored using the CFSQ Quick Scoring Device. When there are multiple respondents, the first step is still to score each individual's responses. For more than one respondent, the individual raw scale scores can be summed and the average determined. The average score can then be converted using the same percentile table.

Instructions

1. In the box labeled A fill in the identifying information taken from the CFSQ cover sheet.
2. In the table labeled B on the Scoring Device, transcribe each of the 30 CFSQ circled responses from the questionnaire (raw data). Note that the numbered blanks are not in consecutive order.
3. Total the raw scores for each column in Box B. Place them along the row labeled Total Scores.
4. Table C contains the percentile scores for each of the six Change Facilitator Style dimensions. Take the first column's (S/I) Total Score from Box B and find it within the Raw Scale Score column of Table C. Look across to the first column ("S/I") and determine the percentile equivalent. For example, if the Raw Score was 20, then the Percentile Equivalent for S/I would be 27. Write the percentile score underneath the S/I column in the row labeled Percentiles under Box B.
5. Repeat step 4 for each of the remaining five columns. Be sure to identify the corresponding column in Box C when identifying the percentile.
6. The CFS Self Scoring Chart on page 325 is provided so that bar graphs can be shaded to represent the height of each percentile column.
7. Interpretation of the resultant bar graphs should be guided by referring to the Six Dimensions of Change Facilitator Style presented in Appendix D. The higher the graph, the more of that aspect of change leadership the respondent(s) views the leader to exhibit.

Change Facilitator Style Questionnaire Scoring Device

A

Date: _____

Site: _____ ID#_____

Innovation: _____

_____

B

S/I	F/M	TiO	AE	DtD	V&P
1 ___	4 ___	5 ___	3 ___	10 ___	2 ___
11 ___	6 ___	7 ___	8 ___	13 ___	9 ___
19 ___	12 ___	16 ___	14 ___	21 ___	18 ___
24 ___	15 ___	25 ___	17 ___	23 ___	20 ___
26 ___	29 ___	27 ___	22 ___	28 ___	30 ___

C   Total Scores   ___ ___ ___ ___ ___ ___

Percentiles   ___ ___ ___ ___ ___ ___

D

Raw Scale Score	Percentile equivalent					
	S/I	F/M	TiO	AE	DtD	V&P
5	1	1	6	1	7	1
6	1	1	10	1	13	1
7	1	1	15	1	19	1
8	1	1	21	1	26	1
9	1	1	28	1	33	1
10	2	1	35	1	42	1
11	2	1	42	1	50	1
12	3	2	49	1	57	1
13	4	2	55	1	64	2
14	5	3	60	2	69	2
15	7	4	66	2	76	3
16	9	5	71	3	80	3
17	12	6	77	5	85	4
18	16	8	81	7	88	6
19	20	12	86	9	91	7
20	27	16	90	12	95	10
21	34	21	92	18	97	14
22	43	28	95	24	99	19
23	52	36	97	31	99	26
24	62	45	98	40	99	33
25	71	56	99	50	99	42
26	81	66	99	60	99	53
27	87	75	99	71	99	63
28	92	85	99	79	99	72
29	97	93	99	87	99	84
30	99	99	99	99	99	99

Chart for Six Dimensions of Change Facilitator Style

Shade each of the bar graphs to the height of the corresponding Change Facilitator Style Questionnaire percentile score.

EXAMPLE INTERVENTIONS FOR
EACH STAGE OF CONCERN

Many possible interventions can be used to address each Stage of Concern (SoC). Interventions that are concerns-based can make a significant positive difference. However, there also are interventions that are likely to be inappropriate. The following are examples of each for each SoC.

Stage 0 Unconcerned. At this stage the types of interventions that may be appropriate certainly depend upon the context. For example, is it the very beginning of a change process, or are many others already using the innovation? Also, is use of the innovation required or even desirable? The following interventions might be relevant.

Appropriate Interventions

    a. Acknowledge that little concern about the innovation is legitimate and okay.

    b. Share some general information about the innovation in the hopes of arousing some interest in it.

    c. Suggest and describe how the innovation might be related to an area that the person(s) is concerned about.

    d. Decree that use of the innovation is required.

    e. Encourage the person(s) to talk with others who are interested in or using the innovation.

Inappropriate Interventions

    a. Communicating lack of concern to others, thereby discouraging their interest.

    b. Continuing to accept/tolerate a lack of concern while others are engaged.

State 1 Informational. Interventions should be designed to provide general descriptive information. Too much detail will not be useful. "Buying them the book" will not lead to their reading all of it. Interventions for this stage should be spread over time and through varied medium and context.

Appropriate Interventions

    a. Share general descriptive information about the innovation through one-legged interviews, e-mail, brochures, short media presentations, and discussions during staff meetings.

    b. Provide information contrasting what the individual is presently doing with potential advantages of use of the innovation.

   c. Express enthusiasm for consideration of the innovation.

   d. Hear from others who are excited about what they are doing with innovation.

   e. State realistic expectations about the benefits, costs, and effort needed to use the innovation.

Inappropriate Interventions

   a. Support travel to a site where the innovation is in use (unless there is careful construction of questions about what to ask before the trip).

   b. Provide in-depth and detailed information at a single time.

   c. Do not provide information about expectations and what use of the innovation will entail.

Stage 2 Personal. Change facilitators need to be extra sensitive in working with persons who have intense Personal concerns. It is quite easy to further raise their Personal concerns. Also, frequently intense Personal concerns are not innovation related. They could be job related (Will I have job next year?) or non–work related (My daughter is going through a divorce). The key to resolution of Personal concerns is to have more information. However, when people have intense Personal concerns, they are not as open to or trustful of the information that is provided. When Personal concerns are clearly innovation related, the following types of interventions may be useful:

Appropriate Interventions

   a. Establish rapport and be empathetic about their feelings of uncertainty.

   b. Be encouraging and offer assurance of their adequacy to engage with the innovation.

   c. Encourage innovation use gingerly; do not push unnecessarily.

   d. Clarify how the innovation relates to other priorities that potentially could conflict in terms of energy and time demands.

   e. Emphasize understanding of personal feelings, and deemphasize talk about the innovation.

   f. Be consistent in what is said about expectations and what is entailed in use of the innovation.

Inappropriate Interventions

   a. Ignore Personal concerns and focus only on presenting advantages of the innovation.

   b. Direct the person(s) to "get rid of those Personal concerns—you should be concerned about students."

   c. Provide inconsistent information over time.

   d. Call a staff meeting so that personal concerns can be shared.

Stage 3 Management. Interventions should focus on the "how-to-do-its." All-day, full-group trainings may not be the most effective method since many Task concerns are idiosyncratic. At one research site, the leaders created informal after-school "comfort and caring" sessions, during which experienced innovation users could provide advice and assistance that addressed specific Management concerns.

Appropriate Interventions

   a. Provide answers in ways that address the person-specific "how-to" issues that are causing concern.
   b. Provide a Web site with answers to the frequently heard Management concern questions.
   c. Provide assigned time for a respected and expert innovation user to meet with and coach those who have Task concerns.
   d. Demonstrate or provide a (video) model for effective use of the innovation, or provide "hands-on" materials for practice.
   e. Send e-mails that provide planning tips, and pace what implementers should be doing "this week."
   f. Establish a buddy system/consulting pair or support group.

Inappropriate Interventions

   a. Provide a lecture or all-day training on philosophy and theory behind the innovation.
   b. Assume there will be no Task concerns, and don't plan any supports or other interventions to address their resolution.
   c. Introduce another major innovation before Management concerns about the first innovation are reduced.

<u>Stage 4 Consequence.</u> Facilitators enjoy persons with Consequence concerns. The concerns of such individuals are targeted toward Impact and how quality of use of the innovation can be enhanced. Persons with Impact concerns appreciate recognition and encouragement for their efforts to improve outcomes.

Appropriate Interventions

   a. Recognize, encourage, and reinforce their ideas and activities.
   b. Drop by and inquire about their ideas for refinements and how things are working.
   c. Share a journal article or book that is related to their efforts.
   d. Provide a professional development session that introduces and supports ways to enhance innovation use.
   e. Encourage the person(s) to reach out to others. They could help by suggesting "how-to-do-its" for those with Task concerns or could develop a collaborative effort with a colleague(s) who also has Impact concerns.

Inappropriate Interventions

   a. Fail to encourage Impact concern innovation users by spending all the time attending to those with Self and Task concerns.
   b. Do not follow up to see what has happened with their efforts to refine use and enhance outcomes.
   c. Reward those with less quality of use of the innovation and not those with Consequence concerns.

<u>Stage 5 Collaboration.</u> The arousal and sustaining of Impact concerns about working with one or more colleagues in relation to use of an innovation is the ultimate. Leaders should do all they can to facilitate the arousal of Collaboration concerns and to support innovation implementers working together.

Appropriate Interventions

    a. Encourage through advocacy and action the arousal of Collaboration concerns.
    b. Arrange a meeting between interested individuals so that there can be an exchange of ideas.
    c. Change schedules, room assignments, and other structures so that those who want to collaborate can do so.
    d. Create opportunities for them to circulate outside their present situation and work with others who have similar ideas.
    e. Celebrate their collaborative efforts.

Inappropriate Interventions

    a. Ignore Stage 5 Collaboration concerns and assume they can work it out on their own.
    b. Change schedules and structures in ways that support those with Self and Task concerns and at the same time reduce the potential for collaboration.
    c. State that "We can't do that. The bus schedule can't be changed."

<u>Stage 6 Refocusing.</u> Individuals at this SoC are self-starters and certainly have their own goals in mind. They have strongly held ideas about ways that the change process and/or the innovation should move in new directions. If the institutional change effort is moving in a direction antagonistic to their opinions and concerns, some fairly directive actions may be necessary to outline the limits within which they may deviate from the mainstream. If their ideas are consistent with furthering use of the innovation and vision for the organization, then encouragement to "go ahead" is appropriate. However, there also should be regular monitoring for unexpected creative adaptations.

Appropriate Interventions

    a. Inquire about how well their ideas match with the vision or strategic directions outlined in the School Improvement Plan (SIP).
    b. Encourage the person(s) to take action while staying within the vision and strategic direction.
    c. Provide the person(s) with resources to access other materials and ideas that could help advance the overall effort.
    d. Encourage the person(s) to test their idea to see if it can increase outcomes.

Inappropriate Interventions

    a. Don't check to see what the person(s) is up to.
    b. Permit them to share their ideas with others who have Self or Task concerns.
    c. Put them in charge of facilitating others' implementation of the innovation. (However, in a few major change efforts we have seen this strategy lead to the Refocusing concerned person owning success of the change process and becoming a very effective leader.)

REFERENCES

Ackoff, R. L., & Emery, F. G. (1972). *On purposeful systems.* Chicago, IL: Aldine-Atherton.

Allen, R. (2003, November). Building school culture in an age of accountability: Principals lead through sharing tasks. *Education Update, 45*(7), 1, 3, 7–8.

Alquist, A., & Hendrickson, M. (1999). Mapping the configurations of mathematics teaching. *Journal of Classroom Interaction, 34*(1), 18–26.

Anderson, B. (1993, September). The stages of systemic change. *Educational Leadership, 51*(1), 14–17.

Anderson, D. L. (2010). *Organization development: The process of leading organizational change.* Thousand Oaks, CA: Sage.

Anderson, S. E. (1997). Understanding teacher change: Revisiting the Concerns Based Adoption Model. *Curriculum Inquiry, 27*(3), 331–357.

Argyris, C. (1982). *Reasoning, learning, and action: Individual and organizational.* San Francisco, CA: Jossey-Bass.

Argyris, C., & Schon, D. (1978). *Organizational learning.* San Francisco, CA: Jossey-Bass.

Ash, P. B., & D'Auria, J. (2013). *School systems that learn: Improving professional practice, overcoming limitations, and diffusing innovation.* Thousand Oaks, CA: Corwin Press.

Banathy, B. H. (1973). *Developing a systems view of education: A systems-model approach.* Palo Alto, CA: Fearon.

Banathy, B. H. (1995). A systems view and systems design in education. In P. M. Jenlink (Ed.), *Systemic change: Touchstones for the future school.* Arlington Heights, IL: Skylight Professional Development.

Banathy, B. H. (1996). *Designing social systems in a changing world.* New York, NY: Plenum.

Bass, M., & Bass, R. (2008). *The Bass handbook of leadership: Theory, research, and managerial applications.* New York, NY: Free Press.

Bavelas, A. (1950). Communication patterns in task-oriented groups. *Journal of Acoustical Society of America, 22,* 725–730.

Beckhard, R. (1969). *Organization development: Strategies and models.* Reading, MA: Addison-Wesley.

Berlin, I. (1953). *The Hedgehog and the Fox: An Essay on Tolstoy's View of History.* London, UK: Weidenfeld & Nicolson; New York, NY: Simon and Schuster.

Bermant, G., & Warwick, D. P. (1978). The ethics of social intervention: Power, freedom and accountability. In G. Bermant, H. C. Kelman, & D. P. Warwick, *The ethics of social intervention* (pp. 377–418). Washington, DC: Hemisphere.

Blake, B. F., Neuendorf, K. A., & Valdiserri, C. M. (2005). Tailoring new websites to appeal to those most likely to shop online. *Technovation, 25*(10), 1205–1214.

Blake, R. R., & Mouton, J. S. (1964). *The managerial grid.* Houston, TX: Gulf.

Bobbett, J. J., Ellett, C. D., Teddlie, C., Olivier, D. F., & Rugutt, J. (2002). *School culture and school effectiveness in demonstrably effective and ineffective schools.* Paper presented at the annual meeting of the American Education Research Association, New Orleans, LA.

Bolman, L. G., & Deal, T. E. (2008). *Reframing organizations: Artistry, choice and leadership* (4th ed.). San Francisco, CA: Jossey-Bass.

Bond-Huie, S., Buttram, J. L., Deviney, F. P., Murphy, K. M., & Ramos, M. A. (2004, November). *Alignment in SEDL's Working Systemically Model.* Austin, TX: Southwest Educational Development Laboratory.

Boyd, V. (1992a). Creating a context for change. *Issues . . . About Change, 2*(2), 1–10.

Boyd, V. (1992b). *School context: Bridge or barrier for change.* Austin, TX: Southwest Educational Development Laboratory.

Boyd, V., & Hord, S. M. (1994). *Principals and the new paradigm: Schools as learning communities.* Paper presented at the annual meeting of the American Educational Research Association, New Orleans, LA.

Bridge, C. A. (1995). *The progress of implementation of the K–3 primary program in Kentucky's elementary schools.* Paper presented at the annual meeting of the American Educational Research Association, San Francisco, CA.

Bridges, W. (2009). *Managing transitions: Making the most of change.* New York, NY: Addison-Wesley.

Bridges, W., & Bridges, S. (2009). *Managing transition: Making the most of change.* Philadelphia, PA: Perseus Books Group.

Caine, R. N., & Caine, G. (1997). *Education on the edge of possibility.* Alexandria, VA: Association for Supervision and Curriculum Development.

Capra, F. (1997, April). *Creativity and leadership in learning communities.* Lecture presented at Mill Valley School District.

Century, J. R., & Levy, A. J. (2002). Sustaining your reform: Five lessons from research. *Benchmarks: The quarterly newsletter of the National Clearinghouse for Comprehensive School Reform, 3*(3), 1–7.

Charters, W. W., Jr., & Jones, J. E. (1973). On the risk of appraising nonevents in program evaluation. *Educational Researcher, 2*(11), 5–7.

Cheung, D., Hattie, J., & Ng, D. (2001). Reexamining the Stages of Concern Questionnaire: A test of alternative models. *Journal of Educational Research, 94*(4), 225–236.

Cheung, D., & Yip, D. (2004). How science teachers' concerns about school-based assessment of practical work vary with time: The Hong Kong experience. *Research in Science & Technological Education, 22*(2), 153–169.

Chin, R., & Benne, K. D. (1969). General strategies for effecting changes in human systems. In W. G. Bennis, K. D. Benne, & R. Chin (Eds.), *The planning of change* (2nd ed., pp. 32–59). New York, NY: Holt, Rinehart and Winston.

Christou, C., Eliophotou-Menon, M., & Philippou, G. (2004). Teachers' concerns regarding the adoption of a new mathematics curriculum: An application of CBAM. *Educational Studies in Mathematics, 57*(2), 157–177.

Clune, W. (1993). Systemic educational policy: A conceptual framework. In Susan H. Fuhrman (Ed.), *Designing coherent education policy: Improving the system.* New York, NY: Jossey-Bass.

Collins, J. (2001). *Good to great: Why some companies make the leap . . . and others don't.* New York, NY: HarperCollins.

Cowan, D., Joyner, S., & Beckwith, S. (2008). *Working systemically in action: A guide for facilitators.* Austin, TX: Southwest Education Development Laboratory.

Cummings, T. G., & Worley, C. G. (2008). *Organization development and change* (9th ed.). Mason, OH: South-Western Publishing.

Danek, J., Calbert, R., & Chubin, D. (1994, February). *NSF's programmatic reform: The catalyst for systemic change.* Paper presented at the Building the System: Making Science Education Work Conference, Washington, DC.

Darling-Hammond, L. (1996). The quiet revolution: Rethinking teacher development. *Educational Leadership, 53*(6), 4–10.

Deal, T. E., & Kennedy, A. A. (1982). *Corporate cultures: The rites and rituals of corporate life.* New York, NY: Addison-Wesley.

Deal, T. E., & Peterson, K. D. (1990). *The principal's role in shaping school culture.* Washington, DC: U.S. Department of Education.

Dunn, K. E., & Rakes, G. C. (2009). Producing caring qualified teachers: An exploration of the influence of pre-service teacher concerns on learner-centeredness. *Teaching and Teacher Education, 26*(3), 516–521.

Dunn, L., & Borchardt, P. (1998). *The Essential Curriculum.* Kansas City, MO: The Teel Institute.

Eden, C., & Huxham, C. (1996). Action research for the study of organizations. In S. R. Clegg, C. Hardy, & W. R. Nord (Eds.), *Handbook of organization studies* (pp. 526–542). Thousand Oaks, CA: Sage.

English, F. W. (2004). *The SAGE handbook of educational leadership: Advances in theory, research, and practice.* Thousand Oaks, CA: Sage.

Entrekin, K. M. (1991). *Principal change facilitator styles and the implementation of consultation-based prereferral child study teams* (Unpublished doctoral dissertation). Temple University, Philadelphia, PA.

Fiedler, F. E. (1978). The contingency model and the dynamics of the leadership process. In L. Berkowitz (Ed.), *Advances in experimental and social psychology* (pp. 59–112). New York, NY: Academic Press.

Fixsen, D. L., Naoom, S. F., Blasé, S. F., Friedman, R. M., & Wallace, F. (2005). *Implementation research: A synthesis of the literature.* Tampa, FL: National Implementation Research Network, University of South Florida.

Floden, R., Goertz, M., & O'Day, J. (1995, September). Capacity building in systemic reform. *Phi Delta Kappan, 77*(1), 19–21.

French, W. (1971, August). *A definition and history of organization development: Some comments.* Proceedings of the 31st Annual Meeting of the Academy of Management, Atlanta, GA.

French, W. L., & Bell, C. H. (1998). *Organization development: Behavioral science interventions for organization improvement.* Upper Saddle River, NJ: Prentice Hall.

Fullan, M. (1993). Innovation, reform, and restructuring strategies. In G. Cawelti (Ed.), *Challenges and achievement of American education, ASCD 1993 Yearbook.* Alexandria, VA: Association for Supervision and Curriculum Development.

Fullan, M., Miles, M. B., & Taylor, G. (1980). Organization development in schools: State of the art. *Review of Educational Research. 50*(1), 121–183.

Fuller, F. F. (1969). Concerns of teachers: A developmental conceptualization. *American Educational Research Journal, 6*(2), 207–226.

Fuller, F. F. (1970). *Personalized education for teachers: An introduction for teacher educators.* University of Texas at Austin, Research and Development Center for Teacher Education.

Fuller, F. F., & Bown, O. H. (1975). Becoming a teacher. *Teacher education 1975.* Chicago, IL: The National Society for the Study of Education.

Gallos, J. V., & Schein, E. H. (Eds.) (2006). *Organization development: A Jossey-Bass reader.* San Francisco, CA: Jossey-Bass.

Garmston, R., & Wellman, B. (2000). *The adaptive school: Developing and facilitating collaborative groups.* El Dorado Hills, CA: Four Hats Seminar.

Garmston, R., & Wellman, B. (2008). *The adaptive school: A sourcebook for developing collaborative groups.* Norwood, MA: Christopher Gordon.

George, A. A., Hall, G. E., & Stiegelbauer, S. M. (2006). *Measuring implementation in schools: The stages of concern Questionnaire.* Austin, TX: Southwest Educational Development Laboratory.

George, A. A., Hall, G. E., & Uchiyama, K. (2000). Extent of implementation of a standards-based approach to teaching mathematics and student outcomes. *Journal of Classroom Interaction, 35*(1), 8–25.

Gonzalez, C. E., Resta, P. E., & De Hoyos, M. L. (2005). *Barriers and facilitators on implementation of policy initiatives to transform higher education teaching-learning process.* Paper submitted for presentation at the annual meeting of the American Educational Research Association, Montreal.

Grantham, A., & Tsekouras, G. (2005). Diffusing wireless applications in a mobile world. *Technology in Society, 27*(1), 85–104.

Hall, G. E. (2013). Evaluating change processes: Assessing extent of implementation (constructs, methods, and implications). *Journal of Educational Administration, 1*(3), 264–289.

Hall, G. E., Dirksen, D. J., & George, A. A. (2006). *Measuring implementation in schools: Levels of use.* Austin, TX: Southwest Educational Development Laboratory.

Hall, G. E., & George, A. A. (1988). *Development of a framework and measure for assessing principal change facilitator style.* Paper presented at the American Educational Research Association Annual Meeting. Retrieved from ERIC database. (ED336401)

Hall, G. E., & George, A. A. (1999). The impact of principal change facilitator style on school and classroom culture. In H. J. Freiberg (Ed.), *School climate: Measuring, improving, and sustaining healthy learning environments.* Philadelphia, PA: Falmer Press.

Hall, G. E., George, A., & Rutherford, W. L. (1979). *Measuring stages of concern about the innovation: A manual for use of the SoC Questionnaire* (Report No. 3032). The University of Texas at Austin, Research and Development Center for Teacher Education. Retrieved from ERIC database. (ED147342)

Hall, G. E., & Hord, S. M. (1984). A framework for analyzing what change facilitators do: The Intervention Taxonomy. *Knowledge: Creation, Diffusion, Utilization, 5*(3), 275–307.

Hall, G. E., & Hord, S. M. (1987). *Change in schools: Facilitating the process.* Albany, NY: SUNY Press.

Hall, G. E., & Hord, S. M. (2006). *Implementing change: Patterns, principles, and potholes.* Boston, MA: Pearson/Allyn & Bacon.

Hall, G. E., Hord, S. M., & Griffin, T. H. (1980). *Implementation at the school building level: The development and analysis of nine mini-case studies* (Report No. 3098). The University of Texas at Austin, Research and Development Center for Teacher Education. Retrieved from ERIC database. (ED207170)

Hall, G. E., & Loucks, S. F. (1977). A developmental model for determining whether the treatment is actually implemented. *American Education Research Journal, 14*(3), 263–276.

Hall, G. E., & Loucks, S. F. (1981). Program definition and adaptation: Implications for inservice. *Journal of Research and Development in Education.* 14(2), 46–58.

Hall, G. E., Loucks, S. F., Rutherford, W. L., & Newlove, B. W. (1975). Levels of use of the innovation: A framework for analyzing innovation adoption. *The Journal of Teacher Education, 26*(1), 52–56.

Hall, G. E., Negroni, I. A., & George, A. A. (2013). Examining relationships between urban principal leadership and student learning. *International Journal of Leadership and Change, 1*(1), 36–46.

Hall, G. E., Newlove, B. W., George, A. A., Rutherford, W. L., & Hord, S. M. (1991). *Measuring change facilitator stages of concern: A manual for use of the CFSoC Questionnaire.* Austin, TX: Southwest Educational Development Laboratory.

Hall, G. E., & Robison, M. (2009). Strategies and themes to district improvement: Keys to all schools achieving AYP. Paper presented at the annual meeting of the Northern Rocky Mountain Education Research Association, Jackson, WY.

Hall, G. E., & Rutherford, W. L. (1976). Concerns of teachers about implementing team teaching. *Educational Leadership, 34*(3), 227–233.

Hall, G. E., Rutherford, W. L., Hord, S. M., & Huling, L. L. (1984). Effects of three principal styles on school improvement. *Educational Leadership, 41*(5), 22–29.

Hall, G. E., & Shieh, W. H. (1998). Supervision and organizational development. In G. R. Firth & E. F. Pajak (Eds.), *Handbook of research on school supervision.* New York, NY: Macmillan.

Hall, G. E., Wallace, R. C., & Dossett, W. A. (1973). *A developmental conceptualization of the adoption process within educational institutions* (Report No. 3006). The University of Texas at Austin, Research and Development Center for Teacher Education. Retrieved from ERIC database. (ED095126)

Hall, J. (1971). Decisions, decisions, decisions, *Psychology Today, 5,* 51–54, 86, 88.

Hallinger, P., & Heck, R. H. (2011). Conceptual and methodological issues in studying school leadership effects as a reciprocal process. *School Effectiveness and Improvement, 22*(2), 149–173.

Hargreaves, A. (1997). Rethinking educational change: Going deeper and wider in the quest for success. In A. Hargreaves (Ed.), *ASCD yearbook: Rethinking educational change with heart and mind* (pp. 1–26). Alexandria, VA: Association for Supervision and Curriculum Development.

Hargreaves, L., Moyles, J., Merry, R., Paterson, F., Pell, A., & Esarte-Sarries, V. (2003). How do primary school teachers define and implement "interactive teaching" in the National Literacy Strategy in England? *Research Papers in Education, 18*(3), 217–237.

Harsh, S. (2013, in press). *A multiple approach to capacity building: Supporting change and reform through capacity building.* Belington, WV: Professional Resources.

Heck, S., Stiegelbauer, S. M., Hall, G. E., & Loucks, S. F. (1981). *Measuring innovation configurations: Procedures and applications* (Report No. 3108). The University of Texas at Austin, Research and Development Center for Teacher Education. (ERIC Document).

Hersey, P., Blanchard, K. H., & Johnson, D. E. (2000). *Management of organizational behavior: Leading human resources.* Upper Saddle River, NJ: Prentice Hall.

Herbert, K. S., Murphy, K. M., Ramos, M. A., Vaden-Kiernan, M., & Buttram, J. L. (2006). *SEDL's Working Systemically model: Final report.* Austin, TX: Southwest Educational Laboratory Develoopement Laboratory. Retrieved from http://www.sedl.org/ws/pdfs/WS-final-report.pdf

Hill, P. W., & Crevola, C. A. (1999). The role of standards in educational reform for the 21st century. In D. D. Marsh (Ed.), *1999 ASCD yearbook: Preparing our schools for the 21st century* (pp. 117–142). Alexandria, VA: ASCD.

Hirsh, S., & Foster, A. (2013). *A school board guide to leading successful schools: Focusing on learning.* Thousand Oaks, CA: Corwin Press.

Hirsh, S., & Hord, S. (2012). *A playbook for professional learning: Putting the standards into action.* Oxford, OH: Learning Forward.

Hord, S. M. (1992). *Facilitative leadership: The imperative for change.* Austin, TX: Southwest Educational Development Laboratory.

Hord, S. M. (Ed.). (2004). *Learning together, leading together: Changing schools through professional learning communities.* New York, NY: Teachers College Press.

Hord, S. M., & Hirsh, S. A. (2008). Making the promise a reality, Chapter 2. In A. Blankstein, P. D. Houston, & R. W. Cole (Eds.), *Sustaining professional learning communities.* Thousand Oaks, CA: Corwin Press.

Hord, S. M., & Hirsh, S. A. (2009, February). The principal's role in supporting learning communities. *Educational Leadership, 66*(5), 22–23.

Hord, S. M., & Huling-Austin, L. (1986). Effective curriculum implementation: Some promising new insights. *The Elementary School Journal, 87*(1), 97–115.

Hord, S. M., & Rousin, J. L. (2013). *Implementing change through learning: Concerns-based concepts, tools, and strategies for guiding change.* Thousand Oaks, CA: Corwin Press.

Hord, S. M., Rutherford, W. L., Huling-Austin, L. L., & Hall, G. E. (2004). *Taking charge of change.* Austin, TX: Southwest Educational Development Laboratory.

Hord, S. M., Stiegelbauer, S. M., Hall, G. E., & George, A. A. (2006). *Measuring implementation in schools: Innovation configurations.* Austin, TX: Southwest Educational Development Laboratory.

Hord, S. M., & Tobia, E. F. (2012). *Reclaiming our teaching profession: The power of educators learning in community.* New York and London: Teachers College Press.

Hougen, M. C. (1984). *High school principals: An analysis of their approach to facilitating implementation of microcomputers* (Doctoral dissertation). The University of Texas at Austin.

House, E. R., Steele, J., & Kerins, C. T. (1971). *The gifted classroom.* Urbana, IL: Center for Instructional Research and Curriculum Evaluation, University of Illinois.

James, L. R., & Jones, A. P. (1974). Organizational climate: A review of theory and research. *Psychological Bulletin, 81*(12), 1096–1112.

Jehue, R. J. (2000). *Development of a measure for assessing military leaders' change facilitator styles* (Unpublished doctoral dissertation). University of Northern Colorado.

Jenlink, P. M. (1995). *Systemic change: Touchstones for the future school.* Arlington Heights, IL: Skylight Professional Development.

Jenlink, P. M., Reigeluth, C. M., Carr, A. A., & Nelson, L. M. (1996). An expedition for change: Facilitating the systemic change process in school districts. *Tech Trends, 41*(1), 21–30.

Johnson, M. H. (2000). A district-wide agenda to improve teaching and learning in mathematics. *Journal of Classroom Interaction, 35*(1), 1–7.

Joyce, B., & Showers, B. (2002). *Student achievement through staff development.* Alexandria, VA: Association for Supervision and Curriculum Development.

Joyce, B., Wolf, J., & Calhoun, E. (1993). *The self-renewing school.* Alexandria, VA: Association for Supervision and Curriculum Development.

Kimberly, J. R., & Nielsen, W. R. (1975). Organization development and change in organizational performance. *Administrative Science Quarterly, 20,* 191–206.

Knapp, M. S., Copland, M. A., & Talbert, J. E. (2003, February). *Leading for learning: Reflective tools for school and district leaders.* Seattle: University of Washington, Center for the Study of Teaching and Policy.

Koon, S. L. (1995). *The relationship of implementation of an entrepreneurial development innovation to student outcomes* (Doctoral dissertation). University of Missouri–Kansas City.

Kourilsky, M. L. (1983). *Mini-society: Experiencing real-world economics in the elementary school classroom.* Menlo Park, CA: Addison-Wesley.

Kuhn, T. S. (1970). *The structure of scientific revolutions.* Chicago, IL: The University of Chicago Press.

Laszlo, E. (1972). *The systems view of the world.* New York, NY: Braziller.

Learning Forward. (2011). *Standards for professional learning.* Oxford, OH: Author.

Learning Forward. (August, 2011). Introducing a new approach to standards that can transform teaching and learning in schools. *JSD, 32*(4).

Learning Forward. (2012). *Standards into practice: School-based roles. Innovation configuration maps for standards for professional learning.* Oxford, OH: Author.

Lee, V. E., Smith, J. B., & Croninger, R. G. (1995, Fall). Another look at high school restructuring. *Issues in restructuring schools.* Madison, WI: Center on Organization and Restructuring of Schools, School of Education, University of Wisconsin.

Leithwood, K., Louis, K. S., Anderson, S., & Wahlstrom, K. (2004). *How leadership influences student learning.* Minneapolis, MN: Center for Applied Research and Educational Improvement, University of Minnesota; Toronto, ON: Ontario Institute for Studies in Education.

Lewis, D. (2011). It's a matter of principal: Examining relationships between leaders' change facilitator style and students' academic achievement (Doctoral dissertation). University of Nevada, Las Vegas.

Lezotte, L. (1991). *Correlates of effective schools: The first and second generation.* Okemos, MI: Effective Schools Products, Ltd.

Lieberman, A. (1995). Practices that support teacher development: Transforming conceptions of professional learning. *Phi Delta Kappan, 76*(8), 591–596.

Likert, R. (1967). *The human organization: Its management and value.* New York, NY: McGraw-Hill.

Lippitt, R., Watson, J., & Westley, B. (1958). *The dynamics of planned change.* New York, NY: Harcourt Brace.

Little, J. W. (1982). Norms of collegiality and experimentation: Workplace conditions of school success. *American Educational Research Journal, 19*(3), 325–340.

Little, J. W., & McLaughlin, M. W. (1993). *Teachers' work: Individuals, colleagues and contexts.* New York, NY: Teachers College Press.

Loucks, S. F., Newlove, B. W., & Hall, G. E. (1975). *Measuring levels of use of the innovation: A manual for trainers, interviewers, and raters.* The University of Texas at Austin, Research and Development Center for Teacher Education. Available from the Southwest Educational Development Laboratory, Austin, TX.

Machiavelli, N. (2005). *The prince* (P. E. Bondanella, Ed. & Trans.) New York, NY: Oxford University Press. (Original work published 1532.)

Mann, F. C., & Likert, R. (1952, Winter). The need for research on the communication of research results. *Human Organization, 11*(4), 15–19.

Marzano, R. J., Waters, T., & McNulty, B. A. (2005). *School leadership that works: From research to results.* Alexandria, VA: Association for Supervision and Curriculum Development.

Matthews, R. J., & Hall, G. E. (1999, November). *Cohort 1: Baseline Data.* Melbourne, Victoria, Australia: Consultancy and Development Unit, Faculty of Education, Deakin University.

Matthews, R. J., Marshall, A. K, & Milne, G. R. (2000, April). *One year on: Report of the notebook evaluation.* Burwood, Victoria, Australia: Deakin University.

McDavid, J. C., Huse, I., & Hawthorn, L. R. L. (2013). *Program evaluation and performance measurement: An introduction to practice.* Thousand Oaks, CA: Sage.

McGill, M. E. (1977). *Organization development for operating managers.* New York, NY: AMACOM.

McGregor, D. (1960). *The human side of management.* New York, NY: McGraw-Hill.

McLaughlin, M. W., & Talbert, J. E. (1993). *Contexts that matter for teaching and learning.* Stanford, CA: Center for Research on the Context of Secondary School Teaching, Stanford University.

Mertler, C. A. (2012). *Action research: Improving schools and empowering educators.* Thousand Oaks, CA: Sage.

Miles, M. B. (1979). Ethical issues in OD. *OD Practitioner, 11*(3), 1–10.

Mills, G. E., (2010). *Action research: A guide for the teacher researcher* (4th ed.). Upper Saddle River, NJ: Pearson.

Mort, P. R. (1953). Educational adaptability. *School Executive, 71,* 1–23.

Nevada IC Teams. (2010). *Sustaining effective instruction through IC teams: A framework for assessment & planning.* Carson City, NV: Nevada Department of Education.

Newlove, B. W., & Hall, G. E. (1976). *A manual for assessing open-ended statements of concern about the innovation* (Report No. 3029). The University of Texas at Austin, Research and Development Center for Teacher Education. Retrieved from ERIC database. (ED144207)

Northouse, P. G. (Ed.). (2007). Leadership: Theory and practice. Thousand Oaks, CA: Sage.

Osher, D. (2013). When planning and implementing multiple interventions, how are the community's needs, each organization's capacity, and specific target population's needs taken into account? Paper presented at the Investing in What Works Project Forum, Washington, DC: AIR.

Park, J. T. R. (2012). *Teacher change in Bangladesh: A study of teachers adapting and implementing active learning into their practice* (Unpublished Ph.D. thesis). University of Toronto, Toronto, Canada.

Park, S., & Yoon, S. (2005). Separating early-adopters from the majority: The case of broadband internet access in Korea. *Technological Forecasting and Social Change, 72*(3), 301–325.

Persichitte, K. A., & Bauer, J. W. (1996). Diffusion of computer-based technologies: Getting the best start. *Journal of Information Technology for Teacher Education, 5*(1–2), 35–41.

Popham, W. J. (2008). *Transformative assessment.* Alexandria, VA: ASCD.

RMC Research Corporation. (2009). *Reading First sustainability: Literature review.* Arlington, VA: Author.

Robins, S. P. (2013). *The truth about managing people* (3rd ed.). Upper Saddle River, NJ: Pearson.

Rogers, E. M. (2003). *Diffusion of innovations.* New York, NY: The Free Press.

Rood, M., & Hinson, R. (2002). *Measuring the effectiveness of collaborative school reform: Implementation and outcomes.* Paper presented at the annual meeting of the American Evaluation Association, Washington, DC.

Rosenfield, S., & Gravois, T. (1996). *Instructional consultation teams.* New York, NY: Guilford.

Rosenholtz, S. (1989). *Teacher's workplace: The social organizations of schools.* New York, NY: Longman.

Rossi, P. H., Lipsey, M. W., & Freeman, H. W. (2004). *Evaluation: A systematic approach* (7th ed.). Thousand Oaks, CA: Sage.

Ryan, B., & Gross, N. C. (1943). The diffusion of hybrid seed corn in two Iowa communities. *Rural Sociology, 8,* 15–24.

Sashkin, M., & Egermeier, J. (1992). *School change models and processes: A review of research and practice.* Paper presented at the annual meeting of the American Educational Research Association, San Francisco, CA.

Saunders, R. (2012). Assessment of professional development for teachers in the vocational education and training sector: An examination of the concerns based adoption model. *Australian Journal of Education, 56*(2), 182–204.

Schein, E. (1985). *Organizational culture and leadership: A dynamic view.* San Francisco, CA: Jossey-Bass.

Schein, E. (1992). *Organizational culture and leadership: A dynamic view* (2nd ed.). San Francisco, CA: Jossey-Bass.

Schiller, J. (1991a, Winter). Implementing computer education: The role of the primary principal. *Australian Journal of Educational Technology, 7*(1), 48–69.

Schiller, J. (1991b). Implementing computer education: The role of the primary principal. *Australian Journal of Educational Technology, 14*(4), 36–39.

Schiller, J. (2002). Interventions by school leaders in effective implementation of information and communications technology: Perceptions of Australian principals. *Journal for Information Technology for Teacher Education, 11*(3), 289–301.

Schiller, J. (2003, July/August). *The elementary school principal as a change facilitator in ICT integration.* The Technology Source Archives at the University of North Carolina. Retrieved March 17, 2010, from http://technologysource.org/article/elementary_school_principal_as_a_change_facilitator_in_ict_integration

Schmoker, M. (1997). Setting goals in turbulent times. In A. Hargreaves (Ed.), *ASCD yearbook: Rethinking educational change with heart and mind.* Alexandria, VA: Association for Supervision and Curriculum Development.

Schmuck, R. A. (1987). *Organization development in schools: Contemporary conceptual practices.* Eugene, OR: Center on Organizational Development in Schools, Oregon University. Retrieved from ERIC database. (ED278119)

Schmuck, R. A., & Runkel, P. J. (1994). *Handbook of organization development in schools.* Prospect Heights, IL: Waveland Press.

Schneider, M., & Somers, M. (2006). Organizations as complex adaptive systems: Implications of complexity theory for leadership research. *The Leadership Quarterly, 17,* 351–365.

Senge, P. M. (1990). *The fifth discipline: The art and practice of the learning organization.* New York, NY: Doubleday/Currency.

Shieh, W. H. (1996). *Environmental factors, principal's change facilitator style and implementation of the cooperative learning project in selected schools in Taiwan* (Unpublished doctoral dissertation). University of Northern Colorado.

Smith, J., & O'Day, J. (1991). *Putting the pieces together: Systemic school reform* (CPRE policy brief). New Brunswick, NJ: Eagleton Institute of Politics.

Spradley, J. P. (1979). *The ethnographic interview.* New York, NY: Holt, Rinehart and Winston.

Staessens, K. (1990). *De professionele cultuur van basisscholen in vernieuwing. En empirisch onderzoek in v.l.o.-scholen.* [The professional culture of innovating primary schools. An empirical study of RPS schools.] (Unpublished doctoral dissertation). University of Leuven, Leuven, Belgium.

Staessens, K. (1993). Identification and description of professional culture in innovating schools. *Qualitative Studies in Education, 6*(2), 111–128.

Stewart, S. K. (2012). Principal change facilitator style and student achievement: A study of schools in the middle (Doctoral dissertation). University of Nevada, Las Vegas.

Stringer, E. T. (2013). *Action research.* Thousand Oaks, CA: Sage.

Tarde, G. (1903). *The laws of imitation* (Elsie Clews Parson, Trans.). New York, NY: Holt (reprinted 1969, Chicago, IL: University of Chicago Press).

Thessin, R. A., & Starr, J. P. (2011). Supporting the growth of effective district-wide professional learning communities. *Kappan, 92*(6), 48–54.

Thornton, E., & West, C. E. (1999). Extent of teacher use of a mathematics curriculum innovation in one district: Years 1 and 2 Levels of Use (LoU). *Journal of Classroom Interaction, 34*(1), 9–17.

Timar, T., & Kirp, D. (1989, March). Education reform in the 1980s: Lessons from the states. *Phi Delta Kappan, 70*(7), 504–511.

Tobia, E. F., & Hord, S. H. (June, 2012). I am a professional. *Journal of Staff Development, 33*(3), 16–20, 26.

Trice, H. M., & Beyer, J. M. (1993). *The cultures of work organizations.* Englewood Cliffs, NJ: Prentice Hall.

Trohoski, C. G. (1984). *Principals' interventions in the implementation of a school health program* (Unpublished Ph.D. thesis). University of Pennsylvania.

Van den Berg, R., & Vandenberghe, R. (1981). *Onderwijsinnovatie in verschuivend perspectief.* Amsterdam: Uitgeverij Zwijsen.

Vandenberghe, R. (1988). *Development of a questionnaire for assessing principal change facilitator style.* Paper presented at the annual meeting of the American Educational Research Association, New Orleans, LA. Retrieved from ERIC database. (ED297463)

Wandersman, A., Chien, V. H., & Katz, J. (2012). Toward an evidence-based system for innovation support for implementing innovations with quality: Tools, training, technical assistance, and quality assurance/quality improvement. *American Journal of Community Psychology, 50*(3–4), 460–461. doi: 10.1007/s10464-012-9509-7

Wandersman, A., Duffy, J., Flaspohler, P., Noonan, R., Lubell, K., Stillman, L., . . . Saul, J. (2008). Bridging the gap between prevention research and practice: The Interactive Systems Framework for Dissemination and Implementation. *American Journal of Community Psychology, 41*(3–4), 171–181. doi: 10.1007/s10464-008-9174-z

Weick, K. E. (1976, March). Educational organizations as loosely coupled systems. *Administrative Science Quarterly, 21*(1), 1–19.

Wheatley, M. J. (1992). *Leadership and the new science: Learning about organization from an orderly universe.* San Francisco, CA: Berrett-Koehler.

Wheatley, M. J., & Kellner-Rogers, M. (1996). A *simpler way.* San Francisco, CA: Berrett-Koehler.

Yuliang, L., & Huang, C. (2005). Concerns of teachers about technology integration in the USA. *European Journal of Teacher Education, 28*(1), 35–48.

Yung, W. Y. A. (2012). Thoughts and practice of a Hong Kong teacher in mathematics alternative assessment via concerns-based adoption model (Doctoral dissertation). University of Hong Kong.

Zmuda, A., Kuklis, R., & Kline, E. (2004). *Transforming schools: Creating a culture of continuous improvement.* Alexandria, VA: Association for Supervision and Curriculum Development.

INDEX